Charles Henry Peck

The Jacksonian Epoch

Charles Henry Peck

The Jacksonian Epoch

ISBN/EAN: 9783744653107

Printed in Europe, USA, Canada, Australia, Japan

Cover: Foto ©ninafisch / pixelio.de

More available books at **www.hansebooks.com**

THE
JACKSONIAN EPOCH

BY
CHARLES H. PECK

NEW YORK AND LONDON
HARPER & BROTHERS PUBLISHERS
1899

Copyright, 1899, by HARPER & BROTHERS.

All rights reserved.

PREFACE

THIS book is an attempt to accomplish two objects: a critical survey of the political history of the United States, particularly in its parliamentary phase, from the Presidential candidacy of Jackson to the accession of Tyler, with a preliminary review of the preceding period beginning with the origin of the War of 1812; and to exhibit the influence of the men who shaped events. The first permits a rapid and independent treatment of the subject from a new point of view; and the second, the introduction of the personal element, which gives to history its keenest interest and its greatest charm.

The epoch treated is the most suggestive and dramatic in our history. It marks the full development of American political methods, and possesses the most distinguished galaxy of public men ever brought together on the political scene in this country. General histories, however useful and excellent, subordinate men, and biographies either magnify individuals beyond their influence and importance, or do not adequately portray their contemporaries and the general perspective. This book, therefore, is an effort to combine and symmetrize both historical elements in order to present a true and lifelike picture of a most animated political epoch.

Much use has necessarily been made of Schurz's *Clay* and Sumner's *Jackson*, each helpful in a distinctly different way. But perhaps it will be perceived that a mass of material never before collected has been utilized for the portraiture of Clay and Jackson and the other leading characters of their time. For the general course of historical events it has not been deemed necessary to cite authorities. Wherever opinions have been expressed at variance with commonly accepted views, a candid effort has been made to submit all the essential facts, that the reader may be in a position to judge for himself.

THE AUTHOR.

CONTENTS

CHAPTER I

Florida and Jackson's Seminole Campaign—The Attempt to Censure the General for his Conduct in the War—The Beginning of the Feud between him and Clay—The Relation of Clay and Jackson to the Ensuing Political Period—Clay's Early History, to his Election as Speaker of the House of Representatives in 1811—The New Political Conditions of the Country..................................Page 1

CHAPTER II

Maritime Aggressions of England and France—The Restrictive System—Clay as Speaker of the House—Preparations for War—Madison Accepts Clay's Programme and is Re-elected—The Embargo and the Declaration of War against England—The Political Aspect of the War—Clay's Reply to Quincy—The Treaty of Ghent—The Effect of the War—The Bank of the United States—Clay's Change of Opinion in Regard to it—The Tariff of 1816—The Policy of Internal Improvements, Madison's Veto, and Monroe's Hostile Position—Clay Opposes Monroe's Administration—He Advocates Internal Improvements and the Recognition of the South American Republics.................................. 46

CHAPTER III

Clay's Political Position—The Missouri Compromise, the Statesmanship of It, and Clay's Agency in Effecting It—He Renews his Efforts for the Recognition of the South American Republics, and Finally Succeeds—He Temporarily Retires, but Returns to the House at the Opening of the Eighteenth Congress—He Defeats a Bill to Pension Commodore Perry's Mother, and Advocates Internal Improvements and Webster's Resolution Concerning the Recognition of Greece—The Monroe Doctrine—The Tariff of 1824 and Clay's Relation to Protection—The Political Situation in 1824—William H. Crawford—John Quincy Adams is

Elected President by the House Through Clay's Influence, and Clay becomes Secretary of State—Clay's Administration of the State Department—The Panama Mission—John Randolph—His Duel with Clay—Adams and his Administration — Jackson is Elected over Adams in 1828—Clay's Home, Family, Personal Appearance, Temperament, and Mind...Page 79

CHAPTER IV

The New Development and Arrangement of Political Forces — Andrew Jackson, and the Significance of his Political Rise—His First Administration—The Spoils System—The "Kitchen Cabinet"—Party Dissension and Reorganization of the Cabinet — The Political Issues — Clay Nominated for President and Re-elected to the Senate—The Political Activity of the Period—The Whig Programme—The Rejection of Van Buren's Nomination for Minister to England — Clay's Plan of Tariff Revision—His Defence of the American System—The Tariff of 1832—The Public Lands—The Effort to Compromise Clay on the Subject—His Land Bill... 123

CHAPTER V

The Controversy over the Bank of the United States—Thomas H. Benton —The Whig Leaders Refuse to Compromise with Jackson on the Question of Rechartering the Bank—The Bank as a Political Issue—The Veto of the Bill to Recharter—The Error of the Whig Policy—The Debate on the Veto—The Presidential Campaign of 1832—Jackson's Triumph—Nullification—The Force Bill and the Verplanck Tariff Bill—John C. Calhoun—Clay's Compromise Bill—It is Substituted for the Verplanck Bill in the House and Passed by the Senate—The Compromise Bill and the Force Bill become Laws, and South Carolina Repeals the Nullification Ordinance—The Wisdom of the Compromise and Clay's Responsibility for it — His Land Bill is Passed by both Houses, but Vetoed by the President.......................... 167

CHAPTER VI

Clay and Jackson make Northern Tours—The Removal of the Deposits—Tactics of the Whigs in the Senate—Clay's Resolutions Censuring the President and the Secretary of the Treasury—The Debate—The Anti-Bank Resolutions of the House — The Distress Petitions — Jackson's Protest against the Censure and the Subsequent Proceedings—Taney's Nomination for Secretary of the Treasury Rejected—Other Phases of the Bank Struggle — Coinage Legislation — The Land Bill — The Deposits Bill — The French Spoliations — The Cherokee Indians — The Four Years Law and the Spoils System........................ 215

CHAPTER VII

Distribution of the Surplus—The French Spoliations—The Slavery Question—The Abolition Petitions and Incendiary Publications—Admission of Arkansas and Michigan into the Union—Texas—Madison's Death and Character—The Colonization Society—Clay and Garrison—Taney Becomes Chief Justice—The Political Situation—The Election of 1836 —Politico-Finance—Jackson's Physical and Mental Traits—Efforts for Further Distribution—The Financial Condition of the Country—The Mania for Speculation—The Specie Circular .... Page 261

CHAPTER VIII

The Recognition of Texas — The Mexican Claims — International Copyright—Slavery—Benton's Resolution to Expunge the Senate's Censure of Jackson for the Removal of the Deposits—The Final Preparations— The Debate—Clay's Speech, Buchanan's Speech, and Webster's Protest—The Resolution Adopted and Executed—Jackson's Gratification— Analysis of his Presidency—Clay Decides to Remain in the Senate. 307

CHAPTER IX

Van Buren's Intellectual and Political Characteristics — His Policy as Jackson's Successor—The Crisis of 1837—The Tactics of the Whigs— Webster's Speech at Niblo's—The Appeal of the New York Merchants to the President—The Extra Session of Congress, the President's Message, and the Democratic Programme—Clay Organizes the Opposition, and Calhoun Supports the Administration—The Opening Debate on the Independent Treasury—The Banks and Resumption—The Regular Session—Renewal of the Excitement Over the Slavery Question—Calhoun's Attitude.. 342

CHAPTER X

The Debate on Calhoun's Slavery Resolutions and Clay's Substitutes—The Independent Treasury again Defeated—Minor Financial Legislation— The Doctrine of Instructions—The Subsidiary Coin—Clay's Set Speech on the Slavery Question and Calhoun's Comments — Clay's Northern Tour—The Obstacles to His Nomination—The Whig National Convention — Harrison and Tyler Nominated — Clay's Disgust and Acquiescence 381

CHAPTER XI

The Financial and Political Situation—Organization of the House—The Independent Treasury Established—Other Proceedings of Congress— Slavery and International Law — The Democratic Convention — The

Campaign of 1840—Clay's Platform for the Whig Party—William H. Harrison and his Opinions—The Election—Harrison and Clay and the Construction of the Cabinet — The Inaugural Address — The Clamor for the Spoils — Strained Relations Between Clay and Harrison — The Death of the President — John Tyler — The Close of the Jacksonian Epoch .... Page 431

THE JACKSONIAN EPOCH

THE JACKSONIAN EPOCH

CHAPTER I

Florida and Jackson's Seminole Campaign—The Attempt to Censure the General for his Conduct in the War—The Beginning of the Feud between him and Clay—The Relation of Clay and Jackson to the Ensuing Political Period—Clay's Early History, to his Election as Speaker of the House of Representatives in 1811—The New Political Conditions of the Country

FLORIDA had long been a prolific cause of trouble. It was the abode of outlaws, hostile Indians, and runaway slaves, constantly increasing in number. During the war with England they had acted, to whatever extent they could, with the British, who left in their possession a fortification on the Appalachicola, known as Negro Fort, containing a large quantity of arms and military stores. It was the source of serious mischief to the adjoining frontier, and particularly to the Georgia slave-owners. In the summer of 1816 our troops, under General Gaines, with the consent of the Spanish authorities at Pensacola, invested the fort and destroyed it. But the condition which had permitted this annoyance still continued, and would continue so long as Spain owned the territory and was unwilling or unable to perform the duties of sovereignty as well as her treaty obligations. The next year after the destruction of Negro Fort the government took similar measures to abate a still greater nuisance

—the occupation of Amelia Island, off the northeast coast of Florida, by pirates, smugglers, and slaves who had overpowered the Spanish garrison stationed there and made it their depot and retreat. Meantime, affrays between the Indians and whites quite as lawless became more frequent, and culminated in an attack by General Gaines and his forces upon the Creeks at Fowltown. Their village was sacked and a few reds were killed. This trivial affair was the beginning of an Indian war which proved to be the origin of a vastly greater political war.

General Jackson was forthwith ordered to the scene. His victory at New Orleans had made him the foremost captain of the country. He had since commanded the Western Department. He had experience in Indian warfare, having won his first military reputation in the Creek war of 1814. He was in cordial relations with the administration. That he should be put in command was a natural consequence. With his characteristic vigor, and assuming authority in disregard of his orders to draw upon State militia in the mode prescribed by law, he raised a body of volunteers, appointed their officers, and pushed with celerity to the Florida frontier. The campaign which followed was all that such preliminaries promised.

With a force of eighteen hundred he plunged into Florida, where he was soon afterward joined by a brigade of friendly Indians. Before this array the enemy vanished into the swamps and forests, leaving only their wretched villages to be destroyed. Not more than sixty of the hostile Indians, who did not number more than a thousand, were killed during the campaign, and these without the loss of a single white soldier. The chiefs were captured by displaying the English flag, and hanged. But for Jackson to execute his orders to pursue and subdue the Indians was not enough. On the supposition that the Spaniards were in complicity with the Indians, he seized St. Mark's and Pensacola, and placed in each an American garrison. The Spanish governor had fled from Pensacola and taken refuge in the fort at Barrancas. This place Jackson bombarded into surrender. He then transported the Spanish officers to Havana, and established a military government.

Among the numerous arbitrary acts of this unique campaign was the execution of Arbuthnot and Ambrister, destined to more conspicuous historical note than any other. The former was an old Scotch trader found at St. Mark's; the latter was a young Englishman taken in one of the Indian towns. Both were tried by court-martial. Arbuthnot was convicted of exciting the Creeks to war and of supplying them with means. He was sentenced to be hanged. Ambrister was convicted of supplying means and leading the lower Creeks. He was sentenced to be shot. For some reason, Ambrister's sentence was reconsidered by the court, and changed to flogging and imprisonment. This, however, Jackson disapproved, and restored the original sentence. Both men were then executed.

Jackson announced that the war was ended, and returned to Nashville. But, upon reflection, he ordered General Gaines to take St. Augustine. This order, if executed, would have completed the conquest of the Floridas. It was sent to the War Department, which by this time had full cognizance of Jackson's proceedings. The Spanish Minister was also apprised, and was already protesting vehemently. The administration was in a predicament. Jackson had grossly exceeded our national rights as well as his instructions. Unless his acts were disavowed the pending negotiations with Spain would be frustrated; and to secure the peaceable cession of the Floridas was, without doubt, the preferable policy. There was plainly but one course to pursue, and that was immediately taken. Jackson's order to Gaines was quickly countermanded. The posts Jackson seized were restored, and the provisional government he had set up was withdrawn.

But Jackson himself was too popular to admit of his being censured by the administration. As so often happens with political administrations, it said one thing and did another. But this course was adopted only after a struggle in the Cabinet. Calhoun, Secretary of War, and Crawford, Secretary of the Treasury, were for censure. Adams, Secretary of State, alone defended the General. The discussion was finally allayed, so far as appearances were concerned, by disavowing in fact what was verbally approved as having been necessary under the circumstances. However bold and arbitrary Jackson's conduct had been, no one supposed that he had been influenced by any other motive than to suppress the frontier troubles, both Indian and Spanish, unless, perhaps, to distinguish himself. The mass of the people believed, with Adams, that Jackson had done the right thing, though possibly in the wrong way. But the politicians with Presidential aspirations were alarmed, professedly for the institutions and character of their country, but really because of Jackson's threatening popularity.

As soon as Congress convened, the subject of the Seminole campaign was taken up. In due time committee reports were made condemning Jackson's operations. In the Senate nothing further was done; but in the House a violent and protracted debate ensued. In this debate

Henry Clay was the principal figure. "But," says Adams, in his Diary, "of that mighty controversy he was no longer the primary leader. He had ranged himself under the Crawford banners." The debate began January 16, 1819, and lasted until February 8th. Thirty-three set speeches were delivered, twenty of them being against the proposed resolutions of censure. One of the resolutions expressed disapproval of the execution of Arbuthnot and Ambrister, and the others proposed legislation to prevent like acts in the future. Clay spoke twice. His first speech was on January 17th. The second was at the close of the debate, and was not reported.

The whole debate is disappointing. It is no great compliment to Clay to say that his speech was the strongest and most striking of the debate; no small part of which was bad declamation. He disclaimed all personal unfriendliness either to General Jackson or to the administration. "Toward that distinguished captain," said he, " who shed so much glory on our country, whose renown constitutes so great a portion of its moral property, I never had, I never can have, any other feelings than those of profound respect and of the utmost kindness. . . . Rather than throw obstructions in the way of the President, I would precede him and pick out those, if I could, which might jostle him in his progress; I would sympathize with him in his embarrassments, and commiserate with him in his misfortunes." To neutralize the effect he had produced in his previous hostility to the administration, he assured the House, with great show of candor but with poor prophecy, that he had not engaged and would not engage in systematic opposition to Monroe, nor to the administration of any other Chief Magistrate. "I will say," he added, "that I approve entirely of the conduct of our government, and that Spain has no just cause of complaint. We having violated no important stipulation of the treaty of 1796, that power has justly subjected herself to all the consequences which ensued upon the entry into her dominions."

He sought the origin of the war, by a far-fetched argument based on imperfect acquaintance with the facts, in the treaty of Fort Jackson, concluded in August, 1814, by which the Creeks were subjected to grinding conditions. This treaty he posted as tyrannical and unconscionable, extorted by the sword. He contended that it served "but to whet and stimulate revenge, and give old hostilities, smothered, not extinguished, by the pretended peace, a greater exasperation and more ferocity. A truce thus patched up with an unfortunate people without means of existence, without bread, is no real peace. The instant there is the slightest prospect of relief from such harsh and severe conditions, the conquered party will fly to arms and spend the last drop of blood rather than live in such degraded bondage." He arraigned the capture of the Indian chiefs "by means of deception—hoisting foreign colors on the staff from which the stars and stripes alone should have floated," and stigmatized as barbaric the retaliation for enormities that the Indians had perpetrated. He examined at length the proceedings under which Arbuthnot and Ambrister were executed, and pronounced the whole transaction to be in flagrant violation of civilized law and principle. He denounced the seizure of St. Mark's, Pensacola, and Barrancas as unauthorized war against Spain, and hence a lawless usurpation of the constitutional powers of Congress. But notwithstanding the severity of his strictures upon the General's acts, he attributed to him no improper motives.

"I must cheerfully and entirely," said he, "acquit General Jackson of any intention to violate the laws of the country or the obligations of humanity. I am persuaded from all I have heard that he considered himself as equally respecting and observing both." And again: "I hope not to be misunderstood; I am far from intimating that General Jackson cherished any designs inimical to the liberty of the country. I believe his intentions to be pure and patriotic." Yet his peroration was as intense as though Jackson had been engaged in conspiracy and treason.

"Against the alarming doctrine of unlimited discretion in our military commanders, when applied even to prisoners of war, I must enter my protest. It begins upon them; it will end on us.... We are fighting a great moral battle for the benefit not only of our country, but of all mankind. The eyes of the whole world are in fixed attention upon us. One, the largest portion of it, is gazing with contempt, with jealousy, and with envy; the other portion, with hope, with confidence, and with affection. Everywhere the black cloud of legitimacy is suspended over the world, save only one bright spot which breaks out from the political hemisphere of the West to enlighten and animate and gladden the human heart. Obscure that by the downfall of liberty here, and all mankind are enshrouded in a pall of universal darkness.... Beware how you forfeit this exalted character. Beware how you give a fatal sanction in this infant period of our republic, scarcely yet two score years old, to military insubordination. Remember that Greece had her Alexander, Rome her Cæsar, England her Cromwell, France her Bonaparte; and that if we escape the rock on which they split we must avoid their errors.... I hope gentlemen will deliberately survey the awful isthmus on which we stand. They may bear down all opposition; they may even vote the General the public thanks. But if they do, in my humble judgment, it will be a triumph of the principle of insubordination—a triumph of the military over the civil authority—a triumph over the powers of this House—a triumph over the Constitution of the land. And I pray most devoutly to Heaven that it may not prove in its ultimate effects and consequences a triumph over the liberties of the people."

The resolutions decisively failed. The sum of the General's acts was advantageous to the country; and whatever they were, they were the acts of the "Hero of New Orleans." However correct it may have been to class the Seminoles within the pale of international law, to the mass of the people they were but a horde of blood-thirsty savages, to be exterminated by any means that offered. Likewise, the effort to convict Jackson of murder by the principles of Vattel seemed to most minds absurdly technical. Even though Arbuthnot and Ambrister were irregularly executed, the suspicious circumstances attending their capture among the red-skins in the wilds of Florida placed them in a precarious position; and this view was subsequently taken by the British government. As not even Jackson's fiercest assailants questioned that he acted, however rashly, as he thought was best and for the public good, a justification sufficient for all practical purposes was conceded. During the debate Jackson was in Washington; but immediately afterward he visited Baltimore, Philadelphia, and New York, and was received with ovations. The attack was ill-advised. It proved the most calamitous and far-reaching of Clay's political mistakes. "The rage and disgust of the General," says Parton, "when he read the speech, were extreme.

The long feud between General Jackson and Mr. Clay dated from the delivery of this speech. Jackson never hated any man so bitterly and so long as he hated Henry Clay."

Such was the origin of the most remarkable contest in our political history. It was the combat of two masterful personalities aided by conditions which had been long maturing. The character and quality of both men had been trained and tried, and through individuality and circumstance they were soon to lead opposing political forces. Clay had been longer in the public eye. His career was solely civic, while Jackson's reputation was solely military. To appreciate the struggle waged under their leadership, it is necessary to understand the respective positions in which they stood in the popular mind when the struggle began; and to do this requires that their previous history should be sketched. We must know the men before we can fully comprehend the events they moulded. Adequate biographies of such men cannot be written; their lives are components of history, and cannot properly be separated from it. At the risk of apparent departure from the purpose of this study, let us first examine at some length Clay's early career and its environment. It will serve the double purpose of depicting the individual and the conditions that produced a new political era.

Clay was born April 12, 1777, in Hanover County, Virginia. Little is known of his ancestry. In the reign of Queen Elizabeth, and soon after the colonization of Virginia, three brothers—Charles, Thomas, and Henry—sons of Sir John Clay, of Wales, came to the colony with Sir Walter Raleigh, who gave each of them ten thousand pounds. They settled near Jamestown. Henry left no children, but

Charles and Thomas became the founders of a numerous family. The future statesman was a descendant of the former.[1] His immediate origin was humble. His father, John Clay, was the pastor of a small congregation of Baptists, to whom he frequently preached from a rock on the shore of the South Anna River, no doubt before administering the peculiar rite of his creed. The sect was then in low esteem in the South; so late as in 1775 its ministers were often arrested as disturbers of the peace. In the preceding year, Madison, disgusted by this intolerant practice, wrote to a Northern friend: "I want again to breathe your free air. . . . That diabolical, hell-conceived principle of persecution rages among some; and to their eternal infamy the clergy can furnish their quota of imps for such purposes. There are at this time in the adjacent county not less than five or six well-meaning men in close jail for publishing their religious sentiments, which in the main are very orthodox."[2]

Kindly tradition represents the Rev. Mr. Clay as possessing some of the oratorical qualities that characterized his famous son. He died in 1781, leaving in straitened circumstances a widow and seven children, one of his five sons having previously died. Henry was next to the youngest child, and the only one to rise from obscurity. Mrs. Clay's maiden name was Hudson. She was an intelligent, estimable woman, and a worthy mother. She lived more than eighty years, surviving most of her fifteen children, having seven by her second husband, whom she married after a few

---

[1] "I believe I have the only reliable record of the Clay family extant. It is written on blank leaves in the 'Works of Samuel Johnson, London, 1713.'"—*Life of Cassius M. Clay*, vol. i. p. 18.

[2] Parton's *Life of Jefferson*, p. 203.

years of widowhood. It is related as indicative of her spirit that she indignantly threw into the fireplace some money left on her table by one of Tarleton's officers to pay for property of hers taken on one of his raids through the county. But the correct account of the incident out of which the story arose was doubtless recounted by Clay himself in a political speech delivered in 1840. "I was born a democrat," said he, "rocked in the cradle of the Revolution, and at the darkest period of that ever-memorable struggle for freedom. I recollect, in 1781 or 1782, a visit made by Tarleton's troops to the house of my mother, and of their running their swords into the new-made graves of my father and grandfather, thinking they contained hidden treasures. Though not more than four or five years of age, the circumstance of that visit is vividly remembered, and it will be to the last moment of my life."

As soon as he was old enough he aided in such ways as he could in the support of the family, which depended on the produce of some indifferent land in the "Slashes," as the region was known. Barefooted and coarsely clad, he often followed the plough. It was his duty to replenish the meal-barrel, which he did by taking the grist to Darricott's mill, on the Pamunky. The bag was his saddle, and with a rope bridle he guided the pony he rode. It is probable that he performed similar errands for others, for he was commonly called by the people along the route the "Mill-boy of the Slashes"—a sobriquet that always clung to him.

In the neighboring district-school, taught in a log-cabin by an intemperate Englishman named Peter Deacon, he received his only regular education, which consisted of the mere rudiments. At the age of fourteen he was placed in a retail store at Richmond, where he worked for nearly a year. He then sought, through the hopeful efforts of his step-father — probably inspired by the boy's budding ambition — a position in the office of the Clerk of the High Court of Chancery. There was no vacancy, but he was nevertheless installed by the influence of a brother of the clerk, who was a friend of Captain Watkins.

His first entrance into the office was long remembered by his fellow-clerks. Plain of features, overgrown and ungainly for his years, and clothed in rustic fashion, he presented a rather curious appearance. "His mother had dressed him up in a new suit of Figinny cloth, cotton and silk mixed, complexion of pepper-and-salt, with clean linen well starched, and the tail of his coat standing out from his legs at an angle of forty-five degrees, like that of a dragoon. The clerks looked askance at each other, and were not a little amused at the apparently awkward chap who had been thrust in upon them."[1] But they were not long in discovering that "Harry" was like the toad in the adage. His natural gifts were even then not wholly undeveloped, and he speedily rose in the estimation of his companions.

It was this early introduction to politics that opened the way to his career. His faithful and competent attention to his duties was observed by all with whom he came in contact, particularly by Chancellor Wythe — a distinguished character in a distinguished time. Wythe was a scholarly, liberal-minded gentleman of the true Virginian school, a signer of the Declaration of Independence, an able jurist, and the Chief of the High Court of Chancery. It was, therefore, no small compliment to Clay that he should be

---

[1] Colton's *Life of Clay*, vol. i. p. 20.

chosen as the Chancellor's amanuensis. He acted in that capacity for four years. His duties at first were very exacting and laborious, as the subject-matter of the Chancellor's dictation—he being unable to write because of a tremulous hand—was strange to him; besides, he was required to copy quotations in Latin, of which he was wholly ignorant.

This situation—or rather relation, from the warm interest of the Chancellor in the promising youth—was an inestimable advantage to him. It might well seem providential were it not that uncommon capacity usually attracts patrons. Besides a livelihood, it gave him character in the community and brought him into constant observation of perhaps the ablest bar in the country. He made the most of the opportunity, which was his only means to remedy his extreme lack of education. His habits were studious and exemplary; his reading, tastes, and aspirations were guided by his venerable friend. His leisure was mostly devoted to books; but his reading appears to have been desultory—Harris's *Hermes*, Tooke's *Diversions of Purley*, Lowth's *Grammar*, and various historical works. Perhaps a further indication of his studies during this time is contained in a letter to his son James, written in 1837. "Your resolution to study," he wrote, "and to begin with history, is a good one, and I hope you will persevere in it. Gillies's *Greece*, with Plutarch's *Lives*; Gibbon's *Decline and Fall of the Roman Empire*; Tacitus; Hume, with the continuation; Russell's *Modern Europe*; Hallam's *Middle Ages*; Robertson's *Charles V., Indies*, etc.; Marshall's *Life of Washington*; Botta's *History of the American Revolution*. These books and others may be read with advantage; and you should adopt some systematic course as to time—that is, to read so many hours out of the twenty-four."

Under these circumstances it was natural that he should decide to pursue the profession of the law. Accordingly, in the latter part of 1796, in his twentieth year, he entered the office of the Attorney-General, Robert Brooke, as a law-student. Within a year he procured a license to practise. While his regular novitiate was of itself inadequate to prepare him for the bar, his long association with the Chancellor was undoubtedly a valuable training in the principles and application of equity jurisprudence, and was probably so considered in hastening his admission to practice.

Concerning this early period of Clay's life there is but little positive information. Though Richmond was a city of but five thousand inhabitants, it was the social and political centre of Virginia. Despite the levelling influences of the Revolution, the subsequent abolition of primogeniture and entail and the progress of Jefferson's political principles, there still remained strong aristocratic tendencies, which largely dominated society. Yet that society was ever ready to open its doors to character and ability, and Clay was accorded the attention and respect of such men as John Marshall, Edmund Pendleton, and Spencer Roane. Instead, however, of remaining in Richmond, he decided to settle in Lexington, Kentucky. "The public attention was at that time strongly drawn to Kentucky as a field especially propitious to the enterprise of the young. Members of the most respectable families of Virginia had already emigrated to that State, and the marvels of its rapid growth and teeming prosperity were recounted with such commendation as to rouse a general fervor in behalf of settlement in this Eldorado of the West."[1] Moreover, Kentucky was still

---

[1] Kennedy's *Life of Wirt*, vol. i. p. 92.

practically a colony of Virginia, most of her people, customs, laws, and institutions being thence derived. Clay's decision may also have been influenced by the removal to that country of his mother and family several years before. But doubtless he sagaciously perceived that the surroundings would yield him congenial opportunities and a better immediate prospect than he would find in Richmond or any other town in his native State.

When Clay settled in Lexington, in 1797, the Indian troubles, which gave the State its name (Indian for dark and bloody ground), had long been subdued by Daniel Boone and his successors. Within a decade the population of the State had trebled, and was then nearly two hundred thousand. The settlement of Lexington began thirty-two years before and had advanced with remarkable rapidity. The original pioneers and their descendants formed but a small portion of the towns-people, who constantly increased in number by fresh arrivals, bringing with them more or less of the cultivation and habits of life acquired in the older States. Schools were soon established and improved. The Transylvania Seminary was founded in 1788, and in a few years developed into a university. But, though Lexington possessed more of the refinements of the East than any other place west of the Alleghanies, it was essentially a frontier town. The free and hearty spirit of the original settlers still prevailed, and with it many of the characteristics of such a population. Drinking, gaming, and horse-racing were general diversions. Social distinctions were practically unknown. To the situation in which Clay now found himself his popular genius was perfectly suited.

The wisdom of his course was soon manifest. "I remember," said he in his old age, "how comfortable I thought I should be if I could make one hundred pounds, Virginia money, per year, and with what delight I received the first fifteen-shilling fee. My hopes were more than realized. I immediately rushed into a lucrative practice."

At that period debating societies were very generally in vogue. Clay had been a diligent member of one in Richmond, and immediately joined another in Lexington. He attended several meetings of the Lexington club without participating in the discussions. One evening, however, after a long debate, and as the question was about to be put, he remarked to some one near him that the subject did not appear to him to have been exhausted. The chairman was informed that Mr. Clay desired to speak. He accepted the invitation then given him and attempted to proceed. In his extreme embarrassment he opened by saying, "Gentlemen of the jury." This caused some merriment in the audience and more confusion to himself, for he repeated the blunder, which was probably caused by his practice of making speeches to imaginary juries in preparation for his début in court. But he quickly recovered his composure, and spoke with such unexpected eloquence and power as to gain enthusiastic applause and admiration. While yet a boy his conversation was noticeable for its ease and propriety, and his earliest efforts in public discussion displayed a singular force and fluency of diction. His associations had been such as to spur and improve this natural gift. He was an eager listener to the eminent counsel who appeared in the Richmond courts; twice he heard Patrick Henry, one occasion being that of Henry's greatest forensic argument, in the case of the British debts, which Wirt so graphically describes. But during this time, what was more directly to the purpose was the efficient exercise he followed privately, as indicated by his mistake in the debating club. The importance he attached to this training, as well as a glimpse of his youthful ambition, is shown by a statement made by him many years afterward before a class of law-graduates. "I owe my success in life," said he, "to one single fact—namely, that at an early period I commenced and continued for some years the practice of daily reading and speaking the contents of some historical or scientific book. These off-hand efforts were sometimes made in a cornfield; at others in the forest; and not infrequently in some distant barn, with the horse and ox for my only auditors. It is to this practice of the art of all arts that I am indebted for the primary and leading impulses that stimulated my progress and have shaped and moulded my entire destiny."[1] His presence was impressive and commanding; his voice the perfection of human tones. With these great gifts he possessed a genial, generous temperament, keen discernment of character, practical judgment, and ready tact.[2] Such qualities found

---

[1] "Oratory was esteemed the first attribute of superior minds, and was assiduously cultivated. There were few newspapers, and the press had not attained the controlling power over the public mind as now. Political information was disseminated chiefly by public speaking, and every one aspiring to lead was expected to be a fine speaker. This method, and the manner of voting, forced the open avowal of political opinion."—Sparks's *Memories of Fifty Years*, p. 22.

[2] "Of all the men I have known, Clay had more of what is called, in modern times, magnetism. He was quite tall, yet commanding, and very graceful in manner and movement. He had the most wonderful voice in compass, purity, and sweetness, and which, with the whole science of gesticulation and manner, he sedulously cultivated. . . . In this Clay had a great source of power. There was also a natural common-sense, which, in him and Abraham Lincoln, outweighed all the culture in books of their great rivals. . . . Thus Mr. Clay, in the backwoods, where men are seen more in their real characters than in older societies and cities, was better able to understand them (and men are at bottom much the same everywhere), or any audience elsewhere. . . . Mr. Clay had a very highly

their best arena in jury practice, where his powers were so transcendent that none of the many persons charged with murder whom he defended were condemned to death. His early professional years abound with anecdotes of his exploits, some of them almost magical and romantic.

He was never deterred from performing his professional duty by fear of consequences. The barbarous arbitrament of duelling to settle personal grievances was nowhere recognized and practised more generally than in Kentucky; and Clay's known disposition to maintain his honor at the peril of the pistol no doubt made his forensic adversaries careful to avoid offence. Only once was he drawn into an "affair" through conduct in court. Colonel Joseph H. Daviess, a prominent Federalist, and the United States district-attorney for that region, had assaulted a tavern-keeper named Bush, at Frankfort. The details of the occurrence are not known, but presumably it grew out of an altercation provoked by politics and whiskey, after the common fashion of that day and country. Such was the awe of Daviess's influence that Bush could not procure an attorney in Frankfort to act for him. He then applied to Clay, who promptly brought suit against Daviess in Lexington. In the course of the proceedings Clay criticised the conduct of the Colonel, who, after the adjournment of the court, sent a note to Clay, remonstrating against his language and expressing the wish that he would not persist in his course. Clay replied that he had undertaken the cause from a sense of duty, and that he would conduct it according to his own judgment, holding himself responsible in

---

developed nervous structure and temperament, by which, as in war, all his forces could be at once rapidly concentrated on one point of attack."— *Life of Cassius M. Clay*, vol. i. p. 88.

or out of court for what he said and did. Daviess then sent a challenge, which Clay accepted. Through the influence of mutual friends the difficulty was settled on the field where the duel was to be fought. Another instance of Clay's fearlessness was in behalf of a man who had suffered extreme hardship by incurring the hostility of a gang of backwoods ruffians known as "Regulators." At the risk of his personal safety, Clay volunteered his services, and by obtaining a heavy verdict for exemplary damages effectually broke up the lawless pest.

Clay was repeatedly urged to accept the office of district-attorney, but criminal prosecution was so distasteful to him that he had declined the position. He was finally induced, however, to take it for a short time, hoping to procure the appointment of a friend whom he desired to have the place. He was immediately called upon to prosecute a slave, who, in defending himself from the brutality of an overseer, had killed his assailant with an axe. The slave was uncommonly intelligent and proud, and his case aroused much interest and sympathy. Had he been free, his act at most would have been manslaughter; but as slaves were required by the law to submit to chastisement, the offence was legally that of murder, whatever the palliating circumstances. The negro was convicted and executed; but he died with such fortitude and manly spirit that Clay deeply deplored his participation in the trial. He immediately resigned his commission; and whenever afterward the subject was mentioned he spoke sorrowfully of the fate of the unfortunate slave.

Clay's extraordinary success as an advocate might be readily imagined from his subsequent public life. It is not surprising, therefore, that so remarkable a man should have made such rapid progress under the circumstances then existing in that frontier country. The fame he soon achieved is evidenced by his being retained (though he declined to accept a fee) by Aaron Burr, himself one of the most adroit of lawyers, when the first efforts were made to indict him in Kentucky, in 1806. And Clay's high personal standing is at the same time illustrated by the fact that Burr's immunity was then largely due to his unqualified pledge to Clay that he was not engaged in any unlawful or improper designs, which Clay implicitly believed. Besides his celebrity in criminal practice, he gained high reputation for his skill in the conduct of causes arising out of the mixed state of the land laws and titles.[1] It is not unlikely, as tradition indicates, that his success in the latter as well as in the former class of cases was occasionally aided by his fertile and dramatic dexterity. In older communities, where conditions and relations are more varied and involved, where property and rights are more secure and valuable, and, consequently, where jurisprudence is matured more to a nicely adjusted science and the practice to a minutely defined system, to say naught of the less emotional temper of the people, the triumphs of mere advocacy and forensic magic are more difficult and rare.

Clay was not a deep student, and never approached the distinction of jurist which marked Webster's intellectual supremacy.[2] Even had his tastes been scholarly, he would

---

[1] "I have heard it stated that the Kentucky bar was at that time superior to the bar of any other State. This was perhaps attributable to the fact that every acre of ground was covered over by conflicting law-claims." —Coleman's *Crittenden*, vol. i. p. 14.

[2] "'In the course of my professional life,' said Mr. Webster, 'it has happened many times that I found myself retained in the same cause with Mr. Clay. He was my senior by several years, in the profession and in

have found little time or necessity for the prolonged and ramified thought essential to eminence at the Eastern bar. But his tastes were not of that kind, except so far as related to the cultivation of his potent art of speech—and that was never distinctly literary. He was convivial, sanguine, and restless. His leading characteristic was action, not reflection. The movement of his mind was rapid and rhetorical; hence it was not laborious and profound. Such a mind is attracted by prominent externals; it sees vividly, but forms its deductions peremptorily: the crystal clearness of its partial perceptions endangers complete and proportioned judgment. Thus Clay's extraordinary gifts were attended by their corresponding defects. Whatever knowledge he acquired was always and entirely at his service; and this frequently had the effect of obscuring the need of more. His fragments of knowledge he wielded as the Titans the rocks; this almost inevitably rendered his principal fault as incorrigible as it was imposing.

It has been urged that his lack of systematic education proved a practical advantage to him by increasing the self-reliance that was the most magnetic and imperial attribute of his leadership. But, on the other hand, so competent a critic as Schurz implies that a thorough early training would have made him more cautious in forming opinions and less commanding in his advocacy of them, but would have led him to avoid grave errors as a statesman. Such

---

age. That fact gave him the right to speak first in all such cases. Often, before beginning my argument, I have had to labor hard to do away with the effect and impression of his. Some of the most labored acts of my professional life have consisted in getting matters back to the starting-point after Clay had spoken. The fact is, he was no lawyer. He was a statesman, a politician, an orator, but no reasoner.'"—March's *Reminiscences of Webster*, p. 217.

conjectures, it may be ventured, have but little value. Men of great genius, which is not least a matter of temperament, are not materially changed by any cause; circumstances may favor, modify, or suppress, but do not transform, their qualities. If Clay's public policy was wrong in any main features, it was not owing to his lack of collegiate training, but to a natural fault or bias of his mind—or to politics. It is doubtless true that with other preparation and surroundings his career would have been different; not in character, however, but in degree. More likely, in that event, we should have been deprived of the historical Henry Clay; the history of the country would be different. As it was, his native powers developed to their fullest pitch speedily and with perfect freedom. The atmosphere in which he moved was charged with the chivalrous and uninquiring spirit of the South and West. There were no customs, standards, or rivalries formidable enough to impede his early growth and rise. But a youth, he plunged into the current of important affairs. Before he reached maturity he had gained the experience of middle age and the prestige of his genius.

The qualities that gave him his peculiar force at the bar were those also to give him popularity and power in the sphere of politics. In truth, the courts were too narrow a theatre for him. Notwithstanding his marvellous skill, the vocation of settling personal and property differences, and keeping the accused from jail or the gallows, could not long be satisfying to a man of his mould, whatever the rewards;[1] and civil litigation in the East, much less in the

---

[1] "Your friend Clay has argued before us with a good deal of ability; and if he were not a candidate for higher office I should think he might attain great eminence at this bar. But he prefers the fame of popular

West, did not involve the wealth and weight concerned in later times when corporate interests began to assert their expansive force in society. That he would take part in politics was inevitable.

His first political efforts were in the cause of abolishing slavery. Soon after his arrival in Lexington a convention was called to meet in 1799 to revise the constitution of the State. Not more than one-fifth of the population (about forty thousand) were slaves; nor was slavery deeply engrafted on the nascent social structure of the commonwealth. It was therefore very practicable to effect by the new constitution the gradual emancipation of the blacks. This plan was adopted in Pennsylvania in 1780, through the characteristic counsel of Franklin; it had already been followed in Connecticut; and was then being agitated in New York, where it succeeded two years later. Clay forthwith joined it, and zealously labored in its behalf. He began by contributing a series of articles to the *Kentucky Gazette*, over the signature "Scævola." He then boldly championed the cause before public meetings. He was prompted both by his feelings and the opinions he had imbibed from Chancellor Wythe, who with other leading characters—among them Washington, Jefferson, Madison, Henry, and Marshall—had vainly sought to extinguish slavery in Virginia in the same mode. In Kentucky, as in the mother State, the movement was confined to a small and select circle, and did not succeed. Clay and his coadjutors were "overpowered by numbers," as he said in a speech at Frankfort in 1829. But he always regarded his action with unchanged convictions.[1]

---

talents to the steady fame of the bar."—*Judge Story to Dodd, March,* 1823.

[1] "The sentiment, however, had taken deep root. It continued with

In the Frankfort speech he expressed his regret over the result, which he admitted had placed Kentucky in the rear of her free neighbors "in the state of agriculture, the progress of manufactures, the advance of improvements, and the general progress of society." For some years he set the example—followed half a century later by Dana, Seward, and other Northern advocates—of volunteering his professional aid, whenever occasion offered, to such as sought their freedom by means of the law. Nevertheless, he very soon became a slave-holder himself, and remained one the rest of his life. Politically, it was fortunate for him that Kentucky continued to be a slave State. It was easy for a slave-holder to avow antislavery sentiments; for a long time they sounded all the more noble at the North, and involved no risk at the South. This hybrid policy, while doubtless sincere, proved a material resource of Clay's political influence.

If he suffered any unpopularity through his course on the slavery question, which is not improbable, it was more than counteracted by his participation at about the same time in the excited opposition to the Alien and Sedition laws. These extraordinary statutes were enacted in 1798 by a Federalist Congress. Although much modified in scope and detail after their introduction, enough remained to give them that despotic character which renders them a notorious topic in our political history. They mark the extreme and

---

increasing strength until the Rebellion, when it proved one of the controlling influences that prevented the State from secession. The increase of free blacks is fairly to be taken as an indication of the antislavery propaganda that began with Henry Clay."—Shaler's *Kentucky*, p. 155.

"In Kentucky, as I am told by several gentlemen of high standing, there is so strong an opposition to slavery that the chief slave-holders have long feared to call a convention to alter the Constitution, though much desired, lest measures should be adopted that might lead to gradual emancipation."—*Niles's Register*, vol. xviii. p. 27 (1820).

fatal stretch of the Federalist doctrine. Among other, but less obnoxious, features, they gave the President power to banish alien residents whom he might judge to be dangerous to the country, and to imprison them if they did not leave within the time he fixed. They also made it a felony to libel the government, either House of Congress, or the President. The principal design was to suppress the chief Republican journalists, mostly foreigners, whose intemperate advocacy of French Republicanism was harassing and hateful to the Federal party. The excitement they kindled, fanned by the adroit management of Jefferson, was more intense in Kentucky than elsewhere.

Kentucky was admitted into the Union but six years before. The struggle for separation from Virginia had been long and acrimonious; to accomplish it, even foreign alliance had been threatened. Separation achieved, the most pressing desire and problem were to free the navigation of the Mississippi, which was under the control of Spain, then allied with England. It was so vital to the development of the State, and so plainly proper, that it seemed a natural right of which the State should not be deprived for any reason; and the demand was loud for the national government to secure it — if necessary, by force.[1] Little concern, however, was apparent in that quarter for this or any of the peculiar interests of the West. This indifference was largely ascribed to Eastern hostility, and therefore to the Federal party. When Genêt, the rashly officious French

---

[1] "There are those now living [1850] in the valley who can remember that the possession of the delta of the Mississippi by Spain was fast separating the East and the West. A delay of five years in the purchase of Louisiana would have dismembered the Union and created a separate government in the valley."—*Democratic Review*, vol. xxvi. p. 11.

ambassador, projected an expedition against Spanish Louisiana, an enthusiastic friendship for France was aroused. Numerous societies were formed, patterned after the Jacobin Clubs, and an active French sentiment soon pervaded the State. But after Genêt's presumptuous follies were quenched by Washington and a treaty with Spain had been effected opening the Mississippi, with a place of deposit at New Orleans, there set in a strong reaction, which was furthered for a time in the early part of 1798 by the piratical demands of the French Directory disclosed by the famous " X. Y. Z. Mission." Nevertheless, at heart, Kentucky was still the most radically anti-Federal of all the States; and when the Federalists, in the over-confidence of their sudden popularity, committed the amazing mistake of enacting the Alien and Sedition laws, Kentucky's former Republicanism vehemently revived. The excitement that soon raged almost reached the pitch of frenzy. All the machinery with which the Kentuckians, through their prolonged efforts for independence, were peculiarly familiar was set in motion. Public meetings were held throughout the State, at which the odious laws were violently denounced. At one of the first and largest of these gatherings, Clay, then in his twenty-second year, was called to speak. George Nicholas, an experienced lawyer and politician, had preceded with a long and able address; but the thrilling power of Clay's impassioned harangue on the menaced liberties of the people so affected the crowd that an opposing orator was silenced, and Clay and Nicholas were shouldered, put in a carriage, and drawn by shouting men through the streets of Lexington. Clay, of course, continued to be a prominent and efficient actor during the commotion, the outcome of which was the celebrated Kentucky and Virginia Resolutions, adopted by the legislatures of those States, and destined to become the canon of the future doctrines of nullification and secession.

After this, aside from speaking in support of Jefferson's election in 1800, Clay devoted his entire attention to the law until 1803, when, in his absence and without his knowledge, he was made a candidate for a seat in the State Assembly. It was induced by a desire to place Clay in a position to oppose a movement which had been started to repeal a law creating a Lexington insurance company. This movement was led by Felix Grundy, who, years afterward, was a Representative and Senator from Tennessee. There was much local interest in the subject, and Clay was selected by the friends of the company as best adapted to perform the desired service. The election had been in progress a day or so before a poll was opened for him. Returning at this juncture, and learning the situation, he accepted the candidacy and was elected. He not only accomplished the particular object for which he was chosen, but his power in debate quickly won for him the leading position in the legislature. Whenever he spoke at length a quorum could not be maintained in the other House. The rapidity of his political progress equalled that which he had made in his profession. So high was his standing that he was elected to the Senate of the United States at the first opportunity. This occurred in 1806, when John Adair resigned his seat because of his complicity with Burr.

When Clay took the oath as Senator, December 29, he had not attained the age of thirty, as prescribed by the Constitution. His eligibility, however, was not questioned; but in after-years he was charged with the act as a wilful violation of the Constitution, and it can hardly be supposed that he acted in ignorance.¹ The vacancy he was elected to fill was only for one session, ending March 3, 1807. He took part in the most important proceedings, served on various committees, and introduced several resolutions, one of them proposing a Constitutional amendment concerning the judicial power. He not only entered freely into the debates, but in his first speech took occasion to rebuke an old member for his manner of assuming superior wisdom, and amused the Senate by quoting from Peter Pindar:

> "Thus have I seen a magpie on the street,
> A chattering bird we often meet;
> A bird for curiosity well known,
>   With head awry, and cunning eye,
> Peep knowingly into a marrow-bone."

He created a favorable impression as an orator, although he had no opportunity to exhibit his powers to the best advantage; yet some grave Senators, unaccustomed to Clay's energetic style in their small chamber, thought it rather declamatory. "This session of Congress," he wrote to a friend, "has not been so interesting as I had anticipated. No questions in relation to our foreign intercourse involving much discussion have been agitated; everything depends upon the result of pending negotiations, and this will not be known, it is probable, until the session expires." His first speech, which was very gratifying to those who were locally interested, was in support of a bill to provide for the erec-

---

¹ "While welcoming Mr. Clay to Boston as chairman of a young men's committee, in the autumn of 1833, I found that he was indisposed to have this early breach of the Constitutional requirements alluded to or inquired into with much particularity. 'I think, my young friend,' said he, 'we may as well omit any reference to my supposed juvenile indiscretions.'" — *Winthrop's Addresses*, vol. iv. p. 41.

Claiborne's election to the House from Tennessee, in 1803, was a similar lapse, for he was not twenty-five years of age.

tion of a bridge over the Potomac at Georgetown. The measure to which he gave most attention was preliminary to the proposed construction of a canal in Kentucky, at the rapids in the Ohio River. By his attitude in regard to these subjects he espoused the doctrine that Congress possessed Constitutional power to promote internal improvements, although in so doing he disagreed with Jefferson, who in his annual message recommended a Constitutional amendment as necessary to give the power. Clay also advocated national aid to the Chesapeake and Ohio canal, and a resolution calling upon the Secretary of the Treasury to submit to the Senate at the next session a report on the policy and plan of a system of improvements. The report was made, but it was not until some years later that the subject assumed political importance. Clay regarded his service at this session as a recreation. He was also before the Supreme Court in several cases. In his social relations, which he cultivated, he was much admired and esteemed.[1] Preferring not to neglect his law practice, he declined a re-election; but he was immediately returned to the State Assembly, despite an unseemly opposition grounded on his having acted as Burr's counsel.

During his former service in the Assembly the discussions had all related to local topics; they now took a wider range. Portentous foreign troubles had begun to disturb the tranquillity which the country had previously enjoyed under Jefferson's administration. Political differences, which had slumbered for some time, were stoutly renewed. The chronic Western aversion for Great Britain was displayed in a senseless, but not wholly novel, way. It was proposed

---

[1] *Life of William Plumer*, p. 351; Adams's *Diary*, January 15, 1807.

to forbid the use of any British legal citations whatever in the courts of the State; and the proposition was favored by a large majority. The administration of justice, it was urged, should not be governed by the decisions of foreign courts, particularly those of Great Britain. Clay had the judgment and courage to oppose the measure, notwithstanding he shared the sentiment that induced it. But his method was the same as that which he employed on several historic occasions long afterward — he proposed a compromise. He moved to limit the prohibition to the period after the Declaration of Independence, and supported the motion by resounding argument and a just and brilliant eulogy of the common law. His motion prevailed, and arrested the demagogic folly that threatened the jurisprudence of the State.[1]

At this session he was Speaker. At the next, Humphrey Marshall, formerly a United States Senator, and the leader of the small contingent of Kentucky Federalists, appeared in the Assembly for the purpose of making war on Clay and the Republican party, and Clay remained on the floor because of the greater freedom it gave him. He did not wait for attack, but soon introduced a series of emphatic resolutions denouncing the conduct of Great Britain toward our maritime commerce, pledging to the government the co-operation of Kentucky in resisting British aggressions, and lauding Jefferson and his policy. Marshall proposed resolutions to the contrary effect; but he had the mortification of voting alone for them after delivering a harsh invective against those which Clay had offered and advocated in his characteristic manner. Following the whim of the day, Clay next

---

[1] A similar law had been enacted in New Jersey in 1801, and the example was followed in Pennsylvania in 1810.

CH. I.] DUEL BETWEEN CLAY AND MARSHALL 31

proposed a resolution declaring that every member of the legislature should wear clothing of domestic manufacture only, to manifest his practical devotion to the policy of encouraging American industry, which was already popular in Kentucky, partly because of the hostile feeling against England. This was Clay's first effort in behalf of the system which he contributed more than any one else to establish as a distinct national policy. Nothing could have been better calculated to inflame Marshall's hostility and to afford him an opportunity to exercise his talent for abuse. He abandoned himself to his violent animosities, and applied to Clay and his resolution a variety of offensive and insulting epithets, to which Clay responded with vigor and freedom. The consequence was a challenge from Marshall to a duel, which Clay promptly accepted. They met and fired at each other twice, each receiving a slight wound. At this point the seconds intervened and ended the combat. Presumably the principals regarded the demands of honor as satisfied.[1]

In the town of Hebron, Ohio, there still lingers the tradition of a peculiar sequel to this duel. For several years subsequent to 1809 the middle counties of Ohio were infested by gangs of horse-thieves. The leader of the Licking County gang was one Eli Marshall, who was generally regarded as the most dangerous desperado in the West, a giant in stature,

---

[1] "It was calculated with certainty by Clay's friends at Louisville (opposite to which, on the Indiana side of the Ohio River, the fight took place) that Marshall would be killed or badly wounded. Mr. Clay, in this event, was to be welcomed on his return from the scene of the combat by a dinner provided by his friends. He was not in condition, of course, to partake of it, but tradition goes on further to relate that he returned the compliment of his friends by giving them card-parties in his room during the whole time he was confined to it by his wound."—*Headlands in the Life of Henry Clay*, No. 1, p. 2.

and a villain every inch. For a long time the farmers near
Hebron had remained unmolested, but finally they were raided and their best horses taken. Of the party that was organized and pursued the gang six were killed, and as a result
the community was in a state of terror. During this excitement, Clay was on his way to Washington over the national
road. He was advised to accept an armed escort, but he
declined. One afternoon immediately afterward he stopped
at the "Licking Arms," a hostelry in Hebron. As a heavy
rain was falling, it was decided to travel no farther until
the next day. In the evening a large number of citizens
gathered at the tavern to pay their respects to Clay; and
in the course of the conversation the subject of the recent
depredations was discussed. Clay freely expressed his opinions on the subject. He said he had no fear of being
molested, and, furthermore, that he would not mind meeting
Marshall and calling him to account.

This remark was probably reported by a spy; at all
events, Marshall and three of his gang came to the tavern
after the people had dispersed. Clay was in his room writing letters when he was informed of the situation by the
landlord, who reported that Marshall demanded to see him.
Clay sent back the reply that he never complied with demands. Marshall forthwith came up the stairs, threw open
Clay's door, and strode into the room—but to look into the
muzzle of a pistol. At Clay's command he halted, deposited
his weapons on a chair near him, and then stepped into an
adjoining store-room. Clay securely fastened the door and
went down-stairs. There the other three desperadoes were
overawed in the same manner, disarmed, and bound. Returning above, Clay released Marshall from the store-room and
bade him sit down and explain his object in perpetrating such

an outrage. He replied that he was a second cousin to Humphrey Marshall, with whom Clay had fought in 1808; that he had been told that the duel was not finished because Clay showed cowardice; and that he had made up his mind to compel Clay to apologize to him for the injury done his kinsman. Clay then proposed that they go to the large room below and take three shots at each other. Marshall agreed and asked for his pistol; but Clay refused to restore it until they were ready to shoot. He directed the landlord and his son to stand with their pistols close to Marshall until the word was given to fire, and to shoot him if he made a move to turn before the word. By this time Marshall was pale and trembling. He showed the craven, and finally refused to fight. Clay then made him get down on his knees and apologize both to himself and to the landlord for the outrage, and to sign a paper acknowledging that he was a coward. This done, he was bound, and, with the other three ruffians, delivered over to the authorities. Whether or not this story is true, Clay was entirely capable of the action ascribed to him, and was so regarded by the people of that region.[1]

The session at which the duel with Marshall occurred terminated Clay's service in the State legislature. He was again elected to the Senate, this time to fill a vacancy for two years. If he had previously hesitated to enter upon a public career in the national arena, it is quite apparent that he had now overcome his indecision. Few details

---

[1] This tradition was first published with considerable detail in the Louisville *Courier Journal*, in June, 1896, and afterward in the New York *Sun*. It is there related that the prisoners managed to escape; but that the gang was soon broken up, Marshall and one other fleeing into Virginia, where they were captured and hanged to a tree. Marshall's sheath-knife, it is said, was sent to Clay, and is still in possession of the family.

of his history during this early period are known, but it may be assumed that his circumstances had improved to a degree that warranted him in yielding to the ambition his brilliant success thus far undoubtedly stimulated.

He re-appeared in the Senate February 5, 1810, and immediately renewed his activity in that body with that independence and initiative which always characterized him. Our foreign relations and maritime troubles were growing daily more threatening, and the warlike spirit, particularly in the West, was rapidly rising. It was doubtless this situation that furnished Clay's main incentive for returning to the Senate. The long-continued system of commercial restrictions—non-importation, embargo, and non-intercourse—was nearly exhausted. It was always obnoxious to one party, and was now becoming unsatisfactory to the other. That Clay was ready to advocate war he soon made manifest. The existing restrictive act was to expire with the session. To meet the situation, a bill proposed by the administration was passed by the House, after much wrangling, to exclude from our ports all British and French vessels, and to admit British and French merchandise only when directly imported in American bottoms; but to permit the renewal of trade, upon the proclamation of the President, with the power that rescinded or changed its decrees so as no longer to violate our neutral trade. Shortly after Clay's return to the Senate the bill was there taken up and an amendment carried striking out all the provisions except those to exclude belligerent ships of war. February 25, Clay moved to recommit the bill, and delivered a passionate speech against the emasculation of it. This is the first of his reported speeches, and it is doubtful whether it was taken fully or with verbal accuracy, though it sufficiently discloses his belligerent views. His motion was defeated, but he voiced a sentiment that soon became controlling. His speech was the inception of the leadership he soon acquired.¹ The bill failed, as the two Houses could not agree; but another bill less stringent in character was enacted in place of it.

Clay spoke frequently, but not again at length until April 6, when he addressed the Senate on the "encouragement of home industry." The question arose on a motion to strike out an amendment to an appropriation bill directing the Secretary of the Navy to give preference, in purchasing sail-duck, cordage, hemp, flax, and the like, to domestic productions, whenever it could be done without material detriment to the public service. It evoked discussion of the general policy of promoting manufactures. Immediately after Clay's speech against it the motion was defeated, 9 to 22. Nevertheless, the House struck out the provision, and the bill became a law without it. It was probably thought more dignified and equally advantageous to leave the matter wholly to the discretion of the Navy Department; indeed, had the provision been enacted it could have had no effect without the concurrence of the department, which was alone to determine what was to the "detriment of the public service." According to Clay's own statement, the progress already made in the production of those articles was good evidence that those industries were quite independent of

---

¹ "Clay's speech marked the appearance of a school which was for fifty years to express the national ideas of statesmanship, drawing elevation of character from confidence in itself, and from devotion to ideas of nationality and union which redeemed every mistake committed in their names. In Clay's speech, almost for the first time, the two rhetorical marks of his generation made their appearance, and during the next half-century the Union and the Fathers were rarely omitted from any popular harangue."
—Adams's *History of the United States*, vol. v. p. 190.

governmental aid. And this view was strongly reinforced in a report on manufactures presented to Congress by Gallatin not long after Clay's speech. The significance of Clay's views at this time is that he was far more moderate in his advocacy of protection than he afterward became; for even then a distinctly protective policy was favored by many. So far as he expressed his opinions, he apparently differed little from those who were free-traders in principle, but who approved such incidental encouragement to domestic production as would not involve extra burdens of taxation.

Besides participating in the debates, he was industrious in the routine duties of legislation. Among numerous subjects that engaged his attention were bills to grant pre-emptive rights to settlers upon the public lands, and to regulate trade and intercourse with the Indians. On each of these bills he drew a committee report which displayed just and sagacious views. He no doubt felt at the close of the session a greater degree of satisfaction than he had experienced during his former service in the Senate. It was unmistakable that he was a rising man. His genius as a parliamentarian and his attractive personal qualities were ungrudgingly admired. He was rapidly perfecting himself in the art that, with his mind and personality, was to make him a potent character in politics and legislation through a long career. The time was propitious—events were approaching a climax suited to bold and self-reliant men. Clay had neglected no opportunity, and could look forward with confidence to a position of conspicuous influence.

The next session of Congress convened December 3. Ten days later Clay was in his seat, and on Christmas Day he delivered the most able and telling speech he had thus far addressed to the Senate.

The southeastern boundary of the Louisiana purchase was not precisely defined; and with the progress of settlement in West Florida, conflicting claims to that territory by Spain and the United States had inevitably arisen, as our negotiations for the purchase of Florida had not succeeded. Spain claimed title to the Mississippi, and the United States to the Rio Perdido. Our government, however, had not taken possession, and the Spanish flag flew unmolested from Baton Rouge to Pensacola, until in the summer of 1810, when the increasing population—composed of various nationalities, with a large portion from the United States — imitating the example of many of the Spanish-American provinces, declared independence, after some confusion, and applied for annexation to the United States. Madison then performed an act that for him was of extraordinary audacity. In October he issued a proclamation asserting our title to the territory, and directing its annexation to Orleans. He professed to be actuated by the desire to prevent further disorder in the district, and announced that the seizure would, notwithstanding, be "the subject of fair and friendly negotiation and adjustment" with Spain. Nevertheless, the declaration of independence and the application for annexation were rebuffed as an impertinence. Measures were at once taken to enforce the edict between the Mississippi and the Pearl rivers; beyond the Pearl the confusion still continued. Madison, of course, stated the situation to Congress at the opening of the session, and a bill in conformity with his proclamation was introduced in the Senate. The proceeding met with intense approval in the West, but was opposed by the Federalists. The principal speech against the bill had been delivered by Horsey, of Delaware. Clay immediately replied. While his animated speech—in which he again vigorously denounced the conduct of Great Britain toward this country—bears some marks of being extemporaneous, its decided superiority over his previous reported utterances suggests that it had been thoroughly considered. Before Madison's proclamation the press of Kentucky and Tennessee had energetically argued the importance of our acquiring exclusive control of the Gulf coast, and that if we did not take possession of West Florida, England, by some means, would. It is probable that Clay's perfect familiarity with the treaties and the President's justification of his course, unsound in law but sound in policy, was derived from Madison, who doubtless selected him to present the case to the Senate. This supposition is aided by his subsequent leadership in the proceedings. Pickering, of Massachusetts, a zealous Federalist, quoted, in replying to Clay, a letter from Talleyrand to Jefferson, which had been confidentially communicated to the Senate by Jefferson in 1805. Clay at once moved a resolution censuring him for his breach of the rules, and procured its adoption.

While this debate was in progress, Madison sent to Congress a secret message asking for authority to take possession of West Florida, and that a declaration be made that the United States could not, unconcerned, see the Floridas pass from Spain to any other foreign power. This message was accompanied by a letter from Folch, the Spanish governor of the Floridas, offering to surrender the whole territory to the United States if Spain should not send him succor by the first day of January. The situation was further complicated by the application of Louisiana (Orleans territory) for admission into the Union. The final result was the enactment of the usual preliminary law for the admission of Louisiana, including the small part of West Florida between the Mississippi, the Iberville, Lake Maurepas, and Lake Pontchartrain; of another authorizing the President to take possession of East Florida if the local authorities assented, or should any foreign power attempt to occupy it; and the adoption of a joint resolution declaring, pursuant to the President's request, that, in view of the situation of Spain and her American colonies, it was impossible to see without alarm any part of the territory pass to any foreign power, and that safety required our occupation of the territory, but subject to future negotiation. By a subsequent law these acts and resolutions concerning East Florida were not to be promulgated before the end of the next session of Congress; and they were not until about the time of the treaty by which Spain ceded the Floridas to the United States, and thus closed the train of controversies which had arisen in relation to this domain. The bill concerning West Florida was dropped, and the situation was left as it was. At the next session, however, all that part of West Florida west of the Pearl was added to Louisiana, which was then admitted into the Union. The rest of the tract was incorporated into the Mississippi territory notwithstanding the Spanish garrison at Mobile. At this session also a bill to authorize the President to take possession of Florida entire, and establish a government over it, was passed by the House; but it was factiously defeated in the Senate.

These subjects gave Clay a rapid experience in the larger statecraft of the period; and this, with the increasing deference shown him, doubtless increased his confidence in his powers. He entered into the discussion of the most important topic before Congress with such assurance and intrepidity that the position he took caused him much embarrassment later.

The charter of the Bank of the United States, enacted in 1791, was about to expire, and the renewal of it was urged upon Congress. Both Madison and Gallatin opposed the bank as unconstitutional when it was established, but had gradually changed their opinions. It had performed important functions in the finances of the government and the country by supplying a sound and uniform currency, facilitating exchanges, aiding in the collection and custody of the public revenues, and in various operations of the Treasury. Hence Gallatin, the ablest financier of the period, deemed it of great moment that the bank should be continued, particularly in view of the possibility of war. Its termination would cause a large export of specie to pay the foreign stockholders, and would produce for a long time a serious contraction of the currency, besides a deterioration in the character of the inevitable issues of the State banks. But notwithstanding the strong support it received from many important business interests, a strong sentiment had arisen against the recharter. The Constitutional objections to a national bank were strongly renewed. The legislatures of several States, and among them Kentucky, instructed their Senators to oppose the recharter. The old cry was raised that the bank was an aristocratic monopoly adverse to the spirit of our institutions. As two-thirds of the stock was held abroad, the bank was charged with being controlled by foreign influence and with sending its profits abroad. It was also accused of favoritism in its accommodations, and consequently of being a political factor—the remaining bulwark of Federalism. The local banks were also clamorous in their opposition, for the policy of the bank imposed a decisive check on their profuse issues of paper, which customers were eager to procure, and, failing, were instructed that their misfortune was due to the hostility of the Bank of the United States to the State banks. The people were thus moved by a desire to put down the institution. Moreover, the proposed plan of recharter was unsatisfactory to many, and opposed for that reason. But underneath all this was a political movement, extending even into the cabinet, to hamper Gallatin and banish him from office. While it is not probable that Clay was influenced by this political design, he did not hesitate to join the motley opposition. On April 6 he expressed himself in the most effective speech delivered against the bill.[1] Several Senators in favor of it had preceded him, Crawford, of Georgia, having spoken with great ability.

Clay, as usual with him at this time, opened his speech in a vein of sarcasm that displayed his self-confidence, which, in the absence of the charm of his personal intercourse, would have been regarded as presumptuous and offensive. His first objection to the bill was that it would not become operative without the assent of the bank's directors, thus placing them superior to Congress. He then, contrary to his previous views in relation to internal im-

---

[1] Concerning this speech, Washington Irving wrote: "Clay, from Kentucky, spoke against the bank. He is one of the finest fellows I have seen here, and one of the finest orators in the Senate, though, I believe, the youngest man in it. The galleries, however, were so crowded with ladies and gentlemen, and such expectations had been expressed concerning his speech, that he was completely frightened, and acquitted himself very little to his own satisfaction. He is a man I have great personal regard for."

provements, took the ground of the strict-constructionist, and argued against the Constitutional power to establish a bank—the chief subject on which, years afterward, he led the great contest with Jackson, but as the advocate of the opposite doctrine. The argument against implied powers of the Constitution has never been more felicitously stated.[1] He denied the utility and expediency of the bank, and pronounced it "a splendid association of favored individuals taken from the mass of society and invested with exemptions and surrounded by immunities and privileges." He also descanted on the danger in the union of the sword and the purse, and allowing foreigners to own stock in the bank. To the suggestion that British capital invested in this country exerted an influence over the British government in our favor, he replied with great fervor, and added: "It has often been stated, and although I do not know that it is susceptible of strict proof, I believe it to be a fact that this bank exercised its influence in support of Jay's treaty; and may it not have contributed to blunt the public sentiment or paralyze this nation against British aggression?" Nevertheless, the commercial and moneyed interests of Great Britain were afterward enlisted in the abrogating the British policy, and they finally exerted a decisive influence in bringing the War of 1812 to a close.[2]

---

[1] In 1837 he said: "I was present as a member of Congress on the occasion of the termination of the charters of both of the banks of the United States, took part in the discussion to which they gave rise, and had an opportunity of extensively knowing the opinions of members; and I declare my deliberate conviction that upon neither was there one-third of the members in either House who entertained the opinion that Congress did not possess the Constitutional power to charter a bank."

[2] Clay admitted this in a speech on the tariff in 1820. "Our late war," said he, "would not have existed if the counsels of the manufacturers in England had been listened to. They finally did prevail in their

The opposition to the recharter succeeded—yet barely succeeded. In the Senate the bill was defeated by the casting vote of the Vice-President. In the House a like bill was rejected by a vote of 65 to 64. Happening at that juncture of affairs, the result proved a serious misfortune to the country; and Clay, who could probably have prevented it, soon regretted his action.[1]

The only other business of importance transacted during the remainder of the session was the enactment of a law reviving non-intercourse with Great Britain. The bill encountered no difficulty in the Senate, but its passage by the House was signalized by the adoption of the rule of the previous question to terminate the dilatory tactics of the opposition. The government had reached a state of truly pitiful weakness. Our foreign relations were in a contemptible plight, while the feebleness of the domestic policy, caused by the timidity of Madison and the want of vigorous support in Congress, had brought the administration into a precarious situation. The time had at last arrived when energy was indispensable. Madison yielded to forceful counsels; there was no other escape from the dilemma in which he was placed. Smith, the inefficient Secretary of State, was dismissed, and Monroe took his place, with a disposition to retrieve our humbled national dignity. But what was still more important, Clay was selected to assume the leadership

---

steady and persevering effort to produce a repeal of the Orders in Council, but it was too late to prevent war."

[1] Martin Van Buren, from the bias of his political principles, ranked Clay's speech higher than it deserves. "It [the bank controversy] gave position to Henry Clay as one of the strong minds of the country, derived from his speech against rechartering the bank, by far the best speech he ever made, and nearly equal to that of Madison in 1790."—Van Buren's *Political Parties in the United States*, p. 413.

in Congress. His hour had come. He decided to retire from the Senate and enter the House. He was readily elected, and on his first appearance in that body, November 4, 1811, in his thirty-fifth year, he was chosen Speaker —the only instance where the position has been given to a new member.

This political rise entitles Clay to rank among the most precocious men notable in civil history; and this is rendered still more remarkable by the age he attained without diminution of his powers and influence. The beginning of the parliamentary career of Fox, Pitt, Canning, or Gladstone is hardly more extraordinary, if we consider the differences in training and surroundings. Although none of Clay's speeches before his second service in the Senate were preserved, they were not less effective, judging from tradition and results, than those of his later years. Certainly his speech "On the Line of the Perdido" is equal in all the elements of skilful debate to any he ever pronounced. Precocious display of this order, however, is not the product of sheer oratorical genius. Capacity for affairs and the management of men that is requisite to success in the higher grades of politics indicates a proportionately superior mind, and is usually accompanied by a considerable faculty for public speech of one type or another; but the period when the powers of such a mind are revealed depends upon favoring circumstances, be it early or late.

At this time Congress had not attained much prestige among the people. The best-known statesmen had acquired their reputation for the most part during the Revolution and the period preceding the adoption of the Constitution. They were not in Congress. A new state of things and a new generation of public men were making their appearance. Since the Revolution, not only the form of the government but the general situation had changed. During the war few of the bearings and necessities of expanding nationality, now rapidly presenting themselves, were disclosed. The establishment of the Constitution was naturally followed by a stage that may be likened to molecular change. Conditions, foreign and domestic, had arisen that called for a new order of statesmanship. Congress, which had thus far been little more than the echo of the executive department, began to assume in the public eye the place belonging to it as the prime political factor under the Constitution. What may be termed the parliamentary period now opened; and the character it soon derived owes much to the example of Henry Clay.

CHAPTER II

Maritime Aggressions of England and France—The Restrictive System—Clay as Speaker of the House—Preparations for War—Madison Accepts Clay's Programme and is Re-elected—The Embargo and the Declaration of War against England—The Political Aspect of the War—Clay's Reply to Quincy—The Treaty of Ghent—The Effect of the War—The Bank of the United States—Clay's Change of Opinion in Regard to it—The Tariff of 1816—The Policy of Internal Improvements, Madison's Veto, and Monroe's Hostile Position—Clay Opposes Monroe's Administration—He Advocates Internal Improvements and the Recognition of the South American Republics

WHEN Clay entered the House, at the opening of the Twelfth Congress, it was perfectly suited, unlike the Senate, for a theatre of debate. It had one hundred and forty-two members and but eight standing committees, and most of its important business was transacted in committee of the whole. It had only lacked the occasion to develop its quality as a debating body, and the occasion was now supplied by the complications that resulted in the war with England.

For nearly thirty years England had harassed our maritime commerce. Prior to 1805 the difficulties so caused had been smoothed or smothered; but with Fox gone and Canning in power her depredations increased in number and her admiralty rulings in rigor, to the havoc of our neutral carrying trade. For twenty years our vessels had been boarded and our seamen impressed into her naval service, both aggressions springing from the unlimited assumption of the right of search. It is not to be doubted, however, that the boldness of our traders, instigated by the immense profits of success, led to the perpetration of gross frauds upon England during the wars of the period, through forged British licenses and the use of the American flag to cover belligerent property. The status of impressment was somewhat similar. It had been practised by England at home from an early period, and notoriously during the American Revolution.[1] And if she had been previously compelled thus to recruit her navy, her need was now the greater. In consequence of the European wars the growth of our commerce was phenomenal, and chiefly at the expense of the British. It had also proved a serious detriment to the British marine, whose sailors were attracted in large numbers to our sea-service, where they were better paid, better fed, and better treated. Few of them were or could be naturalized, and therefore entitled to protection as American citizens. Besides, the British government did not recognize the right of naturalization. In the effort to capture British subjects, many of them being deserters from the royal service, native Americans, whom they closely resembled in speech and appearance, were often taken.[2] Yet such desertions were not discouraged by our government; on the contrary, deserters were knowingly mustered into our naval service and their surrender refused.

In view of the great events occurring in Europe our national interests seemed insignificant, and England, as her own cares increased in the contest with Napoleon, grew more indifferent to our just complaints—if, indeed, she were disposed to regard any as being just. The name of America was still odious to the governing classes. The poignant

---

[1] Hall's *Retrospect*, p. 48.   [2] *Niles's Register*, vol. i. p. 148.

recollection survived of the many millions sterling of confiscated debts and of the millions more appropriated to compensate banished Tories and pension American placemen.

Meantime, Napoleon's treatment of our interests was only less injurious and ignominious. By her Orders in Council, England had first put qualified restrictions upon neutral trade; these had been answered by Napoleon's Berlin decree to similar effect. Then followed still more sweeping Orders in Council, responded to by Napoleon's Milan decree, which was at once imitated by Spain and Holland, his subject nations.[1] The effect of these measures was to place America, as well as most of commercial Europe, under a paper blockade, and subject most of the vessels of our maritime commerce to seizure. There is no period in modern history so characterized by such wide and flagrant disregard of international law. England, by such operations as the piratical capture of the Spanish treasure-ships and the Danish fleet, and the attack on the *Chesapeake*, seemed to emulate on sea Napoleon's example on land; while at home the most stringent and despotic laws were enforced.[2] Nevertheless,

---

[1] "Whatever the merits of the system," says Bourrienne, in his *Memoirs*, "and although it was the cause of war between the United States and England, its execution did most damage to France and England, and to band all Europe against it. . . . The Emperor gave me so many orders for army clothing that all that could be supplied by the cities of Hamburg, Bremen, and Lübeck would have been insufficient for executing the commissions. I entered into a treaty with a house in Hamburg, which I authorized, in spite of the Berlin decree, to bring cloth and leathers from England. Thus I procured those articles in a sure and cheap way. Our troops might have perished of cold had the Continental system and the absurd mass of inextricable decrees relative to English merchandise been enforced."

[2] Spencer's *Principles of Sociology*, vol. ii. pp. 626, 632; Buckle's *Posthumous Works*, vol. i. pp. 230, 242-3; vol. iii. p. 465; Lecky's *England*, vol. iii. p. 581.

a social and intellectual movement, destined to bring in a liberal era, had already well begun; and a conspicuous sign of that movement was Brougham's assault on the Orders in Council, succeeding just too late to avert the war.[1]

Despite our grievances and the contempt with which our diplomatic remonstrances were received, the growth of popular feeling was slow. The mass of the people knew little and cared less about the epistolary discussions of ministers and diplomats, and the commercial depredations were chiefly felt at the seaports. Jefferson was horrified at the possible prospect of war, equally justifiable against England, France, and Spain. The need of some defensive course was recognized, with arbitrary supineness, by a series of commercial restrictions under penalties and forfeitures, beginning in the fall of 1806: first, partial non-intercourse, then non-importation, then non-intercourse, then again non-importation. Madison, whose administration began in 1809, had fallen heir to Jefferson's pacific sentiments and timorous policy. But the restrictive system was extremely unpopular in quarters most directly affected by it. New England, in particular, more generally concerned in shipping than any other portion of the country — perhaps more than all the rest combined[2] — was vehemently opposed to any interference with commercial freedom, whatever the risks of going to sea and whatever the considerations of national honor.[3]

---

[1] *Life and Times of Brougham*, vol. ii. pp. 1, 23; Levi's *History of British Commerce*, p. 118.

[2] "Six towns in New England possessed more than one-third of the tonnage of the whole Union." "A single State then possessed four times as much shipping as was owned by England in the reign of Elizabeth."— Curtis's *Life of Webster*, vol. i. pp. 94, 106.

[3] Garland's *Life of Randolph*, vol. ii. p. 49.

4

Clay professed as his reason for changing to the House of Representatives that he "preferred the turbulence of the House to the ominous stillness of the Senate." This was doubtless true, but it was an open secret that the growing war party, recognizing his peculiar powers, wanted him in the House, where war measures would most effectively originate and the popular ear be best obtained.[1] In fact, the want of efficient Republican leadership in that body had been the main cause of the feeble and dilatory policy more hurtful than war. The leaders of the opposition were John Randolph, nondescript, and Josiah Quincy,[2] Federalist, neither of whom has during the history of Congress been surpassed in caustic, truculent speech. Randolph had been the torment and the terror of the House. He spoke on all subjects, in season and out of season. Able as he was at times, he was desultory and interminable, and his indiscriminating and unsparing invective had become intolerable. To curb him was understood to be a part of Clay's new functions, which the preceding Speakers, Macon and Varnum, had not satisfactorily exercised.[3] In his brief speech on taking the chair he gave a distinct intimation of this purpose. "Should the rare and delicate occasion present itself," said he, "when your Speaker shall be called upon to check or control wanderings or intemperance in debate, your justice will, I hope, ascribe to his interposition the motives only of

---

[1] "Not long after the opening of Congress, Randolph said to a friend concerning Clay and Calhoun: 'They have entered this House with their eye on the Presidency, and, mark my word, sir, we shall have war before the end of the session.'"—Garland's *Life of Randolph*, vol. i. p. 306.

[2] He was first elected to the House, from Massachusetts, in 1800. "He was twenty-eight years old, but this was regarded then as so infantile an age for a member of Congress that the Democratic papers called aloud for a cradle to rock the Federal candidate in."—*Life of Quincy*, p. 60.

[3] Prentice's *Life of Clay*, p. 62; Sargent's *Life of Clay*, p. 41.

the public good and a regard to the dignity of the House." And he was not long in demonstrating the wisdom of his election. Under his guidance debate became orderly and pertinent, and markedly improved in quality. As a presiding officer he has had no superior. Notwithstanding his exuberant temperament, his decided opinions, and his politics, his impartiality was rarely impugned after the rules of the House were settled. He was continued Speaker so long as he remained in the House—with three brief absences, until 1825, longer than any one else who has held the position.[1]

Foreign affairs were, of course, the paramount topic before Congress. After much duplicity, and nearly as much spoliation as England had committed, Napoleon professed to revoke his decrees as to American vessels, although he did not entirely cease to enforce them, while England refused to treat upon any of the difficulties. Thus the war party was ready to accept Napoleon's conciliatory professions, if for no other reason than to direct the energies of the country against England alone, at best an unpropitious undertaking. As a sole policy, restriction could no longer be maintained. The disastrous effects of the system on the business and commerce of the country had wrought a political revolution. Half the members of the House at this session, which was convoked a month earlier than the regular day, were there for the first time, and the ablest of these were young men who were to

---

[1] "He was in a sense a law unto himself. . . . He betrayed to me one of the characteristic secrets of his success, more than thirty years afterwards, when I had the honor of occupying the same chair. 'I have attentively observed your course as Speaker,' said he, to me one day most kindly, 'and I have heartily approved it. But let me give you one hint from the oldest survivor of your predecessors: *Decide—decide promptly—and never give reasons for your decisions.* The House will sustain your decisions, but there will always be some to cavil and quarrel about your reasons.'"—Winthrop's *Addresses*, vol. iv. p. 42.

achieve distinction. They were for war. Clay, by position as well as by ability, was the leader of the war party, and he organized the proper committees to declare its sentiment and initiate its policy. Madison, timid and faltering in the presence of the approaching conflict, was nevertheless nerved to a sufficient degree of belligerent energy to recommend in his message that the country be put "into an armor and attitude demanded by the crisis and corresponding with the national spirit and expectations." Congress soon responded. In the House, the select committee on foreign relations made a stirring report imbued with warlike sentiments, and submitted a series of resolutions in favor of increasing the army, placing the vessels of the navy in commission, and permitting merchant-men to arm. The resolutions were adopted after a vigorous debate, and were followed by an act providing for the addition of twenty-five thousand men to the army for five years. By another act the President was empowered to accept the service of fifty thousand volunteers; but this act was vitally defective, as events proved, by not granting authority to use this force across the borders. A bill was then reported in the House to repair and fit for service the existing navy (which consisted of six frigates and ten smaller vessels, but not a ship of the line), to construct ten new frigates of thirty-eight guns, to purchase timber for future use, and to build a dry-dock. But through the chronic Republican antipathy to a navy and the remarkable lack of appreciation of its utility, the latter provisions were defeated.

For a time the failure of the effort to strengthen the navy had a dispiriting effect. It caused serious dissensions. A bill to provide for a uniform militia was defeated; another to arm the militia was passed by only a small majority; and a resolution for the appointment of a committee to frame a bill for a provisional army of twenty thousand was defeated. Such was the pique of some who favored increasing the navy. The war leaders had temporarily lost control of their party. Some degree of unity, however, was restored in the effort to raise the means to pay for what had already been authorized; and a bill for a loan of eleven millions was enacted. Most that had thus far been accomplished was by the aid of the Federalists, who said little, but did what they could to bring on the war, in the belief that it would be a failure, and by reaction cause the overthrow of the Republican party. They even confided their views to the British minister. But now that the Republicans were brought to the necessity of determining the question of war or peace, they hesitated to take the decisive step. Many were averse to war, but dreaded the disruption of the party; others were indifferent. It required all the energy and fertility of resource possessed by Clay, Calhoun, Cheves, Lowndes, and Porter to hold their wavering ranks together. Their efforts were somewhat aided by the "Henry Letters," which were purchased by the government for fifty thousand dollars from one John Henry, an Irish adventurer, who had prowled through the Eastern States, at the suggestion of the Governor of Canada, in quest of information. It was contended that they disclosed a British design to promote the secession of New England. In fact, they proved nothing except the extreme exasperation of that section against the restrictive system; and this feeling had long been displayed in speech and in print with the utmost license. But to haters of all that was British they served their transient purpose. They were submitted to Congress on March 9.

Madison, naturally, was anxious to be re-elected, and the

time was nearly at hand for the party nomination to be made. That he was reluctant to consent to war was well understood; but his success depended upon the support of the war leaders. He received their support, was renominated by the Congressional caucus, and subsequently reelected. It was common rumor that he was compelled to accept their programme as the condition of his re-election. It is beyond doubt that Clay presented that programme to him, and that it was afterward carried out. Clay denied that he exercised any coercion; but it is not improbable that Madison was influenced by the desires of those whose aid he most needed, however those desires may have been communicated. April 1 he sent a message to Congress, proposing a general embargo for sixty days. A bill in compliance with it was quickly passed by the House, Clay supporting it in a vehement speech "as a direct precursor of war."[1] To give it the appearance of a desire for further negotiations, the Senate extended the time to ninety days. The House concurred in the amendment, and on the 4th it became a law. Had an ultimatum been sent to the British government, as many desired, the delay alone would have averted war.

April and May passed without further important action by Congress. Only by the greatest pressure was a recess from May 28 to June 9 prevented. The war party was in a state of uncertainty and discouragement. The placing of the loan had progressed with disheartening slowness, and the elections in Massachusetts and New York had resulted in favor of the Federalists. The outcry against the embargo was growing daily louder and more angered. Then came the information that the British government persisted in

---

[1] Sargent's *Life of Clay*, p. 39.

its refusal to revoke the Orders in Council. Inaction was no longer deemed possible. "No choice remained," declared Madison, long afterward, "but between war and degradation." June 1 his war message was delivered to Congress. Three days later a bill to declare war was passed by the House, 79 to 49. The Senate was more deliberate; but on the 18th it passed the bill, 19 to 13. The Senate's amendments were forthwith accepted by the House, and the bill was immediately signed by the President. The next day the proclamation of war was issued.

The Republicans had practically exchanged principles with the Federalists. They had gone as far in compassing the Louisiana purchase, under the lead of Jefferson himself, as the Federalists had ever sought to go; and their restrictive system was quite as arbitrary, and far more harmful, than the Alien and Sedition laws. On the other hand, the Federalists, now indeed a faction mostly confined to New England, vociferously opposed the increase of the military as inimical to liberty, and restriction as the tyranny of centralized government. The opposition became so intense in that section that, upon the declaration of war, flags were hung at half-mast, bells tolled, and maledictions hurled from the pulpits. Secession was openly proposed, and later on the famous Hartford Convention debated the proposition.[1]

As insulting and injurious as the course of England toward the United States had been, there is little doubt but that, under all the circumstances—with our want of seasoned

---

[1] When Quincy was asked what the result of the convention would be, he replied: "I can tell you exactly—*a great pamphlet*."—*Life of Quincy*, p. 358. As to the Eastern disaffection, see ibid. p. 356; *Memoirs of Dix*, vol. i. p. 100; *Life of Story*, vol. i. p. 229.

nationality, of resources, unanimity, and preparation — it was unwise to go to war. The worst features of the situation were mainly due to our own inert policy during a long period of years preceding. A vigorous armed assertion of our rights in the beginning would probably have prevented any extensive injuries and saved our character in the eyes of Europe. Certainly, patience for a short time longer, since we had borne so much, would hardly have aggravated our disgrace, and would have settled the difficulties without recourse to war—a dire expedient even under extreme provocation. However outrageous and however stimulating to the patriotism of those in authority, the causes of the war were not so serious or so general as to be superior to the common motives of interest among the people. There was irony in the fact that the concern for "sailors' rights" was most warlike remote from the seaboard. The evils complained of could not be equal to the ravages of war, and the most and worst of them had already been suffered with such feeble resistance as to amount almost to estoppel. The purpose of the leaders far exceeded the power of the nation, as their enthusiasm exceeded that of the people at large. The war was practically a party war. For these reasons there was not the occasion for that type of exalted oratory which springs from a vital national crisis. The supporters of the war were put continually on the defensive. As Clay had most to do with bringing on the war, so he was foremost in sustaining its prosecution, which was attended with great difficulties and little glory, except on sea. The subject was adapted to his genius. It appealed to his lofty and impulsive patriotism; and it offered the means of furthering his ambition and of enhancing the sentiment of nationality, which was the best consequence of the war. He had spoken with great vigor on all the leading measures before Congress, but his reply to Quincy, January 8 and 9, 1813, was incomparably the most brilliant piece of oratory of that period.

The bill declaring war had been hurried through both Houses in secret session, thus preventing a full discussion. Moreover, the opportunity of the opposition was now at its best. While our meagre navy had gained renown, the operations on land had been paltry and unfortunate. The attempt to conquer Canada was an utter failure, and Hull's surrender of Detroit a profound humiliation. When, therefore, the proposition was made to increase the army and invade Canada the occasion was presented for a critical and exhaustive discussion of the causes, conduct, and policy of the war. Quincy had watched his opportunity, and at the right moment he savagely assailed the measure. He had more than plausible grounds. Within a week after the declaration of war, and before knowledge of it had crossed the ocean, the obnoxious Orders in Council had been repealed. Though grievances stood unredressed, the only remaining active cause of war was the impressment of our seamen. Yet the number of these in captivity at the commencement of the war must have been far less than of the lives already lost through the hostilities; and it was now proposed to carry on the war for sailors' rights by marching inland upon Canada. Quincy surpassed his wonted ability, incisiveness, and rancor. He reviewed in his characteristic style the history of our foreign relations. He ridiculed the war leaders as "young politicians, their pinfeathers not yet grown, and however they may flutter on this floor they are not yet fledged for any high or distant flight." He denounced the proposed invasion as wanton and infamous, and exposed with pungent satire the underlying political motives.[1]

The assault was staggering to the war party. Others essayed to meet it, but it was felt that no one but Clay could cope with Quincy on this occasion, and a few days later Clay took the floor. Both speeches were toned down in the report, but they still seem like living voices from the passions of the time. The grave fault in Quincy's speech was its extreme virulence; which Clay was too sagacious to return in kind; his retorts, though harsh, were adroit, and, above all, fused with flaming patriotism. The whole performance was marked by his unrivalled skill and power as a debater.[2] The prodigious effect it produced upon Congress soon spread through the country, invigorating the war spirit.

Patriotic sentiment, however, did not produce success in arms. Aside from the noble strokes of the navy, the cause sorely suffered. The finances were at the lowest ebb. The departments were blighted with incapacity and mismanagement. New England grew more clamorous and threatening. Besides, Napoleon's disasters in Russia would enable England to divert her veteran forces to the United States. At this ominous juncture there fortunately opened an avenue to peace. The Emperor of Russia proposed a mediation between

---

[1] *Life of Quincy*, pp. 256, 294.

[2] Quincy expressed this opinion of Clay: "Bold, aspiring, presumptuous, with a rough, overbearing eloquence, neither exact nor comprehensive, . . . he had not yet that polish of language and refinement of manners which he afterwards acquired by familiarity and attrition with highly cultivated men. . . . Such was the man whose influence and power more than that of any other produced the war of 1812."—*Life of Quincy*, p. 256. A somewhat similar impression was created by Webster's early manner.—*Life of William Plumer*, p. 215.

England, his ally, and this country. So anxious was Madison for peace that he eagerly grasped the opportunity. Forthwith, and before knowing the disposition of the British government, he nominated envoys to St. Petersburg. The news now came that England declined the mediation, but offered to treat directly. The proposal was accepted, and Gallatin, Adams, Bayard, Russell, and Clay were selected as plenipotentiaries.[1]

They arrived at Ghent, the place fixed for the negotiations, July 6, 1814, a month before the British envoys. Some time passed before the two commissions could find any point or possibility of agreement. The British demands were extortionate and humiliating; they appeared to be prompted by the assumption that the United States was vanquished and solicitous for peace at any cost. The conditions were haughtily rejected. The Americans pronounced as useless any further attempt to negotiate: they had come to preserve, not to sacrifice, national independence. Their attitude was so firm that the British government, which was practi-

---

[1] "The following, said to be a letter from Washington, dated February 21, 1814, first appeared in the Boston *Gazette*, and is called 'interesting.' We copy it to preserve a sample of the stuff that floats in the newspapers: 'After the arrival of the *Bramble*, and before the nomination of Clay, the President sent for him and observed, "There is a proposal from the British government to negotiate, and we must have peace. You have driven me into this war; what can you do to help me out of it?" And it was finally concluded that, with a view to conciliate the Southern and Western people to peace, that Clay was to go and make a treaty in which no mention was to be made about the right of impressment, but enter into the best arrangement they could make about the practice. Clay was to stand and bluster about it at first, but eventually agree to the treaty with the other commissioners. In the mean time the warlike attitude was to be kept up and preparations made as if for a vigorous campaign. Clay gave this information himself gratuitously; and I have it from a gentleman upon whom I can place the greatest reliance, and I have not the least doubt of the fact.'"—*Niles's Register*, vol. vi. p. 45.

cally present at the deliberations of its envoys, wisely determined to relax its rigorous demands. It was impolitic to give us just grounds for breaking off the negotiations; and, more than this, the commercial classes, whose pressure had forced the repeal of the Orders in Council, were strenuous for peace. Accordingly, the proposals grew less offensive. At the same time, the necessities of our cause grew more urgent. At length, Madison sent instructions to treat upon a condition that would have existed had the war not occurred. This basis of negotiation was adopted, and on December 24 a treaty substantially to that effect was concluded.[1]

Clay's objections had been the main obstacle to the adoption of this basis of peace. As he had been the chief champion of the war, and had even talked of dictating peace at Quebec or Halifax, it was deep humiliation to sign a treaty silent upon the main causes of the war—impressment and the principles of blockade. Nor were these questions ever settled by treaty. The rules that now regulate the right of search and seizure were eventually established by the progressive practice of nations, and have thus become elementary in the international code.[2] Time was to evolve our sufficient guarantee. Clay strove hard to within a few days before the treaty was signed to break off the negotiations; but when the British commissioners offered to accept a treaty silent as to the Mississippi, for the exclusive control of which the Kentuckian had from the be-

---

[1] "When it is so notorious that the issue of our late war was at best a drawn game, there is nothing but the most egregious national vanity that can turn it to a triumph."—Adams's *Diary*, December 13, 1817.

[2] See Webster's speech on the treaty of Washington, *Works*, vol. v. p. 145; Sumner's speech on the *Trent* case, *Works*, vol. vi. p. 190.

ginning taken an unyielding stand, he was compelled to concur, but with extreme repugnance.¹ One of the several unexpected results of this singular treaty was that its silence upon the British right to navigate the Mississippi, conceded by Jay's treaty in 1794, proved as effectual to liberate the river as though there had been an express provision for that purpose.

Contrary to the fears of the American envoys, the treaty was received with general satisfaction. It was enough that peace was attained; the country was weary of the war. In New England the intelligence was greeted by processions, the ringing of bells, and general jubilation. In other parts of the country it was hailed with less enthusiastic yet grateful demonstrations.

After the conclusion of the treaty Clay visited Paris. It was there that he heard of Jackson's victory at New Orleans, the battle having been fought after the treaty was signed, but before it was known in America.² This suggests the reflection that had Clay been less determined in his opposition to the British overtures, the treaty would have been signed earlier, the battle would have been prevented, and the subsequent course of our political history would have been different; for without the prestige of this

---

¹ Adams's *Diary* (vol. iii. pp. 1-120) contains a minute and entertaining record of this mission.

² "The news of the treaty of peace arrived in New York on the 11th of February, 1815."—Goodrich's *Recollections*, vol. i. p. 503. "We received the news of Waterloo sixty-five days after the event, when Louis XVIII. was on the throne, and Bonaparte was on his way to St. Helena. And how much do you think we got in our papers of the great transactions that followed after Ligny? A leading American journal devoted a third of a column to the subject, sparing five lines for a description of the battle of Waterloo."—Stanton's *Random Recollections*, p. 257.

victory, Jackson would not have been elected President. To Clay, at the time, however, the event was keenly gratifying. "Now," he exclaimed, "I can go to England without mortification!"[1]

After the treaty had been ratified, Adams, Gallatin, and Clay proceeded to London, where they had been deputed to negotiate a commercial arrangement. Several months were thus employed, resulting in a convention, which, besides securing some advantages in the East Indian trade, was the first departure from the system of discriminating duties adopted after the Constitution.[2] Clay reached home in September, 1815, and was unanimously returned to the House.

Congress was in the ascendant. Its superior importance in the scheme of the Constitution had been revealed by the war, and that importance was to become more dominant through the national necessities succeeding the war. Colonialism in American politics ended with the treaty of Ghent. It lends too much importance to the war to say that it produced that result; no single cause howsoever great makes, though it may mark, as the culmination of a tendency, an epoch in national history. The country had nearly outgrown that colonial spirit which lingered with the persistence due to the associations of two centuries. The effect of the war was to hasten the expulsion of that influence. Congress had risen with the progress of the na-

---

[1] "I have heard from undoubted authority that immediately after the signing of the treaty of peace at Ghent, Lord Goulburn, one of the British commissioners, said: 'By this act, gentlemen, you have saved New Orleans from capture.' 'No danger of that,' said Henry Clay; 'Jackson is there.'"—*Recollections of John Binns*, p. 242.

[2] *North American Review*, vol. lvii. p. 318; Lyman's *Diplomacy of the United States*, vol. ii. p. 69.

tion; it was apparent that the course of development our institutions would take chiefly depended on the latitude to be exercised by the law-making power. The first division of parties after the adoption of the Constitution was induced by opposing opinions on this subject. Yet thus far each party had been inconsistent with itself and the principles it had first declared. When in office each had felt the need of power, and so far as possible seized it. But through all their contentions and contortions, there had been a constant activity of foreign sympathies. Each party was in the eyes of the other a French or a British faction. This had excluded an unalloyed American ideal. The long period of restriction and war turned the thoughts of the people upon themselves. They were almost wholly shut off from the foreign world, and when peace reopened the way to normal relations, the former spirit had been exorcised. At home and abroad the country was nationalized. Henceforth the predominant concerns and habits of thought of the nation were domestic.

The foremost problem that confronted Congress at the restoration of peace was the distressed financial condition of the government and the country. At the beginning of the war the finances of the national government were not so considerable and complex as those of a modern metropolis; nor was it long before that the administration of them became methodical and businesslike, and appropriation bills detailed and precise. After the multiplied expenses of the war were encountered, the Treasury was soon in desperate straits. As urgent appeals were made to the people for loans of money as had previously been made to take up arms. The financial weakness of the government became so extreme that Monroe, Secretary of War, was compelled to pledge his personal credit to obtain the means indispensable to the defence of New Orleans. The worst features of this financial distress resulted from the failure to renew the charter of the Bank of the United States, which expired in 1811. Disorder of the currency, the most ruinous of public ills, quickly followed. A horde of local banks sprang into existence, sapping the financial vitality of the country by loaning their spurious issues at extortionate rates of interest. Banks that were solid could remain so only by limiting their operations to a degree that was disastrous to their debtors.

In January, 1815, a bank charter was passed by Congress, but it was vetoed by the President because of its defective plan. He was anxious that a bank should be established on a satisfactory basis. Clay had now come to the same conclusion, reversing the opinions he declared in 1811. He endeavored to shield his change as much as possible by the defects in the plan proposed at that time; but he had nevertheless overcome his Constitutional scruples. And he was not alone in changing his views, for Madison had led the way and was followed by his party. Despite the strong opposition to it, a national bank was probably the only means at that time of restoring financial health. It was necessitated by the situation, and it was soon justified by its operation. Clay's support of the measure marks his complete acceptance of the theory of broad construction toward which he had been steadily tending since his entrance into public life.

Two other subjects, also depending substantially on the same Constitutional doctrine, engaged the attention of Congress at this period — a protective tariff and internal improvements. As to these subjects, Clay's course involved no change, although an expansion, of opinion. So far as both had previously been acted upon, he had given them zealous support. But they were now to assume larger proportions and importance than ever before, and were to find in him their chief champion.

Prior to 1812, numerous tariff laws had been enacted. But while they had to some extent increased both the duties and the number of dutiable articles, the motive was revenue more distinctively than protection. The protective purpose was incidental, yet it was gaining in influence. In view of all the surroundings, at that period as well as afterward, absolute freedom of trade was not a possibility. It was inevitable that for the support of the government, duties on importations rather than direct taxation would be resorted to. Direct taxation for national purposes was not, and never has been, acceptable to the people; yet it was a favorite doctrine with the Republican party, immediately preceding Jefferson's administration, that direct taxes are preferable to duties on imports, because they are more economically collected, and because the burden of them is more accurately known by the people. Thus, with a revenue basis, it was not difficult for prospecting capital to introduce the protective system by a slow and gradual process, and, with such an opportunity, this method of introduction was quite certain to be instituted. It may be that, without the aid of extraneous circumstances, protection would have expanded into a predominant policy. Yet this was not likely, and without reference to the probability of its meeting an overruling opposition from the South before the policy could have acquired sufficient strength and standing to maintain a successful struggle. But it was not the product of deliberate doctrinal choice. It was pri-

5

marily due to other causes not designed to establish protection.

Except for the lurid events that turned the energies of Europe from production to destruction, it is probable that the growth of American manufactures would in the end have mainly depended on the law of natural selection. It was those events that led the Republicans to adopt the series of commercial restrictions which had all the effect of prohibitive tariffs. It is true that those restrictions were flagrantly adverse to sound economics; yet it must be admitted that what is now held by all competent authorities to be elementary in economic science in this regard was not generally received at that time. Non-importation, non-intercourse, and embargo were commonly considered quite as properly defensive measures as armament and fortification. Nevertheless, the fallacy and harm of such measures were then explained in Congress with as much clearness and vigor as they have been anywhere since.

Our people had more or less depended on England for articles alike of fashion, comfort, and necessity. In the same manner England had depended on this country, in a less but increasing degree, for many of our native productions, particularly agricultural. For a time after foreign importations were stayed the inconvenience of being deprived of those habitual supplies amounted almost to hardship. Thus constrained, our people began to supply their own wants at home to an extent never practised before. This private production was soon imitated on a large scale by the establishment of many manufactories of various kinds.[1] At the close of the war they represented a heavy

---

[1] For details of this rapid growth of manufacturing, see *Niles's Register*,

investment of capital. When the channels of trade were reopened there was an immediate influx of cheaper English goods. The news of peace alone sufficed to send prices abruptly down, to the ruin of many merchants.[1] Investments in manufacturing which had prospered through the temporary misfortunes of the country were threatened with disaster. Unless the commercial conditions produced by restriction and war were continued by legislation the "infant industries" would be overwhelmed. So the cry went through the land that capital, labor, and the welfare of the country were in danger. Congress was appealed to for protection. The claims assumed a patriotic hue. New wars might come. Americans should be independent, able at all times to rely upon their own resources. England was our implacable enemy. Her importation of low-priced merchandise, menacing native production, was another hostile invasion. These interests and opinions combined to produce the tariff of 1816. It was the first whose avowedly paramount policy was protection; and it was typical of all subsequent protective tariffs in the character and method of its construction.

In the last of the triad of economic problems — internal improvements — Clay had, as in the tariff, a local interest that early fixed his opinions. The development of the West depended much on good roads, by which to send its productions to the seaboard with all facility possible. In the West communication—to say naught of the transportation of agri-

---

vol. i. pp. 343, 390, 406 ; vol. ii. p. 227 ; vol. v. p. 317 ; vol. vi. pp. 173, 198, 331.

[1] Parton's *Jackson*, vol. ii. p. 255 ; *Diary and Correspondence of Amos Lawrence*, p. 47; Barrett's *Old Merchants of New York* (second series), p. 372.

cultural products by cart and oxen—was at best an arduous effort. The coastwise States, by reason of their older and denser settlement, were better provided, yet they had need of extensive improvements. This need was recognized by the many schemes for the construction of roads and waterways that marked the period. These schemes, however, were those of State and private enterprise, while the nascent West, without the resources of the older East—as well as without the benefits arising from the maintenance of fortifications, arsenals, and ship-yards—pressed for aid from the national government. But what was granted to one section would be demanded by others, and so arose the general question of internal improvements. There was a strong favorable sentiment; but such had been the issue over the interpretation of the Constitution that many who were best disposed toward the policy were forced by their own past arguments to deny the power to execute it. They were willing that the Constitution be amended so as to provide the power expressly; but that course was deemed inexpedient, as it would be in danger of defeat by those who opposed government control of roads and canals in any case, together with those who approved the policy, but who believed the power already existed, and were therefore unwilling to hazard their Constitutional opinions and the political interests dependent on them by a possible adverse vote that would operate as a practical construction against them.

Notwithstanding these difficulties, Clay, as we have seen, had labored from the first in furtherance of internal improvements. Little, however, had been accomplished beyond attracting public interest. After the war the subject took great prominence. Clay at once recurred to it as an important feature of his programme. "I would see," said he, "a chain of turnpike roads and canals from Passamaquoddy to New Orleans; and other similar roads intersecting the mountains, to facilitate intercourse between all parts of the country and to bind and connect us together." This was in January, 1816. In December, Madison, in his last annual message, recommended a comprehensive system of roads and canals. The usual preliminary process of important legislation was immediately started in the House, Calhoun, it should be remembered, being in zealous accord with Clay in his support of the project, as he was also in regard to the bank and the tariff. With all seemly speed a committee report was made, depicting the advantages of such a system and presenting plans and estimates that called for an outlay of twenty million dollars. The report was followed by a bill to make the bonus of a million and a half to be paid by the new bank for its charter and the share of the government in its dividends a permanent fund pledged to the policy. The bill was passed by both Houses, but it met the obstacle least expected. Despite his recommendation, although it was stated in rather vague and general terms, Madison, the day before Monroe's inauguration, vetoed the bill as unconstitutional. It is not improbable that the motive of the veto was political as well as Constitutional—to prevent the prestige that Clay might gain as the successful promoter of the policy of internal improvements. Madison furnished only a brief statement of his objections; but Monroe, in whose interest the bill had been vetoed, supplied the reasoning at length. In his first message to Congress he made bold to announce in advance of further legislation that the power to make internal improvements was not granted by the Constitution; but he proposed, as both Jefferson and Madison had done, the impracticable expedient of a Constitutional amendment. This announcement extinguished all hope of carrying out the policy during his Presidency. But a long debate ensued on resolutions asserting the power of Congress to appropriate money for internal improvements, and also to construct them. The first was adopted, but the others were not. In this discussion Clay took the leading part. He not only defined his Constitutional and political views more fully and clearly than ever before, but used the occasion to declare open opposition to Monroe's administration. He had entered upon a new stage of his public career.

He had returned from Europe with stimulated ambition to become President. He was the most conspicuous figure in Congress, and the foremost of the new generation of public men.[1] He was the acknowledged representative of the West, while by nativity and as a slave-holder he stood essentially with the South. Moreover, his general policy was certain to grow in favor in the East. Such were the elements of his political influence, combined with the most popular genius the country has ever known. He had good grounds for his aspirations.

To Monroe's elevation there had been no substantial opposition. It had been in course of long and assiduous preparation. Political tradition and skilful management had united in his support. But he was the last of the Virginian succession. It was plain that his term of office would wit-

---

[1] "An able writer in the Boston *Patriot* has commenced a series of essays addressed to Henry Clay respecting the peace establishment of the army."—*Niles's Register*, vol. ix. p. 214, November 25, 1815. A similar course was taken by Channing in 1837 to promulgate his views concerning the annexation of Texas.

ness a new disposition of political forces. Clay had determined to succeed him; and to gain the advantage of standing next in line of promotion, according to precedent, he desired to be Secretary of State.

Shortly after Clay's return from Europe, Madison offered him the mission to Russia,[1] and within a year afterward invited him to the Cabinet as Secretary of War. Madison held him in high esteem. In 1813 he would have offered him the command of the army had not his presence in Congress been regarded as indispensable.[2] Yet it is probable that politics more than esteem induced Madison to propose the Russian mission and the Department of War. Clay's acceptance of either, even had he been willing to exchange his notable position in Congress for so slight an official distinction, would have been a tacit consent to the deferment of his hopes; for the offers, coming so late in Madison's term, must have been approved by Monroe, by whom it was doubtless understood that if Clay accepted an appointment it was to be continued. Both were declined; but they were significant that he would not be given the first place in Monroe's cabinet. It was apparent soon after Monroe's election that

---

[1] "Seventeen years later, in 1832, Buchanan, Minister to Russia, wrote: 'To be an American Minister is but a slender passport to the kind attention of the Russian nobility. They know but little of our country, and probably desire to know still less, as they are afraid of the contamination of liberty.'"—Curtis's *Buchanan*, vol. i. p. 156.

[2] "Henry Clay had equal moral courage with Jackson, but he lacked military glory; and with the ignorant majority military glory is appreciable, whilst moral courage and intellectual statesmanship are incomprehensible. In such a conflict, Jackson, of course, triumphed. Had Mr. Clay accepted the generalship-in-chief in the war of 1812, as proposed by his friends—the President, Madison, being out—there is no doubt but he would have made a great and successful general; for of all men who ever came into political rivalry in our country, Henry Clay and Andrew Jackson were most alike in character."—*Life of Cassius M. Clay*, vol. i. p. 49.

Clay's wishes were to be disregarded—that not he but John Quincy Adams was to be the administration candidate for the Presidential succession. Adams was made Secretary of State. Clay was again pressed to take the War Department or the mission to England—practically anything he wanted save the coveted post. But nothing else would suffice.

He was disappointed and angered. Justly or not, in view of Adams's experience and the Northern support he brought to Monroe, Clay held his own claims to be higher.[1] And to be pushed aside by such a man as Monroe added to his spleen. The President was a sagacious, cautious, methodical, and mediocre man, advanced over abler men by political machinery. Both he and Adams had been chiefly occupied abroad in diplomacy, while Clay's service had been for the most part in the gaze of the nation. He assumed that the prominence he had achieved justified his aspirations. But his principal source of influence—his diffused popularity, arising from admiration for the man, his manner, his oratory, and his showy policy — was not alone sufficient to raise him to the Presidency. Popular admiration of the talents of a statesman has seldom been successful in the strife for that position against the concrete interests and material means that aid shrewd but otherwise ordinary men. Immeasurably superior to the horde of brawling, scrambling mediocres that ever throng the ways to preferment, he was impatient of resistance, and often asserted his opinions in a dictatorial and overbearing way. When his

---

[1] MacMaster says (vol. iv. p. 376) that Clay prevented the use of the chamber of the House for the inauguration, which was therefore held outside ; and that he did not attend the ceremonies. In *Clay's Correspondence*, however (p. 53), is a note from Monroe, dated March 4, 1817, thanking Clay for his offer to put the chamber in order for the proceedings.

feelings and prejudices were aroused, they were apt to be too strong and impetuous for calculating prudence and sound judgment. After Monroe's administration was organized these traits came into full play by the independent and hostile attitude that Clay assumed. Henceforth, recognizing no leadership above his own, he was often to commit the error of excess. In making war on Monroe, however good the grounds, he allowed his fervor and his personal grievance to be obtruded too far for circumspect and successful opposition.

His persistence in behalf of internal improvements after Monroe's announcement of his Constitutional objections would have excited no surprise had he gone no further than to urge the legal and economic arguments that he held to be valid. To that extent he would only have been consistent with what he had previously advocated. But he exceeded the necessities of debate by not only harshly combating the President's reasoning, but also denouncing what he chose to regard as gross presumption in vetoing legislation before it had been introduced in Congress. This he did in terms so ill-restrained as to evince personal resentment at his failure to obtain the Secretaryship of State in the new cabinet. Such at least was the construction put upon it—to his serious disadvantage. It was received as the public declaration of revolt against the administration. It was not, however, the first intimation of his designs; for he had at once made his sentiments known through various channels, and had been exerting himself to marshal all his available forces.[1] Nor was his stand for internal improve-

---

[1] Adams's *Diary*, December 25, 1817; July 28, 1818; February 2, 3, 1819. *Niles's Register*, August 29, 1819.

ments, as prominent as that policy was in his plan of operations, more than a preliminary stroke. The principal onset followed immediately. March 24, 1818, but eleven days afterward, he "came out with his great opposition speech," as Adams expressed it, on the emancipation of South America.

The decrepitude of Spain, caused by the subversion of her power by Napoleon, was extreme, and her colonies had taken advantage of it to attain independence. Mexico and the whole of South America—except Brazil, which was under the dominion of Portugal—were in more or less active rebellion. In those countries where the revolution had been successful, republican institutions were organized. Many of the revolutionary movements were stained by cruelty and excess, and among the new states jealousy and discord prevailed. Yet their former condition could justly be urged in palliation of this state of things. Any struggle for liberty, however violent and irregular, on the part of those peoples, who had been long subjected to the most barbarizing despotism that ever existed, was deserving of sympathy. Clay was enthusiastically of that belief. He had proclaimed it early. In January, 1816, he expressed a desire that the government of the United States should interpose in aid of the South American cause. He subsequently opposed a bill to prevent the equipment in our ports of cruisers to be sold to the insurgents. The bill became a law as a measure of neutrality; but after Monroe's administration began, Clay urged the repeal of the law and the assumption of such an attitude as would benefit the struggling colonies instead of Spain, which he deeply detested. The debate on this question prepared the way for his proposal to recognize the patriot flag. To supply the want of exact information as to the condition of the insurgent countries, Madison had sent thither three commissioners on a tour of investigation. They had not yet made their report, but it was proposed to provide for their compensation. To this Clay objected, contending that their appointment was unconstitutional, having been made without the advice and consent of the Senate. He then moved an appropriation for one year's salary and outfit for a minister to the United Provinces of the Rio de la Plata whenever the President should deem it expedient to send one.

His speech on this motion was in his best style. The subject, as he viewed it, was exalted, yet it was not one upon which to form a party division. The proposition involved no existing interests; it simply represented a sentiment, though a large and lofty sentiment. But the subject was fascinating, and Clay was determined to discredit the administration. Perhaps no speech he ever delivered reflects more completely his strongest and his weakest traits.

He deplored his difference with many friends on the question, but found some consolation in that, if he erred, it was "on the side of the liberty and happiness of a large portion of the human family." He was averse to war with Spain, yet he criticised with harshness and asperity the manner in which the long-continued negotiations with Spain had been conducted, and defined a course that would result in war unless the many injuries done us were redressed. He eloquently described the immense region throughout which "the spirit of revolt against the dominion of Spain had manifested itself," its diverse and magnificent resources, the character and promise of its inhabitants, the blighting tyranny they had suffered, and the scenes of atrocity their efforts for freedom had provoked. He urged the commercial interest of the United States in the independence of the revolted provinces, and the likelihood of their adopting institutions modelled after ours. He showed that the states of the Rio de la Plata were already free and independent, and that within their territory there was not a Spanish bayonet to contest the authority of their government. This *de facto* government, he insisted, was entitled to recognition, according to the practice of Washington, Jefferson, and Madison, the established principles of international law and of a true neutrality. Such a recognition, he maintained, would not be to Spain a just cause of war; but he contended that if she should make war on that pretext her weakness would complete her ruin in the Americas—that it would "ensure beyond all doubt the cause of American independence" and "would be attended with the immediate and certain loss of Florida."

Notwithstanding the sentiment evoked and the merit of the speech, which was strikingly superior to the speeches in the debate that followed, the measure he advocated was too premature not to encounter certain defeat. The position of the administration was well understood. While it was unwilling to appear at all precipitate, it was not opposed to recognizing any of the new governments when that could be done with assurance of their independence and the approval of public sentiment. But there was no call for haste, especially as it was proposed to send a minister to a government which had not as yet sought recognition by sending an accredited minister here.[1] Besides, there was the consideration, which Clay had boldly combated, that it was impolitic needlessly to offend the Spanish government pending the negotiations for the acquisition of Florida. The

---

[1] Lyman's *Diplomacy of the United States*, vol. ii. p. 424.

main effect, therefore, of his censure of the administration was, as in the debate on internal improvements, to foment bitterness of feeling. The execution of his aggressive plan might have quickly secured the results he looked for with a great gain of national prestige; but the wisdom of seeking them by diplomacy was shown by the event, and was more in accord with the character of our institutions.

The motion was defeated by a vote of 45 to 115. Though he made two further speeches during the debate,[1] and exhausted every resource, he could hardly have expected a different result, and probably he did not. In this view some allowance should be made for the extent to which he pressed his advocacy. The proposition itself was as limited as it could well be; yet the chief argument used against it was that the Constitutional power to manage our foreign relations is vested in the President, and therefore that it was improper for Congress to interfere.[2] If adopted it would have been merely an expression by Congress of its

---

[1] At a banquet which followed the unveiling of a monument to Clay at Richmond, in 1860, John Tyler had the magnanimity to extol Clay's ability as Speaker and debater. "His gesture," said he, among other things, "was impressive, and he had the faculty of throwing the power of his voice into a single sentence after such a manner as to produce sometimes an electric effect. The late Philip P. Barbour often quoted to me an illustration of this power of voice and expression used by Mr. Clay in discussing the recognition of the Spanish-American colonies. The speaker had drawn a desponding picture of the condition of Mexico in her struggle for independence. Her hopes were reported to be blasted; Mina, her great leader, either killed or captured. At that moment a page put in his hand a morning paper. His eye fell on a paragraph, when his whole manner changed, and holding the paper up, he exclaimed, 'Mina still lives!' The effect was wonderful. Mr. Barbour said, 'I sprang to my feet, and some moments elapsed before I recovered from my trance.'"

[2] An excellent memoir on this subject was submitted to the Senate in January, 1897, in connection with a pending proposition to recognize the independence of Cuba. The Constitutional phase of the debates in 1818,

desire that the specified government be recognized, and a provision of the means for such recognition, leaving the subject otherwise to the discretion of the President. If that government were independent the cause of republicanism demanded its recognition as soon as prudence and propriety would permit. Whatever criticism, therefore, Clay's course warranted, it had the merit of bringing an important and worthy subject into national prominence, and of charging the administration with a responsibility that it could not ignore. A more ordinary and moderate effort would not have produced that result.

Despite the large majority of the administration forces in Congress, Clay's opposition caused Monroe much anxiety and Adams much wrath. It was evident that hostilities had only begun. The subject of South American independence was one to which he could recur as often as he chose, with the probability of improving grounds and increasing popular support.¹ Moreover, another opportunity of attack had already arisen. Even while the South American debate was in progress the events that occasioned the next parliamentary battle were taking place. General Jackson was in the midst of his operations in the Seminole War.

We have now reached the origin of the fateful feud between Jackson and Clay described at the opening of this volume. It remains to sketch the ensuing events to the election of 1828, and to complete the portrait of Clay as he was when he re-entered the Senate to take up the gage of battle with Jackson.

1821, and 1822 is there fully presented. See *Congressional Record*, Fifty-fourth Congress, Second Session, p. 684.

¹ The Supreme Congress of Mexico gave Clay a vote of thanks for his efforts in the cause, and extracts from his speeches were read at the head of the South American armies.

CHAPTER III

Clay's Political Position—The Missouri Compromise, the Statesmanship of It, and Clay's Agency in Effecting It.—He Renews his Efforts for the Recognition of the South American Republics, and Finally Succeeds—He Temporarily Retires, but Returns to the House at the Opening of the Eighteenth Congress—He Defeats a Bill to Pension Commodore Perry's Mother, and Advocates Internal Improvements and Webster's Resolution Concerning the Recognition of Greece—The Monroe Doctrine—The Tariff of 1824 and Clay's Relation to Protection—The Political Situation in 1824—William H. Crawford—John Quincy Adams is Elected President by the House Through Clay's Influence, and Clay becomes Secretary of State—Clay's Administration of the State Department—The Panama Mission—John Randolph—His Duel with Clay—Adams and his Administration—Jackson is Elected over Adams in 1828—Clay's Home, Family, Personal Appearance, Temperament, and Mind.

CLAY's repeated defeats told heavily. Without his peculiar and remarkable powers he would have been undone. His home constituency, however, was always loyal to him. Only once was he threatened from that quarter. In 1816 he voted for a bill increasing the compensation of members of Congress from six dollars per day while in session to fifteen hundred per year, and twice that sum to the Speaker. It met with the stormy but unreasonable opposition of the country. By voting for it many members lost their seats. Clay's return was contested on that ground. After a short and spirited canvass of his district—the only one he ever made—he was successful,[1] though he pledged himself to

---

[1] See *Niles's Register*, vol. xliii. p. 19; *Headlands in the Life of Henry Clay*, No. 1, p. 3.

advocate the repeal of the law and the substitution of a *per diem* compensation. The other candidate had been opposed to the war, and in joint debate with Clay he fared badly. But though secure of his seat in the House, his position there was not so assured. There is always danger of a thwarted statesman degenerating into a political guerilla. Clay's course was still imputed to factious vindictiveness. His character suffered. It was seriously considered by the adherents of the administration whether he should not be retired from the Speakership; but Monroe prudently prevented this action, as magnifying Clay's importance, and also because it would, if successful, deprive the West of official representation, there being no Western man in the cabinet and none in the House of sufficient strength and eminence to contend with Clay for the chair. He was keenly sensible of his decline, and for a time was much depressed by it, even neglecting his duties as presiding officer.[1] Rumor had it that he sought diversion in the excitement of the card-table, a prevalent passion among Southern gentlemen of that period.[2] However this may be, his weakness was of short duration. He soon recovered himself, and through the part he took in the controversy over the admission of Missouri, he won the title of the "Great Pacificator."

The details of that controversy, which extended over three sessions of Congress, need not be recounted here. The expanding cotton culture had largely increased the number and value of slaves, and this was accompanied by a

---

[1] *Niles's Register*, vol. xviii. p. 4.
[2] In regard to the charge that Clay gambled, see Schurz's *Clay*, vol. i. p. 160; Mallory's *Clay*, vol. i. p. 192; *Headlands in the Life of Henry Clay*, No. 1, p. 2.

more general and radical belief in the propriety of their bondage. At the North slavery had gradually become extinct, yet the growth of Northern wealth and population was deranging the political balance with the South. To increase the slave territory had, therefore, become to the South an active political principle, naturally obnoxious to Northern sentiment. The effort of Missouri for admission into the Union as a slave State brought to light this vital difference which had insensibly developed between the two sections of the country.

After an excited struggle during two sessions of Congress, Maine was admitted into the Union, Missouri was authorized to form a State constitution, and slavery was prohibited in all the territory north of thirty-six degrees and thirty minutes, except Missouri. The difficulty was supposed to be settled.

The second session of the Sixteenth Congress convened November 13, 1820. Clay was not in attendance, owing to the pressure of his private affairs.[1] As it was understood at the close of the preceding session that he would do, he resigned the Speakership. A stubborn contest arose over his successor. Twenty-two ballots, with many variations, were required to reach a decision, Taylor, of New York, being elected over Lowndes, of South Carolina.[2] As this

---

[1] Adams's *Diary*, vol. v. p. 58.
[2] "William Lowndes, after Clay, exercised more influence in the House than any other man. . . . He had been elaborately educated, and improved by foreign travel, extensive reading, and research. As a *belles-lettres* scholar he was even superior to Mr. Randolph. Very retiring and modest in his demeanor, he rarely obtruded himself upon the House. When he did, it seemed only to remind the House of something which had been forgotten by his predecessors in debate. Sometimes he would make a set speech. When he did, it was always remarkable for profound reasoning and profound thought. . . . His impression upon the nation had made

indicates, the chief cause of the contest was the renewal of the antislavery agitation. The Missouri question had not been laid. There was deep dissatisfaction in diverse quarters, and for opposite reasons, over the conditions of the Compromise. Many at the North objected to the permission of slavery in Missouri, while many at the South objected to the restriction of it anywhere. It needed only a slight reason to unsettle the arrangement, and this was furnished by the constitution upon which Missouri sought formal admission into the Union. It contained a provision directing the legislature to enact a law "to prevent free negroes and mulattoes from coming to, and settling in, said State on any pretext whatever." This was charged to be a violation of the federal Constitution, which declares that "the citizens of each State shall be entitled to all privileges and immunities of citizens in the several States." The same objection had been urged against the Compromise.

The perturbation that prevailed in Congress was fully shared by the country. The debates, increasing in vehemence and heat, and covering all phases—moral, economic, and Constitutional—of the slavery question, had been everywhere read and discussed with fevered interest. Public meetings held throughout the land fulminated resolutions; legislatures, municipalities, and the people, presented memorials and petitions to Congress praying on one or the other side. The feeling was general that the Union was imperilled. Extremists of the South boldly threatened secession, to be answered with equally violent defiance by extremists of the North.

---

him the favored candidate of every section for the next President; and it is not, perhaps, saying too much that, had his life been spared, he, and not John Quincy Adams, would have been President in 1824."—Sparks's *Memories of Fifty Years*, p. 338.

The question was wrangled over in various forms, but with no other result than to leave the real difficulty, from the temper aroused, more arduous than before. January 11, 1821, when the excitement was at its height, Clay appeared in the House. His coming had been anxiously awaited, in the belief that he could work out some solution of the problem.[1] The belief was not misplaced. While the public excitement constantly increased, the temper of Congress now underwent a gradual change. This was mainly due to Clay's tireless and undiscouraged efforts, which were even more effective in private than in public. From the first he had been steadily gaining converts to a compromise, as well as allaying the violence of opposition that could not be wholly converted.[2] He tried various means to settle the question, but they were unavailing except to prepare the way for his final resort. At length he made a motion for a joint committee of both Houses. February 23 the committee was elected. It was virtually his selection, and he was chairman of it. This was on Friday. On the following Monday he presented the report of the committee, which recommended the admission of Missouri practically on the terms of the former compromise, and on the further condition that no law should be passed abridg-

---

[1] Sparks's *Memories of Fifty Years*, p. 230; Goodrich's *Recollections*, vol. ii. p. 395.

[2] An instance of his persistent energy on the floor was related by Crittenden. Clay had made a motion to allow some members to vote who were absent when their names were called. The Speaker ruled that the motion was out of order. Clay then moved to suspend the rules forbidding it. This motion was likewise ruled out. "Then," said Clay, exerting his voice beyond its highest wont, "I move to suspend all the rules of the House! Away with them! Is it to be endured that we shall be trammelled in our action by mere forms and technicalities at a moment like this, when the peace, and perhaps the existence, of this Union is at stake?"
—Coleman's *Crittenden*, vol. ii. p. 53.

ing the right of any citizens to settle in the State. On the same day, with little debate, the resolution reported was adopted by the House, and on the next day by the Senate.[1] The condition was in due time complied with, and Missouri became a State.

The settlement of this portentous controversy brought profound relief. The struggle had reached a pass that would have impelled the secession of the slave States had Missouri been denied admission; and secession would not, could not, have been prevented. When the excitement was highest, Clay repeatedly expressed his doubt as to the continuance of the Union. The hypercritical complain because the antislavery principle yielded to compromise, and impugn the policy that effected it. Compromise, it is said, was but an expedient to put off the inevitable crisis; instead of multiplying both terms of the equation, the problem should have been solved while yet the forces were small. This answer should be sufficient — compromise preserved the Union. Thus far politics more than the altruistic sentiment of liberty was the motive of the antislavery movement; and it was politics that eventually constrained the compromise. Love for the Union was not a general and in-

---

[1] In a political speech in 1844, Clay said: "I moved for the appointment of a committee of one from each State, and that they should be elected by ballot—a means of designating a committee then unknown in the House. On that committee I placed the names of several that had voted against the reception of Missouri into the Union, and had the influence to have them elected; eighteen on the first ballot, and the remaining six were, upon my suggestion, made up of those having the highest number of votes. The committee met and readily agreed to report favorably to the reception of the new State into the Union. But this did not satisfy me. I urged on A, B, and C the question, 'Will you vote for it in the House?' and had the happiness to wring from them the positive promise I desired. This gave the turn to the scale in the House, and I now knew that the question was settled."

veterate instinct in any section of the country. The duration of the Union and the consequences of its dissolution were freely and coolly discussed by public men. Had the South seceded, slavery would have received a still greater impetus and protection, not to speak of the manifold evils that must have followed in the wake of separation, which would have increased and strengthened the territorial demands of slavery. The future of our political institutions was at stake; and they were wise who trusted that the right would profit most by time, and in the end prevail.

It may be that Clay's persistent efforts to effect the compromise were not governed by the deliberate calculation of remote consequences. At such a time those considerations are secondary, if entertained at all. Clay was not a philosopher, but a man of action. His paramount impulse throughout his career was to maintain and glorify the Union. He was intensely patriotic, and ambitious to become President of the Union intact. He was a Southerner and a slave-holder, and as such was imbued to a large degree with Southern sentiments; yet his instinctive feeling was adverse to slavery. But it was certain that slavery could not be eradicated in his day. As a practical man he met each condition as it arose, with an incidental but not unworthy view to his own elevation. To solve the present and urgent problem, in a way to preserve and expand our nationality on the existing basis, was therefore the leading principle of his statesmanship; and when instant action is imperative, only that type of statesmanship is efficient. Clay was the sole possessor of the genius and influence to quell the storm that would otherwise have destroyed the Union. He felt his responsibility and fully met it. So far as one man can achieve so great a result, Clay saved the Union at that crisis.

In the midst of the Missouri struggle, Clay recurred to his favorite subject—the recognition of the South American republics. At the preceding session he assailed the administration for negotiating a treaty with Spain for the purchase of Florida with the Sabine instead of the Rio del Norte as our southwestern boundary, which had the effect of relinquishing our claim to Texas as a part of the Louisiana purchase.[1] But the treaty was not ratified by Spain within the stipulated time, and Clay attempted to prevent a renewal; he introduced resolutions declaring the treaty invalid inasmuch as it amounted to a cession of Texas to Spain, thus requiring the joint action of both Houses of Congress; and that the consideration from Spain for the territory west of the Sabine was inadequate.[2] The resolutions were defeated; but in the course of his speech in support of them he again brought into full view his South American policy, and not long afterward he made a direct effort in its behalf by moving a resolution declaring that it was expedient to provide by law for sending ministers to the South American governments then maintaining their independence. This resolution was adopted,[3] but no further action was taken

---

[1] Adams's *Diary*, vol. v. p. 25; Monroe to Jackson, May 22, 1820.

[2] "We want Florida," said he, "or rather we shall want it; or, to speak more correctly, we want nobody else to have it. We do not desire it for immediate use. It fills a space in our imagination, and we wish to complete the *arrondissement* of our territory. It must certainly come to us. The ripened fruit will not more surely fall. Florida is enclosed between Alabama and Georgia, and cannot escape. Texas may. Whether we get Florida now or some five or ten years hence, it is of no consequence. I would not give Texas for Florida in naked exchange. We are bound by the treaty to give not merely Texas, but five millions of dollars also, and the excess beyond that sum of all claims upon Spain, which have been variously estimated at from fifteen to twenty millions of dollars."

[3] "It is, no doubt, an indication of Clay's influence in the House, and of his increasing popularity in the nation, as the great antagonist of the administration."—Adams's *Diary*, May 14, 1820.

during the session. In February, 1821, he moved an appropriation for the purpose. This narrowly failing, he proposed a resolution declaring the interest of the people and the House in the South American cause, and the readiness of the House to co-operate with the President in recognizing the independent nationalities. It was adopted by a large majority, and was presented with somewhat of triumph to the President by a committee of the House headed by Clay.[1] But Monroe still halted, to avoid, it may be supposed, the appearance of coercion; and it was not until March, 1822, that he formally recommended the recognition of the independent governments. Congress then took prompt action, and ministers were subsequently sent to several of the new states.[2]

At the close of the session Clay retired from Congress, and with much *éclat*.[3] His embarrassed financial circumstances, caused by the failure of a friend whose paper he had endorsed to a large amount, rendered it necessary for him to resume his practice, which his great prestige now made weighty and lucrative. He was retained by the Bank of the United States in much important litigation. He was also retained at this time by the legislature of Kentucky to assist in arranging with the legislature of Virginia a mode of settling disputed land-titles arising out of the former relations between the two States. This engagement recalled him to the scenes of his youth; and the dramatic use he made of it attracted considerable attention.[4] During this period he actively opposed the agitation against the State court, caused by its holding unconstitutional cer-

---

[1] Colton's *Clay*, vol. i. p. 242.
[2] Lyman's *Diplomacy of the United States*, vol. ii. p. 447.
[3] Adams's *Diary*, March 9, 14, 1821.   [4] Sargent's *Clay*, p. 98.

tain acts that had been passed to afford "relief" to distressed debtors, and to create a "new court" designed to uphold the popular movement. The people were suffering the consequences of paper inflation, which they did not comprehend. For several years this agitation was promoted by demagogues; but it finally subsided, as all such political manias do, under the sustained efforts and influence of the conservative elements, which formed Clay's chief political support. For a time his great popularity was seriously menaced; but his district did not waver in its loyalty to him. In the fall of 1823 he was re-elected to the House, and there to the Speakership.[1]

The business of the session had much variety and interest,[2] and in it Clay evinced his usual spirit and initiative, notwithstanding he was a candidate for the Presidency, having already been nominated by the legislatures of Kentucky, Ohio, Missouri, and Louisiana. At the outset his habitual and critical watchfulness of legislation, to which the Journal of the House amply testifies, was shown in an instance somewhat perilous to him as a Presidential aspirant. By a speech said to have had overpowering effect, he defeated a bill to pension the indigent mother of Commo-

---

[1] This *jeu d'esprit* appeared in the *National Intelligencer*:

"As near the Potomac's broad stream, t'other day,
  Fair Liberty strolled in solicitous mood,
  Deep pondering the future—unheeding her way—
  She met goddess Nature beside a green wood.
'Good mother,' she cried, 'deign help me at need!
  I must make for my guardians a Speaker to day:
The first in the world I would give them.'—'Indeed!
  When I made the first Speaker, I made him of Clay.'"

[2] The growing importance of the House and the increasing amount of business it transacted are shown by the fact that the number of standing committees had now reached twenty-five.

dore Perry, as proposing an expensive and dangerous precedent, which, besides exalting the military above the civil service, was against the policy and principle of the pension system, inasmuch as Perry neither fell nor was wounded in battle. It is apparent, however, from some of his remarks on military glory, that the spectre of General Jackson's candidacy was before his eyes. "If you wish," said he, "to make your country illustrious you must diffuse your glory. It is not your heroes—God knows we have had enough of them within the last twenty years, every man is now a hero—it is not your heroes, but the body of the people, the men who fight your battles, to whom you are indebted for your safety and your eminence as a nation."[1]

The subject of internal improvements was again reopened. In 1822, while Clay was out of Congress, Monroe had vetoed an appropriation for the Cumberland road. It was the only considerable work the government had ever undertaken; and it was the result almost entirely of Clay's exertions, which, indeed, were recognized by a monument on the road, inscribed to him. But it had at length encountered opposition in Pennsylvania, where a turnpike from Philadelphia to Pittsburgh, with which it competed, had been constructed by private capital.[2] In vetoing the appropriation, Monroe had communicated a long exposition of his Constitutional opinions; and though the discussion in which Clay participated was upon a bill to provide for the preliminary plans of a general system—which, being harm-

---

[1] "Mr. Hamilton said that in rising to reply to the gentleman from Kentucky, he could not but feel a foreboding how hopeless the attempt must be to break the spell of that eloquence for which, if he might so speak, the House had a sort of habitual deference and admiration."

[2] Curtis's *Buchanan*, vol. i. p. 82; *Madison's Works*, vol. iii. p. 54.

less, became a law—he made it the occasion to renew his efforts in support of the policy and in hostility to Monroe.

Shortly after this he warmly advocated Webster's resolution, modelled after his own previous propositions touching the South American States, to provide for the recognition of Greece, then in the midst of her revolution, which naturally challenged very general and enthusiastic interest. He also introduced a joint resolution asserting the principle he had before repeatedly declared, and which was announced in the President's message at the opening of the session, now familiar as the "Monroe Doctrine." This portion of the message and Clay's resolution were both provoked by the designs imputed to the so-called "Holy Alliance" to aid Spain to reconquer the revolted provinces. Neither his nor Webster's resolution, however, was acted upon. The friends of Adams, Jackson, and Calhoun were not disposed to allow Clay to gain any further political advantage from championing the doctrine Monroe had declared, but of which Clay was in a large degree the author.[1]

The engrossing topic of the session was the tariff. The act of 1816 had not proven satisfactory to the manufacturers. With the exception of an increase of the duties on iron in 1818 and a reduction of those on wines in 1819, the schedule remained unchanged. An effort was made in 1820 for a general increase, but it was defeated in the Senate. Since 1819, when a severe financial crisis occurred as the natural consequence of the conditions produced by the war, the country had been suffering a period of extreme and general depression. There had been a great decrease in the export trade, and hence a ruinous decline in prices, accompanied by

---

[1] Von Holst's *Constitutional History of the United States*, vol. i. p. 412.

all the symptoms that flow from a vicious currency. All this had created a strong protection movement, notwithstanding the natural process of recuperation had already well set in, and if left to itself would have brought a slow but steady and ultimately complete restoration of financial and industrial health. The manufacturing interests took advantage of the situation on much the same plea that prevailed at the close of the war.

Early in the session a bill more thoroughly and systematically protective than any ever before proposed was reported to the House. In the middle of February discussion of it began, first over details, then developing into a vigorous and elaborate debate on the policy and principle of protection. It was really the first of the many great debates on the subject. Clay strongly favored the bill of 1820, and made an elaborate speech which may be taken as the general introduction to the series of disquisitions pronounced by him in behalf of what he denominated with singular inaptness, but efficient popular effect, the "American system." He took the lead in support of the bill of 1824. Prompted by a truly powerful speech in favor of free-trade by Philip P. Barbour, one of the ablest members of Congress during that period,[1] Clay delivered the most ambitious and exhaustive

---

[1] "James Barbour was a member of the Senate; Philip P. Barbour of the House. They were brothers, and both from Virginia. They were both men of great abilities, but their style and manner were very different. James was a verbose and ornate declaimer; Philip was a close, cogent reasoner, without any attempt at elegance or display. He labored to convince the mind; James to control and direct the feelings. A wag wrote upon the wall of the House:

"'Two Barbours to shave our Congress long did try.
One shaves with froth; the other shaves dry.'"

—Sparks's *Memories of Fifty Years*, p. 238. See also Benton's *Thirty Years' View*, vol. ii. p. 202.

speech he had thus far made in his Congressional career. This speech best reflects the protection arguments then current, and it is also marked by some of his most powerful rhetorical effects. After defining the division of sentiment on the tariff question, he described a state of the most stifling and paralyzing distress that he asserted to prevail throughout the country. Previous to the delivery of this speech the debate had been in progress over a month, yet nothing in the discussion suggested the existence of any such direful condition as that which Clay depicted. As Webster said, the country could not be "represented in gloom, melancholy, and distress, but by the effort of extraordinary powers of tragedy."[1]

The speech was far superior to any other on his side of the question delivered during the debate; but it cannot be classed as a valuable contribution to economic science. Even extreme protectionists have abandoned most of the arguments he employed. Despite the statesmanlike cast of his mind, he was not a profound reasoner on purely financial and economical subjects. In this respect he was far inferior to Webster.[2] In 1824 protection was not deep-

---

[1] "The paragraphs devoted to distress in this speech are more likely than any others Clay ever uttered to give those who shall deeply ponder them a generation or two hence any adequate conception of the orator's power. In fact, it is well remembered still how hundreds, not of members merely, but of those who on that occasion crowded the lobby, were agonized at their own and their country's distress, themselves having forgotten it till then."—*Democratic Review*, March, 1843, vol. xii. p. 302.

[2] The strongest speech in reply to Clay was made by Webster—indeed, it was one of the ablest he ever pronounced, although he subsequently abandoned the position he then took. In 1846 he made a speech on the tariff question at a dinner in Philadelphia. The next morning one of the Democratic newspapers reprinted his great speech of 1824, and many thousand copies "were sold before the joke was discovered. The Democrats were delighted—the Whigs furious, especially Mr. Greeley, of the *Tribune*,

ly rooted in the policy of the country. It had not as yet affected the sensitive and complex tissue of society. Against it there was a strong drift of instinctive disfavor, which needed only popular guidance to rule the national policy. The *Wealth of Nations* had been written half a century.[1] Clay admitted familiarity with its commercial doctrines, and stated them with exquisite precision. He had stretched his opinions far beyond their original scope. A few years more and the disorder and depression following in the train of war and bad finance would have disappeared, and national health would have been restored by natural processes, with increased vigor and vitality. A Presidential election was close at hand. The candidates were numerous, and their following was largely personal.[2]

---

who had come over to hear Mr. Webster, and who bought several copies of the old speech, thinking it the new one. But Mr. Webster enjoyed it hugely; and when his friend Ashmun handed him my extra, he laughed heartily, and said, 'I think Forney has printed a much better speech than the one I made last night.'"—Forney's *Anecdotes of Public Men*, p. 10.

[1] In a speech during this debate, Randolph said: "In the course of this discussion I have heard, I will not say with surprise, because *nil admirari* is my motto—no doctrine that can be broached on this floor can ever hereafter excite surprise in my mind—I have heard the names of Say, Ganilh, Adam Smith, and Ricardo pronounced not only in terms, but in tones, of sneering contempt, as visionary theorists, destitute of practical wisdom, and the clan of Scotch and Quarterly Reviewers lugged in to boot. This, sir, is a sweeping case of proscription. With the names of Say, Smith, and Ganilh I profess to be acquainted; for I, too, am versed in *title-pages*. But I did not expect to hear in this House a name with which I am a little further acquainted treated with so little ceremony, and by whom? I leave Adam Smith to the simplicity and majesty and strength of his own native genius, which has canonized his name—a name which will be pronounced with veneration, when not a man in this House will be remembered."

[2] "At present we chiefly know the names of those who are said to be candidates; and none of them stand committed, that I know of, to any particular policy or general principle as to national affairs."—*Niles's Register*, March, 1822, vol. xxii. p. 1.

The rivalry was intense. Clay seized the opportunity that his position gave him to rally and organize the scattered forces of protection. Without his support the bill must have failed. As it was, with every combination of interest and politics that could be devised, it was passed only by the scant majority of five in the House[1] and four in the Senate. Had Clay thrown against it the weight of his great influence and authority, protection in the United States, with all its attendant and lineal evils, would have met a signal and probably an abiding repulse. To aid him in his efforts to attain the glittering but transient distinction of the Presidency, he sacrificed one of the noblest opportunities of modern times, not only to benefit his country, but the world, and to earn a place among the few whose names are jewels in the crown of statesmanship.

The dominating influence that Clay exerted at the first session of the Eighteenth Congress was displayed at the next in relation to a subject which, though far less important than the tariff, was far more spectacular—the election of President by the House of Representatives. Clay's course was destined to peculiar historical interest, and to produce an unpropitious and enduring effect upon his political fortunes.

The prospect at the beginning of Monroe's Presidency had been realized. Federalism, so far as concerned party

---

[1] "After the passage of the bill on Friday, when the House adjourned and the Speaker was stepping down from his seat, a gentleman who had voted with the majority, said to him, 'We have done pretty well to-day.' 'Yes,' returned Mr. Clay. 'We made a good stand, considering that we lost both our Feet.' Alluding to Mr. Foot, of Connecticut, and Mr. Foote, of New York, who both voted against the bill, though it was thought some time ago that they would both support it."—*Niles's Register*, vol. xxvi. p. 143.

organization, was quite extinct; and the reigning party, if party it could be called, was in a state of disintegration, which caused the misnomer of the period, the "era of good feeling." The Congressional caucus, which for a time hitherto had governed the Presidential succession, had fallen into disrepute. National politics had lost all semblance of system or control. Four candidates for the Presidency, not materially differing in the political views they professed, had entered the field, and no one had secured a majority of the Electoral College. The election was thus devolved upon the House of Representatives, the choice to be made from the three candidates—Jackson, Adams, and Crawford—who had received the most electoral votes, 99, 84, and 41, respectively. This debarred Clay, who had received but 37.[1] Had he been one of the three he would unquestionably have been elected through his popularity in the House. As it was, his preference would determine the result. He was accordingly beset by the friends of the several candidates.

But for Crawford's relation to the election of 1824 he would now be quite unremembered, though he had been prominent in public life for a long period. He was a native of Virginia, whence he emigrated to Georgia in early life. He maintained himself by teaching school while preparing for the bar; and upon his admission he settled in the village of Lexington. He soon became the chief personage as well as the first lawyer of upper Georgia. His rising influence brought him into collision with the clique which had long controlled politics in that part of the State. Out of this arose between him and one of the old faction a duel in which he

---

[1] It was charged that Clay was unfairly deprived of the five votes of Louisiana.—Colton's *Clay*, vol. i. p. 291. For Vice-President, Calhoun received 182 of the 261 votes.

killed his adversary, and thus opened a feud the consequences of which influenced the political history of Georgia for more than forty years. In 1807 he was elected to the Senate. He there exhibited much ability and wise moderation, opposing the restrictive measures, but finally, along with Madison, supporting the war. In 1813 he succeeded Livingston as Minister to France. Livingston was very deaf, and Crawford could not speak French. This led Napoleon to remark that the United States had sent him one minister that was deaf and one that was dumb. Yet Napoleon was much impressed by Crawford, and once said of him, " No government but a republic could foster so much truth and simplicity of character as I find in Mr. Crawford." He would have been a formidable, if not successful, candidate for the Presidency against Monroe, had he not declined to oppose him. He served in Monroe's cabinet as Secretary of War for a short time and then as Secretary of the Treasury. He held the latter post at the time of the election, with full control of what was left of the party machinery. He possessed an exceptionally fine presence and a profound mind; but he must be regarded as an able politician rather than a statesman. Save the reminiscences of his political acumen, his long continuance in public affairs, and the fact that he received more votes than Henry Clay, there is little to distinguish his name from the ordinary obscurity of the civil lists. Nevertheless, it was alone the loss of health that prevented him from attaining the Presidency. In the latter part of 1823 he suffered a shock of paralysis so severe that for over a year he was unable to sign his name. Clay much preferred him, with good reason, to either of the other candidates; and beyond doubt it was solely Crawford's shattered health that determined Clay not to support him. The circumstance was scarcely a greater misfortune to Crawford than it proved to be to Clay. Crawford retired from public life. He afterward partly regained his health, and served as a circuit judge in Georgia from 1827 until his death, in 1834.[1]

As Clay regarded both Jackson and Adams, to choose between them was, in truth, as he expressed it, a choice of evils. But he at once decided to support Adams; he could not do otherwise, with decent respect for consistency. When his determination became known, and after all other means to change it had been exhausted, some of Jackson's friends attempted to drive him from it by a performance quite characteristic of American politics.

Some days before the election took place in the House a letter appeared in a Philadelphia newspaper asserting that Clay had agreed to support Adams on the condition that Clay be made Secretary of State. It was further alleged that the same terms had been offered to Jackson's friends, but that none of them would "descend to such mean barter and sale." Although anonymous, the letter purported to be written by a member of the House. Clay forthwith published a card. He pronounced the writer "a base and infamous calumniator, a dastard and a liar; and," he continued, "if he dare unveil himself and avow his name I will hold him responsible, as I here admit myself to be, to all the laws which govern and regulate men of honor." Two days later, in the same paper in which Clay's card appeared, the letter was acknowledged by one Kremer, a witless member from Pennsylvania, chiefly known at the capital by a

---

[1] Sparks's *Memories of Fifty Years*, pp. 40, 41, 60; Adams's *Gallatin*, p. 598; Sumner's *Jackson*, p. 83.

leopard-skin overcoat that he commonly wore. He asserted that the statements he had made were true, and that he was ready to prove them. A duel with such a character would have been ridiculous. The tragedy had turned to farce. Something, however, had to be done. Clay immediately demanded an investigation by a special committee of the House, and retracted his hasty challenge by stating that the charges, "emanating from such a source, this was the only notice he could take of them." After two days of discussion, such a committee was elected. It was composed of seven members, none of whom had supported Clay for the Presidency. Kremer at once announced his willingness to meet the inquiry; but on the morning of the day of the election in the House the committee reported that Kremer had declined to appear before it, sending a communication in which he denied the Constitutional power of the House to compel him to testify. No further action was taken. Adams was elected, and Clay became Secretary of State.

By Kremer's own admissions he had been induced by others to undertake this business. At one time, affrighted by the turmoil he had created, he repented and disclaimed; but again stimulated by his prompters, he returned to their bidding. The contemptible outcome of the scheme gave Clay reason to think that it had been sufficiently exposed and could safely be ignored. His mistake was soon apparent. Never was a groundless political scandal more effective. It was at once revived with intensified force and persistence. A strong effort was made in the Senate to reject his nomination; fifteen Senators, including Jackson himself, voted against it. This attempt failing, the cry of "bargain and corruption" was industriously started to in-

CH. III.]   CLAY AS SECRETARY OF STATE   99

fluence the next election. The extreme propriety of the appointment was entirely lost sight of, as was also the fact —then well known in Washington, and now on all hands admitted—that the only attempt at bargain was made by Jackson's friends. However plain it was to those in position to know the facts, it was natural that the rank and file of those who favored Jackson should regard Clay's appointment as the absolute demonstration of a deal. By accepting it he deliberately made himself the victim of circumstantial evidence. And to hostile minds the unfortunate appearance was heightened by the differences between him and Adams during the negotiations at Ghent, his subsequent attitude concerning a public controversy between Russell and Adams as to what took place there, and his severe criticism of Adams and the policy of Monroe's administration toward the South American states.

For several days he hesitated to accept the place, which Adams had immediately tendered. His friends were at first divided in their opinions regarding it, but they finally concurred in advising its acceptance. Even friends of Crawford and Jackson joined in this advice, although Crawford himself refused Adams's tender of the Treasury Department. For the position itself Clay was not desirous, and he assumed its duties with reluctance. What chiefly determined him was the belief that, if he did not accept, it would be argued that he dared not. The prospect of such an accusation was more obnoxious to him than the other horn of the dilemma. He, therefore, took the alternative of bold defiance.

With one exception, Clay's administration of the Department of State was not marked by any event of much historical importance. More treaties, principally commercial arrangements with the lesser powers, were concluded during his term than during the previous existence of the government, a result somewhat due to Clay's personal popularity with the foreign ministers at Washington.[1] Urgent efforts were also made to perfect a mutually satisfactory adjustment of our commercial relations with Great Britain and her dependencies; but the efforts were unavailing, except to keep palpably alive the questions involved. As the chief exponent of protection, Clay shared the theory that almost universally prevailed in commercial diplomacy—an eye for an eye and a tooth for a tooth. By an Order in Council in 1826 the British government prohibited all commercial intercourse between the West Indies and the United States, our government having failed to take advantage of an opportunity for reciprocity for which provision had been made by an act of Parliament, if made within a year thereafter; Clay, and also Gallatin, then minister to England, were unable to obtain the repeal of the order, despite the ability with which they presented our side of the case. In 1827, under an act passed four years previously, the President issued a retaliatory proclamation. One difficulty of long standing with England, however, Clay succeeded in settling: he secured an indemnity for slaves forcibly taken by the British during the War of 1812. In another instance, also, the interests of the slave-holders, which had now begun to appear on the surface of most of our public affairs, sought diplomatic aid. The House adopted a resolution requesting

---

[1] "In his intercourse with foreign ministers Mr. Clay had an opportunity to display all the charms of his unequalled courtesy; they remained his friends long after he retired. His Wednesday dinners and his pleasant evening receptions were remembered for many years."—Parton's *Famous Americans*, p. 39.

the President to open negotiations for the recovery of slaves that had escaped into Canada, in return for deserters from the British army and navy. The proposition was advanced, but the British government very decently declined the barter. With Mexico a boundary treaty was effected; but with Spain nothing could be accomplished, much as Clay then desired to purchase the province of Texas. He also endeavored to procure the mediation of the Emperor of Russia to induce Spain to recognize the independence of the South American republics, on condition that she retain her sovereignty over Cuba and Porto Rico, as our government desired that they should not come under the dominion of any other foreign naval power, because of their command of the Gulf.

The most prominent feature of his diplomatic administration was the Panama mission. The subject was opened early. The Spanish-American republics had arranged for a congress, which was to meet on the Isthmus. The principal objects were to secure co-operation against Spain, which had not recognized their independence, to frame a system for the regulation of their commercial and other relations, and to counteract the operations of the Holy Alliance. After Clay had been sounded in regard to it our government was invited to send plenipotentiaries. The project received his cordial approval. Adams, who, as Secretary of State, had opposed Clay's early manœuvres to procure the recognition of the South American states, now readily assented to his views on the subject, and the invitation was accepted. The Congress seemed to promise great possibilities, despite the hazard of European embroilment. If guided by the counsels of our government it would combine the international interests of the entire American hemisphere, carrying into practical and complete effect the Monroe Doctrine, and further the principles of religious liberty and the extermination of the slave-trade.[1]

The nomination of the envoys was at length confirmed by the Senate and an appropriation for their salaries and expenses passed after strenuous opposition on every available ground. Yet, to Clay's sincere sorrow, the whole project was finally frustrated. The delay caused by the prolonged debates prevented our representatives from reaching the Isthmus in time for the congress. When they arrived it had adjourned to meet at a later time in Mexico; but when the time came the renewed dissensions among the Southern republics rendered the congress impossible. Thus failed Clay's darling plan. Nor was it until sixty-five years later that it was revived, by Blaine, when the conditions had radically changed. The reason for its early failure and the slow progress of republican institutions in the Spanish-American countries lay in the unschooled character of the peoples who were barbarously struggling to adopt them. Since that time those peoples have been gradually fused with intelligent enterprise from the United States, which, like the influence of ancient Greece upon all her surroundings, has been slowly transforming the general character of the other American populations from Canada to Chili.

It was the President's announcement of the Panama mission to Congress that occasioned the first assault on his administration. It was politically necessary for his eager adversaries to find some ground of attack, and this was the

---

[1] "My Panama instructions were the most elaborate, and (if I may be allowed to speak of them) the ablest state paper that I composed while in the Department of State. They contain an exposition of liberal principles regulating maritime war, neutral rights, etc., which will command the approbation of enlightened men of posterity."—*Clay to Ullman, September 26, 1851.*

first that offered. Besides, the whole subject was distasteful to the slave-holders generally, as there were many negroes and mulattoes among the revolutionary leaders in the new republics. There was also some possibility of the scheme leading to a movement to procure the independence of Cuba, Hayti, and Porto Rico, where the colored population was large. A negro republic in the vicinity of the Gulf States was a most repulsive prospect.

In the course of one of the several debates concerning the Panama mission, John Randolph delivered against the administration in general, and Clay in particular, an harangue of such unbridled truculence that it resulted in a duel. It was the climax of an antipathy which had existed between them since Clay's first entrance into the House.[1]

Randolph is the most unique figure in our political history. So long as the period with which his life is mingled retains its interest he will be remembered and his utterances will be quoted. No man ever had a more curious political career, and no man ever used the English tongue with more pungent power. He came into the House in 1799, and remained in Congress, with two brief interruptions, until 1830. In 1801 he became the administration leader in the House. His opportunities and his influence for a time were very great. He then fell out with the Jefferson regime, and in 1806 began his long career of opposition. His party had pushed him aside. His temper and eccentricities had much to do with it, yet candor must admit that his stanch ad-

---

[1] "Mr. Randolph sat near Mr. Seaton, and on one occasion when Mr. Clay, speaking in his not unusual personal and self-sufficient strain, said among other things that his 'parents had left him nothing but *indigence* and *ignorance*,' Randolph, turning to Mr. Seaton, said in a stage whisper to be heard by the House: 'The gentleman might continue the alliteration and add *insolence.*'"—*Life of Seaton*, p. 152.

herence to his original principles had more. The exigencies of politics and the possession of power had gradually drawn Jefferson and the Virginian school from their pristine faith. Randolph was never again to represent authority, but he remained to the end of his days the most consistent advocate, barring his occasional extravagancies and aberrations, of the true theory of government. It is one of the seeming paradoxes of politics that the ablest early exponents of democracy were slave-holders.[1]

Some notion of Randolph's quaint appearance and strange personality may be derived from nearly every political history and biography relating to his times. Many a stretch of otherwise barren and dreary annals is enlivened by the magic of his wonderful, but eccentric and at times maniacal, genius. His touch usually left a gleam of light or a dash of color.[2] It was, however, seldom the radiance of poetic imagination, but rather the flash of almost supernatural insight, the glare of satirical wit, or too often the stain of cruel and malignant invective, like the trail of the knout upon human flesh. There is no more stupid reading in all the wide range of ambitious print than is con-

---

[1] "Jefferson was a States-rights man and a strict constructionist because he was a Republican, Randolph because he was a Virginian; Jefferson thought that government should be small that the people might be great, Randolph thought that government should be small that Virginia might be great. . . . Here we have the explanation of the great puzzle of American politics—the unnatural alliance, for sixty years, between the plantation lords of the South and the democracy of the North, both venerating the name of Jefferson, and both professing his principles."—Parton's *Famous Americans*, p. 191. Edmund Burke's explanation is more profound. In speaking of the Southern colonies, he said: "Freedom is to them not only an enjoyment, but a kind of rank and privilege. . . . In such a people the haughtiness of domination combines with the spirit of freedom, fortifies it, and renders it invincible."

[2] See Garland's *Randolph*, vol. ii. p. 300; *Life of Quincy*, p. 343.

tained in the Congressional debates. A truly good speech is such a rarity that it fairly shines from the dingy, double-columned pages. But Randolph's speeches, rambling and disjointed as they are, seem like glittering nuggets amid the arid sands. From his letters and speeches could be collected a volume of passages equal in style and force to anything in the language. When at his best, however discursive, he was terse, simple, and direct, epigrammatic and scintillating. His delicate idiom and the range of his illustration betoken a critical acquaintance with the classics and a vast variety of reading. The first book he read was Voltaire's *Charles XII.;* the next was the *Spectator*. So remarkable was his precocity that he was familiar with Shakespeare, Plutarch, Fielding, and Cervantes before he was eleven years of age.

On no occasion did he make much preparation for his speeches, usually none at all. He would leisurely enter the chamber and then give close attention to the business in progress. If it attracted his interest he would rise at the first opportunity and speak perhaps for three or four hours, with absolute ease, in tones that were silver except when emphasis or passion made them shrill. Yet the greater part of what he said in his later years had little or no connection with the subject that called him up.[1]

He was essentially dramatic. His interested presence

---

[1] "I heard him between three and four hours. His speech, as usual, had neither beginning, middle, nor end. Egotism, Virginian aristocracy, slave-scourging liberty, religion, literature, science, wit, fancy, generous feelings, and malignant passions constitute a chaos in his mind from which nothing orderly can ever flow."—Adams's *Diary*, vol. iv. p. 532. An accurate idea of his style and manner, its piquancy, desultoriness, and irrelevancy to the subject of debate may be obtained from *Niles's Register*, vol. xxx. pp. 186, 451.

could transform routine into a spectacular episode.[1] Nor were his most peculiar effects always produced by a speech; his acting was sometimes even more efficient. A striking instance of it took place in 1806. A new member, Barnabas Bidwell, of Massachusetts, had come into the House; and from his high reputation at home he was supposed to be a potent acquisition to the administration forces. On the occasion of his first speech, which had been duly advertised, Randolph was present. He always rode to the Capitol followed by a black servant, both being finely mounted. "He was dressed," says Quincy, "in his usual morning costume— his skeleton legs cased in tight-fitting leather breeches and top-boots, with a blue riding-coat, and the thick buckskin gloves from which he was never parted, and a heavily loaded riding-whip in his hand. After listening attentively for about a quarter of an hour he rose deliberately, settled his hat on his head, and walked slowly out of the House, striking the handle of his whip emphatically upon the palm of his left hand, and regarding poor Bidwell, as he passed him, with a look of insolent contempt, as much as to say, 'I have taken your measure, sir, and shall give myself no further concern about you!' It helped to extinguish effectually the new light from whom the administration had hoped so much. Mr. Bidwell acquired no weight in the House, and left Congress at the end of his term."[2]

Randolph's family was one of the oldest, most numerous, and wealthy of Virginia. It was always a source of pride with him that he was a descendant of Pocahontas. There is a touch of, perhaps, fanciful suggestiveness in the fact that until 1810 he resided on one of his plantations called,

---

[1] *Recollections of John Binns*, p. 240.   [2] *Life of Quincy*, p. 95.

and before his birth, Bizarre.¹ He must have been without strong ambition for preferment; for, by separating from the only party he could ever expect to co-operate with for any length of time, he deliberately flung away every future chance. Throughout his career a faithful constituency, which revolted but once, made him without effort secure of a seat in the House. Thus the extreme independence of his position, with the increasing plague of bodily infirmity and an uncontrollable tendency to morbidness of mind, produced what appeared like arrogance, but was, in truth, despairing discontent and total indifference to the ordinary considerations of policy.² In a speech in 1824 he casually remarked, " I have not the honor to know personally, or even by name, a large portion of the members of this House." There is no reasonable doubt that the extreme eccentricities and corrosive malignities that began early to characterize him were the

---

¹ "In 1810 he removed to Roanoke. . . . On Sunday, March 21, 1813, the house at Bizarre took fire. 'I lost,' says he, 'a valuable collection of books. In it was a whole body of infidelity; the Encyclopædia of Diderot and D'Alembert, Voltaire's works, seventy volumes; Rousseau, thirteen quartos; Hume, etc., etc.'"—Garland's *Randolph*, vol. ii. p. 9.

² "My powers, such as they are, have not been improved by culture. The first time I ever dreamed of speaking in public was on the eve of my election, in March, 1799, when I opposed myself (fearful odds) to Patrick Henry. My manner is spontaneous, like my matter, from the impulse of the moment; and when I do not feel strongly I cannot speak to any purpose. These fits are independent of my volition. . . . During the last four or five years I have perceived a sensible decline of my powers, which I estimate with as much impartiality as you would; in a word, as if they belonged to another. I am not better persuaded of the loss of my grinders or of the wrinkles in my face—and care as much for the one as the other."— *Randolph to Key, February* 17, 1814. " This letter is written as children whistle in the dark, to keep themselves from being afraid. I dare not look upon that 'blank and waste of the heart' within. Dreary, desolate, dismal—there is no word in our language, or any other, that can express the misery of my life. I drag on like a tired captive at the end of a slave-chain in an African coffle."—*June* 12, 1821.

brood of partial and increasing insanity, despite the common assertion, a relic of the antislavery struggles, that he was an instance of total depravity, a demon in human form. Whatever may be said of his errors and his faults, while he sat in Congress buncombe and dishonesty stood in wholesome terror of his scathing and merciless tongue.

With the events that caused the strife over the admission of Missouri, Randolph had begun to recover a degree of personal influence. He soon became the recognized leader of the slave-holding interest, which was rapidly growing in purpose and power as a political factor.[1] He was organizing the South to a systematic defence of that interest and formulating the political theory by which it was to be maintained. It was wholly derived from the political doctrines with which he had begun his public life, but which were to be shorn of their noble virtue by being cramped and distorted in the service of slavery. Clay was the chief obstacle to the political union of the slave power. His efforts in bringing about the Missouri Compromise, against Randolph's untiring opposition, fanned the slumbering flame of his old hatred into a frenzy that burst forth with every opportunity, and an opportunity presented itself with every general subject that came before Congress. During the debates on internal improvements and the tariff he assailed Clay with vehemence and venom; but when the discussion of the Panama mission opened the way he gave full vent to his unparalleled power of invective. He repeated in his characteristic style all the motley aspersions against Adams and

---

[1] "The two words, 'dough faces,'" said Clay, in 1838, in reference to Randolph's hostility to the Missouri Compromise, "with which that gentleman rated and taunted our Northern friends, did more injury than any two words I have ever known."

Clay. Among them he insinuated that the invitations to participate in the congress were practically a fraud because they had been written or inspired by the State Department. Later on, in reference to another affair, he uttered a sentence that is one of the most famous ever spoken in Congress: "I was defeated, horse, foot, and dragoons—cut up and clean broke down by a coalition of Blifil and Black George—by a combination, unheard of till then, of the Puritan with the blackleg." He then descended into such malevolence as to berate Clay's parents for bringing into the world "this being, so brilliant yet so corrupt, which, like a rotten mackerel by moonlight, shines and stinks."

The more vicious bits of this flagrant diatribe were soon retailed through Washington. Clay was enraged, and forthwith challenged Randolph to a duel. An effort was made by friends to effect a reconciliation, but it failed: Randolph's language was never of doubtful meaning. The duel, however, which came off in the most high-toned fashion, proved harmless. Randolph had determined not to fire at Clay, and Clay was inexpert with the pistol. Two shots were fired. Before the first one, Randolph changed his mind and tried to disable Clay; with the second shot he recovered his original purpose and fired in the air. Fortunately, Clay did nothing worse than to spoil Randolph's coat by sending two bullets through it. Then, in an affecting scene, the men made up.[1] This was Clay's last experience as a duellist.

Although Clay's efforts while Secretary of State in be-

---

[1] Benton's *Thirty Years' View*, vol. i. p. 77; Prentice's *Life of Clay*, p. 299. For a curious parallel between this duel and a contemporaneous one between the Duke of Wellington and Lord Winchelsea, see *Life of Quincy*, p. 169. Randolph was Minister to Russia in 1830. He died in 1833.

half of the South American republics did not attain immediate results, they were not in vain. His zeal in that office was the culmination of his long-sustained interest in the subject; and time alone could produce the full fruition of his labors. It was the impulse he originated which matured into the Monroe Doctrine, and must eventually render the influence of the United States dominant in the western hemisphere. To him more than to any one else belongs the credit of this result. With egregious vanity, but in brilliant phrase, Canning claimed this distinction. In the House of Commons in 1826 he asserted that he "called the New World into existence to redress the balance of the Old." As Premier of the British government he did indeed materially aid the South American cause; but Clay was the first to espouse and elevate it, and it was he that contributed most to make it popular and powerful.[1]

Like that phase which came within the compass of the State Department, Adams's entire administration was quite unsignalized except by its general excellence. It yields but little to animate the interest of the curious reader. Rush, of Pennsylvania, was Secretary of the Treasury; Barbour, of Virginia, Secretary of War; McLean, of Ohio, Postmaster-General; and Wirt, of Maryland, Attorney-General. Nothing disturbed the tranquillity and steadily advancing prosperity of the country. In this respect no administration has ever been more colorless. The affairs to which the turbulent condition of politics gave rise were small and

---

[1] Rush, to Clay, June 27, 1827. In 1827 Bolivar wrote to Clay a letter expressing his appreciation of Clay's services to South American independence. In his reply, Clay took occasion to admonish Bolivar that "ambitious designs" had been imputed to him, but with delicate earnestness affirming his confidence in Bolivar's patriotic purposes.

transient, and mostly confined to Washington: there were no railroads or telegraphs to distribute the daily guess-work and piecemeal that mainly fill the columns of the modern newspaper. The principal topic that engrossed the public mind was the next Presidential election; but the general discussion was conducted upon the same lines as it was on the day of Adams's election by the House. There being nothing in his administration to excite popular disapproval, the only contributions to the discussion were new personal scandals and fresh versions of the old ones.

Adams came into office exempt from party or personal pledges, yet in a manner very unsatisfying to his pride and ambition. He entered upon the discharge of his duties with an ideal appreciation of his responsibilities; and no Chief Magistrate, here or elsewhere, has ever surpassed his austere and unswerving efforts to banish politics from the performance of his public duties. He has often been denominated one of the few statesmen who have held the Presidency. Most of his life had been devoted to the public service in distinguished positions — diplomatic, legislative, and executive. He may be said to have begun his public career at the age of fourteen, as secretary to the American envoy to Russia. Then, in a like capacity, he served his father and Franklin when they negotiated the Treaty of 1783, by which England formally recognized the independence of the United States. Instead of continuing as secretary to his father, who was then appointed Minister to the Court of St. James, he wisely decided to return home and finish his education.

Although his reading was extensive and thorough, and he had enjoyed the invaluable advantage of mingling with some of the greatest men of both Europe and America, his schooling had been confined to such snatches as he could get while sojourning at Paris, Amsterdam, and Leyden. He prepared himself as quickly as possible and entered the junior class at Harvard. Graduating, he qualified for the bar and began practice at Boston. But he soon acquired more reputation for his contributions to the press on international topics than he gained in the profession. He was then sent as Minister to The Hague, whence he was transferred to London, and thence to Berlin. On Jefferson's election he again returned to Massachusetts and was successively elected to the State Senate and the Senate of the United States.

Thus far he had been a stanch Federalist; but he now entered upon a course that soon identified him completely with the Republicans. To the astonishment of the New England Federalists, he approved the Louisiana purchase. This departure from party fealty, although it involved no change of principles, was followed by his supporting Jefferson's restrictive measures. The intense anger and disgust of the Federalists, who stigmatized his conduct with all the epithets that can be applied to apostasy and treason, led him to resign before his term expired. But he was not abandoned by the Republicans. Madison straightway appointed him Minister to Russia, where he remained over four years, thence going to Ghent and to London, and then entering Monroe's cabinet as Secretary of State.

Had he joined the Republican party because of the better prospects it afforded him, he could not have done so at a more propitious time and with better results; and to minds inclined to be cynical, his immediate preferment, under the circumstances, is convincing proof that he was actuated by material motives. This fact led a great number to believe him to the end of his days entirely capable of doing anything necessary to further his designs. Nevertheless, from the ample evidence by which to judge him, most critics, however hostile, unite in imputing to him no unworthy motives. And besides this, to those practically conversant with the ways of politics, the conduct he pursued while President demonstrates that he was entirely without political art. It may be safely asserted that, without his hereditary advantages, he would not have achieved a distinguished public career. He possessed extraordinary powers of mind in some respects, yet he was curiously limited in others. In a large and practical sense he was not a statesman. He had no faculty whatever for political leadership; and in the world as it is the statesman must in a large degree possess it. His long and varied experience seemed only to intensify his narrow and unbending Puritanism. He was so rigidly and minutely true to his convictions that his marvellous honesty was incredible to the strifes and passions of his time. It was inevitable that such a rare man should be thought by many to be a knave and hypocrite. His main fault was that he was not callous enough to the minor defects in the minds and characters of those about him, and to the petty evils of one kind and another, always present and unavoidable, and which must be philosophically recognized and utilized to accomplish any considerable results in public life.

As much as Adams desired and deserved a second term at the hands of the people, he not only abstained rigorously from doing aught to aid his chances, but acted with such apparent indifference to them that he ruined any possibility he might have had.[1] He flatly refused to make any removals

---

[1] "Mr. Adams, during his administration, failed to cherish, strengthen, or even recognize the party to which he owed his election ; nor, so far as

from office except for breach of duty. He thus, and against the urgent protests of Clay and others, wholly deprived himself of any assistance that might be gained from the bestowal of patronage. He went so absurdly far in this course as to allow to remain in office even those who had passed the bounds of decency in reviling him and his administration. This lost to him the support of a large body that would have stood by him had he offered any prospect of advantage. He offered none. He put himself without the pale of politics. He seemed barren of any sentiment of appreciation for personal services. His temperament was cold and acrid; his manner abstracted and ungracious.¹ In his opinion whatever ought to be granted required no other reason; and whatever ought not to be deserved no civility. His refusal was like a blow in the face, and no one receiving it forgot or forgave. His entire conduct partook of his character—it was devoid of policy. He was the complete obverse of the popular politician. In whatever

---

I am informed, with the great power which he possessed did he make a single influential political friend."—Thurlow Weed's *Autobiography*, vol. i. p. 180.

¹ "I was told that when he was a candidate for the Presidency his friends persuaded him to go to a cattle show. Among the persons who addressed him was a respectable farmer who impulsively exclaimed, 'Mr. Adams, I am very glad to see you. My wife, when she was a gal, lived in your father's house; you were then a little boy, and she has often combed your head.' 'Well,' said Mr. Adams, in a harsh voice, 'I suppose she combs yours now!'"—Ames's *Ten Years in Washington*, p. 210. "The two candidates, Mr. Adams, the elect, and General Jackson, the defeated, accidentally met in the East Room. General Jackson, who was escorting a lady, promptly extended his hand, saying, pleasantly, 'How do you do, Mr. Adams? I give you my left hand, for the right, as you see, is devoted to the fair. I hope you are very well, sir.' All this was gallantly and heartily said and done. Mr. Adams took the General's hand, and said, with chilling coolness, 'Very well, sir; I hope General Jackson is well.'"—*Reminiscences of B. P. Poore*, vol. i. p. 26.

policy he advocated—as, for instance, his scheme of internal improvements—he went to the uttermost of his convictions, apparently indifferent to the prospect of success and without effort to qualify or accommodate, thus driving into the swelling ranks of his adversaries all those whose views were not as radical and uncompromising as his own. But, with the most popular genius and politic judgment, it would have been difficult for him to obtain a second term. From the hour of his election, war without scruple was waged against him. With the first general election after his term began, and for the first time in the history of the government, a majority of both Houses of Congress came in against the administration. The opposition grew constantly in strength and violence. There being no important policy or principle in party controversy, the sole issue was Adams or Jackson in 1828. The campaign was the longest and the most scandalous American politics has ever known. Everything that rancorous and conscienceless partisan invention could concoct was fused into the noisome atmosphere.[1] Nor were Adams and Clay the sole objects of this pestilence of slander. Charges of the most infamous character were made against Jackson; and his variegated career was full of unique and serviceable material upon which to found campaign calumny. So serious were some of the charges that it was deemed needful formally to refute them by means of a "whitewashing committee," as it was dubbed, composed of several eminent citizens of Tennessee. Even Jackson's wife, a plain and inoffensive woman whom he in early life had married,

---

[1] "I am alternately diverted and disgusted with the scenes which are passing around me. Such working, toiling, and sweating; such mining and countermining; such lying, abusing, quarrelling, and almost fighting for a little short-lived distinction."—*Wirt, to Pope, March* 23, 1828.

and had been obliged to remarry because she had not been fully divorced from her former husband, was not exempt from attack; soon after the election she died of the grief occasioned by the abuse to which she had been subjected during this shameless canvass. This rankled in Jackson's mind to the close of his life and inflamed his animosity against his opponents in that campaign to a degree that approached insanity.

His hatred of Clay was fierce and implacable. He fully believed him capable of anything of which he could be accused, and he himself gave currency to the "bargain and corruption" cry. Nothing could quell it. It was printed, placarded, and harped upon throughout the land.[1] It was disproved time and time again as effectually as any such charge can be disproved. Every person ever named as having any actual knowledge concerning it, even those nearest Jackson and the most ardent in his support, admitted their inability to substantiate a single particular.[2] Clay wrote elaborate addresses and made exhaustive speeches in which he demonstrated the utter groundlessness of the accusation. Several times it was thought to be annihilated; but that was a mistaken notion; it still thrived, in company with a variety of congenial aspersions against his personal habits and character.[3] Argument had little force against the potent

---

[1] Baldwin's *Party Leaders*, p. 309.

[2] Benton furnished conclusive evidence of Clay's innocence.—*Thirty Years' View*, vol. i. p. 48. Even Buchanan, to whom Jackson referred as his only source of information, disclaimed all knowledge.—Colton's *Life of Clay*, vol. i. p. 352. See also a letter from Lafayette in *Clay's Correspondence*, p. 180.

[3] Among the many slanders against him was the misrepresentation of his financial condition. "I am not free, absolutely, from debt," he wrote to a friend. "I am not rich. I never coveted riches. But my estate would even now be estimated at not much less than $100,000."

fact that he had elected Adams and was Secretary of State. On the Kentucky stump he was unable to pursue the line of dignified refutation; his language lost all moderation and restraint and became the vehicle of raving wrath.[1] The complete history of that lie would form many volumes. What Clay alone wrote and spoke about it would fill several. For a generation a large portion of the people believed the charge; and many thought that, although it might not be true, Clay's support of Adams, after Jackson had received a plurality of the electoral votes, was a political crime—a conclusion that will not bear analysis.

The result of the contest was Jackson's signal triumph. Even Kentucky went for him. Adams retired in the shadow of deep humiliation; and Clay, with broken health and spirits.[2] Yet before both of them lay the most arduous, yet the most brilliant part of their careers.

Clay at once returned to Ashland, his home. It was neither his desire nor intention to resume the practice of law, and after this period his appearance in court was only occasional. His chief interest, aside from politics, was in agricultural pursuits, which he enjoyed as an expert, with all the means to indulge his skill and inclinations. His estate was one of the best in Kentucky. It contained some six hundred acres of land near Lexington. It was originally owned by Daniel Boone, and finally came by descent into the possession of Lucretia Hart, whom Clay married in 1799. Here, ten years later, he erected the mansion that became one of the historic homes of America. Mount Vernon and Monticello are scarcely more famous. The

---

[1] Parton's *Jackson*, vol. iii. p. 180.
[2] Adams's *Diary*, vol. vii. pp. 439, 517; *Life of George Ticknor*, vol. i. p. 381.

site is on a slight eminence overlooking the city two miles distant. The house was built of brick, in a plain style of architecture, staid and comfortable in appearance rather than imposing. At either end of the oblong and spacious main building, two stories and a half in height, is an ample one-story wing; and all are topped with tall, substantial chimneys. The interior, somewhat peculiar in arrangement, was finished and furnished with admirable effect. The grounds and surroundings were in picturesque harmony with the house. Thus Ashland was in all respects worthy of the distinction it was soon to acquire as the Mecca of the Whigs and a point of attraction to notable visitors from abroad.[1]

Clay's success as a farmer was quite equal to that as an advocate. He was a judge of fine-bred horses and stock,[2] and in the Blue-Grass Region of Kentucky this means much. Though he was chiefly interested in stock-raising, agriculture was not slighted. The products of the garden and dairy were sufficient to meet the expenses of the farm. He conducted many experiments of various kinds, and made fertilization and hemp the subjects of considerable study. He wrote a pamphlet on the cultivation of hemp, an article which he always sedulously protected by his tariff policy. The labor on the estate was performed by slaves, of whom he had about fifty. His chief assistant was his wife, who was accounted as good a farmer as any in the neighborhood.[3] She was thoroughly domestic, seldom accompanying her husband to Washington to participate in the society of the capital. During his protracted absences she competently administered the affairs of Ashland. Indeed, we may well sur-

---

[1] *Century Magazine*, vol. xxxiii. pp. 163, 169.
[2] *Niles's Register*, vol. xlviii. p. 362. [3] Colton's *Clay*, vol. i. p. 34.

mise that the success of the establishment was largely due to the intelligence and skill with which she executed Clay's agricultural policy. She was the mother of eleven children—five boys and six girls.[1] Her last child was born in 1821. In 1845 she had fifteen grandchildren. She survived her husband and most of her children.

Clay's personal appearance and bearing were not especially distinguished. He did not arrest the attention of strangers by any unwonted cast of countenance or peculiarity of manner. He was tall, rather thin, with somewhat narrow and sloping shoulders. He was seldom entirely robust, having a tendency to consumption, that betrayed itself at intervals through his life, and of which he finally died. His head was not large, but symmetrical and well poised, the forehead full and slightly retreating.[2] In early life his hair was quite flaxen, and though in later years when hoary it grew sparsely in front, it was abundant enough to prevent all appearance of baldness. He had the gray eyes so common to genius and fine intelligence. In repose they were not markedly expressive, but with excitement or emotion they flamed with various lights. His features were plain, even homely. They were nowise peculiar or striking, with the exception of the mouth, which was unusually large, with thinnish, straight, and closely set lips. His complexion to the last was very fair and smooth. The facial muscles were extremely flexile and in the highest degree responsive to his thoughts and feelings. This latter

---

[1] Amos Kendall's *Autobiography*, p. 115.
[2] "Considering the volume of the brain, or size of the head, it has the best adjusted faculties I have ever seen. The skull, after death, will give no idea of his power, as he derives the whole of it from his temperament." —*Life of Horace Mann*, p. 282.

was the one physical attribute, besides his voice, that gave distinction to his presence when he spoke or was moved. It was this harmony of movement and expression, in combination with a voice marvellous in its richness, variety, and power, that produced the singular spell he exerted. His entire composition seemed plain and neutral, that his highly emotional nature might have a perfect instrument of manifestation.

As might be supposed from these characteristics, his manner had great charm. It gave the impression of frankness, freedom, and generosity, and was ordinarily coupled with a contagious buoyancy and sanguineness of spirits. He was extremely convivial, keenly enjoying the society of his friends. He was far from being an epicure, yet he was fastidious in his tastes. He indulged moderately in wine, took snuff, after the fashion of the period, and used tobacco freely. In earlier days he lost and won large sums at play; but in consequence of the censure he encountered, he ceased the practice of gaming, though he always remained inveterately fond of whist. In most respects, so far as manners and habits were concerned, he was a typical Southern gentleman.[1] Placed in elevated positions and thrown among able men at an early age, he soon acquired that ease and grace which follow capacity and experience of the world. This

---

[1] "His sentiments were always fine, and his animal passions weak. In all the animal proclivities, Webster and Clay were wide apart. Webster was like a catfish—gross and omnivorous; Clay like a brook-trout—fastidious even in taking the gilded fly. . . . I have never seen him perform a disrespectful action, or heard from his lips a sensual word in regard to women in my life; yet his sympathy with intellectual, virtuous women was intense and his magnetism pre-eminent. With homely features, he had the plastic radiation of countenance which at times seemed like inspiration. Women were crazy in his presence, and grave men filled with unusual enthusiasm."—*Life of Cassius M. Clay*, vol. i. p. 96.

may be almost necessarily implied from his elocution; for great power and smoothness of speech are quite incompatible with angularity of mind or manner. While he had superiors in various departments and particulars, in his generation there lived no man who rivalled his peculiar combination of heart, mind, and address. There were many who surpassed him in range, variety, and solidity of learning; many, in closeness and severity of logic; many, in calculation and shrewdness of judgment; many, in purity and finish of diction: but in that general excellence and complete harmony of faculties which unify body and mind, on a lofty scale, he had no peer. It is that balance, allowing the most free and perfect play of the faculties, which produces the subtle attribute of personal magnetism; and no more striking instance of it is found in history than that exhibited by Henry Clay. He was entirely devoid of pettiness and vanity; he was of too large and strong a mould to be in any way cheap. Long before the age of fifty, and when the most brilliant part of his career was yet to come, his experience in the highest realm of public affairs had destroyed all sense of novelty in his situation and that self-consciousness which attends the assumption of power; his habit of mind had become that of the statesman and party chieftain. His greatest defect of manner was his involuntary assumption of authority when his views met with opposition; at such times he inclined to be dictatorial, not with coarse arrogance, but with lofty and courtly assurance.[1] Yet he would have been more than human if, with

---

[1] From the many sources whence this description is derived, the following should be cited: Martineau's *Retrospect of Western Travel*, vol. i. pp. 172, 176; Hilliard's *Politics and Pen Pictures*, p. 8; Greeley's *Recollections of a Busy Life*, p. 250; Parton's *Greeley*, p. 166; Parton's *Famous Ameri-*

his peculiar and wonderful abilities and fascinating hold on his adherents, he had been otherwise in this regard. The growth of his personal influence doubtless had much to do with developing this temper of mind, and it is not unlikely that it tended to his gradual adoption of the Federalist creed, which was soon to become the basis of the Whig party, of which Clay, from its origin to his death, was the foremost figure and lawgiver. It was to the formation of this new party that his efforts were at once devoted after the election of Jackson. At the head of it he designed to contest the field with Jackson in 1832.

---

cans, p. 11; Pierce's *Sumner*, vol. i. p. 316; Winthrop's *Addresses*, vol. iv. pp. 59, 60; Thurlow Weed's *Autobiography*, vol. i. pp. 181, 207; *Reminiscences of B. P. Poore*, vol. i. p. 85; *Appleton's Encyclopædia of American Biography*, article "O. E. Dodge," vol. ii. p. 194; *Democratic Review*, vol. xii. p. 302; *Century Magazine*, vol. xxxiii. p. 179.

CHAPTER IV

The New Development and Arrangement of Political Forces—Andrew Jackson, and the Significance of his Political Rise—His First Administration—The Spoils System—The "Kitchen Cabinet"—Party Dissension and Reorganization of the Cabinet—The Political Issues—Clay Nominated for President and Re-Elected to the Senate—The Political Activity of the Period—The Whig Programme—The Rejection of Van Buren's Nomination for Minister to England—Clay's Plan of Tariff Revision—His Defence of the American System—The Tariff of 1832—The Public Lands—The Effort to Compromise Clay on the Subject—His Land Bill

THE time had at length arrived for a regular and militant arrangement of political forces. The chaos of politics had reached the stage of crystallization. The preceding conditions had naturally led to it. It is easy to discern from the literature and characteristics of the period the changes that were coming over the public mind. The effects of the war and of the causes that produced it were becoming distinctly visible. The steady expansion of wealth and population had begun strongly to manifest itself in the political thought and movement of the time. The disseminations of the press were constantly increasing in variety and volume. The stream of politics was rapidly gathering in expanse and momentum from the new and numerous tributaries of private interest; it was becoming a wide and turbulent current, and even to many thoughtful observers who did not perceive the true meaning of the phenomena, it threatened calamity to our national character and institutions.

In all nations and all times, politics, whatever the kind or quality, is primarily the avenue to personal advantage. Whether it be in the seemingly petty strifes for court favors or the greater struggles of able statesmen over policies that affect the world, personal ambition for power and position is the ruling motive; desire for the national weal, how deep and genuine soever, is seldom paramount. But in nations whose concerns have weight and whose peoples have power, personal rivalries are forced to conform to the processes of party organization, which alone can press the discordant interests and elements that inevitably exist into orderly and efficient union. If adequate issues do not exist they are created; for without them there can be no systematic and seemly operations. All this is plain enough now; but in 1828 party warfare, in the full modern sense, was unknown in the United States. Necessity is the mother of political invention and progress. After 1828, system and intricacy speedily developed in our politics. The ensuing thirty years form the most interesting and remarkable period of our political annals. From a superficial and cynical point of view it was the struggle of ambitious ability, supported by the wealth and conservatism of the country, with pushing mediocrity, supported by the multitude and lighted up toward the last by the lurid glow of the antislavery agitation.[1] The most significant indication of the changing political temper of the times was the rise of Andrew Jackson.

---

[1] "In these Jacksonian contests we find nearly all the learning, nearly all the ancient wealth, nearly all the book-nourished intelligence, nearly all the silver-forked civilization, united in opposition to General Jackson, who represented the country's untutored instincts."—Parton's *Jackson*, vol. iii. p. 150.

Concerning Jackson there is an antipodal difference of opinion, both extremes being equally wrong, owing to partisan prejudices, without critical understanding of his career and the general causes that made it possible. There should, however, be little disagreement as to either, for the historical quality of both is easily ascertained.

To say that Jackson's political career was the product of circumstances would not be strictly accurate, yet it is more nearly so than is usually supposed. It is of course true, in a general sense, that every distinguished career is proximately due to circumstances; but in most cases the reputations acquired by men of superior ability are only modified or colored by their surroundings. It is altogether probable that had Shakespeare, Newton, and Burke lived in other ages than those which they adorn, their great powers would in some way have been conspicuously displayed. So also would it have been with Franklin, Hamilton, and Clay; but not with Jackson. His eminence was the consequence of his being the chance instrument by which the forces that had been long in gathering were to assert themselves. Undoubtedly no other man would have done exactly, or perhaps even approximately, as he did; yet certainly the general results of the period would have been practically the same. His potent personality, indeed, singularly adapted him to the conditions, but he affected rather the hue than the texture of the political fabric.

Most of the men who attained authority in the early settlement of the West were untutored, restless, and daring. The new communities were chiefly composed of these semi-barbarians, who naturally gravitated to the pioneer regions, which were constant scenes of Indian depredations and ruffianly *mêlées*. One of the incentives to this early immigration was the conditions that always exist where the restraint of law is lax. The populations being small and scattered, the man who possessed the common character, along with pronounced capacity, at once became prominent. If Jackson was not precisely of this class, it was thoroughly congenial to him.

His parents—who were of the humblest station of life—came to this country from the North of Ireland in 1765. Andrew was born two years later. His father died at about the same time, in poverty. Until his mother's death, when he was fourteen, he lived most of the time with an uncle. He worked for some three or four years at the saddlery trade, and then began to read law at Salisbury, North Carolina, not far from the place in which he had always lived. But he was neither by turn of mind nor application a student, and much of the time that should have been devoted to preparation for the bar was given up to the exciting and boisterous sports of the neighborhood. According to an old resident of the place, who informed Parton, young Jackson " was the most roaring, rollicking, gamecocking, horse-racing, card-playing, mischievous fellow that ever lived in Salisbury." From the scanty accounts of this period of his life, we learn that the most marked talent he exhibited was his power of profanity, which for originality, variety, and violence was unsurpassed by any of his contemporaries. He developed the faculty of ferocity to such a degree that it became with him an art which he employed as one of his principal weapons, albeit, on most occasions, he had little need of simulation—for his natural temper was terrible and overpowering.[1]

---

[1] Parton's *Jackson*, vol. i. pp. 64, 463.

In 1788 one of his friends was appointed Superior Court judge of the district of Tennessee, and Jackson, then twenty-one, was appointed prosecuting attorney. There was no difficulty in procuring the post, for its functions were extremely dangerous and undesirable. If knowledge of the law had been the first requisite, Jackson probably would not have presumed to seek the place. The qualifications demanded were fierce resolution, dauntless courage, and the power of terrorizing the lawless elements of the border. An idea of Jackson's native spirit of fearless independence may be drawn from an incident that happened when he was a lad. He boldly, and doubtless insolently, refused to clean the boots of one of Tarleton's troopers, who several times raided the region, and for his refusal received a sabre-cut on the head that left for life an ugly scar. The promise of the youth was amply fulfilled by the man. It sufficiently illustrates his character to say, without recounting the many belligerent and bloody affairs during his service, that he proved himself the man for the place; he used process and pistols with equal readiness and facility. Nor was he long in acquiring the lion's share of such civil business as there was in the primitive town of Nashville and the neighboring country.

After eight years of this sort of life he had gained an influential standing. He was a member of the convention in 1796 that framed the original constitution for the new commonwealth, and was elected its first Representative in Congress. He served in that capacity for a year, and was then appointed to fill a vacancy caused by the expulsion from the Senate of one of the Tennessee members. His appearance, dress, and deportment were uncouth. Gallatin described him as a "rough backwoodsman"; and Jefferson said of him that "he could never speak on account of the rashness of his feelings; that he had seen him attempt it repeatedly and as often choke with rage."[1] His appointment to the Senate was largely in recognition of his success in securing the passage of a bill to reimburse his State for expenses it had incurred in warfare with the savages, a subject of much complaint on the frontier because of the indifference of the federal government. His legislative service was subsequently remembered only by his having voted with eleven others against the laudatory address to Washington at the close of his Presidency. Jackson shared intensely in the prevailing Western friendliness for French democracy and hostility to Federalism, and the small part he took in the proceedings of Congress was governed by these sentiments. He remained in the Senate only a year, withdrawing in 1798, to become a Supreme Court judge in Tennessee.

It is evident that during this period he was quite without political ambition and wholly without the qualifications to rise in politics in the ordinary way. His service as judge suggests the conclusion that he was equally without juridical ambition. He held the judgeship six years, and then resigned. Beyond this nothing is known about his judicial

---

[1] Jefferson further said of him: "I feel very much alarmed at the prospect of seeing General Jackson President. He is one of the most unfit men I know for the place. He has had very little respect for laws or constitutions, and is, in fact, an able military chief. His passions are terrible. . . . He has been much tried since I knew him, but he is a dangerous man."—Webster's *Correspondence*, vol. i. p. 346. When, in 1818, Monroe asked Jefferson whether it would be wise to give Jackson the mission to Russia Jefferson exclaimed: "Why, good God, he would breed you a quarrel before he had been there a month!"—*Niles's Register*, vol. xxiv. p. 280. Jackson was offered and declined the mission to Mexico in 1823.

CH. IV.] QUALIFICATIONS OF FRONTIER JUDGES 129

service, either as to the amount and kind of business in his court or the manner in which he despatched it. None of his decisions, if he wrote any, were preserved; but it is probable that he wrote none, for his letters during this time were crudely composed, and it would have been characteristic of him to dispose of all questions before him summarily, according to the view he took of them at the time. His mind was so unjudicial that the incongruity of his being a judge would be amusing were it not for the probability that, however else his conduct may have appeared, it was never amusing to suitors and criminals in his court. Still, there was not much need of learning and refinement in the tribunals of the frontier, and it may fairly be presumed that Jackson's directness and knowledge of the people rendered his service efficient. Under the conditions of the time and place judicial fitness, in the proper sense, had little to do with judicial appointments. The idea was not present. This is strikingly shown by the circumstance that while Jackson was judge he was elected major-general of the militia after a sharp and close contest with ex-Governor Sevier, the most prominent man in the State. No doubt the pecuniary compensation—six hundred dollars per year—was the controlling motive for Jackson's going upon the bench; and that he desired the position was sufficient reason for his obtaining it.

He retired from the bench in 1804. He was in embarrassed circumstances. He had been concerned in trade and land speculations which had proven unsuccessful. To repair his misfortunes, he abandoned the law and devoted several years to various business enterprises,[1] but at length

---
[1] Jackson was charged with having been in early life a dealer in slaves. "This charge was strictly true, though abundantly disproved by the oaths

confined his attention to planting. During this interval of private occupation he evinced the same violent and undisciplined traits which had characterized his previous course. He was usually involved in quarrels and personal difficulties. In 1806 he fought a duel in which he killed his opponent and barely escaped death himself; the ball that struck him broke two ribs, and was thus deflected from its mortal errand. For a time he was engaged in boat-building; and in 1805 he contracted to provide Burr with boats for his uncertain project. He took a conspicuous share in lionizing Burr at the outset, and was loath to believe him guilty of any unlawful design. He vacillated somewhat, but finally appeared during the trial at Richmond as one of Burr's most zealous champions. He went so far as to deliver a foaming harangue against Jefferson. Spleen was the principal cause of his conduct. He disliked Jefferson because he had refused to appoint him governor of the Orleans territory; and Burr's chief accuser, the shallow and unprincipled Wilkinson, who commanded there, he loathed.

At the outbreak of the war with England, Jackson had passed his forty-fifth year. He had withdrawn from politics, if his brief Congressional experience could be called political; he had tired of the judgeship, if his position could be called judicial; he had forsaken his profession, if his practice could be called professional. His business ventures had been futile. "Nothing really prospered with

---

of some, and even by the certificate of his principal partner. Jackson had a small store or trading establishment at Bruinsburgh, near the mouth of the Bayou Pierre, in Claiborne county, Mississippi. It was at this point he received the negroes, purchased by his partner at Nashville, and sold them to the planters of the neighborhood."—Sparks's *Memories of Fifty Years*, p. 149.

him," says Parton, "but his farm and his horses, both of which he loved, and therefore understood." He was merely a planter and a militia general. He had achieved nothing to distinguish him from the numberless and forgotten legion of the sometime prominent; or, if he escaped oblivion, it would be in consequence of his connection with Burr. If he had ever had any but military ambition, which is doubtful, it must have subsided. His hopes, whatever they had been, had reached their compass of satisfaction. His character had hardened in its original mould. Beyond question, without war he would have continued in the same course as that which he had pursued during the six years preceding. But the war came, and he instinctively embraced the belated opportunity of his life. He forthwith offered himself and his division of the Tennessee militia to the service of the government.

It was supposed that the British would at once attack New Orleans. In due time Jackson assembled his forces at Natchez. But when it appeared that no attempt would be made against New Orleans he was ordered by the War Department to disband, without any provision being made to pay, ration, and return his men, who were five hundred miles from home. Jackson was furious. Instead of obeying his orders, he marched the division in regular form back to Tennessee, pledging his own credit to secure the auxiliary transportation. His drafts went to protest, and he would have been financially ruined had not the great popularity of his conduct compelled the administration, as a matter of politics, to rectify the wrong or oversight it had committed. Still full of warlike ardor, he again tendered his forces to the government for an invasion of Canada; for "Old Hickory," as he was now familiarly styled, was idolized by his men for his fierce and soldierly devotion to their interests. His offer was ignored, and he dismissed the troops. During this episode his pugnacious propensity was not diverted from his private affairs. While at Natchez he had a violent dissension with General Wilkinson over a question of rank, and after returning to Nashville he started a barbarous affray with Colonel Coffee and the Bentons that almost cost him his life. Weapons were freely used, and in the *mêlée* Jackson received a terrible wound in the shoulder from which he never fully recovered.[1]

Meantime the Creek war had broken out in the Mississippi territory. To Jackson this was a most fortunate circumstance: it continued his military career. While yet unable to quit his bed on account of his wound, he recalled his disbanded volunteers to service, and obtained authority from the legislature to proceed. As soon as he was able, he advanced, though with great physical suffering, into the Indian country. The ensuing campaign was thoroughly Jacksonesque. The hinderances he encountered were numerous and embarrassing. He was not in supreme command, and was therefore impeded by other officers until he acquired the ascendency to guide the operations to suit himself. The troops were ill provided with food and munitions, and most of them were on short enlistments. Several times some of them were in open mutiny. On one occasion, when some of the men proposed to march homeward, Jackson seized a musket and, standing before them, said he would shoot the

---

[1] "It was quite a curious coincidence that on one of these fine mornings when Colonel Benton was so fiercely battling for the President in the Senate Chamber the President had to submit to a surgical operation for the extraction of the bullet he had carried in his left arm ever since the time of the Benton affray in Nashville, twenty years before."—Parton's *Jackson*, vol. iii. p. 415.

first man who refused to perform his duty. During these troubles he committed acts that subsequently received severe criticism. Among them was the arrest of General Cocke, professedly for inciting his division to mutiny, but really to remove a jealous and inefficient officer. He also caused a private to be shot for insubordination, not so much that the man deserved it as to make an example of him. But with appalling energy and celerity, as well as skilful management of his wayward troops, which showed a truly high order of combative military genius, he surmounted all obstacles and forever broke the warlike power of the Creeks. He afterward wrested from the friendly part of the tribe—for the hostiles had fled—the treaty that Clay stigmatized as the real origin of the Seminole war. However this may be, the so-called treaty was a cruel extortion; and, strictly considered, it was illegal, as not more than one-third of the entire tribe was represented by the signers. It compelled them to surrender two-thirds of their lands as an indemnity for the expense of the war; and, besides other severe exactions, it required them to retire to the unrelinquished tract, which was so located as to isolate them from all external influences that might incite them to future war.

The campaign was finished in April, 1814, and the militia discharged; but so considerable was the service Jackson had performed that in May he was commissioned a major-general in the regular army and placed in command of the Southern Department. He fixed his headquarters at Mobile, whither he proceeded in August. Until a short time before this no British force had appeared during the year in the Gulf region. A small number had then arrived at Pensacola in several sloops-of-war. The purpose was to stir up the Florida Indians and divert attention from New Orleans, against which the long-delayed expedition was now being prepared. Of this, however, Jackson then had no intimation, nor did he even surmise it.

The Spanish occupation of Florida was obnoxious to the people of the Southwest, whose old hatred of Spain, occasioned by the troubles over the navigation of the Mississippi, was intensified through the unhindered use of Florida by the savages and the English. Thus the principal and popular object that Jackson desired to achieve was to take forcible possession of the territory. This was his prime motive at the outset of his military career, and it continued to be until he finally succeeded in his purpose during the Seminole war. When he first offered himself and his volunteers for service, in 1813, he assured the Secretary of War that they were "the choicest of our citizens, . . . who have no constitutional scruples, and, if the government orders, will rejoice at the opportunity of placing the American eagle on the ramparts of Mobile, Pensacola, and St. Augustine." Just before the British appeared at Pensacola Jackson wrote for leave to seize the place. For some reason the despatch denying his request did not reach him until long afterward. Meanwhile a naval attack was made on Fort Bowyer, at Mobile Point. This was thoroughly repulsed, if, indeed, it was intended to be more than a demonstration, and the enemy returned to Pensacola. In the absence of orders, Jackson pursued his own course. Two weeks later he marched over the border with 4100 men, nearly all his forces. November 7 he took Pensacola without resistance. The British had retired to the Appalachicola: their main function was performed. Jackson left one thousand men in Florida and returned to Mobile, where he remained several days. He then proceeded leisurely to New Orleans with only part of his army. He was regardless of the impending danger, of which he had now been warned from Washington.

He reached the city December 2. Already the British expedition, fifty sail, had been for a week under way from its rendezvous at Jamaica. Before Jackson arrived nothing had been done for the defence of the city; and after he came he made no haste to improve its condition. He was ill. His forces were scattered. The authorities were heedless. In the place there were no arms and no military stores. Jackson's conduct thus far betrays an astonishing ignorance of the science of war. Mobile, in any case, was not worth the trouble he had taken; without New Orleans it was totally worthless. In fact, it would have been strategic so to fortify New Orleans and its approaches that the British would be induced to land at Mobile and then advance through the wilderness. Had this been done the invading army might have suffered the experience of Braddock sixty years before. December 10 the fleet was sighted; within a week our gunboats had been taken; by another week, the enemy had approached within seven miles of the city. Jackson's remissness was more glaring than that of any other of the generals whose inefficiency had rendered the war inglorious and abortive. His whole power was in his genius for combat. It was only when an enemy or an opposition was visible that his unquestioning and tremendous energy appeared. So abnormal was this attribute that it diminished prudence, calculation, and judgment. His potent characteristic now came to the rescue. He assumed military dictatorship, made resounding proclamations, and filled the torpid populace with enthusiastic vigor. Aided by Packenham's bad generalship, he was victorious. The treaty of Ghent, signed fifteen days before the final assault, prevented further hostilities, except the capture of Mobile Point. How Jackson would have fared in the field had the war continued can only be conjectured. As it was, he was the " Hero of New Orleans." His success, even less brilliant than it was surprising to the nation, which expected his overthrow, gave him that prestige which was soon to be exploited in the service of politics. It was this alone that saved him from condemnation for his rash conduct in the Seminole war and his short governorship of Florida, to say naught of the many violent acts and quarrels that would have disgraced and destroyed any other man.

Such are the outlines of Jackson's history before he became a Presidential candidate. About it there is no room for material disagreement. The leading facts depict his character as clearly as a few skilful strokes portray a visage. His military career was the compound of that character and remarkable chance. It was his good fortune that the Creek war broke out just at the time it did; that New Orleans was not taken before he could defend it; that the war had been a disheartening failure nearly everywhere else and ended with his victory. That he should attain political popularity and power invincible against an opposition unparalleled in our history for the elements it included and the ability of its leaders, would be inconceivable apart from a political movement so deep and general as to make it a matter of minor consequence who its representative might be. But Jackson's peculiar character and achievements doubtless hastened the supremacy of that democratic sentiment which was to overwhelm all barriers and carry him on its crest.

Broadly speaking, the political institutions of a country

are the reflection of the theory prevailing among its people. That theory is necessarily influenced by old associations and the degree of intelligence and independence diffused among the masses. In a general sense, the form of any government has but little to do intrinsically for a long period with the larger popular rights. The same principle is discovered in the vicissitudes of political parties under the freest republican constitutions. In the nature of things, the long retention of power by a party tends to develop an increasing disregard of the views of the minority touching particular questions. But the fundamental character of a government is not radically affected by mere politics; in legislation and administration, errors and excesses are quite certain to be eventually rebuked and corrected by popular revulsion. This causes that oscillation from and to its fundamental tenets which has marked the history of every political party that has survived a decisive defeat. Every sustained departure from the true theory of republics—non-interference with private rights—sooner or later begets a popular revolt and a return to democratic principles. To understand the events of our political history, these elementary truths must be applied in the same manner as the first rules of arithmetic to all mathematical calculations.

Prior to the adoption of the Constitution, the United States could scarcely be called a nation. Each of the States in the fragile confederation was but a fragment of a prospective nation; for had not the general Union been formed, it is quite certain that sectional ones would. The confederation was vitally incompetent to produce nationality either in sentiment or in power, although it performed a momentous service in staying the centrifugal jealousies that must otherwise have resulted in several republics, or, what was not altogether improbable, a consolidated monarchy. During this stage the "rights of man" were freely proclaimed; yet the idea of democracy was singularly incomplete. The generation that achieved our independence had been subjects of a king of whom they had once spoken with regard as "His Majesty." In dress, customs, respect for class and government, they were still Englishmen. It mattered not that political relations were severed; the old habits of thought and feeling continued of their own momentum. Thus comparatively but a small number of the people were immediately affected in any marked degree, so far as political ideas were concerned, by the success of the Revolution; nor could they be materially changed except by a gradual and necessary adaptation to the new conditions arising from the practice of self-government. It is well known that after the confederation had proven a failure there was a strong monarchical sentiment—not that monarchy was deliberately preferred by many to a republic, but that the latter was a hazardous experiment, while limited monarchy was understood and familiar. It is equally well known that Hamilton, the chief founder of the Federalist creed, earnestly favored monarchy before the adoption of the Constitution, and afterward bent his great abilities to make the government so powerful as to be regarded for itself alone instead of being merely the organ of administering the will of the people in affairs strictly national.

It has been said with much wit and some truth that at Washington's inauguration the government consisted of himself and a roll of parchment. To distend the implied powers granted by that instrument until they were practically commensurate with the discretion of Congress was the policy of the Federalists; and it was enforced with such vigor, as we have seen, that it brought about the democratic reaction which overthrew that party. Nevertheless, after the popular success of Jefferson's principles the earlier ideas and impulses still continued. "No person," says MacMaster, "could, in 1803, look over our country without beholding on every hand the lingering remains of monarchy, of aristocracy, of class rule." Notwithstanding the fact that the Revolution was principally caused by the imposition of taxation without representation, for a long time subsequently, in nearly every State, the right of suffrage was dependent upon property qualifications. It is not surprising, therefore, that Jefferson's principles proved to be in the main merely abstractions, and that the Republican party soon applied the Federalist theory with far greater effect than the Federalists had ever presumed to do. Still, the democratic doctrine was promulgated as a general creed, and the people began to appreciate and exert their power, though it was not until 1824 that popular sentiment gave promise of becoming the controlling factor in political affairs. The elections of Madison and Monroe were not the results of popular movements for their elevation, but chiefly of a custom that alone almost dominated the succession. The war and the events that gave rise to it arrested the progress of the democratic sentiment. For the same reasons the necessities that followed had much the same, though steadily diminishing effect. But by the time of the Presidential election of 1824 that influence had gained sufficient force to prevent mere precedent or political machinery from determining the result. Under these circumstances it was natural that the popular movement should gather about some personage who aroused popular admiration, and without much regard to mere politics. Such a personage was General Jackson.

But the underlying cause of Jackson's political success was not recognized by his opponents. To such men as Clay, Calhoun, Webster, and their admirers and adherents, Jackson's candidacy was at first absurd and then outrageous. In their view his election was contrary to the best traditions of the republic, inconsistent with respectable government, and boded social and political calamity. They ascribed his elevation solely to his military exploits, and deplored it as the dangerous ascendency of a military chieftain destitute of civic qualifications. They seemed not to consider the fact fully that his rise was not due to a sudden and spontaneous popular desire to reward a military hero, but was slowly compassed by dexterous management operating on the new conditions; and that his chief counsellors were men of sagacity and ability. Their want of insight into the true meaning of his success led them into fatal errors of judgment in their policy of opposition. They did not wait for Jackson to exhibit the alarming unfitness they proclaimed, but forthwith imitated the example that Jackson's promoters had set when Adams was elected. They augured evil and disaster before any threatened, and ultimately adopted the tactics of forcing Jackson into the course they regarded as the most advantageous to themselves to condemn. Nearly every cause he gave for censure during his Presidency was thus induced; yet for the most part the policy he was compelled to pursue deserves greater credit than belongs to that of the opposition.

The general condition of the country was prosperous. The Southern and Western States were being developed with marvellous rapidity, to the corresponding benefit of the other sections. At no period of our history have the people been so individualized as during that which had now begun. The democratic awakening was as thorough as it had finally been rapid. In the popular mind Jackson's mission was to infuse the democratic spirit into the administration of the government. The prevailing and potential idea of Jackson was that he was "of and for the people," and it was prodigiously aided by the criticism that he was without training, and on that account barbarously unfit for President. Nor was the popular notion of him wrong. He was thoroughly homespun. Despite his martial bearing and the belligerent vigor of his administration, he was accessible and unaffected. To all but his declared enemies he was sincerely cordial and winning.[1] His advanced age and later experience had subdued and improved his manner. He was in all things entirely direct; and such a man is necessarily free from cant and pretension. As during his previous career, he seemed without strong personal ambition, and his ferocious energy after he entered the contest was far more the consequence of his pugnacious temperament than of his desire for the honor of being elected. During his Presidency the same assertive self-reliance which had always characterized him still governed his conduct. In this he displayed one of the prime elements of

---

[1] "After dinner we went to the President's; the rooms were all filled, and the company consisted, as usual, of all varieties of rank and station—foreign ministers and shopkeepers, heads of departments and dressers of heads, Senators and office-hunters. The President was sociable and courteous, and the ladies of his family performed their parts with great propriety; on the whole, it was an affair not to be missed."—Hone's *Diary*, March 15, 1832, vol. i. p. 48. Webster wrote in 1824: "General Jackson's manners are more Presidential than those of any of the candidates. He is grave, mild, and subdued. My wife is for him decidedly."—*Webster's Correspondence*, p. 346.

superiority. Intrinsically there is little difference between a so-called great question and a small one. What renders the one more onerous and apparently more difficult is usually the wider and weightier importance of its consequences. Generally an imposing public question admits of an easier solution than a private one, because it is amenable to the science of political economy. A strong mind operates unawed by the magnitude of results. Jackson, with the same freedom as though he were deciding which fields of his farm should be ploughed, simply applied his common-sense, so far as he could, with his acute personal prejudices, to the various subjects that arose or were forced upon him. No one thought him venal, and few thought he had any moral obliquity. Hence, however violent and vindictive he might be, a large majority of the people believed him honest and well meaning; and his dreadful independence, directness, and force prompted them equally to believe that he fully understood what he was about and was sufficiently right in his course.

The first feature that signalized his administration was the establishment of what is familiarly known as the "spoils system." As this subject is still one of living interest, Jackson is persistently and vehemently criticised for his course; and any approval or disapproval of it is taking side in a present and pressing controversy. Nevertheless, an accurate estimate of Jackson and his period is quite impossible without a critical consideration of the causes that led to the introduction of the practice of removals from the inferior public offices for political reasons.

Most of the evils that afflict republics are caused by the lack of sustained interest in political affairs among the larger part of the people. The vicious and incompetent would seldom be elected to office if the intelligent and right-minded had a proper sense of citizenship and duty toward their political institutions. Their sins of omission surpass those of commission by the ignorant and unfit, who are thus permitted to work themselves into public positions. If the mooted topic of "civil service reform" were a legal one, the doctrine of estoppel would to some extent apply. But, as it is, the public administrative business is performed, with comparatively few exceptions, with honesty and reasonable competency. Those who have most occasion to transact business, or to observe the manner of its transaction in the public offices, find the least substantial cause for criticism. The man is rare, in all the grades of the public service which it is contended should be placed beyond the reach of partisan appointment, who is not actuated by a decent desire to perform his duties properly. It is safe to say that there is more proud loyalty to duty on the part of the mass of such office-holders than there is to their employers among the mass of men in private occupations. In the nature of the case, it is impossible that the immense and diversified public business should be conducted with the same economy as an ordinary private business. Its orderly and systematic despatch necessitates division and subdivision of functions. But this enables clerks and other similar subordinates to become quickly familiar with their narrow scope of duty. And the fact that the integrity of those classes is, as a rule, entirely untempted by opportunity goes far to insure the efficiency of the service. " Civil service reform," therefore, has no financial aspect aside from obtaining an adequate return of work for the salaries paid; and even if it could effect any substantial result in this respect, which is doubtful, the cost of attaining it would more than offset the saving. The serious injury to the public is not perpetrated by the dishonesty and incompetency of the lesser servants, but by those whose opportunity is bestowed, directly or indirectly, by the ballot. One year of vicious financial or economic policy instituted by an ignorant or wilful majority of Congress exceeds, as a plague exceeds the common ills, a century of petty evils in subordinate administration. Besides these considerations, a force which is not subject to removal almost inevitably becomes more or less self-sufficient and insubordinate. And the same principle supplies, in a wider application, the paramount argument why there should not be established under our institutions a great class practically secure for life of official position and dependency on the government. The genius of our institutions is the equality of opportunity to all the people. So long as the routine business of government can be performed with reasonable efficiency without special training or prolonged experience, the greater the number of those who gain, if only a brief, acquaintance with official duties the better; for it is in some sense a means of education in popular government, which in the largest degree possible should be of the people, by the people, and for the people.

Such is the true argument in behalf of the spoils system. That it is inherently susceptible of abuses is undeniable; yet bad appointments in consequence of the practice in this country have never been alone sufficient to warrant its overthrow. The most serious evil it produces is its effect on political activity. It renders partisan service subordinate to the public welfare, and thus tends to make party contest a venal quest for office instead of a sincere and elevated contention over large questions of political principle and public policy, with the effect of aiding mediocre and unfit men to push themselves into public life. Doubtless the better opinion on the whole case is that the competitive system with fixed tenure—treating the civil service as merely the mechanical means of administration—is wiser and more productive, in a large sense, of the best results. Yet the rise and long continuance of the opposite practice was inevitable, and must be regarded as a natural outgrowth of our political system. This view reconciles theory and fact, and tempers acute prejudices that are detrimental to just historical judgment.

For many years the total number of appointees to the minor offices under the government of the United States was less than the number now appointed under that of New York or Pennsylvania. There was no urgent and general rivalry for such positions. But at length the increase of the population, with all that it signifies, and the corresponding expansion of the business of the government, naturally attracted the attention of the constantly increasing class desiring employment that was not manual. Politics was inevitably affected by its influence. But it was first felt in State politics, especially in the two States mentioned and in Massachusetts, where the "spoils system" speedily developed, not indeed through the instrumentality of party, but as the consequence of changing conditions.

From the time of the administration of Jefferson to that of Adams there had been little occasion to make removals for political reasons. For twenty-four years there had been but one Presidential dynasty. The opposition being at no time sufficiently strong and coherent to deserve the title of party, there was no opportunity for the office-seeking class to develop in the national arena; there was nothing upon which to found claims as the reward for services, and, if there had been, those installed were mainly the faithful. Moreover, it necessarily required some time for the system being rapidly established in the several States to appear in national politics; but in those States eventually the numberless influences that produced a new political epoch operated perforce to evoke efforts that would secure the minor appointments as the reward for partisan zeal. While Jackson's administration marked the beginning of this element of party organization in national politics, any other man at that time representing the Democratic party would have pursued substantially the same course. In truth, it would be more accurate to say that John Quincy Adams was the proximate cause of the system; for his absolute refusal to allow political considerations to influence the retention or selection of appointees stimulated the clamor and the efforts of the multiplying "outs." But though the situation had rendered proscription inevitable, Jackson was not reluctant to enforce it. In this, as in all he did, he proceeded with vigor and celerity. During the first year of his Presidency he made as many removals for political reasons as had been effected by all his predecessors, mostly for cause; and, besides, there was the still greater number made by heads of departments and the like.[1] This policy was greeted by a loud

---

[1] "'The gloom of suspicion,' says Mr. Stansbury, himself an officeholder, 'pervaded the face of society. No man deemed it safe or prudent to trust his neighbor, and the interior of the Department presented a fearful scene of guarded silence, secret intrigue, espionage, and tale-bearing. A casual remark dropped on the street would within an hour be repeated at headquarters; and many a man received unceremonious dismission who could not for his life conceive or conjecture wherein he had offended.'" "So numerous were the removals in the city of Washington that the business of the place seemed paralyzed."—Parton's *Jackson*, vol. iii. pp. 212, 214. See also Shepard's *Van Buren*, p. 180.

chorus of denunciation and direful prophecy; and by no one with such latitude of indignant phrase as by Clay, notwithstanding he had been much disappointed by the attitude Adams had taken in regard to the subject.

Jackson took a novel view of the functions of the cabinet. In his hands it was shorn of much of the dignity it had before possessed. During previous administrations it was composed principally of distinguished men who influenced the policy of the government. Under Jackson the cabinet officers were no longer the "Constitutional advisers" of the President. He held no cabinet councils. The members practically resembled military staff-officers. With the exception of Van Buren, they were not men of conspicuous ability, although possessing much political experience. Jackson's actual advisers were confined to a small coterie of friends who, with one subsequent exception, were not in the cabinet. During the first years these advisers were William B. Lewis,[1] Amos Kendall,[2] Isaac Hill, and Duff Green. Green, however, because of his devotion to Calhoun, was soon replaced by Francis P. Blair, one of Clay's

---

[1] "Among all the remarkable accidents which opened his way to the first position in the country it was not the least that he had William B. Lewis for a neighbor and friend. Lewis was the great father of wire-pullers."—Sumner's *Jackson*, p. 77.

[2] "He is supposed to be the moving spring of the whole administration—the thinker, planner, and doer; but it is all in the dark. Documents are issued of an excellence which prevents their being attributed to the persons who take the responsibility of them; a correspondence is kept up all over the country for which no one seems answerable; work is done, of goblin extent and goblin speed, which makes men wonder; and the invisible Amos Kendall has the credit of it all. . . . He is undoubtedly a great genius. He unites with his 'great talent for silence' a splendid audacity. . . . The extreme sallowness of his complexion, and hair of such perfect whiteness as is rarely seen in a man of middle age, testify to disease. His countenance does not help the superstitious to throw off their dread of him."—Martineau's *Retrospect of Western Travel*, vol. i. p. 155.

former friends, who established the *Globe*, the organ of the administration. They had all been obscure men, but were clever writers and consummate politicians of the new school. They constituted the famous "Kitchen Cabinet."[1]

It was not until toward the close of his first term that Jackson furnished solid ground for the opposition. Soon after the beginning of his administration a violent dissension arose in his own party. It was occasioned by a rivalry between Calhoun, Vice-President, and Van Buren, Secretary of State, each of whom sought to succeed Jackson in the Presidency. It began by a contest between them to strengthen their positions by means of patronage, and speedily reached a pass that wanted only small provocation to cause open disruption. The provocation was soon supplied.

John H. Eaton, Secretary of War, and previously for ten years a Senator from Tennessee, had recently married Mrs. Timberlake, the widow of a purser in the navy who had committed suicide. She was the comely daughter of a Washington tavern-keeper, and, as "Peggy O'Neil," had at one time enjoyed much popularity among the gallant frequenters of the capital. Before her husband's death Eaton had been more attentive to her than was good for her reputation. Under these circumstances the wives of the Vice-President and the cabinet officers refused to recognize her socially. Jackson, smarting under the recollection of the charges that his own matrimonial experience had occa-

---

[1] "The General's misfortune is that his confidence is reposed in men in no degree equal to him in natural parts, but who have been of use to him heretofore in covering his very lamentable defects of education; and as he is very unwilling to make these defects known to any others, he is compelled to keep these gentlemen about him."—*Reminiscences of J. A. Hamilton*, p. 104. Concerning the "Kitchen Cabinet," see Sumner's *Jackson*, p. 142.

sioned, strove to coerce the recognition of Mrs. Eaton. Even his own niece, who was mistress of the White House, refused to comply, and was sent back to Tennessee in consequence. As Van Buren was a widower he profited by the affair.

This hastened the impending breach that other events served to increase. A circumstance hitherto concealed now came to light. It will be remembered that after the Florida campaign, Calhoun, then Secretary of War, favored the proposed censure of General Jackson, who was now apprised of the fact by a letter written by Crawford to one of Jackson's friends. Jackson at once enclosed a copy of it to Calhoun, with a request for an explanation; but as there could be no explanation satisfactory to Jackson, open war between them was declared. Three members of the cabinet were partisans of Calhoun. A reorganization of it was, therefore, decided upon. To bring this about, Eaton set the example which it was desired the others should follow. He resigned, and was appointed governor of Florida. Van Buren immediately did likewise, and was sent as Minister to England. The obnoxious members were then disposed of, and a new cabinet was constructed. Such was the internal condition of the Democratic party on the eve of the campaign of 1832, in which it had been determined that Jackson was to be a candidate for re-election.

By this time Jackson's policy had developed distinct outlines. It gave Clay precisely the opportunity he most desired. Jackson was now hostile to the system of internal improvements, and to every sort of special legislation. While he was not strongly opposed to the policy of protection, his inclinations were that way; he assumed a neutral attitude that encouraged the South without alarming the

North.[1] Inasmuch as the public debt was nearly paid, he favored such a revision of the tariff as would reduce the revenue without radically disturbing protected interests. Clay was thus driven to a policy far more extreme than he had ever before advocated. Rather than to impair protection, he preferred to maintain the debt, and favored an elaborate system of internal improvements, or, as an alternative, to diminish the revenue by making many of the duties prohibitive, and entirely removing the duties on many articles not competing with those produced here.

Besides these questions, another had made its appearance. In his first message to Congress, Jackson intimated his disfavor of renewing the charter of the Bank of the United States, which was to expire in 1836.[2] With the bank, Jackson's opponents were indissolubly allied. It was the embodiment of their Constitutional doctrine and the representative of the moneyed interests of the country. The issue, however, did not become formidable until just before the election of 1832, although the threatening attitude of Jackson and some of his supporters, notably Benton, had provoked discussion and caused the bank and the anti-administration party to do all that could be done to insure the recharter.

---

[1] Bolles's *Financial History of the United States*, vol. ii. p. 394; Greeley's *Recollections of a Busy Life*, p. 67.

[2] This message was the work of several hands. It was revised by Hamilton, who abridged and rewrote the part relating to the bank. "When I stopped here, he [Jackson] said, 'Do you think that is all I ought to say?' I answered, 'I think you ought to say nothing at present about the bank.' He replied, 'Oh! my friend, I am pledged against the bank, but if you think that is enough, so let it be.'" Van Buren expressed himself as agreeing with Madison, that the Constitutional power to establish a national bank had been settled by practical construction.—*Reminiscences of J. A. Hamilton*, p. 150.

By common consent of that party—then called the National Republican party, for it did not take the name of Whig until 1834[1]—Clay was to be its candidate for the Presidency. This was generally understood after the election of 1828. He was formally nominated by the national convention held at Baltimore in December, 1831; the nominee for Vice-President was John Sergeant, one of those who had advocated the prohibition of slavery in Missouri. After Clay retired from the Department of State he made several tours in Kentucky and the neighboring States. In the larger towns he usually made speeches, sometimes of considerable length, on political topics. The demonstrations with which he was everywhere greeted made him confident of success. But he received a very distinct warning of disaster in the results of the Kentucky election in the early part of 1831; Jackson's popularity in the State showed no decline. Clay's adherents obtained only a narrow majority in the State legislature, which was to elect a Senator. Clay was prevailed upon to accept the post.[2]

---

[1] "The term 'Whig' was a nickname applied to the Scotch Presbyterians. It began at the time when the Cameronians took up arms for their religion, and was derived from 'whey,' refuse milk, which their poverty obliged them to use; or, according to another version, from 'whiggam,' a word employed by Scotch cattle-drovers of the West in driving their horses."—Lecky's *England in the Eighteenth Century*, vol. i. p. 19. It is stated in Barnes's *Life of Weed* (vol. ii. p. 48) that the name was first suggested at a public meeting of the anti-Jackson men by James Watson Webb; Philip Hone, however, says in his *Diary* (vol. ii. p. 34), that to the name "I stand godfather, having been the first to use it at a political meeting of which I was president, at Washington Hall." See also *Niles's Register*, vol. xlvi. p. 101; Seward's *Autobiography*, p. 287.

[2] "There is much anxiety, too, for the election in Kentucky, which was fixed for yesterday. Mr. Clay wished J. J. Crittenden to be elected; but he cannot be chosen but by voting for himself. The election will fall, therefore, upon a Jackson man, or Clay himself must be elected by Crittenden's vote, even this being of so doubtful issue that Clay is unwilling to

There was urgent reason. The mutter of the coming storm was growing more ominous. It was evident that Congress was to be the scene of a fierce and protracted struggle. However autocratic Jackson's behests, and however compliant the fealty of his party, Congress, which had now attained the full measure of its importance, was to be the seat of war. There the opposition was to show its boldest front. Clay had refused a seat in the House, and was reluctant, as a Presidential candidate, to make himself the needless target of his foes. But it was the general desire of his party that he should command in person. Under these circumstances he returned, at the opening of the Twenty-second Congress, to the body in which he had won his first national distinction.

That the new epoch which Jackson's elevation indicated had begun was everywhere visible. Everything that tells the history of the time bespeaks a transition so distinct as to seem almost abrupt. Events assumed a new mould and complexion.

Never in the history of the country has public life absorbed so large a proportion of the talent adapted to it as during the twenty years beginning with the Twenty-second Congress. Much of the talent that afterward sought the channels then newly opening—journalism, literature, corporate enterprise, and the like—was devoted to the profession of the law, and thence to politics. As a result, political activity became so intense that many of the performances

---

take the chance."—Adams's *Diary*, January 5, 1831, vol. viii. p. 268. Clay was elected, however, by a majority of eight. Crittenden wrote to his daughter: "I *could* have gone to the Senate; it was but for me to express the wish and Mr. Clay would not have been the candidate. There was no collision, no rivalry between us. All that was done was with my perfect accordance."—Coleman's *Crittenden*, vol. i. p. 81.

enacted in the public arena only escaped being ridiculous by the great ability displayed and by their harmful consequences to the country; for the people were hardly less frenzied in their partisanship than were their representatives.

Clay's presence in Congress was necessarily the signal for energetic warfare against the administration. The qualities he had exhibited in his previous course of opposition not only reappeared in all their vigor, but were enhanced by his commanding position and the confidence he felt and inspired. The principal features of the party policy were to procure the recharter of the bank and to perpetuate protection. As to the latter, Clay asserted in a conclave of his friends that "to preserve, maintain, and strengthen the American System, he would defy the South, the President, and the devil."[1] The other features of the party policy were to conform to exigencies. Whatever opportunity offered was to be vigorously utilized.

The session began December 5. January 9 Clay submitted a resolution declaring his plan of tariff revision—to abolish all duties on articles not competing with domestic productions, except duties on wines and silks, which were to be reduced. This would permit the maintenance of the existing or increased duties on other articles. The Committee on Finance was to report a bill framed on that basis. On the same day the memorial of the bank for the renewal of its charter was presented. This was to be the occasion of a bill for that purpose. But before the discussion of these paramount subjects had well begun the Senate carried out a preliminary detail of the Whig programme—the rejection

---

[1] Adams's *Diary*, vol. viii. p. 447; McCulloch's *Men and Measures of Half a Century*, p. 506.

of Van Buren's nomination as Minister to England. It was the first of a series of calamitous mistakes.

Inasmuch as it was settled that Van Buren was to be the Democratic candidate for successor to Jackson, it was supposed by the Whig leaders that the rejection of his nomination as minister would injure him politically. To make it appear proper and just, however, was a troublesome task. Having been a Senator, he was entitled to the benefit of the "Senatorial courtesy." There was absolutely no personal ground on which to justify the action, for his character was irreproachable and his deportment ineffably amiable. Moreover, the indignity would be poignantly severe, as he was sent after the adjournment of Congress, and had already been at his post several months. But after a painstaking delay the votes were procured and the *modus operandi* arranged. Twelve set speeches against the nomination were pronounced with dramatic solemnity. Had the occasion been the impeachment of the President the oratory would have displayed about the same quality, if not quantity, of patriotic bathos. Clay, Webster, Hayne, and the rest of the dozen all asseverated their painful reluctance, which a profound sense of public duty alone could constrain them to overcome. Van Buren was guilty of political misdeeds that rendered him unfit to represent the nation at a foreign court. To advance himself, he had embroiled the President and Vice-President and caused the disruption of the cabinet. He was chiefly responsible for introducing the system of political proscription. And, worst of all, he had stultified the nation by the instructions he had given as Secretary of State to McLane, Minister to England, to govern his negotiations touching the West Indian trade, which had long been interrupted through needless differences between the two governments. The fact is that he, or rather the President through him, had directed a frank avowal of the errors on our part that had impeded the adjustment of the subject, in order to "obviate as far as practicable the unfavorable impression they had produced." These were the charges preferred. They were variously treated, according to the histrionic powers of the different speakers. The two latter were made most of by the Whigs, and the other, by the adherents of Calhoun, who had zealously joined the cabal.

Had it been true that Van Buren fomented the breach between Jackson and Calhoun, no dishonorable means being used, it would not justify the rejection of his nomination. But it is obvious from the facts already narrated, and without regard to Jackson's express declaration, that Van Buren was not the cause of the trouble, which originated in Crawford's disclosure of Calhoun's course concerning the Seminole campaign. That Van Buren profited by it was immaterial to the question; some one necessarily would. Indeed, it is probable that in any event he would have received Jackson's preference. He was at the head of the dominant power in New York State, not by accident or mere force of circumstances, but in consequence of his capacity, political sagacity, and singularly attractive personal qualities. He had begun at the bottom. Before attaining his majority he was conspicuous in local politics, and at an early age was a commanding personage in the councils of his party. At the same time his learning and skill as a lawyer won him at the bar a reputation equally wide and solid. The bare list of the successive steps of his rise to eminence and influence in the midst of politicians of remarkable ability—for in this respect the political history of New York during this period

is altogether unrivalled—is sufficient proof of his powers.
In 1808, at the age of twenty-six, he became surrogate of
his county. In 1812 he was elected to the State Senate,
which was then also the court of last resort. Two years
later he was made Attorney-General of the State, at that
time a very high professional distinction. In 1820 he was
elected to the Senate of the United States. In 1828 he was
nominated for Governor and was elected, carrying the State
for Jackson. This made his entrance into Jackson's cabinet inevitable; and once there, it would have been singular
had he not won Jackson's cordial respect and friendship.[1]
In any case, therefore, to oppose his nomination as minister
because of Jackson's attitude toward Calhoun was unjust
and unseemly.

It was scarcely less improper to charge upon him, for
such a purpose, Jackson's policy of political appointments.
Whatever the difference of opinion as to the propriety of
that course, it had no relation to Van Buren's nomination,
and hence it was not a legitimate ground of opposition to it.
But, as before shown, that policy was not the result of the
advice or efforts of any individual, even assuming the impossible theory that Jackson could have been governed in
that regard by Van Buren or any one else; Jackson needed no stimulation, and, if he did, it was supplied by the
general political situation in which he found himself, and
the demands upon him from every quarter. Merely political differences between the President and a majority of
the Senate have never been urged as a reason for reject-

---

[1] Hamilton asserts that at this period Van Buren's historical information was meagre, and that in the composition of his state papers he depended on his son John and B. F. Butler, his law partner and subsequently Attorney-General.—*Reminiscences of J. A. Hamilton*, pp. 68, 97, 216.

ing the President's nominations; if they were, he would often be unable to form a cabinet. No doubt Clay was not a little actuated by the fact that Jackson and some of his friends had voted against his nomination for Secretary of State; but it would have been more worthy of him to remember that Van Buren was then in the Senate and had not opposed him.

The last charge—that directing the acknowledgment of undeniable error was in derogation of national honor, requiring the minister to uphold his country right or wrong—does not deserve refutation. It was a noble, as it was a very successful, departure from the common course of diplomacy, which has always been to obtain advantage rather than justice. The fault that Van Buren committed was in supporting this consideration by the far-fetched and superfluous suggestion that the question had been virtually determined by the people, whose judgment was unfavorable to the policy of the last administration. This, it was contended, made the minister the representative of his party, not of the country. And there was much force in the criticism; still, if the instructions were otherwise proper, this error was not sufficient to justify the rejection.

The defence was not conducted with the thoroughness and vigor that the opposition warranted. But four Senators spoke in Van Buren's behalf, and they failed to take due advantage of the merits of the case, allowing them to be obscured by debating irrelevant considerations. Some of the most ardent supporters of the administration shared Benton's view of the matter. They voted to confirm, but said nothing, preferring that the nomination be rejected, on the assumption that instead of Van Buren being injured he would be materially strengthened, as the people would attribute the affair entirely to personal rivalry.¹ And the sequel proved this view to be correct.

This electioneering episode finished, the Senate recurred to Clay's tariff resolution. Two days after offering it he called it up and delivered a speech in its support. As it was announced that he would speak, the floor and galleries were thronged. It was six years since he had been heard in Congress by the public; for the debate on Van Buren's nomination was in secret session, though the speeches were immediately published, having been made for that purpose. But the speech on the tariff resolution was neither long nor showy.² His manner of introducing it, however, betrayed an affectation, despite his disclaimer, that provoked comment. "I have a few observations, Mr. President," he began, "and only a few, to submit to the Senate on the measure before you, in doing which I have to ask all your indulgence. I am getting old; I feel too sensibly and unaffectedly the effects of approaching age, and have been for some years very little in the habit of addressing deliberative assemblies. I am told that I have been the

---

¹ "Mr. Calhoun, as Vice-President, presiding in the Senate, could not speak; but he was understood to be personated by his friends, and twice gave the casting vote, one interlocutory, against the nominee—a tie being contrived for that purpose, and the combined plan requiring him to be upon the record." "I heard Mr. Calh.un say to one of his doubting friends: 'It will kill him, sir, kill him dead. He will never kick, sir, never kick.'"—Benton's *Thirty Years' View*, vol. i. pp. 215, 219.

² "Clay's presence in the Senate this winter is providential. Surely he is needed more than in 1824, if possible, and he has a cordial, most able, and sufficient support in the Senate. His speech was not showy, nor vehement, but cool, plain, paternal, grave, conciliatory."—*Choate to Nichols*, January 14, 1832. Yet Adams recorded: "I found much excitement among the Senators from the South upon the doctrines of Mr. Clay's speech yesterday. Mr. Tyler, of Virginia, and General Smith, of Maryland, spoke of dividing the Union by the Potomac."—*Diary*, January 12, vol. viii. p. 455.

cause—the most unwilling cause, if I have been—of exciting expectations, the evidence of which is around us. I regret it; for however the subject on which I am to speak in other hands might be treated, to gratify the presence and attention now given, in mine I have nothing but a plain, unvarnished, and unambitious exposition to make." The comments on this exordium were mostly in line of compliment, though with covert humor. One Senator, however—Smith, of Maryland—made the rather tart observation that he could not complain of the infirmities of age, though older than the Senator from Kentucky, nor could he find in his years any apology for the insufficiency of his speech. This gave Clay some offence; and to his retort Smith made this amusing reply: "The gentleman from Kentucky is the last who should take the remark as disparaging to his vigor and personal appearance; for when that gentleman spoke to us of his age I heard a young lady near me exclaim, 'Old! why, I think he is mighty pretty!'"

In his speech Clay assumed the "established policy of protection," contenting himself with some reference to the history of it, and the benefits he alleged to be its fruits. He adverted to the suggestions of the Secretary of the Treasury, which pointed to a general reduction of the tariff, and explained his own plan to the contrary, touching incidentally the subjects of internal improvements and the public lands. He opposed a rapid reduction of the public debt, and urged the adoption of the system of home valuation of goods subject to *ad valorem* duties. He also spoke of the Southern hostility to the protective policy, but held that the importance of the system to the rest of the Union required its maintenance. Yet he professed to act "in a spirit of warm attachment to all parts of our beloved country, with a lively solicitude to restore and preserve its harmony, and with a firm determination to pour oil and balm into existing wounds rather than further to lacerate them."

He was much mistaken if he supposed that protection was so firmly established as to be secure from serious assault. While he was Secretary of State the tariff of 1828 was enacted. It has always been known as the "tariff of abominations." In its day it was also styled the "black tariff." It flagrantly betrayed the most pernicious tendencies of protective legislation. It was the motley and undisguised product of politics and sectional and private interests. The tariff of 1824 had hardly gone into effect before the woollen interests began to clamor and strive for more protection. On the eve of the ensuing Presidential election a tariff bill was introduced as an administration measure. Its main object was to increase the duties on wool and woollen goods; but as that object could not be attained without bartering with various other interests, these interests also were admitted to the benefits of the bill. Even Webster, who previously figured among the ablest advocates of commercial freedom, changed his ground. To win favor with the East, he supported the bill, though a majority of the Eastern Representatives opposed it. His plea was that inasmuch as protection had apparently become a settled policy, and New England capital had been invested on the strength of it, he was bound to support it. Yet he hesitated for some time before he decided to vote for the bill. He then accepted the admittedly vicious provisions in order to save those that were satisfactory to him. The tariff of 1828 thus became a conglomeration of monstrosities, some of which were unwisely introduced by the opponents of the bill in the expectation that they would prevent its passage.[1] Even Van Buren, who was then in the Senate, voted for it. It was extremely obnoxious in the South, upon which it bore with uncompensated and defiant injustice. Hence the proposition to make the entire revenue system subservient to protection and perpetuate and increase the heaviest and most irksome burdens upon the South was very far from pouring "oil and balm into existing wounds": it added insult to injury. Strenuous resistance was at once resolved on.

January 16, five days after Clay's speech, Hayne offered an amendment to the resolution, by which he proposed the immediate reduction of the import revenue, according to the existing scale, to an amount sufficient to defray the expenses of the government after paying the public debt, and the gradual adoption of a general average of duties. He supported his proposition in a speech of great ability. The profound impression it produced impelled Clay to reply. The result was his notable "Defence of the American System." It ranks among the most conspicuous contributions to the literature of protection in this country. For years this speech and Hamilton's celebrated Report were regarded as the most authoritative expositions of the protective policy. After much further debate, Clay's resolution was adopted and a bill modelled on the plan it proposed became a law. But it was soon to bear bitter fruit.

The next subject of debate was that of the public lands.

---

[1] Clay wrote to Crittenden, February 14, 1828 : "We shall have the tariff up in Congress next week. I anticipate a tremendous discussion. The Jackson party are playing a game of brag on the subject. They do not really desire the passage of their own measure, and it may happen in the sequel that what is desired by neithei party commands the support of both."—Coleman's *Crittenden*, vol. i. p. 67.

Like the tariff, it was perennial. Though a large portion of the public domain had been slowly disposed of by gift and sale, vast areas, amounting at that time to 1,090,000,000 acres, still remained, chiefly in the Southern and Western States. They had always been a source of scheming, which constantly increased with the development of the country: public property is always viewed with eager and ingenious eyes. For some years this growing interest in the subject had prompted a variety of plans for dealing with it. Protectionists wanted the government to retain control of the lands and maintain prices sufficiently high to impede the rapid occupation of them. This would "protect agriculture" and not divert attention from manufacturing. It would hinder any material increase in the wages of labor by confining the working classes to the East, as the new lands would be rendered less alluring. Thus free lands and free trade became allied policies, and as such were denounced by the protectionists. But the subject was now introduced mainly to embarrass Clay.

The principal champion of the free-lands policy was Benton, who began his crusade in its behalf in 1824. His plan was that of graduated prices and gratuitous grants to actual settlers—the system of pre-emption. In 1826, he says, he first read Edmund Burke's great plea for the disposition of the crown lands, in which he argued that the principal revenue to be derived from these uncultivated wastes would "spring from the improvement and population of the kingdom." This furnished Benton with a broader reason for his plan than he had before conceived, as well as an imposing authority which won Jackson's approval when brought to his attention. Benton labored zealously from year to year in furtherance of his policy, and his bills and speeches were at

THE DISPOSITION OF THE PUBLIC LANDS

length instrumental in making it a part of the Democratic creed.

The Secretary of the Treasury, McLane, proposed in his annual report for 1831 that the public lands within any of the States should be sold to those States and the proceeds be apportioned among all the States. Six of the new States petitioned Congress for the cession of the lands so situated. In March, 1832, one Senator moved an inquiry into the expediency of reducing the price of the lands, and another, into that of McLane's proposition. The whole subject was then referred to the Committee on Manufactures, of which Clay was chairman. As there was a standing Committee on Public Lands, this course was manifestly improper and fraught with great danger to Clay as a Presidential candidate. As he himself put it: "Although any other member of that committee could have rendered himself, with appropriate researches and proper time, more competent than I was to understand the subject of the public lands, it was felt that from my local position I alone was supposed to have any particular knowledge of them. Whatever emanated from the committee was likely, therefore, to be ascribed to me. If the committee should propose a measure of great liberality toward the new States, the old States might complain. If the measure should seem to lean toward the old States, the new might be dissatisfied. And if it included neither class of States, but recommended a plan according to which there would be distributed impartial justice among all the States, it was far from certain that any would be pleased."

The proceeding long rankled in his mind. "I strenuously opposed the reference," said he in a speech in 1835. "I remonstrated, I protested, I entreated, I implored. It was in vain that I insisted that the Committee on Public Lands was the regular standing committee to which such reference should be made. It was in vain that I contended that the public lands and domestic manufactures were subjects absolutely incongruous. The unnatural alliance was ordered by the vote of a majority of the Senate. I felt that a personal embarrassment was intended me. I felt that the design was to place in my hands a many-edged instrument which I could not touch without being wounded. Nevertheless, I subdued all my repugnance and I engaged assiduously in the task which had been so unkindly assigned me." In a speech in 1841 he expressed himself in the same strain.

The report of the committee was soon forthcoming. It was a long document, giving the devious history and the status of the subject, together with the argument for the plan proposed. The plan was embodied in an accompanying bill. It was against reducing the price of the lands or ceding them to the States. But as the political exigencies of the situation required some new departure which would at least tend to neutralize conflicting views and interests, it was proposed that Ohio, Indiana, Illinois, Alabama, Missouri, and Mississippi should receive twelve and a half per centum of the proceeds of the lands sold within their limits, to be applied to schools and internal improvements. The remainder of the proceeds was to be distributed among all the States according to their population, for the same purposes and for colonization, as their legislatures should direct. The act was to remain in force five years. There were other details, but these were the principal features of the scheme. It would leave the existing relations of the public lands to the economic conditions of the country substantially unaltered, yet it would satisfy the East, yield something to the West, and effectively further the policy of internal improvements.

It encountered determined resistance. The process that begot it necessarily made it an important part of the Whig policy, and a prominent issue between the parties. The report and bill were immediately referred to the committee to which the subject should have gone originally, the Committee on Public Lands. A few days afterward that committee made a voluminous report sharply combating all phases of Clay's plan. It was for the most part Benton's production. It proposed the reduction of the minimum price to one dollar per acre, and after five years to fifty cents, fifteen per centum of the proceeds to be divided among all the States. There were also to be provisions for pre-emption. The whole subject had become so involved through the various and unequal benefits which the different States, old and new, had derived from the public domain that no general plan could be adopted that would accomplish a perfectly equitable adjustment among all the States. But, looking at the subject broadly, there is little doubt that Benton's plan, while open to some criticism, would have produced a more just and beneficial result. Whatever its minor consequences, it would throw open the wilderness to population and development, and thus prove of much greater, though indirect, benefit to the nation than would follow treating the subject as a matter of revenue.

A spirited debate ensued. Clay's bill was finally passed by the Senate, but it failed in the House. The subject, however, was now placed in a position of political importance it had never before occupied. The immediate purpose of bringing it forward was accomplished—Clay was irretrievably injured in the West.

Meanwhile, the great topic of the session had reached its climax. July 4, the President received the bill to recharter the bank; on the 10th he returned it with his veto.

CHAPTER V

The Controversy over the Bank of the United States—Thomas H. Benton—The Whig Leaders Refuse to Compromise with Jackson on the Question of Rechartering the Bank—The Bank as a Political Issue—The Veto of the Bill to Recharter—The Error of the Whig Policy—The Debate on the Veto—The Presidential Campaign of 1832—Jackson's Triumph—Nullification—The Force Bill and the Verplanck Tariff Bill—John C. Calhoun—Clay's Compromise Bill—It is Substituted for the Verplanck Bill in the House and Passed by the Senate—The Compromise Bill and the Force Bill become Laws, and South Carolina Repeals the Nullification Ordinance—The Wisdom of the Compromise and Clay's Responsibility for it—His Land Bill is Passed by both Houses, but Vetoed by the President

No topic in our political history, except slavery and the tariff, has been the subject of so much controversy as the subversion of the Bank of the United States. It was the chief exploit of Jackson's Presidency, and, like most of his political acts, it has been glorified or denounced according to the political bias of the critic. The literature of the subject is almost endless. For several years the bank was the source of frequently recurring investigation, report, and debate in Congress, and discussion outside. Nor did the struggle cease after the bank was gone; it was even more violent over the efforts to establish the Independent Treasury to meet the public functions which the bank had performed. Besides the records, the multitude of government documents, and the current literature bearing on the subject, every historical and biographical work relating to the political and economic history of the period treats of it more or less. To examine it in detail, however, is needless to the present survey; the principal facts and general considerations will afford a sufficiently clear and satisfactory view of the question.

Jackson's prejudice against a national bank was of long standing. It is said that Clay's speech in 1811, in opposition to the recharter of the original bank, fixed Jackson's opinions on the subject.[1] Certainly the main grounds of his objection to the recharter in these later years were substantially the same as Clay advanced in that speech.

The new bank, chartered in 1816, after some years of bad administration, which precipitated the crisis of 1819 and the ensuing period of general liquidation, partly accomplished the objects for which it was established. Had it been well conducted at the outset it would soon have materially aided in restoring the government and the country from the decrepit financial condition into which they had fallen during the war. It did finally effect the resumption of specie payments, against the opposition of the State banks, and supplied a currency that was uniform and acceptable, though far from perfect. After the first years it was not open to any just charge of insolvency or of not properly performing all its business with the government according to the terms of its charter. In all this it was powerfully aided by the general recuperation of the times; yet it was fairly entitled to the credit of performing some valuable service. The latent evil in the character of the institution did not appear until 1829.

Jeremiah Mason, a noted and able New England lawyer and a close political friend of Daniel Webster, had been

---

[1] Parton's *Jackson*, vol. ii. p. 654.

previously appointed president of the Portsmouth branch. In the extremely rigorous, but probably faithful, performance of his duties he had incurred the ill-will of some of the patrons of the bank, by compelling—in an unnecessarily austere manner, it was charged—the payment of certain protested paper, presumably held against Democrats. This led to an effort on the part of Isaac Hill—who, it will be remembered, was one of Jackson's "Kitchen Cabinet"—and other New Hampshire adherents of the administration to cause Mason's removal. Then followed a protracted correspondence over the matter between Nicholas Biddle, the doughty and over-fluent president of the bank, and Ingham, Secretary of the Treasury. The discussion at length developed into a severe and general encounter. But the bank pursued its own course in all respects notwithstanding. Jackson had immediately and very characteristically taken up the quarrel, and in his message to Congress soon afterward gave the ominous announcement of his hostility to the renewal of the charter.[1] But to prevent the recharter was a difficult undertaking. As it was several years since the bank had been seriously challenged from any quarter, many of Jackson's chief supporters were friends of the institution; and many others of his party were interested in one way and another in its continuance. It was at this juncture that Benton earned his first promotion toward the leadership of the administration forces in Congress which he soon attained.

---

[1] "In the Presidential campaign of 1824 the bank was not so much as mentioned, nor was it mentioned in that of 1828. In all the political pamphlets, volumes, newspapers, campaign papers, burlesques, and caricatures of those years there is not the most distant allusion to the bank as a political issue."—Parton's *Jackson*, vol. iii. p. 257.

At the beginning of Jackson's administration, March 4, 1829, Benton lacked but ten days of being forty-seven years of age; he was in the prime of his powers, with eight years of experience in the Senate. While he had not yet risen to a position of imposing influence, he had laid the foundation for it. The Senate never contained a more robust personage. He was neither unique nor brilliant. His moral and mental integrity were sterling. His large, solid frame was in harmony with his intellectual qualities. He was a man of momentum. He served in the Senate thirty years continuously, during the most variously exciting political period the country has ever seen; and by his straightforward and energetic devotion to the principles he had early imbibed, he obtained a respect that the more brilliant but vacillating talents of his most distinguished compeers in public life could not command.

His father was a North Carolina lawyer of standing. He died in the boy's early youth, leaving as part of his estate a tract of forty thousand acres near Nashville, Tennessee, whither the widow with her several children soon afterward removed. The land was well located, and about the settlement begun by her grew up in the course of a few years the village of Bentonville. Before the family went West, Thomas had attended good schools and developed a strong and abiding love of learning. His mother had education, strength of character, and a refined moral sense. She exerted much influence over him and effectually fostered his intellectual tastes. Though he did not attend school after leaving North Carolina, he acquired by assiduous reading and study at home an extensive and available knowledge of history and literature. Barring his defects in the niceties of the classics, he subsequently ranked with the most accomplished statesmen of the East. In due time, after serving a successful apprenticeship as a planter, he took up the study of the law and was admitted to practice. In 1811 he served a term in the Tennessee legislature, where he exhibited the same traits that marked his Senatorial career. Like most Western men, he was enthusiastic for war with England. He raised a regiment of volunteers for Jackson's first army, which did little more than organize before it was disbanded. He was afterward appointed lieutenant-colonel by the President; but before he could reach Canada, where he was to serve, peace was declared and he resigned his commission. In 1815 he removed to St. Louis, continuing the practice of the law and publishing a newspaper. His practice was lucrative and his newspaper productive of quarrels that led to several duels, in one of which he killed his adversary. There were few men of any influence in the Southwest in those times who did not engage in these affairs; readiness to face the pistol when the "code of honor" required it was one of the essentials of popular respect. That Benton never outgrew this chivalrous sentiment is shown by the zest of his minute account, in the *Thirty Years' View*, of the Clay-Randolph duel, which he witnessed. He closes by saying: "Certainly duelling is bad and has been put down, but not quite so bad as its substitute—revolvers, bowie-knives, blackguarding, and street assassinations under the pretext of self-defence."

He was thoroughly in touch with the people of his region. Possessing in an eminent degree the qualities that characterized the prevailing type, his ability and attainments naturally advanced him to the rank of influence he so long held in Missouri and the West. He was not the inventor of political theories and projects, but the representative of the Western people and the exponent of the Western policy. In the contest over the admission of Missouri he took chief command of the local movement against the restriction of slavery, which finally overcame all opposition. Though he was a slave-holder, his sentiments were adverse to slavery. He opposed restriction in Missouri because slavery existed there by the general choice of the people. But the compromise through which Missouri came into the Union met his cordial favor, as it quieted a dangerous agitation and fixed a limit to the extension of slavery. He was elected one of the first Senators from the new State, and remained the dictator of its politics until the heroic course he took in opposition to the extension of slavery caused his overthrow.

He at once assumed an active part in the proceedings of the Senate. He was not an orator in the sense that Clay was, but a skilful and prolific debater, sometimes tedious and often pompous. His capacity for labor was prodigious, hence his speeches usually displayed wide and accurate investigation. His peculiar strength lay in his mastery of facts and details—and the impressive boldness with which he presented them. He steadily improved, and, what best indicates his genuine and tenacious powers, he continued to improve to the end of his career. On most of the numerous questions, arising in various ways, that related to the expansion and development of the West, he took a vigorous initiative. It was this which gave him by degrees that Western character and influence which made him an important factor in national politics. During the canvass of 1824 he supported Clay; but after the election devolved upon the House he supported Jackson, because he was a Western man and because he had received the highest popular and electoral vote. Thenceforth he co-operated with the Democratic party, which soon began to receive the impress of his views.

Before the war, Jackson and Benton were warm friends. After the war began, Benton was Jackson's aide-de-camp until the first disbandment of his troops. It was Benton who induced the President, by political threats, to meet the obligations that Jackson had incurred to provide for the return of the troops at Natchez. For some years after the affray between Jackson and Coffee and the Bentons the two were estranged; they then resumed their friendly relations. Before Jackson's declaration in his message against the bank, Benton had made several futile attacks upon the bank, and the subject had been repeatedly discussed between him and Jackson. As they thoroughly agreed in their opinions concerning the institution, Benton was ready to lead the contest against it when the time arrived.

The bank and its friends, taking the alarm which the message had sounded, exerted all possible efforts to create public sentiment in its behalf. A committee in each House of Congress made a long and vigorous report upholding the bank. In the House adverse resolutions were quickly and silently tabled. The press, with few exceptions, teemed with articles in favor of the recharter. Besides these means, every resource of politics was brought to bear. Little, however, was done to counteract the effect of this agitation. "The current was all setting one way," says Benton. "I determined to raise a voice against it in the Senate, and made several efforts before I succeeded—the thick array of the bank friends throwing every obstacle in my way, and even friends holding me back for the regular course, which was to wait until the application for the renewed charter was presented, and then oppose it. I foresaw that if this course was followed the bank would triumph without a contest—that she would wait until a majority was installed in both Houses of Congress—then present her application—hear a few barren speeches in opposition—and then gallop the renewed charter through." In February, 1831, he asked leave to submit a resolution declaring that the charter ought not to be renewed, and supported the application in an extended speech.

The charter was similar to that of the original Bank of the United States founded by Hamilton. One-fifth ($7,000,000) of the capital stock was subscribed by the government by a stock-note bearing five per centum interest; the remainder was subscribed by the public—one-fifth in specie and three-fifths in United States stocks. Five of the twenty directors were appointed by the President, subject to confirmation by the Senate. The Secretary of the Treasury was vested with certain important discretionary powers over the government's relations with the bank. The principal powers and privileges of the bank were exclusive; and besides the great benefits derived from its currency functions and the prestige of its partnership with the government, it and its twenty-five branches were depositories of the public moneys, the undrawn balances of which were steady and considerable and bore no interest.[1] The bonus to the government of a million and a half, exacted by the charter, was more than offset by the interest paid by the government on loans from the bank. The amount of the dividends received by the government was nearly one hundred thousand dollars less than the interest on the stock-note, which

---

[1] The average monthly balance to the credit of the government in the bank and its branches from 1818 to 1832 was $6,700,000.

was not paid until 1831. Other losses, indirect, were easily traced. These leading facts furnished the topics for Benton's harangue. It was an indictment in several distinct and subdivided counts, all put in plain terms for popular effect.

His method of attack, as well as many of his arguments, were drawn from the debates in Parliament over the re-charter of the Bank of England, which presented many points of resemblance to the issue here. He did not touch on the Constitutional question, but assailed the bank solely on the score of its general character. He denounced it as "an institution too great and powerful to be tolerated in a government of free and equal laws"; because "its tendencies were dangerous and pernicious to the government and the people"; and because of "the exclusive privileges and anti-republican monopoly it gave to the stockholders." These considerations he explained and illustrated in various ways and with graphic, though sometimes rather demagogical, effect. He closed with one of his pleas for hard money, which eventually gave him the sobriquet of "Old Bullion."

As soon as he had finished his speech his application to introduce the resolution was denied without discussion. "The debate stopped with the single speech," says Benton, characteristically; "but it was a speech to be read by the people—the masses—the millions; and was conceived and delivered for that purpose; and was read by them; and has been complimented since as having crippled the bank, and given it the wound of which it afterward died, but not within the year and a day which would make the slayer responsible for the homicide."

In his annual message at the opening of the Twenty-second Congress, Jackson merely declared that he still held the same opinions concerning the bank which he had stated in his previous messages. "Having thus discharged a conscientious duty," he added, "I deem it proper on this occasion, without more particular reference to the views of the subject there expressed, to leave it for the present to the investigation of an enlightened people and their representatives." At the same time the Secretary of the Treasury, in his report, strongly favored the bank.[1] The effort to procure a recharter at this session was contrary to the wishes of the bank and its non-political friends. Its political friends arbitrarily compelled it. The bank policy had been made one of the principal features of the Whig platform adopted at the Baltimore convention, held only a few days after the session began, and Clay declined to recede from the fatuous plan of campaign to overthrow Jackson on that issue. It is related that Jackson himself tried about this time to settle the question amicably, by proposing a compromise through the conditions of a recharter. "Shortly before the bank applied to Congress for a recharter," says Thurlow Weed, "the Honorable Louis McLane, the Secretary of the Treasury, invited Mr. Biddle, the president of the United States Bank, to Washington. At their interview the Secretary informed Mr. Biddle that he was authorized by the President to say that if the proposed recharter of the bank contained certain modifications, which Mr. McLane handed to Mr.

---

[1] "It is now generally admitted, I think, after a considerate examination of Mr. McLane's views, that he does not express any opposition to those entertained by myself; although it is obvious that his solicitude to obtain a new charter, so modified as to free the institution from the objections of the Executive, springs from convictions much more favorable than mine of the general character and conduct of the institution. Mr. McLane and myself understand each other, and have not the slightest disagreement about the principles which will be a *sine qua non* to my assent to a bill rechartering the bank."—*Jackson to Hamilton, December* 12, 1831.

Biddle in writing, the bill would be approved. Mr. Biddle returned to Philadelphia, and submitted the proposed modifications to Mr. John Sergeant, a director of the bank and its counsel, and to one or two other influential directors, by each one of whom the modifications were accepted. But before announcing such acquiescence to the Secretary of the Treasury, it was deemed proper to confer with the leading friends of the bank then in Congress. Mr. Biddle and Mr. Sergeant, therefore, called upon Messrs. Clay and Webster, submitting to these gentlemen the modifications required to secure the approval by the President of a recharter of the bank. After much discussion and consideration, Messrs. Clay and Webster came to the conclusion that the question of a recharter had progressed too far and had assumed aspects too decided in the public mind and in Congress to render any compromise or change of front expedient or desirable. Messrs. Biddle and Sergeant retired for consultation, but returned in the evening of the same day, confirmed in their convictions that it was wise to accept the offer of the Secretary of the Treasury. Messrs. Clay and Webster replied that they had borne the brunt of the battle so far, and that they were confident of their ability to carry a bill through Congress rechartering the bank, even though the bill should encounter a Presidential veto; but that they could not be responsible for the result if in the heat of the contest the bank, abandoning its reliable friends, should strike hands with its foe."[1] This very significant account finds strong confirmation in the brief and perfunctory manner in which Jackson had touched the bank question in his last message, and in the report of the Secretary of the Treasury. One of

---

[1] Thurlow Weed's *Autobiography*, vol. i. p. 373.

12

the chief political considerations of the Whig leaders in precipitating the issue was the expectation of winning Pennsylvania from Jackson. As the bank was located at Philadelphia, it was supposed that it would exert a decisive influence on the popular opinion of the State.

Upon the presentation of the bank's memorial for a re-charter it was referred in the Senate to a select committee, and in the House to the Committee on Ways and Means, both committees having a majority of pro-bank men. Some days after this Benton returned to the attack. This time he asked leave to introduce a resolution declaring that the "branch drafts" were illegal and ought to be suppressed. This was the text for another speech. These drafts were an imitation of a Scotch invention which came into common use in Great Britain. They were prohibited by an act of Parliament in 1826, the same year in which the Bank of the United States adopted the contrivance. The drafts were issued by the branches, most of them by the branches in the South and West, and payable at the main bank in Philadelphia. They would be paid on presentation at any of the branches, however; but as they were in small denominations they became the principal currency of the region in which they were issued, and were rarely redeemed. In 1832 the amount of them in circulation was over seven million dollars. Able lawyers had pronounced them legal, yet it was a serious question whether they were justified by the terms of the charter, which guarded with scrupulous care the emission of paper expressly designed for currency. Certainly, whatever the instruments might be styled, they possessed most of the attributes of an unrestrained paper currency, and no one denied that they might lead to dangerous results. Benton's attack was sharp and vigorous; but it met the same immediate fate that had befallen the former one.

Though Jackson had been willing to avoid the bank issue by a compromise, the course of his opponents could not have been better calculated to stimulate his combative energy to its highest tension. He and his advisers were no doubt actuated in their desire to take the question out of the pending election by an appreciation of the tremendous and ramified power the bank could wield against him. But when his conciliatory proposition was defiantly rejected, for political reasons solely, it was a political necessity, and would have been with any candidate in the same situation, to enter the contest with all his power. He did so, and with keen delight. Benton now assumed authoritative command of the anti-bank forces. His assault on the branch-draft system was only a preliminary skirmish; an organized and concerted campaign followed. "It was seen," says Benton, "to be the policy of the bank leaders to carry the charter first and quietly through the Senate, and afterwards in the same way through the House. We determined to have a contest in both places and to force the bank into defences which would engage it in a general contest and lay it open to side blows as well as direct attacks. With this view a great many amendments and inquiries were prepared to be offered in the Senate, all of them proper or plausible, recommendable in themselves and supported by acceptable reasons, which the friends of the bank must either answer or reject without answer, and so incur odium. In the House it was determined to make a move which, whether resisted or admitted by the bank majority, would be certain to have an effect against the institution—namely, an investigation by a committee of the House as provided in the charter. If the investigation was denied, it would be guilt shrinking from detection; if admitted, it was well known that misconduct would be found. I conceived this movement and had charge of its direction."

This plan was diligently prosecuted. Two things were certain: the recharter would be passed by both Houses, and the President would veto it. All the operations of both parties, therefore, had for their exclusive object the production of campaign material. Under these circumstances, had any one desired an impartial, accurate, and exhaustive investigation and presentation of the subject, necessary to the complete solution and settlement of a momentous question of national finance, it could not have been accomplished. One party was bound to continue the bank at all hazards; the other, to destroy it. Any means that promised utility to either of the combatants was certain to be employed.

Inasmuch as the several prior reports of committees went for naught, and as neither of the committees to which the memorial of the bank had been referred was directed to conduct a detailed inquiry into the management and condition of the bank, the appointment of a select committee for that purpose was moved in the House. Benton had drawn the charges and specifications, twenty-two in number, and they were boldly preferred by the member who made the motion for a committee. After an acrimonious discussion, in which it soon developed, as had been foreseen, that the partisans of the bank deemed it impolitic to prevent the investigation, the committee was appointed. It spent some time in taking evidence, and then made three reports. The majority report was against the bank, the minority reports— one of which was drawn by John Quincy Adams, who began his remarkable career in the House at the preceding session

—were in its favor. Though most of the charges were not adequately sustained by proof, sufficient maladministration —and it required but little — was shown to exist as to affect the public mind. But above all now stood out as it had never done before the dangerous possibilities of a gigantic financial corporation invested with functions that should alone be exercised by the government.

The bill to recharter the bank on essentially the old plan was in due time reported to the Senate. After a protracted debate over separate provisions and proposed amendments, it was passed. According to the programme, it went through the House without much delay. No doubt when it reached the President the veto message was ready. The space of six days, during which he held the bill, was suited to the double effect he desired to produce—the appearance of respectful consideration, yet unhesitating decision.

The message contained little that was new to the controversy, but presented the old arguments best adapted for popular effect. It was the perfection of political art, to which even its errors contributed.

The President favored a bank, but not this bank. The monopoly bestowed by the original charter operated as a gratuity of many millions by greatly increasing the value of the stock. The renewal would still further improve the stock to fifty per centum above its par value, rendering the market value of the monopoly $17,000,000. "It appears," said the message, "that more than one-fourth of the stock is held by foreigners, and the residue by a few hundreds of our own citizens, chiefly of the richest class. For their benefit does this act exclude the whole American people from competition in the purchase of this monopoly, and dispose of it for many millions less than it is worth. . . . If our government must sell monopolies, it would seem to be its duty to take nothing less than their full value; and if gratuities must be made once in fifteen or twenty years, let them not be bestowed on the subjects of a foreign government nor upon a designated and favored class of men in our own country."

That the termination of the existing charter might cause embarrassment by requiring the bank to call in its loans was no reason for the renewal of the charter; otherwise the bank might justly claim to be perpetual. Besides, there was ample time for it to close its business without distressing its debtors; if it caused distress the fault would be its own. The proposed modifications of the charter were of little value or importance. "All the objectionable principles of the existing corporation, and most of its odious features, were retained without alleviation." The provision that the paper of the bank, though made payable at one place, should nevertheless be received at any of the branches if tendered in liquidation of a balance due from any other incorporated bank, would give to the banks a privilege withheld from all private citizens, and was therefore "most odious, because it did not measure equal justice to the high and the low, the rich and the poor." Several forcible considerations were presented against the holding of stock by foreigners, 'both as to the effect upon taxation of the stock under the proposed provisions, and the dangers that might attend the control by aliens of the finances of the nation. Then followed an argument against the constitutionality of the scheme, a part of which was directed to showing that the provisions would result in exempting a large portion of the stock and all the property of the bank from taxation.

The message referred to the charges against the bank

and spoke of the investigation by the House as too brief to be complete and satisfactory. "As the charter had yet four years to run, and as a renewal was not necessary to the successful prosecution of its business, it was to be expected that the bank itself, conscious of its purity and proud of its character, would have withdrawn its application for the present, and demanded the severest scrutiny into all its transactions." This furnished another reason why the government should proceed with "less haste and more caution" in the renewal of the monopoly. Moreover, the "executive branches of the government," as the agent of which the bank "was professedly established," had no need for it; on the contrary, it was then regarded as "not only unnecessary, but dangerous to the government and the country."

The close of the message contains these just and eloquent observations, which were not hackneyed then, and probably had greater effect on the popular mind than was produced by the merely argumentative parts of the document:

"Distinctions in society will always exist under every just government. Equality of talents, of education, or wealth cannot be produced by human institutions. In the full enjoyment of the gifts of Heaven and the fruits of superior industry, economy, and virtue, every man is equally entitled to protection by law. But when the laws undertake to add to these natural and just advantages artificial distinctions, to grant titles, gratuities, and exclusive privileges, to make the rich richer and the potent more powerful, the humble members of society, the farmers, mechanics, and laborers, who have neither the time nor the means of securing like favors to themselves, have the right to complain of the injustice of their government.

There are no necessary evils in government. Its evils exist only in its abuses. If it would confine itself to equal protection, and, as heaven does its rains, shower its favors alike on the high and the low, the rich and the poor, it would be an unqualified blessing. . . . Most of the difficulties our government now encounters, and most of the dangers which now impend over our Union, have sprung from the abandonment of the legitimate objects of government by our national legislation and the adoption of such principles as are embodied in this act. Many of our rich men have not been content with equal protection and equal benefits, but have besought us to make them richer by acts of Congress. By attempting to gratify their desires we have, in the results of our legislation, arrayed section against section, interest against interest, and man against man."

Strange as it now seems, the message was rapturously received by the Whig party, which industriously aided in circulating it among the people. The history of politics does not exhibit a more preposterous delusion than the idea which possessed that party that there would be a popular uprising to save the bank from the vindictive tyrant in the White House. The whole proceeding was founded on that hallucination. The Whig leaders were still blind to the forces which had elected Jackson, and which, from the sense of mastery they had derived, would thenceforth dominate the politics of the country. From Jefferson to Jackson, politicians had been little in the habit of considering, so far as Presidential elections were concerned, how the masses generally view any given national policy; the probable attitude of sections and interests had been the main factors in their calculations. The men who had organized victory for Jackson were for the most part an entirely new order of politicians. Unlike the anti-Jackson leaders, they were free from the influence of those ideas and prepossessions usually begotten by long continuance in public office. They were of the people, familiar with the drift of popular sentiment, which they constantly and involuntarily consulted. Their opponents, oblivious to these new elements or underrating them, clung in the pride of their talents to their accustomed theories and methods.

When the message was received by the Senate the final scene in the bank programme was enacted. As the bill could not be passed over the veto, the occasion was only of spectacular importance; it was the formal appeal of the bank to the people. Jackson was denounced as a despot and destroyer, and his message was dissected and arraigned as no other message except his has ever been. Webster,[1] Clayton, Ewing, and Clay were the bank's Senatorial champions. Clay closed the case for it with a speech that was to be taken as his manifesto in the approaching election. It was not long, but it displayed deliberation and a nicer accuracy of phrase than was common with him. He spoke with haughty freedom, perhaps more so than became his position as Jackson's nominated rival.

He assailed the veto as the ordinary use of an extraordinary power. "The veto," said he, "is hardly reconcil-

---

[1] Martin Van Buren very justly places Hamilton and Clay superior to Webster in "genius and eloquence." "But," he adds, "as a close and powerful reasoner, an adroit and wary debater—one capable of taking comprehensive and at the same time close views of a subject, who surveyed all points in his case, the weak as well as the strong, and dealt with each in a way best calculated to serve his purpose and to reduce the advantage of his antagonist to the lowest allowable point, and who was withal unscrupulous in the employment of his great powers—he was in his day unsurpassed."—*Political Parties in the United States*, p. 319.

able with the genius of representative government. It is totally irreconcilable with it if it is to be frequently employed in respect to the expediency of measures as well as their constitutionality. It is a feature of our government borrowed from a prerogative of the British king. And it is remarkable that in England it has grown obsolete, not having been used for upward of a century." Nevertheless, it is obvious as a legal proposition that since the President possesses the unqualified Constitutional right, his exercise of it is wholly discretionary. If it were improper for the President to veto a bill as inexpedient, it might be asserted with equal correctness that he should not veto a bill as unconstitutional, because the validity of laws is to be determined by the courts. Considering the veto in its purely legal aspect, as the exercise of a power expressly granted by a written constitution, reference to the British practice had no force; for the British constitution is chiefly tradition and precedent. Clay's argument, therefore, only went to the propriety of the Constitutional provision. Jackson was condemned for doing what his adversaries had forced him to do; and his action was not in opposition to the popular will, but to prevent Congress from subverting it, for the charter once granted was irrevocable.

Despite the propriety of the veto, the argument of the message against the constitutionality of the bank could not stand. The Supreme Court, in a suit arising under the existing charter, had sanctioned the power to establish such an institution. Had not the question—which belonged to the old radical difference of political opinion as to the latitude to be given the implied powers of the Constitution—been thus authoritatively settled, Jackson's argument, principally that of Clay's speech in 1811, would have been legally appropriate. But respect for the law as declared by the ultimate tribunal demanded acquiescence.

Clay did not enter into a general examination of the Constitutional question. But as his speech in 1811 had been read to the Senate during the debate, he was led to speak of his change of opinion after the war, and to read extracts from his speech in 1816 in justification. He asserted, in contradiction of the statement in the message that Congressional precedents as to the constitutionality of a national bank were equally divided, that at no time was there a majority against the legal power, although bills failed in 1811 and 1815. Undoubtedly, as he maintained, they failed on other grounds. Various other acts in relation to the bank after it was established were to be regarded as a practical construction in favor of the power.

Jackson's disregard of judicial construction led him to announce a doctrine totally indefensible. "Each public officer," said the message, "who takes an oath to support the Constitution swears that he will support it as he understands it, and not as it is understood by others. . . . The opinion of the judges has no more authority over Congress than the opinion of Congress has over the judges; and on that point the President is independent of both." This doctrine taken literally would lead to a chaos in administration — the least of its consequences. It was refuted by Webster with grave logic, and rebuked by Clay with vivid energy. The only apology for it is that Jackson could not have intended precisely what the message made him say; but that the President, in considering bills presented to him for approval, should take his own view as to whether or not they violate the true spirit of the organic law, independent of Congress or the courts. Indeed, the

President can seldom perform a better service than to arrest a tendency to make and uphold laws that depend for their validity upon legislative powers practically equivalent to the discretion of Congress. But preventing the enactment of such laws is entirely different from nullifying them after they are enacted and voiding transactions based upon them.[1]

Clay defended the policy of allowing foreigners to hold bank stock, which he placed in the same category as the stock of other corporations. He also defended the operations of the bank against the charge that they were injurious to the West, and predicted ruinous consequences if the bank should be compelled by the termination of its charter to enforce the payment of its Western loans. The message stated that had the Executive been called upon to furnish the project of a bank that would obviate his objections, the duty would have been cheerfully performed. Clay criticised this with caustic severity. "Does the President," he asked, "wish to introduce the initiative here? Are the powers of recommendation and that of veto not sufficient? Must all legislation, in its commencement and its termination, concentrate in the President? When we shall have reached that state of things the election and annual sessions of Congress will be a useless charge upon the people, and the whole business of government may be economically conducted by ukases and decrees." He closed, as Webster did, in a strain of lurid prophecy of the downfall of our institutions if the course Jackson had begun were not checked, setting a fashion of Whig oratory that was to prevail for years to come.

---

[1] See Lincoln's first inaugural address; Tyler's *Taney*, p. 410; Sumner's *Works*, vol. iii. p. 375; Van Buren's *Political Parties in the United States*, p. 316.

Benton at once took the floor. As a campaign speech his reply was a skilful performance. His retorts and political appeals showed the art of a master. An uninformed stranger, however, might well have supposed that in any case the country was doomed; for Benton's prediction of a moneyed aristocracy and monarchy as the ultimate result of continuing the bank outvied the prophecies of Webster and Clay. The weightiest part of his speech was in answer to the reiterated pleas that the West would be ruined by the dissolution of the bank. He asserted that since the subject of renewing the charter had been agitated the bank had increased its loans over thirty million dollars. This increase had been largely in the politically doubtful states, particularly in the South and West, one-third of it being in Louisiana, Kentucky, and Ohio. He then referred to certain curtailments recently made by some of the Western branches, through the alleged dearth of funds, caused mainly by decrease of the public deposits, and pronounced this reason a mere pretence; for the bank had ample funds, and was then increasing its loans in other quarters at the rate of $1,250,000 per month. "The true reasons," said he, "were political; a foretaste and prelude to what is now threatened. It was a measure to press the debtors—a turn of the screw upon the borrowers—to make them all cry out and join in the clamors and petitions for a renewed charter. . . . All this for political effect, and to be followed by electioneering fabrication that it was the effect of the veto message." Nor was this the only expedient adopted by the bank. "Numerous promises for new branches," said Benton, "is another trick of the same kind. Thirty new branches are said to be in contemplation, and about three hundred villages have been induced each to believe that itself was the favored spot of location; but always upon the condition, well understood, that Jackson should not be re-elected, and that it should elect a Representative to vote for the recharter."

In the course of the speech he intimated that Clay had not shown proper courtesy toward the President; and, as soon as he had concluded, Clay responded in a manner that would have won admiration in a frontier court-room. It led to an angry passage of recriminations that boded another duel.[1] The question was then put, and the bill failed, not receiving the requisite two-thirds vote. On the 16th Congress adjourned. The Presidential campaign was begun.

The contest of 1828 was mild in comparison with it. It was scarcely impeded by the cholera, which raged in several cities during the summer. Detraction, misrepresentation, buncombe, rioted unrestrained. All the slanders and perversions of 1828 were renewed and reinforced. Yet the more flagrant characteristics of the campaign, instead of denoting, as many supposed, a decline of public morality, were due rather to the license naturally attending the novel political conditions of the time. It has taken many years to lessen the barbarous asperity of Presidential contests; not that the masses have improved in their public morals, but that among a very large proportion of the people passionate and unbridled partisanship has to a great extent exhausted itself. The larger experience of the country has rendered the people less emotional in politics; they have grown more wary of the "campaign lie," which has therefore lost much of its former efficacy. In 1832, personal vilification was not confined to either party; the epithets and imputations with which Jackson was assailed were not less scurrilous

---

[1] Benton quotes the whole of this fierce colloquy in the *Thirty Years' View*, vol. i. p. 203.

and unfounded than those from which Clay suffered.¹ Indeed, Jackson doubtless got the worst of it in this regard; for the great majority of the newspapers were Whig, and their columns were constantly laden with all that partisan ingenuity could invent.²

But apart from these vicious phases of the struggle, the important issues involved gave it a character and significance that the preceding elections did not possess. And each of these issues, although of Clay's own making, worked to his detriment. His tariff policy was hateful to the South; his public-lands policy was unsatisfactory to the West; while the bank policy was altogether the most ill-advised political issue that could have been conceived. Had there been no other question before the people, it alone would have been fatal to his success. Aged men long afterward related with keen enthusiasm the part they took in "slaying the monster." It was in vain to call the "Hero of New Orleans" a public enemy; the question, as it was put, whether he or a gigantic corporation supported by a moneyed aristocracy were the more dangerous to our institutions, could receive but one answer by the popular voice. The spectacle of the bank

---

¹ Hunt's *Livingston*, p. 369.

² "Caricatures, poorly designed and worse executed, were published in great numbers in the course of the season. A favorite idea of the caricaturists was to depict Mr. Van Buren as an infant in the arms of General Jackson, receiving sustenance from a spoon in the hand of the General. One popular picture represented the President receiving a crown from Mr. Van Buren and a sceptre from the devil. Another showed the President raving at a delegation. Another gave Clay and Jackson in the guise of jockeys riding a race toward the White House—Clay half a length ahead. Another represented Jackson, Van Buren, Benton, Blair, Kendall, and others attired as burglars, aiming a huge battering-ram at the bank's impregnable front door. Another portrayed General Jackson as Don Quixote tilting at one of the pillars of the same marble edifice, and breaking his puny lance against it."—Parton's *Jackson*, vol. iii. p. 423.

openly using every possible means to preserve its existence was the most powerful argument against it. Its conduct during the campaign justified the chief objection to such an institution. In reaching a correct view of the subject it matters not whether Jackson or the bank was the first assailant, nor what were the motives that led to the issue; that the bank could under any circumstances become the subject of a political contest was reason enough why it should not exist.

Many subsequent elections have occasioned much speculation as to the effect minor things had or might have had in determining the result; but in 1832 the outcome was inevitable. The Anti-masonic movement figured conspicuously in the canvass, but it had no decisive effect.[1] Jackson's election was an overwhelming triumph. Clay received but 49 out of 286 votes. The disparity in the popular vote was not so marked, though sufficiently emphatic: Clay received 530,189 to Jackson's 687,502. The humiliation was intensified by Van Buren's election to the Vice-Presidency by nearly the same vote. The rejection of his nomination for Minister to England had produced precisely the opposite effect from that intended. Yet so completely were the Whigs deceived that they continued boastfully confident until the result of the election was known. And with most of the press and the cultivated classes enlisted in the Whig cause the external appearances seemed promising. The sentiment of the " plain people " had no means of spectacular display: its mode of expression was the ballot.[2]

---

[1] Kennedy's *Wirt*, vol. ii. p. 330.

[2] "An English election, instead of the tranquil, dignified scene we witness in this country, presents nothing but riot and misrule. The opening of the poll is the signal for the prostration of legal restraint and the

A man of less elastic temperament than Clay would have been disheartened by the utter defeat he had sustained. Under less vigorous and alluring leadership his party would have been long in recovering from its total rout. But acutely as he felt the defeat, he wrote and spoke of it stoically. For some time his health had not been good. In April he wrote to a friend: "Naturally ardent, perhaps too ardent, I cannot avoid being too much excited and provoked at the scenes of tergiversation, hypocrisy, degeneracy, and corruption which are daily exhibited. I would fly from them and renounce forever public life if I were not restrained by a sentiment of duty and of attachment to my friends. . . . I will endeavor to moderate my interest in public affairs." Nevertheless, he did not curb his political zeal. Congress reassembled December 3. A few days later he appeared on the scene.

The topic of the hour was "nullification." The excitement of the Presidential election had merged in that which the attitude of South Carolina had aroused. The dissatisfaction of the South generally with the tariff of 1828 had been driven wellnigh to exasperation by the tariff of 1832; but in none of the Southern States, except South Carolina, had the anti-protection sentiment led to any new mode of opposition. The novelty of nullification was confined to that State. This unique doctrine, first promulgated in 1828, had rapidly matured to action. Before the tariff of 1832 was enacted the course of the State was virtually decided; the people were at least two to one in favor of nulli-

---

commencement of the reign of anarchy. The contest frequently lasts for several days, and during this time the unfortunate borough is given over to the mob. The shops are all closed—business is at an end—parties attracted to the different candidates are parading the streets and frequently meeting, when desperate battles are sure to ensue."—*North American Review*, vol. xiii. p. 356.

fication. In November a convocation in the nature of a constitutional convention, which had been regularly called and empowered, adopted an ordinance declaring the acts of 1828 and 1832 null and void, and prohibiting the payment of any duties under them within the State after February 1, 1833. It made any appeal to the Supreme Court of the United States touching the validity of the ordinance a penal offence; and required all State officers, civil and military, and all jurors, to take an oath to support the ordinance. It further asserted the determination to maintain the ordinance at every hazard, and threatened secession from the Union if any attempt were made to coerce the State.

In his annual message, December 4, the President devoted but one short paragraph directly to the subject. He merely stated that "in one quarter of the United States opposition to the revenue laws had risen to a height which threatened to thwart their execution, if not to endanger the integrity of the Union," but that it was hoped to overcome peaceably any obstructions that might be thrown in the way of the judicial authorities; and in any case it was believed that the laws themselves were fully adequate to the suppression of such attempts as might immediately be made. But the preceding part of the message bore indirectly upon the question, which was the only shadow upon the general picture of harmony and prosperity presented by this politic paper. The entire public debt was to be extinguished during the ensuing year; this would permit a reduction of the revenue, as proposed by the Secretary of the Treasury. Then followed some judicious and carefully guarded considerations against the protective system, with the recommendation that "the whole scheme of duties be reduced to the revenue standard as soon as just regard to the faith of the government and to the preservation of the large capital invested in the establishments of domestic industry will permit." In short, while the administration meant to execute the laws and to preserve the Union, it admitted the justice of the Southern complaints, and proposed to ameliorate the cause of them. These views on the tariff indicated Jackson's abandonment of the protective system, to which he had not until then been avowedly opposed, although gradually tending in that direction. In his messages prior to that of December, 1831, he had expressed himself as favoring protection to a moderate degree; but he then advised a reduction of the revenue, in consequence of the approaching extinguishment of the public debt. It was on this theory, to some extent, that he had approved the act of 1832. Thus far, however, the tariff question had not materially entered into the Jacksonian policy.

Considered as a whole, the message was apparently as favorable to South Carolina as the most hopeful nullifier could reasonably expect; for not only was the avowed policy of the administration pledged to a reduction of the tariff, but all the principles laid down in the message relating to the powers of the government were those of the strict-construction school. It was a thoroughly Democratic document. The Whigs thought it the complete espousal of the extreme State-rights doctrine. But in this they were mistaken. Its true meaning and its consummate art were not perceived until six days later, when the President's proclamation to the people of South Carolina appeared.

The leading arguments of this celebrated manifesto were drawn from Webster's reply to Hayne,[1] in 1830, denying

---

[1] Benton gives an appreciative sketch of Hayne in the *Thirty Years' View*, vol. ii. p. 186. See also *Life of Silliman*, vol. ii. p. 119.

that the Constitution forms a league and not a nation, and that it is incompetent for a State lawfully to annul an act of Congress or to withdraw from the Union. The people of South Carolina were eloquently adjured to retrace their steps and warned that the Constitution and the Union would be maintained even at the cost of blood.

The fact that no Southern State would join South Carolina[1] might suggest that the Northern sentiment against nullification was intense. It was so. Politics was quite forgotten in the patriotic fervor with which the President's proclamation was greeted throughout the North. The impetuous loyalty to the Union there exhibited might well have terrified South Carolina in her wayward course. The determination and unanimity of the opposition were a surprise to the leaders of the nullification movement, who expected some degree of co-operation in the South and no vigorous and general resistance in the North; and undoubtedly this result influenced their subsequent action. No small share of Jackson's peculiar fame at the present day is due to the effect produced by that proclamation.

Clay, of course, was in no mood to join in the fervid approval of the President. Two days after the proclamation he wrote in a letter with somewhat of petulance: "One short week produced the message and the proclamation—the former ultra on the side of State-rights, the latter ultra on the side of consolidation. How they can be reconciled I must leave to our Virginia friends. As to the proclamation, although there are some good things in it, especially as to

---

[1] The legislatures of Virginia, Mississippi, Alabama, and North Carolina declared against the doctrine of nullification. The Virginia legislature sent Leigh as a commissioner to counsel moderation, and he accordingly addressed the South Carolina legislature. Cass, Secretary of War, at once ordered troops to Charleston.—Smith's *Cass*, pp. 269, 274.

what relates to the judiciary, there are some entirely too ultra for me and which I cannot stomach. A proclamation should have been issued weeks ago, but I think it should have been a different paper from the present, which, I apprehend, will irritate instead of allaying any excited feeling."[1]

Meantime Calhoun resigned the Vice-Presidency and was elected to the Senate to fill the vacancy caused by the resignation of Hayne, who had become Governor of South Carolina. The State showed no sign of receding from its position. Its strongest men were at the front. Though Calhoun took the most responsible and arduous post, he was supported by the whole machinery of the State government, Hayne boldly issuing a proclamation of defiance, and the legislature adopting a series of resolutions to the same effect. January 16, the President sent to Congress another message. It was a long one, accompanied by all the documents relating to the subject. It closed by recommending various legislation, including a grant of additional powers to the Executive to enforce the collection of duties. On the 21st a bill in compliance with the message was reported to the Senate. On the next day, Calhoun met the whole issue by introducing a set of resolutions declaring his theory of the nature and powers of the government.

Soon after the opening of the session the Verplanck bill, as it was called, was introduced in the House. It was an administration measure, framed on the recommendation of the President's annual message and the report of the Secretary of the Treasury. Its avowed object was to reduce the revenue from $27,000,000, which had been the average annual income of the government for several years

---

[1] To Tyler he pronounced it an "ultra-Federal black cockade."—*Letters and Times of the Tylers*, vol. iii. p. 75. See also *Life of Story*, vol. ii. p. 121.

preceding the tariff of 1832, to $15,000,000 within two years. The latter tariff had effected some reduction, though not nearly so much as had been expected; but it was estimated that the proposed bill would work a further reduction of $7,000,000. "To the great opponents of the tariff (the South Carolina school)," says Benton, who unquestionably states the views of the subject then entertained by the administration, "it was also bound to be satisfactory, as it carried back the whole system of duties to the standard at which that school had fixed them, with the great amelioration of the arbitrary and injurious minimums. The bill, then, seemed bound to conciliate every fair interest—the government, because it gave all the revenue it needed; the real manufacturers, because it gave them an adequate incidental protection; the South, because it gave them their own bill, and that ameliorated." It was assiduously debated until Clay's "compromise bill" was suddenly projected into the House.

Between the demands of the nullifiers and the policy of the administration the protective system was in extreme jeopardy. Should the inevitable revision of the tariff be made by the enemies or the friends of protection? To this question Clay had at once addressed himself. In December he visited Philadelphia, where, after conferring with various manufacturers, he devised a plan of adjusting the controversy. He then submitted it to a few of his immediate friends, and also to Webster and Calhoun. The former refused, but the latter determined to support it. The combination of Clay and Calhoun would ensure its passage.

The political career of no other public man of that eventful period inspires the candid student with such mingled feelings of respect and regret as Calhoun's. He entered the arena of national politics in 1811, in his thirtieth year, after a brief service in the South Carolina legislature. He was a graduate of Yale College, and finished his law studies at Litchfield. He began the practice of law, but did not long continue it; a competency relieved him of that necessity. His instinctive interest in public affairs, which indeed was conspicuously displayed in college, soon led him into public life. Able men were quickly recognized in the South, and seldom experienced much difficulty in procuring and retaining seats in Congress—a fact that accounts for the uniform superiority in talents and training of the Southern members, as a class, over the Northern.

He at once took a leading position in the House. He was eager for war; and Clay, quick to appreciate his ability and alliance, assigned him to the most appropriate place—on the Committee on Foreign Relations, from which emanated the declaration of war. In this capacity he became the leader of the war party on the floor of the House. His only difference with that party was in regard to the restrictive system, which he strenuously opposed. After the war he zealously co-operated with Clay in his entire domestic programme—a national bank, a protective tariff, and extensive internal improvements. Nor did Clay ever go to greater lengths in advocating those policies than Calhoun went at that period. The Constitution then offered no obstacles to him. All his views were characterized by the utmost liberality and freedom from sectional interest. The nation and a strong national government were the prime objects of his solicitude. He was much admired generally for his personal and intellectual qualities. His style of speech was pure, poised, and strong. It did not possess the eloquent energy and fervor of Clay's, nor the terseness and solid power of Webster's, yet it had more elegance and finish than either. During this period he freely employed historical illustrations and evinced a strong tendency to generalize. His early speeches are interspersed with philosophic maxims and comments which indicate the wide and profound thought he bestowed upon the subjects of his attention in all their relations; and so marked is this trait as to suggest familiarity with the works of Edmund Burke. These qualities of style and method, however, he gradually relinquished, until his speeches became, for the most part, the naked exposition of his own reasoning undeviatingly directed to the subject before him.

In 1817 he became Secretary of War under Monroe, and retained that post until he entered upon the duties of Vice-President in 1825. During this time his political and economic opinions underwent no change; they were emphatically reiterated whenever occasion offered. He now openly aspired to the Presidency. Though his administration of the War Department received some criticism, mostly due to the warm rivalry of Presidential candidates during the political chaos of Monroe's last term, he had gained ground in popular favor. While it was soon manifest that he could not succeed Monroe, it was equally clear that he would be raised to the second place. But, unknown to the political world, there had been sown the seeds of a difficulty that was to frustrate the great ambition of his life.

He was elected Vice-President by a combination of the Adams and Jackson electors, probably because of his neutrality. But as soon as the effect of Adams's election by the House became apparent, Calhoun joined the opposition. Discerning Jackson's rising star, he sought its auspicious influence. The prospect seemed flattering. He was re-elected with Jackson in 1828. Nevertheless, the catastrophe was close at hand. Soon came the disclosure of the fact, until then kept secret, that as Secretary of War he had favored the proposed censure of Jackson for his proceedings in the Seminole war. This was followed by the disruption of the cabinet, the banishment of Calhoun's adherents, and the plain indication that Van Buren was destined to the Presidential succession.

Another cause of dislike, however, had been working in Jackson's mind. Calhoun had concurred in the Southern hostility to the tariffs of 1824 and 1828: he could not have done otherwise and be countenanced in the South. That course once taken, he labored with all his might to make the cause succeed. Naturally he was regarded as the leader-in-chief. The "South Carolina Exposition," adopted by the legislature of that State in 1828, and the first formal declaration of the doctrine of nullification, was his handiwork. Though couched in rather vague and covert terms, it found no favor with Jackson. Calhoun undoubtedly believed that Jackson would cast his influence against protection; but he utterly mistook Jackson if he imagined that he would tolerate any scheme that savored of disunion. Events now rapidly conspired to put Calhoun hopelessly without the pale of Presidential possibility. The Hayne-Webster debate took place in January, 1830, Hayne being, as every one knew, the spokesman on his side, because Calhoun was not in a position to speak. In April following a banquet in celebration of Jefferson's birthday was held at Washington. It was attended by many leading Democrats, including Jackson and Calhoun. The tenor of the toasts and speeches indicated that the affair had been arranged to promote principally the nullification movement. After the regular speeches, the

President was invited to propose a toast. He did so, and in a manner that left no doubt as to his sentiments on the subject—"The Union: It must be preserved." Calhoun gave the next toast—"The Union: Next to our liberty the most dear: may we all remember that it can only be preserved by respecting the rights of the States and distributing equally the benefit and burthen of the Union."

The die was cast. As a candidate for President, Calhoun was undone; and no one recognized it more clearly than himself. Henceforth he was the political head of the slave interest, acting apart from the two great parties, except as particular objects led him into temporary combinations. He took up the work where the disjointed efforts of Randolph had left it, and pursued it with fanatical energy to his latest day. Politics and personal interests no longer influenced him. He had become a changed man. From the broadest latitudinarianism he had gone to the opposite extreme. Without motive to temporize or dissemble, or occasion to deceive himself, he saw the inevitable result that was to come from the divergent elements then taking undisguised form and force. While he did not devote his labors to cause disunion, he strove in every way to protect and strengthen the institution of slavery and its political power. Yet his course cannot be justly charged to vindictiveness. He was the victim of circumstance. With a wonderfully acute, analytical, and subtly logical mind, it was a necessity with him to carry to the last result the conclusion that his enforced premises required. His manner gradually assumed a cold and distant dignity. His intense, sustained thought, the consciousness of his isolated position, and the perpetual struggle against odds creased and hardened his visage, upon which dwelt the shadow of his thwarted hopes.[1]

On February 12, Clay asked leave to introduce his tariff bill. Having given notice of his purpose the day before, he had a large and eager audience to hear his explanatory speech. He professed two objects—to save the protective system from the destruction designed by the administration in any event, and to allay the South Carolina outbreak, and thus prevent the calamities that might follow it in consequence of the general Southern discontent. "I am anxious," said he, "to find some principle of mutual accommodation, to satisfy, as far as practicable, both parties—to increase the stability of our legislation, and at some distant day—but not too distant—to bring down the rate of duties to the revenue standard for which our opponents have so long contended." This basis was to be one of time. His plan was to reach the revenue standard in a little less than ten years. One-tenth of the excess of duties above twenty *per centum ad*

---

[1] For the less familiar sources of this sketch of Calhoun, see *Life of Silliman*, vol. i. p. 309; Webster's *Works*, vol. v. p. 369; Tyler's *Taney*, p. 185; Kennedy's *Wirt*, vol. ii. p. 161; *Life of Story*, vol. i. p. 426; Quincy's *Figures of the Past*, p. 264; Adams's *Diary*, vol. v. p. 361; vol. vii. p. 447; vol. viii. p. 536; vol. ix. p. 461; Godwin's *Bryant*, vol. i. p. 268; Martineau's *Retrospect of Western Travel*, vol. i. p. 147. "His head was long rather than broad, the ears were placed low upon it, the depth from front to back was very great; his forehead was low, steep, and beetled squarely over the most glorious pair of yellow-brown, shining eyes that seemed to have a light inherent in themselves; they looked steadily out from under bushy eyebrows that made the deep sockets look still more shrunken. He lowered them less than any one I have ever seen; they were steadily bent on the object with which he was engaged; indeed on some people they had an almost mesmeric power. . . . No dignity could be more supreme than Mr. Calhoun's. . . . He always appeared to me rather as a moral and mental abstraction than a politician, and it was impossible, knowing him well, to associate him with mere personal ambition. His theories and his sense of duty alone dominated him."—*Memoir of Jefferson Davis*, pp. 209-211.

valorem was to be removed after September, 1833; one-tenth biennially thereafter until 1841; one-half of the remaining excess the following year; and the residue the next. If in 1842 there should be a surplus of revenue, it could be devoted to internal improvements. The free list was to be somewhat extended, and the credit system, which had always obtained, was to be abolished.[1] In case of war or other emergency, Congress was to be at liberty to lay whatever duties it saw fit. While there could be no absolute guarantee that the scheme would be held inviolate during the proposed period, there was a practical assurance that it would be. "If the measure," he argued, "should be carried by the consent of all parties, we shall have sufficient security; history will faithfully record the transaction; narrate under what circumstances the bill was passed; that it was a pacifying measure; that it was oil poured from the vessel of the Union to restore peace and harmony to the country. When all this is done, what Congress, what legislature, will mar the guarantee? What man who is entitled to deserve the character of an American statesman would stand up in his place and disturb this treaty of peace and amity?" He also contended, to appease the stubborn partisans of protection, that his plan was not the abandonment of that system. It was at most provisional, to allow differences of opinion to be adjusted. After 1842, any plan could be adopted that circumstances and the demands of the people might dictate. The bill did "not touch the power of protection"; on the contrary, the free admission of raw materials distinctly "extended and upheld" it. As reluc-

---

[1] "For eighteen or twenty years, John Jacob Astor had what was actually a free-of-interest loan from the government of over five millions of dollars."—Barrett's *Old Merchants of New York* (first series), p. 82.

tantly as he yielded so much of what he held to be the true method of protection—raising the necessary revenue " from the protected and not from the unprotected articles—it was preferable to the immediate and total destruction of the policy."

Such were the leading ideas of his exposition of the bill. His reasoning thus far was wisely tempered and judicious. But to meet the rebuke that his plan was a surrender to the threats of South Carolina was a more difficult task. His treatment of this phase of the matter partook of forensic ingenuity. Although he pronounced the course of South Carolina "rash, intemperate, and greatly in error," he sought to palliate it on the theory that the State was not really threatening forcible resistance, but was appealing to law. "From one end to the other of this continent," said he, "by acclamation, as it were, nullification has been put down in a manner more effectual than by a thousand armies: by the irresistible force, by the mighty influence of public opinion. Not a voice beyond the single State of South Carolina has been heard in favor of nullification, which she has asserted by her ordinance; and I will say that she must fail in her lawsuit."

His argument against peaceable nullification was brief, and practical rather than Constitutional. It is not possible, he maintained, to devise a system of State legislation that cannot be successfully counteracted by federal legislation. Congress is expressly empowered to pass all laws necessary to carry into effect the powers vested in the government. If the government be administered with prudence and propriety, the responsibility of employing force must rest with the State government. "I am ready," said he, "to give the tribunals and the Executive of the country, whether that Executive has or has not my confidence, the necessary measure of power to execute the laws of the Union. But I would not go a hair's-breadth farther than what was necessary for those purposes." According to the apologetic view he had taken, South Carolina was doing no more than Ohio had done in attempting to tax the branch of the bank in that State, and no more than Virginia had done in attempting to deprive the federal courts of jurisdiction in cases arising under certain lottery laws. Moreover, the 1st of February was passed. South Carolina had practically postponed the operation of the ordinance, and if the question were not at once settled she would further postpone it. It was impossible, for various practical reasons which he recounted, that she should wish to become a separate and independent state. If the existence of the ordinance were a sufficient motive for not passing the bill, she could defeat all legislation by postponing the ordinance from time to time. The condition of South Carolina was only one of the elements that rendered it expedient to resort at that session to some measure to tranquillize the country. He closed with a persuasive appeal.

The motion for leave to introduce the bill was stoutly opposed by several Senators, Webster being the most aggressive and formidable.[1] He did not content himself with merely announcing his disapproval of the bill and then awaiting the opportunity of debate upon it, but on the next day he offered an elaborate set of resolutions declaring against the scheme. Calhoun, on the other hand, at once gave evidence of his partnership in the design to compromise by expressing his entire approbation of the "object"

---

[1] Curtis's *Webster*, vol. i. p. 443; *Clay's Correspondence*, pp. 351, 352.

and "general principles" of the bill. Nor was Jackson averse.[1]

The motion was successful, and the bill was referred to a select committee, of which Clay was made chairman. It was reported on the 19th. Meantime the debate on the revenue collection bill grew more heated. It was in connection with this subject that Calhoun, on the 15th, delivered his notable speech in exposition of the doctrine of nullification. It was immediately answered by Webster, in a speech that, as a legal argument, is superior to his reply to Hayne. Even to those most friendly at the present day to the theory of the utmost rights of the States consistent with the nationality of the Union in purely national concerns, it is remarkable that so fine and strong a mind as Calhoun's should have evolved and advocated with all its powers so impracticable a theory as nullification. Whatever the opinion as to the origin of the leading features of the Constitution, the ultimate question involved in the controversy was simply as to where the power was vested to pronounce upon the constitutionality of laws. From any possible point of view, the doctrine that a State can exercise that power as a finality is to render the Constitution merely the evidence of a provisional acquiescence in a national government that shall cease in and over any State at its own discretion.

During the early years of the Constitution there was diversity of opinion as to the fundamental nature of the national organism—whether it is a dissoluble compact between sovereign States or a perpetually consolidated nationality. This necessarily arose from the extraordinary con-

---

[1] Jackson to Hamilton, February 23, 1833.

ditions that produced it, the divergent purposes that entered into it, and hence the novelty of the political system it created. In the nature of things it could not have been otherwise. Fortunately the question was almost wholly speculative; no actual and general emergency had arisen to compel its practical determination. The subjects of difference were settled as merely political questions. The Virginia and Kentucky resolutions and the proceedings of the Hartford Convention, subsequently cited as authorities, are to be regarded, so far as they may seem to warrant the theory of Constitutional nullification and secession, as little else than *obiter dicta*, inasmuch as there was no real design to accomplish more than an emphatic protest, for political effect, against objectionable acts of the government. The evolution of the principles of the original Democratic party lay in the distinct separation of the functions of State and federal government, giving to each its true sphere and operation—preserving the autonomy of the States, yet maintaining adequate national power and dignity. The gradual growth of the national sentiment is, perhaps, no better illustrated than by the changed use of the word "Union." Until after the civil war it was the common appellation of the United States. It has since assumed a poetic significance, and is mostly employed for sentiment or euphony.

To the last the revenue collection bill encountered bitter opposition. It was branded as the "force bill" and the "bloody bill," and denounced with extreme asperity even after the Compromise was virtually assured and the bill thus rendered hardly more in practical effect than a mere declaration of principle. While little was openly said, the deeper motive of the opposition was plainly insinuated—it was the practical beginning of the struggle to fortify the slave interest. Clay did not speak on the subject. He could not well have voted against the bill, and he withdrew before the vote was taken. The bill was passed by the Senate on the 20th, the day after Clay, from the select committee, reported the compromise bill.

When the proposed Compromise was first announced the manufacturing interests were stricken with consternation. That Clay should propose it confounded them. *Et tu, Brute!* Their representatives hastened to Washington to remonstrate; but on learning the true situation many of them were converted: a half-loaf was better than no bread. When the bill was reported, various amendments to it were proposed, the principal one being to adopt home valuation instead of foreign, which had always prevailed. The importance of this amendment, although not to take effect until 1842, is shown by a remark Clay made years afterward. "Give me," said he, "but the power of fixing the valuation of the goods, and I care little, in comparison, what may be the rate of duties you propose."

The amendment at once provoked violent opposition. It was pronounced unconstitutional, because of the inequality of its effect, goods being cheaper in the Northern than in the Southern markets; and besides this, was the possibility that the duties themselves might be made to enter into the valuation. The obnoxious feature had not formed a part of the original scheme, and Calhoun revolted. Amid great excitement he announced that if it were insisted upon he would not support the bill. Clayton, who was mainly instrumental in proposing the amendment, moved to table the bill. Under the circumstances, if this were done, the bill would have been killed. He was induced to withdraw the motion. After an ineffectual attempt to qualify the amendment, an adjournment was taken. But the contrivers of the amendment remained inexorable. The next day, Calhoun acquiesced, veiling his coercion with the thin pretext that he felt himself "justified in concluding" that no valuation would be adopted that would come in conflict with the Constitution, and that the duties would not form an element of the valuation. This was on the 22d.

The debate proceeded. The Constitutional objection was now raised that a revenue bill could not originate in the Senate; but instead of its operating to obstruct the bill, it hastened its success by prompting a *coup-de-main*. But few days of the session remained. Whatever was done must be done quickly. On the 25th a motion was made in the House by Letcher[1] to strike out all after the enacting clause of the Verplanck bill, which was still under debate, and substitute the Senate bill. None but those favorable to this extraordinary operation had notice of it. Without regard to the astonished protests of the opposition, the design was accomplished. This occurred late in the afternoon of Tuesday. The next day debate was stifled by carrying the previous question. The bill was then passed, 119 to 85. It was at once taken up by the Senate, and on Friday, March 1, passed, 29 to 16. On the preceding Wednesday the House passed the force bill. On Saturday both bills were signed by the President. On the 16th the South Carolina Convention, which had adjourned to that time, repealed the ordinance, but adopted another against the force bill—a harmless fulmination for spectacular effect.

Whatever the opinion concerning the wisdom of the Com-

---

[1] Concerning Letcher, who was one of Clay's chief lieutenants in both compromises, see *Life of Cassius M. Clay*, vol. i. p. 215; Adams's *Diary*, vol. viii. p. 336; Coleman's *Crittenden*, vol. i. p. 182.

promise, the responsibility for it rests mainly upon Clay, not only as the originator of the plan, but as the chief agent in carrying it through. While his principal motive, as he always affirmed, was to preserve all that was possible of the protective system, he was doubtless stimulated by the imposing effect of his action and a desire to prevent Jackson from executing his militant threats against South Carolina. No act of his career called out more signally all his peculiar resources. He labored night and day—pleading, manipulating, bartering, threatening. In the closet, in committee, on the floor, he was the controlling spirit.[1] With the protected interests at stake he had the *matériel* to undermine the plan of the administration. Though the secret history of the transaction is not known in detail, the various means that were successfully used are evidenced by the vote. A more variegated combination of diverse elements was never fused in a legislative act. Every interest, influence, and device that could gain a supporter without impairing the general purpose of the scheme was unhesitatingly resorted to.

The main obstacles that Clay encountered were the efforts of Benton and Webster, the latter giving the original policy of the administration, in regard to nullification, such support as to create the impression that he had permanently abandoned his former party affiliations. He achieved great renown by his speeches on the subject of nullification, his position compelling him to take an uncompromising stand for the nationality of the Union. He, therefore, favored putting the question to the test of arms if necessary rather than yield anything to the menace of nullification and

---

[1] Sargent's *Clay*, p. 144; Garland's *Randolph*, vol. ii. p. 362; *Clay's Correspondence*, p. 352.

secession. He did not favor the Verplanck bill; but had it reached the Senate it is not unlikely that he would have supported it, provided he could have obtained such amendments as would reasonably satisfy the New England interests. He was in a peculiar predicament in regard to the tariff. Having forsaken his early principles through political exigency, he desired to gain all the advantage he could for the interests for which he had practically sacrificed those principles, and yet disclaim all responsibility for protection. He sought to blend the necessary reduction of the revenue with the retention of the utmost protection possible under the circumstances. His chief objections to the Compromise were that a horizontal reduction would prevent the discrimination essential to protection, and that to bind the action of Congress for a long term of years was unwise and unconstitutional.

For years after the Compromise there was much dispute between the principal parties to it as to which of them got the best of the bargain. The truth is that the arrangement afforded a convenient escape for all concerned. Protection, which would otherwise have soon been eradicated, retained a considerable measure of vitality, with the chance of complete restoration; nullification, which had proven odious and impracticable, had nevertheless effected a large part of the actual object at which it was aimed; and the administration had gained a substantial modification of the tariff, and upheld the national theory of the Union and the right of the government to resort to force to maintain it.

From no practical point of view can the Missouri Compromise be justly condemned. Although the reasons that justified it were more imposing in appearance than those which induced the Compromise of 1833, they were not more urgent and important; in reality they were much the same. The time had not arrived to effect by force—and it could be done in no other way—a complete and final settlement of the difference that lay at the bottom of all the sectional controversies. Had the existing tariff system been maintained intact, and force successfully exerted to prevent the secession of South Carolina, the result could have been but temporary. The underlying motives that prompted the action of that State were quite as powerful in all the Southern States. Discontent pervaded the South, and but little would have been required to rally the entire section to the aid of South Carolina, which would have been moved to new efforts by the terrible incentives of humiliation and revenge. At that period the North could not have preserved the Union against the concerted withdrawal of the South.

Critics exceed their prerogative when they condemn by an ideal standard those who partake in such a transaction as this Compromise.[1] The question is not whether this or that man or set of men was theoretically right or wrong, but what was the most practicable expedient to adopt, considering the whole situation — the clashing interests of the sections, the immaturity of the republic, and the untried quality of the Constitution. The imperfect human nature that governs all the affairs of a people demands allowances that critics no less than public men who represent hostile elements and bear the practical responsibilities are bound to make. If they who criticise and carp had been placed in the same situation with those who

---

[1] This presentation of the subject cannot well ignore the comment of Von Holst (*Constitutional and Political History of the United States*, vol. i. p. 505), who, notwithstanding the ability of his work, so often betrays the peevishness and lack of insight characteristic of the idealist and bookman.

shaped events at that perilous juncture, and had employed the logic of their present criticism, their voices would not have been heard above the mutter of the impending storm.

Precisely two months before he offered the compromise bill, Clay introduced the land bill which had failed at the preceding session. It formed a part of his general plan for dealing with the financial situation mainly caused by the tariff. After a vigorous debate the bill was narrowly passed by the Senate. It was finally passed by the House also, but with amendments, which were not concurred in by the Senate until just before the close of the session. The President did not sign it, but retained it until the beginning of the next session, when he returned it with his veto, and thus furnished one of the topics that made the Twenty-third Congress memorable.

CHAPTER VI

Clay and Jackson make Northern Tours—The Removal of the Deposits—Tactics of the Whigs in the Senate—Clay's Resolutions Censuring the President and the Secretary of the Treasury—The Debate—The Anti-Bank Resolutions of the House—The Distress Petitions—Jackson's Protest against the Censure and the Subsequent Proceedings—Taney's Nomination for Secretary of the Treasury Rejected—Other Phases of the Bank Struggle—Coinage Legislation—The Land Bill—The Deposits Bill—The French Spoliations—The Cherokee Indians—The Four Years Law and the Spoils System

THE session over, Clay returned to Ashland and resumed his rural pursuits. He had planned to make an extensive tour through Canada and the Northern States, intending to set out in July. Part of this plan, however, he relinquished. In October he went to Baltimore, and thence northward, visiting various points in New England and New York.[1] He also stopped at several cities on his way to Washington. The tour was a continuous ovation, flattering to his pride and stimulating to his purpose to renew the Whig war against the administration.

In the summer, Jackson had preceded him over much the same ground and amid similar demonstrations,[2] which like-

---

[1] Adams's *Diary*, vol. ix. pp. 25, 43; *Niles's Register*, vol. xlv. p. 176; *Clay's Correspondence*, p. 371.

[2] When Jackson visited New England on this tour, Harvard University conferred upon him the degree of LL.D., which excited the deepest contempt of Adams, who was a member of the Board of Overseers.—Adams's *Diary*, vol. viii. p. 576. " A few years ago one of the universities conferred the honorary degree of LL.D. on Henry Clay . . . and *Dr.* Clay, *Doctor*

wise encouraged him to carry out the policy upon which he was resolved. About the time that Clay started north, Jackson performed the culminating act of his design to destroy the bank—the removal of the government deposits.[1] An inkling of the great struggle that was soon to follow was given by Clay in a note, October 14, declining a public dinner which was proposed to be held in his honor at Philadelphia. "The time has arrived," he wrote, "which I long ago apprehended, when our greatest exertions are necessary to maintain the free institutions inherited from our ancestors. Yes, gentlemen, disguise is useless. The time is come when we must decide whether the Constitution, the laws, and the checks which they have respectively provided, shall prevail, or the will of one man shall have uncontrolled sway. In the settlement of that question I shall be found where I have ever been."

Congress convened December 2. Ten years of increasing political agitation had made Congress the centre of popular interest, with the effect of bringing into both Houses an unwonted number of men of marked talent and ability.[2] The proceedings, particularly of the Senate, where the Whigs still had a majority, were watched like a gladi-

---

Clay was said and sung a million of times by noisy fools who affected much pride in remembering Doctor Franklin as one of their countrymen—and who obtained the title in the same way that it was conferred on Mr. Clay, and on the same principles. Well—this degree has been bestowed on Andrew Jackson, and it is pretty near 'treason' to call *him Doctor*. . . . Mr. Clay did not present himself to receive the degree, as General Jackson did."—*Niles's Register*, vol. xliv. p. 323.

[1] Van Buren accompanied Jackson on this tour, and was induced to change his opinion in regard to the removal of the deposits. He had previously been adverse to it.—*Reminiscences of J. A. Hamilton*, p. 258.

[2] "Of the members of this Congress five have been President; five Vice-President; eight Secretary of State; twenty-five Governor of a State; besides other men of note."—Parton's *Jackson*, vol. iii. p. 537.

Ch. VI.] JACKSON'S PURPOSE TO RUIN THE BANK 217

atorial combat.[1] Undaunted by defeat and the apparent odds against them, Clay and the Whig leaders determined to persist in the policy of sustaining the bank. The removal of the deposits was now the gage of battle. Thus began the famous "Panic Session."

The action of the President, through the Secretary of the Treasury, in withholding further deposits of the public moneys from the bank and its branches, was prompted by no sudden impulse. It was a very natural stroke in Jackson's crusade against the institution, which he flatly declared in his message to Congress was "converted into a permanent electioneering engine." It was hardly to be expected, in view of all which had preceded, that he would spare so efficient a means to hasten and complete its destruction. Sumner, his ablest biographer, asserts, after the manner of most of those who have since written on the subject, that "Jackson's animosity towards the bank, in the autumn of 1832, had gathered the intensity and bulldog ferocity which he always felt for an enemy engaged in active resistance." Not satisfied with this energetic metaphor, the same writer also ascribes Jackson's procedure to the "impulse of the passions which animate the Indian on the war-path." Such characterizations are not calculated to promote a just and complete view of the matter; they resemble the splenetic exaggerations of Von Holst, and display somewhat the same temper of mind as such writers impute to Jackson. Starting from the proposition that the scheme of the bank was fundamentally wrong, by reason of its partnership of public with private interests, which left

---

[1] It was during this period that James Brooks introduced the practice of writing regular letters from Washington to distant newspapers. His correspondence was regarded as a revelation in journalism.

the institution open to political influences, it follows that to prevent the recharter on that basis was right. If Jackson acted like a bulldog or an Indian in the subsequent contest, the bank and its champions were hardly less savage and inconsiderate of the business interests of the country. The bank had entered into an alliance, offensive and defensive, with the Whig party, and was using its prodigious power to that end. Refusing to compromise upon a modified plan of recharter, the allies prematurely projected the issue into a Presidential election as a means of party success. The result proving disastrous, they sought to coerce a change of popular opinion by furthering a financial stringency, which would be charged to the removal of the deposits, and which in truth would alone tend to some extent to produce that result. Certainly the bank would not be likely to mitigate the consequences when it was supposed that great political advantages could under the circumstances be derived from them. While these considerations, too often lost sight of, do not lessen any just criticism of Jackson, they will aid in apportioning the blame between him and the bank party.

The authority for the removal was contained in this provision of the charter: "The deposits . . . shall be made in said bank or branches thereof, unless the Secretary of the Treasury at any time otherwise order and direct; in which case the Secretary of the Treasury shall immediately lay before Congress, if in session, and if not, immediately at the commencement of the next session, the reason for such order or direction." The bank of course had not been unmindful of the danger in which it stood from this provision. Soon after Jackson's re-election it was rumored that he meditated removing the deposits. Another investigation by a committee of the House took place, resulting as usual in a majority and minority report. The latter report, however, did not recommend the removal of the deposits; it only brought to view some bad practices of the bank, yet nothing of sufficient importance to show that the bank was insolvent, and that the deposits were insecure. Indeed, it may be conceded, in the full light of subsequent information, that at this period the bank was solvent, and such was the general opinion without regard to party lines. On the heels of these reports, two days before Jackson was inaugurated, a resolution was adopted by the House, by a large majority, declaring that the deposits might be safely continued in the bank. This was done confessedly to stay the hands of the President.

But his purpose was not so easily frustrated. The House resolution was the least of the difficulties he encountered. He found himself in the same position in which he was placed when he first announced his opposition to renewing the charter—the majority of his party, so far as they had any opinion on the subject, as well as the majority of his immediate advisers, were opposed to the plan. To remove the deposits was viewed as an unnecessary and dangerous proceeding. But when at length he determined that it should be done, opposition, even in his own party, did not deter him. Despite all evidence that had been adduced, he believed that the bank was unsound and was using every means, including the public moneys on deposit with it, to perpetuate its existence contrary to the expressed will of the people. It must not be forgotten that tangible evidence of the operations of the bank that were politically most effective is not attainable. The motives that governed its officers in making loans and discounting paper were generally inscrutable. But the slightest insight into financial affairs suggests not only the possibility but the practical certainty that at this juncture at least the business of the bank was conducted with a view to its political interests, and hence that its favors were bestowed only upon its tried friends and those who became its friends through the accommodations they received. Undoubtedly considerations of this kind controlled Jackson's decision more than any fears he may have entertained concerning the safety of the public funds. At all events, having made up his mind to remove them, he forthwith proceeded to execute his purpose. But he was now met by obstacles more difficult to surmount than adverse counsels. McLane, Secretary of the Treasury, refused to issue the necessary order. He was promptly transferred to the State Department to take the place of Livingston, who was made Minister to France. Duane, of Philadelphia, was then appointed Secretary of the Treasury. He had thus far been a warm supporter of the President in his opposition to the renewal of the charter. It was therefore assumed, without inquiry, as it seems, that he would be willing to make the desired order; but the President was immediately surprised and chagrined to find himself mistaken in the new Secretary. Without delay or equivocation Duane refused to make the order; and no argument or persuasion could shake his resolution. And not only did he refuse to make the order, but he also refused to resign his place voluntarily. He preferred political martyrdom for the good of the cause he had espoused. He was then summarily dismissed, and he retired denouncing the President and the "irresponsible cabal," as he charged, under whose influence the President acted. Taney, the Attorney-General, was at once appointed in his stead. This time no mistake was made. The order was issued with alacrity. In fact, Taney had from the first strongly advocated the measure and contributed materially to strengthening the President's purpose.¹

The order was issued September 26. It did not affect existing deposits, which amounted to nearly ten millions; they were left to be drawn in the usual course of disbursement, and after a lapse of fifteen months there still remained a balance with the bank of about four millions. The order related exclusively to moneys to be henceforth collected, and these were to be deposited with specified State banks. The bank at once began to curtail its discounts and to increase its clamor. The Whig press furiously joined the cry, assailing Jackson with increased license and rancor. The State banks were compelled to curtail, while the "pet banks" were not as yet able to relieve the pressure. The result was a serious disturbance of business, with the usual incidents of general financial fright. Such in brief was the situation at the opening of the "Panic Session."

Although Benton had not been consulted by the President as to the policy of removing the deposits, it received his exuberant approval. "I felt," he says, "an emotion of the moral sublime at beholding such an instance of civic heroism." As before, he took command of the anti-bank forces in Congress. December 5, he submitted a resolution calling on the Secretary of the Treasury for a statement of the public funds in the bank at the end of each month during the whole period. On the 10th the resolution was amended on Clay's motion so as to call also for detailed information touching the State banks selected as the new

¹ The internal history of the measure is given in detail by Amos Kendall in his *Autobiography*, p. 374 *et seq.* For Van Buren's estimate of Taney, see his *Political Parties in the United States*, p. 364.

depositories. On the same day, Clay offered a resolution requesting the President to inform the Senate whether a certain paper, purporting to have been read by him at the cabinet meeting in September, was genuine, and if so that a copy of it be laid before the Senate. The paper had been published for months. It had been formally prepared by Taney, according to the President's views, and was little more than an animated restatement of the considerations which had already been expressed in his official message, together with certain facts which had been brought out in the "investigations," showing the political activity and mismanagement of the bank. It closed with an assumption of personal responsibility for the proposed act and its consequences. The resolution met with the criticism that the Senate had no right to demand the paper; that it was not an official document, but precisely the same as a speech made by the President at a cabinet meeting. Clay virtually admitted that if the paper had not been published the Senate would have no right to it, but as it had been, the case was altered —a distinction without a difference. The resolution was adopted, Calhoun and his friends voting with the majority.

The imprudence of this move immediately appeared. The President responded in a curt message declining to comply with the request. And there is no doubt that he was entirely justified in doing so. The publication of the paper presented merely a question of propriety. It was the President's mode of making public the motives for doing an act that was violently assailed. It was one of the symptoms of the intense political strife—and not materially different in character from the various reports and communications issued by the bank for political effect. That he would refuse to comply with the resolution must have been foreseen, and that the advantage of the affair would lie with him ought to have been.[1]

For several days after this incident the time of the Senate was mostly given to organizing the standing committees and to other preliminary and routine business. Clay was elected to but one committee—Public Lands—and was not made chairman of that. This was undoubtedly from choice, so that his functions of leadership might not be interfered with. He was almost invariably present during the sessions of the Senate, and participated in the discussion of nearly every question of any importance that arose. His extensive experience usually gave controlling weight to his views when the subjects were not political. When politics was concerned his opinions were practically law to his side.

Meantime he was perfecting his preparations for the main assault. On the 18th he offered resolutions calling on the Secretary of the Treasury for further specified information in regard to the deposits question. They were amended next day on Benton's motion, so as to call for additional facts. In explaining his reasons for submitting the resolutions, Clay severely criticised Taney, who, he alleged, had erroneously cited Crawford as an authority for controlling the deposits. But especial interest was given the speech by his statement of his past relations with the bank. It had been charged that he had a pecuniary interest in supporting the bank. He said that he had not subscribed for any of the stock when the bank was created, and did not own any until a few years afterward, when five shares were purchased for him and he was made a director without consultation. He paid for the shares, but soon afterward ceased

---

[1] Adams's *Diary*, vol. ix. p. 51.

to be a director and sold his stock. Since then he had not owned a single share. At one period he had acted as counsel for the bank in a large amount of litigation, and had received the usual compensation, and no more. He had also owed the bank in consequence of the failure of a friend whose paper he had endorsed. But he had paid the debt and had not acted as counsel for the bank during the previous eight years.

At the beginning of the session the President nominated the five government directors of the bank as provided by the charter. Four of them had already served a year, and being friendly to the administration had brought to light some facts showing misconduct on the part of the bank; and these facts had been used in the minority report of the investigating committee and in the paper read by the President to his cabinet. The four nominees were immediately rejected. The President then replied in a message arguing the propriety of the nominations and returning the names. The message and renominations were referred to the Finance Committee. The report was adverse and grounded on the absolute right of the Senate to reject all nominations in its discretion without giving reasons. The report was adopted. The debates, having taken place in executive session, were not published; but the action of the Senate heightened the animosity of the contending parties.

December 26, Clay opened the great debate of the session in the presence of a crowded and eager audience. The speech was in support of two resolutions which he submitted at the outset. They were as follows:

"*Resolved*, That by dismissing the late Secretary of the Treasury because he would not, contrary to his sense of his own duty, remove the money of the United States on deposit with the Bank of the United States and its branches, in conformity with the President's opinion; and by appointing his successor to effect such removal, which has been done, the President has assumed the exercise of a power over the Treasury of the United States not granted to him by the Constitution and laws, and dangerous to the liberties of the people.

"*Resolved*, That the reasons assigned by the Secretary of the Treasury for the removal of the money of the United States deposited in the Bank of the United States and its branches, communicated to Congress on the 3d of December, 1833, are unsatisfactory and insufficient."

"We are in the midst of a revolution," he began, "hitherto bloodless, but rapidly tending toward a total change of the pure republican character of our government, and to the concentration of all power in the hands of one man. The powers of Congress are paralyzed, except when exerted in conformity with his will, by frequent and extraordinary exercise of the Executive veto, not anticipated by the founders of our Constitution and not practised by any of the predecessors of the present Chief Magistrate. And to cramp them still more, a new expedient is springing into use, of withholding altogether bills which have received the sanction of both houses of Congress, thereby cutting off all opportunity of passing them, even if after their return the members should be unanimous in their favor. The Constitutional participation of the Senate in the appointing power is virtually abolished by the constant use of the power of removal from office without any known cause, and by the appointment of the same individual to the same office after his rejection by the Senate. . . .

"The judiciary has not been exempt from the prevailing

rage for innovation. Decisions of the tribunals, deliberately pronounced, have been contemptuously disregarded, and the sanctity of numerous treaties openly violated. Our Indian relations, coeval with the existence of the government and recognized and established by numerous laws and treaties, have been subverted and the rights of the helpless and unfortunate aborigines trampled in the dust, and they are brought under subjection to unknown laws, in which they have no voice, promulgated in an unknown language. The most extensive and valuable public domain that ever fell to the lot of one nation is threatened with total sacrifice. The general currency of the country—the life-blood of all business—is in the most imminent danger of universal disorder and confusion. The power of internal improvement lies crushed beneath the veto. The system of protection to American industry was snatched from impending destruction at the last session; but we are now coolly told by the Secretary of the Treasury, without a blush, 'that it is understood to be conceded on all hands that a tariff for protection merely is to be finally abandoned.' By the 3d of March, 1837, if the progress of innovation continues, there will be scarcely a vestige remaining of the government and its policy as they existed prior to the 3d of March, 1829. In a term of eight years, a little more than equal to that which was required to establish our liberties, the government will have been transformed into an elective monarchy — the worst of all forms of government."

This exordium set the key of the entire performance. The first step of the argument, which was graphically presented, was that the removal of the deposits was not the independent act of the Secretary of the Treasury, but was done at the dictation of the President. While it was true that the primary cause of the measure was the will of the President, the fact afforded no foundation for the use Clay sought to make of it. He maintained that the office of the Secretary of the Treasury was wholly independent of the President; that the Treasury, therefore, was not one of the Executive Departments over which the President had control, and further, that the President's Constitutional duty "to take care that the laws be faithfully executed" had no application to the subject, because that clause means nothing more nor less than that if resistance is made to the laws he shall take care that the resistance cease—a construction plainly too restricted. He asserted that the bank and the President were likewise independent of each other, and that the powers possessed by the President in relation to the institution were only to nominate the government directors and to take proceedings to annul the charter if he apprehended that it had been violated. This consideration, however, did not aid his argument, which was thus far radically unsound. Had it been made in a suit to test the validity of the order removing the deposits it would not have been even plausible. He apparently lost sight of three things absolutely conclusive against him: that the President had unquestionable authority to dismiss Duane; that Duane's successor had express power to remove the deposits, and that it was his actual order that was issued; and that the law does not consider the motives that lead to the exercise of a legal power.

He also argued that the removal of the deposits in accordance with the will of the President was practically a union in his hands of the sword and the purse, the possibility of Executive encroachment against which Patrick Henry had inveighed in opposing the adoption of the Constitution; and he used more neatly than appositely the familiar anecdote of Julius Cæsar in seizing the treasury of Rome from Metellus, the tribune. But here also he was in palpable error. By the removal of the deposits the President had asserted and acquired no more control over the use and expenditure of the public moneys than he possessed before, which was solely to approve or disapprove legislation appropriating them.

But if Clay had travelled beyond the limits of solid argument, the President had to some extent done likewise in some of the reasons declared by him in his paper. "The responsibility," said he, "has been assumed, after the most mature and deliberate reflection, as necessary to preserve the morals of the people, the freedom of the press, and the purity of the elective franchise." Clay pungently asked whence the President derived his functions as public guardian. The statement was induced by the President's not unfounded belief that the bank was using the government deposits to win supporters in order to procure a renewal of the charter. It nevertheless laid him open to the criticism that he was assuming an unwarranted paternalism over the people, and this gave some color to the charge that, whether or not he had violated the letter of the Constitution and the laws, he had violated their spirit. However, had the Secretary of the Treasury removed the deposits contrary to the will of the President and been dismissed in consequence, and had they then been restored by the President's dictation, Clay would have found the task of defending those acts far more easy and congenial.

The first part of the speech thus outlined was delivered on Thursday. The Senate then adjourned to the following Monday, when Clay resumed. He concluded on the next day. On resuming he proceeded to examine the legal power of the Secretary over the deposits. The Secretary asserted the power to be absolute and unconditional. This Clay denied, using the same line of argument that he had previously employed. He failed utterly to demonstrate that the provision of the charter under which the removal was made did not authorize it. That the condition of the bank was not such as to make the removal necessary as a prudential measure did not in the least affect the naked question of legal power. The language of the charter was too plain to call for any extrinsic considerations by way of construction or interpretation. Nor did the act of the Secretary, as Clay maintained, interfere with the power of Congress to pass other laws to regulate the custody of the deposits or even to restore them to the bank.

He then considered at length the various reasons presented by the Secretary in his report as justifying the removal. They were substantially the same as those contained in the President's paper. This was the strongest part of the speech, some of the strictures being entirely just. Though it was ineffectual as an argument against the legality of the removal, it was a spirited and forcible presentation of the case against the expediency of it, and as such was not improved upon during the debate.

He concluded by reviewing the manner in which the Secretary had exercised his power over the deposits. He asserted that in selecting the new depositories the Secretary had unfairly discriminated in favor of banks at the Atlantic seaports, which would thus receive most of the public moneys; and, further, that these banks had been chosen without adequate information as to their financial condition. Moreover, he argued that inasmuch as there was a law prohibiting the Secretary from entering into any contracts except by special authority, this law had been violated in making the new depositories, for the reason that in so doing he had necessarily made contracts with those banks. He denied that the power to remove *from* implied the power to designate the places *to* which the deposits should be removed, a contention too clearly erroneous to require any argument to refute it. It may be that in some of the details of the new arrangement the Secretary had exceeded his strict legal authority; but this did not militate against the validity of the main act nor prevent Congress from making any laws it deemed advisable to protect the public funds. Clay closed in the same strain as he began.

"The eyes and the hopes of the American people are anxiously turned to Congress. They feel that they have been deceived and insulted, their confidence abused, their interests betrayed, and their liberties in danger. They see a rapid and alarming concentration of all power in one man's hands. They see that by the exercise of the positive authority of the Executive, and his negative power exerted over Congress, the will of one man prevails and governs the republic. The question is no longer what laws will Congress pass, but what will the Executive not veto. The President, and not Congress, is addressed for legislative action. . . . We behold the usual incidents of approaching tyranny. The land is filled with spies and informers, and detraction and denunciation are the orders of the day. People, especially official incumbents in this place, no longer dare speak in tones of manly freedom, but in the cautious whispers of trembling slaves. The premonitory symptoms of despotism are upon us; and if Congress do not apply an instantaneous and effective remedy the fatal collapse will soon come on, and we shall die, ignobly die! base, mean, and abject slaves—the scorn and contempt of mankind—unpitied, unwept, and unmourned!"

The speech was received by the Whigs with unbounded approval and admiration. The effect upon Jackson was, of course, the extreme reverse.[1] "Oh!" he exclaimed, upon reading it, "if I live to get these robes of office off me, I will bring the rascal to dear account!" To those who heard the speech Clay fully sustained his oratorical reputation.[2] Many passages were pronounced with that magnetic effect which always made the more animated parts of his speeches so striking to his listeners. The applause was so frequent that, after he had finished, the Vice-President announced that upon any further manifestations of the kind the galleries would be cleared.

It is unnecessary to trace the course of the prolonged debate that ensued. Benton followed Clay, completely answering his legal argument and presenting the anti-bank side of the question with his usual thoroughness and force. Calhoun continued in the alliance he had formed at the preceding session, and gave Clay earnest co-operation. Webster resumed his former affiliations and renewed his powerful support of the bank. He spoke many times on various phases of the controversy and wrote the elaborate report of the Finance Committee approving the second resolution.[3]

---

[1] "The action of the Senate . . . was a fearful shock to Jackson's strong nervous system. It produced more than anger. This word faintly conveys the idea."—Smith's *Cass*, p. 284.

[2] A few days after Clay's speech, and perhaps somewhat influenced by it, Judge Story wrote: "I seem almost, while I write, to be in a dream, and to be called back to the last days of the Roman Republic, when the people shouted for Cæsar, and liberty itself expired with the dark but prophetic words of Cicero."—*Life and Letters of Story*, vol. ii. p. 154.

[3] He also proposed a bill to continue the charter of the bank for six years under certain limitations; but it was not acceptable to either party

Most of the Senators took an active part in the debate, which continued until March 28. It was closed by Clay, who began his speech by saying: "It was just three months yesterday since I opened the debate in the Senate which is now drawing to a close. The period which has since elapsed is long enough for a vessel to have passed the Cape of Good Hope or to have made a return voyage from Europe. It is the longest period which has been occupied in a single debate since the organization of the government." The second resolution was adopted in its original form. The first was not entirely acceptable to Calhoun, Webster, and others, who could not deny that the President had the power to remove Duane; they held that he had abused, but not usurped, the power of removal. The resolution was accordingly modified so as to read: "*Resolved*, That the President, in the late executive proceedings in relation to the public revenue, has assumed upon himself authority and power not conferred by the Constitution and the laws, but in derogation of both." In this form it was adopted.

During this time the House had not been inactive toward the subject. There the administration had a majority, by which to counteract, to some extent, the more imposing operations of the Senate. After a long discussion the report of the Secretary of the Treasury in regard to the deposits was referred to the Committee on Ways and Means, of which James K. Polk was chairman. March 3, the committee reported. The majority sustained the administration on all

---

and nothing came of it. Sumner wrote from Washington, March 3, 1834: "Webster is doing the labor in court which should have been done out of court. In fact, politics has entirely swamped his whole time and talents. All here declare that he has neglected his cases this term in a remarkable manner."—Pierce's *Sumner*, vol. i. p. 136.

points and proposed four resolutions: that the bank ought not to be rechartered; that the deposits ought not to be restored to the bank; that the State banks ought to be continued as the depositories, under a law prescribing the mode and terms of their selection and the securities to be taken; and that a committee be appointed to ascertain the causes of the commercial depression, and particularly whether the bank had furthered it. Discussion of the resolutions was twice postponed, probably for the Senate to conclude its proceedings on Clay's resolutions. The debate then began and continued vigorously until April 4, when the previous question was ordered and the resolutions were adopted.

That the President would take official notice of the Senate's censure was not generally expected; but it was soon understood that he would not remain silent. That there was no precedent to guide him was regarded as not likely to deter him more than it ever had in any of his undertakings. While his counter-stroke was preparing, and after the formal debate on the removal of the deposits had ceased in both houses, another phase of the proceedings in relation to the subject continued unabated. From the beginning of the session to its close memorials and petitions were presented almost daily, picturing in the most sombre hues the calamity and distress which had befallen the country as the result of removing the deposits, and praying their restoration. They were met by others of contrary character, but they were more numerous and were presented with more display.[1]

In these proceedings Clay was very active. He spoke often, using the memorials he presented as the subjects of a variety of comment. On one occasion he endeavored to

---

[1] See Benton's *Thirty Years' View*, vol. i. p. 421.

affix the name "Tory" to the Democratic party, but it made no progress; on another he made an appeal to the Vice-President to intercede with Jackson to rescue the country from the pitiable condition which he pathetically described. In some quarters this ingenious harangue was taken more seriously than it was by Van Buren. "As Clay closed his eloquent philippic, Van Buren called a Senator to the chair and went straight across the chamber to Clay's seat. The tall Kentuckian stared at the 'Little Magician' while the perturbed spectators awaited the result with undisguised anxiety. Van Buren bowed gracefully to Clay and said: 'Mr. Senator, allow me to be indebted to you for another pinch of your aromatic maccoboy.' Clay waved his hand towards the gold snuff-box on his desk and took his seat, while Van Buren took a deliberate pinch and leisurely returned to the Vice-President's chair."[1] Charles Sumner was present on one of these occasions when Clay spoke. "His eloquence," wrote Sumner, "was splendid and thrilling. Without notes or papers of any kind, he seemed to surrender himself entirely to the guidance of his feelings. He showed *feeling;* to which, of course, his audience responded. There was not one there whose blood did not flow quickly and pulse throb quickly as he listened. He delivered a violent attack upon Jackson and a vehement exhortation to the people to continue their memorials and remonstrances. His language, without being choice, is strong; but it is his manner, or what Demosthenes called *action— action*—ACTION—which makes him so powerful. The opposition have now a majority of members in the Senate and much the heaviest weight of talents. Van Buren sits

---

[1] Stanton's *Random Recollections*, p. 206.

like a martyr under the torrents of abuse that are poured upon his masters and followers."[1]

There was an organized effort by the friends of the bank throughout the country to create excitement and alarm, and to bring about public meetings at which inflammatory speeches were made and the distress petitions were circulated and signed. In many cases these petitions were taken to Washington by large delegations that besieged the White House and the halls of Congress. The effort was successful. What would have been at most but a short financial flurry was thus aggravated to a severe panic and depression disastrous to many business interests and harmful to all.

In the face of the facts, conceding that the policy of the administration was wrong, the subsequent action of the bank in intensifying the financial distress was worse. Jackson should at least be acquitted of any design to cripple commerce and finance for political effect.

His reply to the resolutions of censure came April 17, in the form of a message to the Senate. It was a well-constructed document, admirable in temper and style. He challenged the propriety of the censure, because it was not a joint resolution of both houses, and asserted no legislative powers and proposed no legislative action. He maintained that it was unconstitutional, because it was virtually an attempt to impeach him by a majority of less than two-thirds of the Senate, without observing any of the requirements in impeachment proceedings, and without contemplating any of the consequences of a regular impeachment. He adverted caustically to the modification of the resolution

---

[1] Pierce's *Sumner*, vol. i. p. 137.

originally introduced, in order that it could obtain a majority of the Senate. He then argued. that the Treasury Department was an Executive Department, and therefore under his supervision, and also that he had unrestricted power to remove cabinet officers. He quoted resolutions adopted by the legislatures of Maine, New Jersey, and Ohio approving the proceedings that effected the removal of the deposits. This was done for the moral effect of showing that if four Senators from those States who had voted for the censure had complied with those resolutions they would not have been adopted, although he was careful to disclaim any implication that Senators could be bound by such instructions. He criticised the tendency of the doctrines asserted by the Senate, and formally protested against the right of the Senate to adopt the resolutions. He closed with an eloquent passage appealing to his personal history and public services as a vindication from any imputation against the purity of his motives and purposes. He requested that the "message and protest" be entered on the journal of the Senate.

As soon as it was read it met with violent opposition. Poindexter moved that it be not received. One paragraph of his remarks in making the motion will illustrate the acrimony that the protest instantly aroused. "This is no message," said he; "it is merely a paper signed by Andrew Jackson; and much more dangerous in its tendency than the same man sent here in 1819, and which the Senate kicked out-of-doors. Then he held the military power only; now he holds both the civil and the military. This is a measure calculated to produce no general good. It is merely an attack on this body. It will make a good article for a certain official journal; but it is unfit for the serious consideration of the Senate. I would spurn it from the Senate. It is an attempt to use the Senate as the medium through which to assail itself—this body which stands as a barrier between the people and the encroachments of Executive power—upon which liberty may repose without danger to the remotest posterity. Destroy this branch, and with the aid of the Blue Book no limit can be set to the extent of Executive power. It is a most miserable attempt to sustain that power. But it is nothing more than what the Executive has said in his private chamber and what appears daily in the columns of the Executive journal itself."

He was followed by two other Senators who spoke in the same temper. Benton then took the floor, speaking at considerable length and confessedly after much deliberation: he was manifestly prepared for what had taken place. His main object was to announce the intention to move to expunge from the journal the resolutions of censure and to persevere in that purpose until it was accomplished. In replying to the motion not to receive the protest he used one argument that was an effective answer. "The President," said he, "in the conclusion of his message has respectfully requested that his defence might be entered upon the journal of the Senate—upon the same journal that contains the record of his conviction. Will they refuse this act of sheer justice and common decency? Will they go further, and not only refuse to place it on the journal, but refuse even to suffer it to remain in the Senate? Will Senators exhaust their minds, and their bodies also, in loading this very communication with epithets, and then say it shall not be received? Will they receive memorials, resolutions, essays, from all that choose to abuse the President, and not receive a word from him?" After some further discussion carried on with the same asperity the Senate adjourned on motion of Leigh, who said: "I cannot now discuss this question without giving utterance to feelings of passion which would be thought by others unbecoming the occasion and my station—feelings which I now feel boiling in my bosom."[1]

The motion to reject was formulated in a series of resolutions declaring that the protest was not authorized by the Constitution; that it was calculated to destroy the independence of the Senate and degrade it in public opinion; and that it be not received. Subsequently a different set was substituted at Clay's request. The language of the preliminary resolutions was materially modified, though the purport was similar; but the last was radically changed, being made to read, "that the aforesaid protest is a breach of the privileges of the Senate, and that it be not entered on the journal." Benton's criticism had taken effect.

Though severe and exciting, the previous debate had been conducted with dignity. But the sequel, which the protest provoked, raged with a violence of feeling and invective then unparalleled in the proceedings of Congress. The Whigs were exasperated beyond restraint. In their eyes the proceedings by which the deposits were removed were

---

[1] On the next day Leigh made his speech; but the delay did not subdue his feelings. Here are some of his remarks: "He has a presumption which no mortal man has ever before been cursed with, which no monarch since the days of King Henry the Eighth ever claimed before. . . . I suppose that never has a hero, in any age, obtained such a mass of military renown from a single victory as the President has received for that [New Orleans]; and I venture to say that I will find five hundred brigadier-generals in the Revolution of France who have equally distinguished themselves. As to the President's gray hairs, on which he draws inspirations of heavenly blessings, I know him too well to believe that the frosts of age have quenched the boilings in his bosom. He rather reminds me of Mount Ætna, whose summit is capped with eternal snow, but which is always vomiting forth its liquid fire."

moderate assertions of Executive power when compared with the doctrines of the protest. Had Jackson threatened to disperse the Senate at the point of the bayonet, he would hardly have been assailed with more vehemence and stigmatized less as a usurper and tyrant. Legal argument now played but a secondary part; denunciation, crimination, and recrimination characterized the debate, from the furious tirade to the studied philippic, for Jackson was defended with the same vigor and license exhibited by his assailants. No theatrical performances were ever attended with more excited interest. Spectators came from afar to witness the proceedings, and no one followed them with more acute attention than did Jackson himself, although, of course, he did not visit the chamber. "Nothing escaped him," says Parton; "no matter to how late an hour of the night the debates were protracted, he never went to sleep till Major Lewis or Major Donelson came from the Capitol and told him what had been said and done there."

The debate continued until May 7, when the resolutions were adopted. But Calhoun, whose hostility to Jackson was even more rabid than Clay's, was not content with merely refusing to enter the protest on the journal. He was unwilling to relinquish the original proposition not to receive it. He therefore submitted two additional resolutions—that the President had no right to protest to the Senate against any of its proceedings, and that the protest be not received. The first was adopted, but the latter failed, receiving but seven votes.

In opening his speech on the resolutions of censure, Clay made a statement that now seems an exaggeration. "It is not," said he, "among the least unfortunate symptoms of the times that a large portion of the good and enlightened men of all parties are yielding to sentiments of despondency. There is, unhappily, a feeling of distrust and insecurity pervading the community. Many of our best citizens entertain serious apprehensions that our Union and our institutions are destined to a speedy overthrow." The statement contained some truth; but the apprehensions were confined to the Whig party, which shared the opinions of its leaders in Congress, that Jackson's conduct toward the bank and the Senate was autocratic and unconstitutional. From this the conclusion that our institutions were in danger was a natural consequence. At that period the people were accustomed to hearing or holding such sentiments. Very many remembered with sharp distinctness when George III. reigned over the colonies. Hence to those who opposed it every departure from familiar conditions and practices was sufficient to invoke the spectres of monarchy and subverted liberty. The controversies over the Alien and Sedition laws, the embargo, the admission of Missouri, and nullification had kept keenly alive the fear of disunion and its possible consequences. That Jackson's bold and novel doctrines and methods should excite genuine alarm in many intelligent and able minds made sensitive by intense party feeling is not surprising therefore, however unfounded the cause may now appear to have been. To reprimand the Senate as he did was entirely characteristic of the arbitrary independence with which he always acted. Certainly his right to protest was quite as clear as the right of the Senate to censure. But undoubtedly the safer judgment upon the whole affair is that strict propriety would have been better observed had the Senate and the President both kept within their ordinary and acknowledged spheres of action. Nevertheless, this is one of the cases where criticism is futile except to disclose the topography of the field of political battle. Under the circumstances battle was inevitable; and the character of the combatants made it equally certain that no obstacles of mere form would hinder their operations. Whatever differences of opinion may exist as to any feature or tendency of the strife, there is one overshadowing agreement — neither party harbored a sinister design against the institutions or the liberties of the country.

The session was drawing to a close. Comparatively little of the time had been devoted to general legislation. But notwithstanding all that had taken place in connection with the absorbing deposits question, the struggle was not yet entirely over. Early in the session the President had sent a short but sharp message assailing the bank for its refusal to surrender to the control of the War Department the pension fund and the books and papers connected with it. He desired to terminate every financial relation between the bank and the government. The direct question involved was merely a legal one arising under a special statute. Both parties seemed unmindful in all the proceedings where the bank was concerned that the appropriate place to determine questions of legal right was in the courts. In the Senate the message was referred to the Judiciary Committee, which at length reported in favor of the bank. After the action on the protest this matter came up for discussion, and resolutions sustaining the bank were adopted by the usual majority. Clay then recurred to the principal subject. He had evidently become convinced that the criticism upon the resolutions of censure, that they were but the fulmination of a majority of the Senate and did not contemplate any legislative action, could not be wholly disregarded. Accordingly, on May 28, he submitted two resolutions. The first reaffirmed the one before adopted, that the reasons of the Secretary of the Treasury for removing the deposits were unsatisfactory and insufficient; the other was that after July 1 the deposits should be restored. They were offered as joint resolutions of both houses. In view of the certain failure of the resolutions in the House he admitted that his purpose was to avoid the technical objection that the previous resolution was abstract and could lead to no practical results. He professed the opinion that the objection had no force, yet he desired to meet it and leave nothing undone to regain the lawful custody of the public treasure. The avowed reason why the resolutions of censure were not joint was because the House would reject them. Clay now acknowledged that this consideration ought not to influence the Senate, which owed to itself and to the country the discharge of its whole duty regardless of any other branch of the government. We may well wonder why he did not pursue this course originally. Had the resolutions of censure been joint or the debate centred on a bill to restore the deposits, Jackson would have had no opportunity to defend himself and attack his accusers, a dangerous advantage before the people. This retreat from the former procedure may be taken as a tacit admission that Jackson was not entirely wrong in the doctrines of the protest. The resolutions were stoutly opposed, but they were soon adopted. In the House they were summarily laid on the table and remained there.

There was another mode of rebuking the President and the Secretary of the Treasury far more efficient than any resolutions. In his remarks on submitting the joint resolutions, Clay plainly intimated it. "To-morrow," said he, "will be one year since any head of the Treasury Department has been appointed by and with the advice and consent of the Senate. Gentlemen have said, Why this anxiety for these nominations? I answer, No other reason but that the Constitution requires them to be made. Gentlemen ask if we want to reject them. I do not acknowledge a right to make such an inquiry into motives, but if it may be made I may with equal propriety ask, Are they withheld from a fear of their being rejected?" June 23, Taney's nomination was sent to the Senate. It was rejected forthwith. Taney at once resigned, and the first clerk of the Treasury became by law the acting Secretary. Subsequently, Woodbury was appointed and confirmed. The other nomination to which Clay alluded was that of Butler for Attorney-General. It was sent in with the nomination of Taney; but as Butler had taken no official action in regard to the deposits, his nomination was confirmed.

Meantime the investigating committee appointed by the House made its report. It was a prolix description of utter failure. The committee had endeavored to get evidence from the bank on the subjects of investigation, but every effort was frustrated. It first met with technical legal objections, and finally with the absolute refusal of the officers to testify or produce the books. It was thus forced to give up the task and return empty-handed. The report proposed resolutions asserting the right of either house of Congress to investigate the affairs of the bank and to compel the production of its books and the testimony of witnesses, and directing the Speaker to issue his warrant for the arrest of the president and directors of the bank that they might be brought to the bar of the House to answer for contempt. The resolutions were not acted upon because it was believed that the bank would suffer seriously in public opinion for its conduct without the House entering upon a protracted trial of the refractory officers. This course proved judicious. The bank had done itself far greater injury than any investigation or any punishment of its officers could have accomplished. The effects were so soon apparent that it was determined on the last day of the session to have the Finance Committee of the Senate conduct an investigation. With one exception, the committee was composed of Senators friendly to the bank. The anti-bank member refused to serve. As might have been expected, this "whitewashing committee," as it was termed, failed to aid the tottering cause of the bank.

The most important legislation enacted at this session was to regulate the coinage of money. For years the currency of the country had consisted chiefly of bank-notes. In 1834 that currency was in a very sound condition, owing to the safeguards upon the circulation issued by the Bank of the United States and the general security of the State banks; but the administration, influenced largely by Benton, favored the retirement of paper currency and the restoration of specie. The coinage was still governed by the original laws on the subject, which were enacted in 1792 and 1793. Several attempts had been made to change the mint ratio between gold and silver (1 to 15) established by those laws, but nothing had been accomplished. Gold in the mean time had somewhat enhanced in value, and in consequence had nearly disappeared from circulation,[1] while the volume of small notes had pro-

---

[1] "A golden piece of money was a curiosity at that time. It was a distinction in the country places to possess one. Clay and eternal rag-money, Jackson and speedy gold, was diligently represented as the issue between the candidates [1832]. Storekeepers responded by announcing themselves as anti-bank hatters and hard-money bakers."—Parton's *Jackson*, vol. iii. p. 421.

duced a similar, though not so extensive, effect upon silver. The ratio was now fixed at 1 to 16.002 by a law passed during the last days of the session. The majority for it was very large in both houses, notwithstanding the opposition of the paper interest. In the Senate only seven voted against it, Clay being among the number. By this law, as it proved, gold was slightly overvalued. This soon had the effect of banishing silver. Such is the delicacy of the monetary relation between the two metals, which renders the "double standard" so difficult of practical operation.

One other topic of the session remains to be noticed. The President's veto of the land bill was sent to the Senate soon after the opening of Congress. Had the bill been returned immediately after its passage during the previous session it would doubtless have been passed over the veto. But it was sent to the President on the last day but one of the session, and failed by reason simply of not receiving his signature. His message, therefore, was rather a manifesto than a veto. It roused Clay's ire that his pet measure should be balked in this manner, and he expressed his opinion with much freedom. He introduced the bill again. It was referred to the Committee on Public Lands, which later reported it with a commentary written by Clay in the same tenor as his remarks when the President's message was received. No further action was taken. On June 20, the session ended.

Clay's reflections on the results of the session must have suggested little cause for exultation. The labors of himself and his coadjutors had been exacting and exciting, but were in vain. The bank was doomed. The administration had already begun to regain the ground it had lost through the panic. The financial distress was fast subsiding, and there was a corresponding revulsion of popular sentiment against the Whig party. The prospect was that the Senate itself would soon be Democratic. Yet there was one consolation in which Clay probably found some degree of comfort— the redoubtable Jackson would soon pass off the scene.

The next session, which began December 1, was short, only lasting until March 3, when the Twenty-third Congress expired. However, a large amount of business was transacted, but most of it was of a non-political character. The bank was but a subordinate topic, although the President, in his message, resumed hostilities against the institution. He recommended the sale of the government stock, the suspension of the receipt of the bank's notes for public dues, the regulation by law of the public deposits in the State banks, and the termination of all connection whatsoever between the bank and the government. The Finance Committee of the Senate, which was directed at the last session to make an investigation of the bank and its operations, presented a long, defensive report, written by John Tyler. None of the recommendations, either of the President or the committee, were embodied in legislation. A bill to regulate the deposits had been passed by the House at the last session, but it failed in the Senate. The same bill was now reintroduced. It received a large majority in both houses, and became a law.

For many years the "French spoliations" had been a subject of much importunity and discussion. In 1800 a treaty between France and the United States was concluded, by which the claims asserted by each power against the other for injuries to commerce prior to that year were mutually relinquished. In consequence, our government was incessantly besought for redress by citizens who had sustained injuries for which France had been released from compensation. The claims against our government were based on the theory that, by releasing France, it had assumed the payment of these claims. The agitation had now gained sufficient momentum to demand action by Congress. As the public debt was nearly extinguished, there was no reason why the claims, if just, should not be paid. A bill was introduced in the Senate to provide for them to the extent of $5,000,000. It was supported chiefly by the Whigs, and was passed by the Senate after a debate that displayed much ability and research. It was defeated in the House by a substantially party vote. The entire discussion of the subject, however, evinced nothing of a partisan nature. Whether our government was justly bound to pay the claims was by no means clear; indeed, the case against them, on the law and facts, was undoubtedly the stronger. That the Whigs should advocate the payment was a natural result of their party policy of high tariffs and high prices for the public lands. Surplus revenues must be spent. The claims continued to be pressed for many years, but the effort was always unsuccessful. There was another branch of the same general subject of much greater importance and urgency.

The depredations upon our maritime commerce after 1800, through the piratical policy of Napoleon, were more grievous and extensive than those which had preceded. After the close of the war with England our government demanded reparation on behalf of those of our citizens who had suffered from the spoliations. Some fifteen years of diplomatic fencing ensued over the question. The justice of the claim was to some extent uniformly conceded by the different administrations of the French government; but from one cause or another a treaty settling the controversy was not reached until 1831. To enforce this claim was one of the first things that Jackson proposed after the beginning of his Presidency. In his first message he directed attention to it in very emphatic language. The result of the negotiations soon instituted was the treaty of 1831, by which the French government agreed to pay an indemnity of 25,000,000 francs. This sum was to be paid in six annual instalments, the first of which became due in February, 1833. Although King Louis Philippe was anxious to maintain relations of cordial amity with the United States, the French Chambers failed to pass the necessary appropriations to meet the two accrued instalments. Jackson was wroth. He sharply reviewed the situation in his message of 1834, and went so far as to recommend a law authorizing reprisals if provision were not made for the payment of the debt at the next session of the French Chambers. The attitude of the President created alarm throughout the country, for France would undoubtedly view it as virtually a recommendation of war. Parton relates that before the message was sent members of the cabinet argued against this extreme measure and urged the President to modify several passages which they regarded as needlessly irritating and menacing; but he refused to change them. "No, gentlemen," he exclaimed, "I know them French! They won't pay unless they're made to."[1]

The feeling of alarm excited by this energetic message was shared even by many of the President's stanchest ad-

---

[1] "After the message had been written some of its expressions were softened by a member of the cabinet before the MS. was sent to the printer, without the President's knowledge. When it was in type the confidential proof-reader of the *Globe* office took the proof-sheets to the President; and he afterwards said that he never before knew what profane swearing was. General Jackson promptly restored his own language to the proof-sheets."—Curtis's *Buchanan*, vol. i. p. 235.

herents in Congress. In the Senate the subject was referred to the Committee on Foreign Relations, of which Clay was elected chairman. Perceiving that something should be done to allay the certain bad effect of the message upon the French, he took the matter in hand. On January 6 he presented the report of the committee. It was prepared by him, and was an exhaustive, temperate, and politic treatment of the subject. It firmly sustained the justice of the indemnity, the binding obligation of the treaty, and the patriotic duty of enforcing our rights; yet it skilfully excused the delay of the French government, and qualified the harshness of the President's recommendation. It proposed this resolution: "That it is inexpedient at this time to pass any law vesting in the President authority for making reprisals upon French property, in the contingency of provision not being made for paying to the United States the indemnity, as stipulated by the treaty of 1831, during the present session of the French Chambers." On the 14th the resolution came up for consideration. Clay spoke briefly in its support, but he did not now restrain the criticism that the President had gone too far in proposing reprisals. Some discussion followed, in which objections were made to the wording of the resolution. Clay, however, expressed his willingness to accept any phraseology consistent with the object he had in view—suspending action until further developments. This harmonized the entire Senate. The resolution was then put in this form: "That it is inexpedient at present to adopt any legislative measure in regard to the state of affairs between the United States and France." In this form it was unanimously adopted.

The temper of the House was somewhat different. Its Committee on Foreign Affairs, to which that part of the message concerning the relations with France had been referred, did not report until February 27. The report was very short. It proposed resolutions declaring that the House would insist upon the execution of the treaty, that contingent preparations ought to be made to meet any emergency growing out of our relations with France, and that the committee be discharged from further consideration of the message. They caused a spirited debate, in which John Quincy Adams advocated them with especial vigor. The first resolution was finally amended so as to read : " That in the opinion of this House the treaty of the 4th of July, 1831, should be maintained and its execution insisted upon." This patchwork of resolutions—not different in practical effect from the Senate's resolution, though more complimentary to the President—proved acceptable to the House, and was unanimously adopted on the day before adjournment. For the time the course of Congress quieted the fear of hostilities. The rates of marine insurance, which had been largely increased through the influence of the message, resumed their former level; and commerce, relieved from danger, put to sea. Here the matter rested until the next session of Congress.

On February 4, Clay presented the memorial of a council of Cherokee Indians, and made it the occasion of a speech on the relations between the government and the tribes in the Southwest. In that region the Indians had been an unceasing source of trouble. The spread of the white population and the planting interest pressed upon the boundaries of the Indian lands, which were gradually narrowed by successive treaties, not always obtained by fair means. Most of the Cherokees were located in Georgia, where the desire and the efforts for their removal approached ferocity. In 1802, in consideration of the cession by Georgia of the territory forming the present States of Alabama and Mississippi, the United States agreed to extinguish the Indian titles in Georgia whenever it could be done peaceably and on reasonable terms. It had not yet been accomplished, and consequent difficulties and controversies had produced an extreme degree of exasperation against both the Indians and the government. During his administration, John Quincy Adams, emulating Jefferson's example, favored the firm protection of the Indians in all their treaty rights, and so far as he could he afforded it. His policy in this respect excited such ill-will toward him among the people of Georgia that he did not receive a vote in that State in the election of 1828. At that time, Clay shared the prevailing opinion of those who lived in the vicinity of Indians—that the race could not be civilized, that it was destined to extinction, and the sooner it was extinct the better; yet he advocated humane treatment and protection.

Of all the tribes the Cherokees were the most advanced in civilization. They had established an elective government wholly independent of State laws, as they had the right to do under the treaties. They had a written language, and churches, schools, and courts. The features of Indian life were not remarkable except by the fact that they existed at all. This community, promising as it was, considering the general character of the aboriginal tribes, was chiefly interesting as a curiosity of embryo civilization. Many of its members were not reclaimed from their savage instincts, and the lawless elements of both races came into frequent collision. This annoyance was much aggravated by the want of jurisdiction of the State over the Indian country, which thus became the refuge of the unruly. This situation finally became so obnoxious to the people of Georgia that they were ready to take any course to be rid of it. In December, 1828, a law was passed by the State legislature dividing the Indian lands into several parts and annexing them to adjacent counties. It declared the native customs and usages of no valid effect, and made the Indians incompetent to act as witnesses. The real object was to extend the sovereignty of the State over the whites who lived in the reservation; and Indian institutions were not further molested. It was the preparatory step to ascertain the policy that Jackson would adopt, though it was expected that he would not interfere. Only a short time before Jackson's inauguration, Adams was formally appealed to by the Cherokees for protection. He left the subject to his successor, who refused to take any action and advised them to submit to the laws of Georgia or remove beyond the Mississippi, whither a part of the tribe had gone in 1818. With this immunity from Executive interference, the legislature of Georgia enacted a series of harsh and arbitrary laws calculated to destroy nearly all the rights of the Indians and drive the unfortunate people from the State. Most of their lands were taken and disposed of by lottery. Application was then made by the Cherokee nation to the Supreme Court of the United States to restrain the State of Georgia from executing these laws; but jurisdiction was refused by the court on the ground that the Cherokees were not a "foreign state" within the meaning of the Constitution, and could not, therefore, maintain a suit against a State of the Union. Not long after this the question as to the validity of these laws was again brought before the court, but this time in a manner that gave it jurisdiction, and they were declared null and void because in violation of the Constitution, laws, and treaties of the United States. The State court refused to conform to the decision. The case arose through the arrest and conviction of two missionaries who refused to obey the State laws in question. Before the next session of the Supreme Court, at which an application could be made to enforce its decision, the prisoners agreed to submit to the State laws and were pardoned. Through all this the President remained passive. Thus at the very time he was resisting the doctrine of nullification proclaimed by South Carolina, he tolerated actual nullification in Georgia.

The helpless situation of the Indians appealed to Clay's sympathies so strongly as to outweigh all political considerations. He consented to bring the subject before the Senate, and he did so in his most effective manner. His speech was admirable. He first presented the rights of the Indians under a long succession of treaties, and then depicted with affecting eloquence the wrongs to which the Cherokees had been subjected by the State of Georgia. At the conclusion of the speech he submitted resolutions directing inquiry into the expediency of further provisions of law enabling the Indians to maintain their rights in the federal courts, and also of provisions setting apart a district west of the Mississippi for such of the Cherokees as would occupy it, and securing their undisturbed possession of it.

The speech of course was offensive to the Georgia Senators, and one of them, Cuthbert, immediately protested against it in a manner that shows the sympathetic effect it produced on those who heard it. "The subject," said he, "has been introduced altogether unnecessarily. It is a subject that cannot be tried here. Georgia does not plead before this tribunal. I do not stand here to plead in her behalf. The case does not admit of that minute examination which the gentleman from Kentucky would give it. To what purpose, then, was the address of the Senator from Kentucky? Was it to secure to himself that praise which all had been previously so ready to yield to him — the praise of splendid rhetoric, of studied eloquence, of measured tones, of theatric starts, of pathos of manner? He had already the credit of these. No one disputes his unrivalled claim to them. If the gentleman intended to play a theatrical part, the opportunity has been afforded him. What part does Roscius next enact?"

He was followed by White, of Tennessee, who took the ground that the Indian treaties were not treaties within the meaning of the Constitution, and could not legally deprive the States of sovereignty over their entire areas, nor of the right to judge whether their laws were adapted to the conditions and wants of the people. He favored the removal of the Indians to the West, with a guarantee of permanent security in their new abode. Benton spoke briefly to the same effect. Clay then replied with his consummate skill.

"The finest speech," says Martineau, "I heard from Mr. Clay in the Senate was on the sad subject of the injuries to the Indians. . . . It was known that he would probably bring forward this great topic that day. Some of the foreign ambassadors might be seen leaning against the pillars behind the chair, and many members of the other House appeared behind and in the passages; and one sat on the steps of the platform, his hands clasped and his eyes fixed on Mr. Clay as if life hung upon his words. As many as could crowd into the gallery leaned over the balustrade; and the lower circle was thronged with ladies and gentlemen, in the centre of whom stood a group of Cherokee chiefs listening immovably. I never saw so deep a moral impression produced by a speech. The best testimony to this was the disgust excited by the empty and abusive reply of the Senator from Georgia. This gentleman's speech, however, showed us one good thing, that Mr. Clay is as excellent in reply as in proposition; prompt, earnest, temperate, and graceful. The chief characteristic of his eloquence is its earnestness. Every tone of his voice, every fibre of his frame, bears testimony to this. His first sentences are homely, and given with a little hesitation and repetition, and with an agitation shown by a frequent putting on and taking off of the spectacles and a trembling of the hands among the documents on the desk. Then as the speaker becomes possessed with his subject the agitation changes its character, but does not subside. His utterance is still deliberate, but his voice becomes deliciously winning. Its higher tones disappointed me at first; but the lower ones, trembling with emotion, swelling and falling with the earnestness of the speaker, are very moving, and his whole manner becomes irresistibly persuasive. I saw tears, of which I am sure he was wholly unconscious, falling on his papers as he vividly described the woes and injuries of the aborigines. I saw Webster draw his hand across his eyes; I saw every one deeply moved except two persons, the Vice-President, who yawned somewhat ostentatiously, and the Georgian Senator, who was busy brewing his storm. I was amazed at the daring of this gentleman, at the audacity which could break up such a moral impression as this Cherokee tale, so told, had produced, by accusing Mr. Clay of securing an interest in opposition to Georgia 'by stage starts and theatric gesticulations.' The audience was visibly displeased at having their feelings thus treated in the presence even of the Cherokee chiefs; but Mr. Clay's replies both to the argument and abuse were so happy and the Georgian's rejoinder so outrageous that the business ended with a general burst of laughter."[1]

The resolutions were adopted, but no further action was taken. In December following a treaty was made with the Cherokees by which the titles to their lands were extinguished. The tribe was afterward removed to Indian Territory, which was established in 1834. By this process the Indian question in the South was solved, although it involved a long and expensive war with the Seminoles in Florida.[2]

Another important topic of the session was the proposed repeal of the so-called "four years law," passed in 1820 at the instance of Crawford to aid him in his candidacy for the Presidency. This law limited the tenure of office of several classes of federal officials to four years, and thus insidiously introduced the spoils system into the national government. In 1825, the practical effects of the measure having become distinct, an effort was made, but unsuccessfully, to repeal it; it was too thoroughly in harmony with the new political tendencies. Under Jackson, as we have seen, the system had developed into an avowed policy. It had become so obtrusive that another attempt was now made to arrest it. Calhoun took the initiative. Early in January he moved the appointment of a select committee to inquire into the extent of Executive patronage, the causes of its recent increase, and the expediency and means of reducing it. He was made chairman of the committee, and a month later presented its report—a sombre and surcharged

---

[1] Martineau's *Retrospect of Western Travel*, vol. i. p. 177.
[2] Benton's *Thirty Years' View*, vol. i. pp. 624, 626; Kennedy's *Wirt*, vol. ii. p. 251; Sumner's *Jackson*, p. 174; Shepard's *Van Buren*, p. 312.

account of the powers and practices of the Executive branch of the government in regard to its patronage. It proposed retrenchment, and alleged the existence of supernumerary offices and the general application of proscriptive political reasons in the making of appointments and removals. Bad as the system was, it was not so direful and far-reaching as Calhoun painted it. Not only the civil service in all its grades, but likewise the army and the navy, and even the pensioners, were treated by him as the active agents of Executive influence and encroachment—"supple instruments of power" and "subservient partisans ready for every service however base and corrupt." Had this been true, even as a prevailing tendency, the conclusion drawn by him that our institutions were in imminent peril would have been justified; but his assertions were too general and too morbid. The character of the mass of those engaged in the service of the government does not deserve so low an estimate. The average office-holder, though more or less a partisan, is above baseness and corruption, even if any wrongful act were asked of him, which must seldom occur. Besides this, the chief posts in the administration of government are generally filled by men of integrity and honorable ambition. Any theory is fallacious that disregards the ordinary facts of life.

Yet much of the criticism upon the spoils system, so far as that system was actually practised, was just. Some effects of the system are undeniably pernicious, however meritorious the great majority of the officials in the service may be. The spoils system tends to make politics a trade by which to gain the emoluments of place—to officer from colonel to corporal the forces of party with men whose paramount object is not the public interest. It indirectly pays for menial partisan service out of the public purse. It, therefore, introduces a motive and an element that should not enter into political contests. It is not a factor of aggressive harm, but it is a hinderance to the best results of representative government It is a vice rather than a direct and radical danger. Its effects are not concentrated —they are widely diffused. It roils the current of popular institutions, but does not change its course.

In accordance with the recommendations of the report, a bill was introduced to repeal the evil features of the four years law, and to provide that nominations to fill vacancies caused by removal should be accompanied by a statement of the reasons for removal. Even this measure did not go far enough to suit Clay. He offered an amendment to provide that officials appointed "by and with the advice and consent of the Senate" could only be removed with the concurrence of that body. It soon became evident, however, that this amendment could not succeed, and Clay did not bring it to a vote; but it evoked discussion as to the power of the President to remove such officials regardless of the Senate. At the outset of Washington's first administration this question was discussed, and it was decided by the casting vote of the Vice-President in favor of the Presidential power. The precedent thus established had governed all subsequent cases. The correct opinion, therefore, was undoubtedly that pronounced by Webster, that long usage had sanctioned the power, although it was questionable in the beginning, but that Congress could, nevertheless, impose conditions upon the tenure of office.

The debate on the bill was general and earnest. Little was left to be said on the subject of the spoils system. Most of the discussion of civil service reform at the present day is but a repetition of the arguments used in that debate. The principal difference between the conditions then existing and those which now exist lies in the fact that at that period the main source of the evils of political patronage was that office-mongering was not yet a leading function of Senators and Representatives. The healthy sentiment on the subject that still prevailed in the Senate is shown by the strong support the bill there received. It was passed by a vote of nearly two to one, and would doubtless have received a larger vote had not the administration been so severely assailed. As it was, Benton voted for it, although he vigorously defended the administration against the charge of extravagance. The ablest and most adroit speech in opposition to the bill was made by Silas Wright. Buchanan also bore a prominent part in opposition to the bill. Calhoun's defence of the report and of the bill was philosophic and excellent. It was superior to the report itself, because less elaborate and more moderate. The case against the spoils system has never been stated with more breadth and force.

Clay's speech was chiefly directed to the power of the President to remove officials appointed with the concurrence of the Senate. His attitude toward this subject would alone indicate his opinions concerning official patronage generally. No one was more pronounced in favor of removing as far as possible the public service from politics. His speech was bold and animated. He began by reviewing from his habitual point of view what he regarded as the centralizing tendency of Jackson's Presidency, and fully presented the argument against the implied Constitutional power of the President to dismiss officials, sharply challenging the precedent of 1789. His remarks on the spoils system itself were made incidentally through the argument. His convictions in regard to it were so intense that instead of reasoning against it he fiercely denounced it. The speech is one of the best specimens of his skill as a debater; but considered as a permanent contribution to the subject of patronage, it is open to the same criticism as that which Calhoun's report compels. It was delivered toward the close of the debate. The subject was not complex or many-sided, and it had been thoroughly canvassed. Yet Clay's speech was fresh and graphic. One of the most significant marks of his genius was the ease and facility with which he lifted out of the commonplace whatever engaged his attention. The bill reached the House too late for action upon it, even had there been a majority in its favor, which is doubtful. Many years passed before this reform was again attempted.

CHAPTER VII

Distribution of the Surplus—The French Spoliations—The Slavery Question—The Abolition Petitions and Incendiary Publications—Admission of Arkansas and Michigan into the Union—Texas—Madison's Death and Character—The Colonization Society—Clay and Garrison—Taney Becomes Chief Justice—The Political Situation—The Election of 1836—Politico-Finance—Jackson's Physical and Mental Traits—Efforts for Further Distribution—The Financial Condition of the Country—The Mania for Speculation—The Specie Circular

THE first session of the Twenty-fourth Congress opened December 7. On the next day Clay made his appearance, having passed the recess at Ashland. He was again elected Chairman of the Committee on Foreign Relations. The post was still especially important, as the difficulty with France had not yet been settled. He had been in Washington but a few days when he received information of the death of his only surviving daughter, Anne, the wife of James Erwin, a gentleman of high standing and character, residing at New Orleans. She was Clay's favorite child. Her letters to him, published in his *Correspondence*, indicate that she possessed refined intelligence and a most amiable disposition. Her death affected Clay more keenly throughout his life than any other of his numerous domestic bereavements. On reading the letter conveying the sad tidings he fainted. For several days he did not leave his apartments.

Upon his return to the Senate, December 29, he again introduced his familiar bill to distribute the proceeds of the public lands. He delivered a speech on the subject, briefly presenting in new form the old arguments in favor of the measure. He closed the speech with the following passage, unique on such an occasion:

"I confess I feel anxious for the fate of this measure, less on account of any agency I have had in proposing it, as I hope and believe, than from a firm, sincere, and thorough conviction that no one measure ever presented to the councils of the nation was fraught with so much unmixed good and could exert such powerful and enduring influence in the preservation of the Union itself. If I can be instrumental in any degree in the adoption of it I shall enjoy in that retirement into which I hope shortly to enter a heart-feeling satisfaction and a lasting consolation. I shall carry there no regrets, no complaints, no reproaches on my own account. When I look back upon my humble origin, left an orphan too young to have been conscious of a father's smiles and caresses, with a widowed mother surrounded by a numerous offspring in the midst of embarrassments, without a regular education, without fortune, without friends, without patrons, I have reason to be satisfied with my public career. I ought to be thankful for the high places and honors to which I have been called by the favor and partiality of my countrymen, and I am thankful and grateful. And I shall take with me the pleasing consciousness that in whatever station I have been placed I have earnestly and honestly labored to justify their confidence by a faithful, fearless, and zealous discharge of my public duties."

The bill went in due course to the Committee on Public Lands, and was reported a month later. Debate upon it began in March and continued fitfully until May 4, when it was passed by the Senate. In the House, after considerable discussion, it was laid on the table. The effort, however, to effect some sort of distribution did not end here. Clay's plan failed, partly because the principle of it was bad, but chiefly because it was his. Yet something had to be done. The public debt was paid. The revenues of the government from all sources continued to be much in excess of its needs, and were increasing. The situation was embarrassing. The recent adjustment of the tariff by the Compromise produced no reduction of the customs revenue,[1] and the Whigs prevented a reduction of the receipts from the sales of the public lands. One proximate cause of the peculiar condition of affairs was undoubtedly the vicious policy of depositing the surplus in the "pet banks." This policy operated inequitably among the different sections of the country, and, favoring the West, it promoted an abnormal speculation in the public lands. From a preceding annual average of $2,500,000, the receipts from the land sales had within three years risen to nearly ten times that amount. This mania for speculation, however, was not confined to the public lands, but spread rapidly to everything that could be made a medium for speculation.[2] It was a distemper of the public mind, engendered by several causes and destined to produce speedily the most severe and wide-spread havoc the country had ever experienced. In short, all the chief evils of the prevailing public policy, for which both parties were about equally responsible, had conspired to create another more serious and alarming.

The surplus had become so large as to be viewed with deep anxiety, not less by the opposition than by the ad-

---

[1] On the contrary, it increased. In 1834 it was $16,200,000; in 1835, $19,400,000; and in 1836, $26,400,000. June 1, 1836, the surplus amounted to $41,500,000.

[2] *Diary of Philip Hone*, vol. i. pp. 173, 204.

ministration; for not only were the Whigs influenced by the bad economic policy of the deposit system, but by the powerful political leverage it placed in the hands of the administration. Its harmful effects were becoming daily more apparent. Under these circumstances some mode of disposing of the surplus was a peremptory necessity — it had to be either expended or distributed. Various schemes were proposed. Calhoun was for a Constitutional amendment authorizing the distribution of the surplus among the States; Benton, for expending it in fortification and other means of national defence; Wright, for investing it in State bonds; Grundy, for purchasing from the railroads perpetually free transportation of the mails and war munitions. But none of these propositions gained much support. It was, of course, known that Clay's bill would fail in the House: the administration was pledged against it. Yet no other measure for distribution was reported until a few days before Clay's bill was tabled.

A bill to regulate the deposits had been reported by the Finance Committee. The propriety of such a measure was undeniable, and there was comparatively little difficulty in devising a bill satisfactory to all. Calhoun had in the mean time overcome his Constitutional scruples, and proposed an amendment to the deposit bill to direct a division of the surplus, beyond five million dollars, among the States, in proportion to their population. This amendment was at length adopted by the Finance Committee, largely through the influence of Webster. After some discussion the ratio of distribution was changed to that of the representation of the States in Congress. In this form the bill went to the House. It there met with strenuous opposition. While the provisions of the bill relating to the deposits were approved, the proposed distribution was not. An effort was made to separate the incongruous provisions into two bills, but without success. An amendment was then offered to the section for distribution, by which instead of donating the surplus to the States, it was to be deposited with them as a call-loan, to bear five per centum interest in case the certificates were assigned by the government to raise money. The amendment prevailed and the bill was passed by a vote of four to one. The Senate quickly concurred, only six members voting in the negative—Benton, Black, Cuthbert, Grundy, Walker, and Wright. The President signed the bill, but not with a very good grace. He professed to do so reluctantly, and doubtless he did so at the instance of Van Buren's friends, who feared that political disadvantage would follow a veto. It was the same motive that gained for the bill so large a vote in both houses. But little time elapsed before the ill effects of this vicious measure became apparent.

Before the original deposit bill had been transformed into a distribution bill several other questions of moment had arisen. The first was the renewal of the difficulty with France, which had been allayed at the preceding session. After the action of the two houses, already recounted, the French Chambers passed a bill appropriating the amount of the indemnity, but with the proviso that it would not be paid until their government had received a satisfactory explanation of that part of the President's message which recommended reprisals—that is to say, until he apologized for his belligerent affront to the dignity of France. The more ominous resentment of the alleged insult was the recall of the French Minister; at the same time our Minister received his passports, and left France. A large part of the President's annual message was devoted to the subject. In January he sent a special message stating that our *chargé d'affaires*, who remained in France after our Minister had left, had, pursuant to his instructions, demanded payment of the money without apology; that payment had been refused, and he had returned. It also stated that the French *chargé d'affaires* had been recalled, and all diplomatic intercourse between the two countries was suspended. The tone of the President's message was more spirited and warlike than that of his preceding messages in regard to the matter. He refused to recede from the position he had taken; he had offered all the "explanation" that could reasonably be expected of him. The money was admittedly due, and payment had been withheld beyond any excusable delay. If Jackson had been a little less vigorous and if the French government had been as regardful of its obligation as of its sentiment, there would have been no trouble. As it was the rupture was now complete.

In the Senate the whole subject was again referred to the Committee on Foreign Relations. While it was under consideration, all the correspondence having been furnished, the President sent another message, conveying the information that the British government had offered to mediate, and that the offer had been accepted. When the correspondence relating to this offer was laid before Congress, Clay made a brief speech in which he could not resist taunting the President with the course he had pursued in the affair. "In his message of December last," said Clay, "he made an explanation almost in the very language required by the Duc de Broglie. This explanation was made with two objects in view. The first was to get with France all the merit of making an explanation; and the next was to get with the people of the United States the merit of not making any explanation at all. I am truly glad that France saw the subject in the true light. The moment she saw the explanation, she made arrangements to pay the money. France saw that while the President protested that he would not explain, he did explain; and that while protesting that he would not apologize, he did apologize." The offer of mediation was as eagerly accepted by the French government as by that of the United States, and soon resulted in a satisfactory adjustment of the difference. It enabled both parties to cloak their indiscretion in a cloud of verbose palaver, the usual medium of diplomacy for effecting an honorable outcome in such cases. This accomplished, the money was paid.

It is now necessary to approach a subject which, though not new, assumed at this session an unwonted and persistent importance in public attention.

Much of the literature pertaining to our political history has, in a sense, been written backward. The history of the entire period preceding the Civil War has generally been treated as the preliminary to that great struggle. Nearly every event, however small or remote, showing the existence of a more or less active antislavery sentiment, has been magnified beyond its real significance. This is the necessary result of history written to maintain a proposition and of biography to create seers and heroes. A history of the country is, of course, inadequate that fails to trace the slow development of the antislavery movement until it attained the proportions of a distinct and continuous political factor; but a like consideration applies to each of the numerous elements that enter into the history of a people. The error of omission is not greater than the fault of distension.

It is not designed here to resurvey this over-cultivated field. It is only needful to restore the salient facts to the proportions they then had in the popular mind.

It is probable that slavery would have become extinct in the South, as it did in the North, but for the cotton culture, which rapidly increased after the invention of the cotton-gin and machinery for the production of cotton fabrics. It does not heighten the glory of the North that the opposition to slavery there had its origin in the humane and philosophic opinions of the early Southern statesmen, and developed only after slavery had become extinct in that section because free labor was more profitable. Until the slave-trade had fallen under the ban of the law and the decent opinion of the world it was prosecuted to a large extent by New-Englanders.[1] But it was certain that when any considerable class came to have no material interest to serve in maintaining or ministering to slavery a crusade against it would begin: the natural instinct of aversion to it would be liberated and the abolitionist become inevitable. Nevertheless, open and active opposition grew but slowly. The powerful interests of commerce and manufacture profited by the striking difference in the economic conditions of the free and the slave States. In the latter, planting was almost the sole interest; hence the business of the former was not only relieved of Southern competition, but was there given a large and virtually exclusive market besides so long as the policy of protection survived. Moreover, odious as slavery was in some of its phases, and in all so repugnant to natural justice and the first principle of our polity, every practical mind knew that it could not be

---

[1] *Butler's Book*, p. 81; Tyler's *Taney*, p. 337; *Democratic Review*, vol. xxvi. p. 4.

CH. VII.] GROWTH OF ANTISLAVERY SOCIETIES   269

abolished without force, and that force was out of the question. The Constitution recognized and indirectly legalized it; thus in the common opinion the moral responsibility for it rested alone upon the South—the North was absolved. This general situation, combined with politics, long reconciled the body of the Northern people to slavery in the South.

Antislavery societies were not a novelty. Such organizations had existed from an early period, but they were not numerous, and exerted no appreciable influence. Their usual object was the advocacy of gradual emancipation. After 1830, through the fanatical ardor of such zealots as Garrison, the formation of antislavery societies received a new impetus. By 1837 no fewer than twelve hundred of them had been organized, and, for a year or so, at nearly the rate of one a day. The purpose, boldly proclaimed, of most of them was to agitate immediate and unconditional abolition. The seat of this movement was in the Eastern States and its chief medium the New England Antislavery Society, formed in 1832. Garrison's *Liberator*, published at Boston, soon became the leading organ of the radical abolition element, although it was some years before it gained much circulation. It made him the most conspicuous of the extreme abolitionists. He was a man of small talent and an eccentric of the most pronounced type. His power lay in his fearless and tireless energy, which made him proof against hardship and persecution. His writings had some merit, but for the most part they were verbose, frothy, and ranting. Had he and his followers been more practical they would have acquired a stronger and speedier influence. Not content with preaching abolition, Garrison urged so many other things having no relation to slavery that he repelled many who were disposed in principle against slavery, but who did not care to be in such bizarre company. Most of the early abolitionists resembled Garrison in eccentricity of mind, which displayed itself in a variety of ridiculous ways, and thus brought the whole class into general contempt.[1] Their combined efforts produced little else, besides bringing slavery into discussion, than local irritation here and there, which was intensified by the ferocious feeling they aroused in the South. So strongly were their operations deprecated by the mass of the Northern people that frequently the apostles of abolition were mobbed and maltreated. In some places it was impossible to procure rooms and buildings in which to hold their meetings and conventions. Even the churches were generally closed against them.

The vital weakness of the Garrison element was the recognition, which could not be avoided, of the Constitutional warrant of slavery. This compelled the agitators to assail the Constitution itself, which they styled in Biblical phrase, a covenant with death and an agreement with hell. Instead of directing their efforts to some practical mode of furthering their object, they merely clamored. The consequence was that as the antislavery element increased in number and ability a schism developed. It was perceived by the more sagacious that nothing substantial could be accomplished save through political means—the organization of an antislavery party of voters. And there was little wisdom or method in the cause until this was done, and restriction rather than abolition was the ostensible policy.

---

[1] Stanton's *Random Recollections*, p. 69; *Life of R. H. Dana*, vol. i. p. 69; Adams's *Diary*, vol. ix. p. 255; Goodell's *Slavery and Antislavery*, p. 460; *Life and Times of Birney*, pp. 256, 278, 292.

This dissension hampered and delayed the cause for some years. So slow was its political progress that in 1840 the Liberty party cast but one vote in three hundred and sixty.

From these facts it is apparent that until the Twenty-fourth Congress the antislavery agitation was but a ripple on the general surface of affairs. Most people paid little attention to it, and it did not enter as a direct factor into the common currents of thought and activity. But now the Southern Senators and Representatives adopted a course that forced the subject into novel prominence and unwittingly aided what it was intended to suppress.

From the beginning, one of the principal means of fomenting the agitation was the dissemination of abolition writings through the mails; and they ranged through every degree, from temperate argument to the wildest paroxysms of arraignment. Great quantities of such matter, including inflammatory prints, were thus sent into the South.[1] This was not only exasperating to the intense pride of the Southern people, but it was believed by them to be designed to incite the slaves to insurrection. The fear of such a possibility was unfeigned, although the conduct of the slaves during the Rebellion proves that it was unfounded. The insurrection led by Nat Turner in 1831 prompted the dread that this most horrible of all calamities might be generally precipitated. For this reason the extreme feeling against

---

[1] "These pictures were smuggled amongst the slaves in many ways. The wrappers of packages of goods, such as tobacco and other articles consumed by slaves, were upon their inner sides covered with pictures representing the slaves in chains and rags, with lordly masters holding scourges in their hands; and many other designs of like character were impressed upon articles of dress and pieces of paper smuggled into goods consumed by the blacks and thus sent amongst them."—Ormsby's *History of the Whig Party*, p. 272.

the abolitionists was not without palliation; it was natural that their reckless operations should be viewed as incendiary and infernal. Another cause of the sensibility of the South on the subject of slavery was the consciousness that wherever the institution existed in other countries it was losing ground. The sentiment of civilization was gradually crystallizing against it. In Great Britain a movement had been started some years before to abolish slavery in the colonies, and in 1833 it ended in success. This freed the slaves in the West Indies and brought closely home to the South the possible danger of the agitation in the North, which had its immediate inception in the British example.[1] But though the growing sentiment of the world against slavery was recognized at the South, it did not change the conviction there as to the propriety of the institution. The consequence was only to harden opinion and render the South more watchful of hostile influences. The Southern people had from their infancy been accustomed to negro slavery. Most of them had been nursed by slaves, and were as familiar with the aspect of slavery as with the natural conditions of existence.[2] It had become the foun-

---

[1] "Wilberforce and his coadjutors commenced their labors in the anti-slavery cause just at the period of the adoption of the United States Constitution. It was about that period that Parliament, under the Wilberforce movement, began to agitate the abolition of the slave-trade; and the speeches of the British orators, the books and essays of British authors, and the songs of British poets, vividly portraying the foul sin of slavery, were instantly reproduced, perused, and wept over in New England. Cowper's spirited poem, which came forth at that period, no doubt inspired millions of hearts with hatred of slavery."—Ormsby's *History of the Whig Party*, p. 83.

[2] Calhoun told Adams in 1820 that "domestic labor was confined to blacks, and such was the prejudice that if the most popular man in his district were to keep a white servant in his house his character and reputation would be irretrievably ruined."—Adams's *Diary*, vol. v. p. 10.

dation of their social fabric and represented a great part of their wealth. They had come to look upon it as absolutely essential to them, and on the whole as more beneficial than freedom to the slaves, whom they regarded as an inferior race, fit only for bondage; and doubtless the majority of the slaves were well treated and contented. While these considerations do not justify the institution, they must be borne in mind in judging fairly the temper and attitude of the South.

Another phase of the agitation were the abolition petitions. They were in many forms and urged various proceedings, from the most tentative and restricted to the most radical and irrational. Most of the petitions, however, were for the abolition of slavery in the District of Columbia. They were often couched with violent license of language, describing slavery and the slave-holders in a manner that aroused the deepest ire of the Southern members. It was asserted on the floor of the House that during the session the number of the signers of the petitions was about thirty thousand, of whom one-half were women and a large proportion of the remainder minors. For several years this mode of bringing the subject before Congress had been resorted to, but the petitions were received and laid on the table without comment. This silent reception did not in the least discourage the petitioners. More and more of the documents were prepared and offered until at this session their unusual number, together with the progress of the agitation in other ways, provoked a protest. The abolitionists had at last penetrated the Capitol.

In the House the petitions were challenged very soon after the opening of the session and gave rise to frequent scenes of angry discussion and disorder. They were so irritating that some of the Southern members strenuously sought to prevent the reading and reception of them, and in some cases were successful, notwithstanding the outcry that the procedure was against the Constitutional right of petition. But as new provocations were continually arising by the appearance of fresh petitions, it became necessary to adopt some general rule in regard to them. At length, on February 8, Pinckney, of South Carolina, introduced a resolution from which was finally evolved what has always been known as the "gag" rule. It was afterward divided into three: (1) that Congress had no power to interfere in any way with slavery in any State; (2) that it ought not to interfere in any way with slavery in the District of Columbia; and (3) that all petitions, memorials, resolutions, propositions, or papers relating in any way to the subject of slavery should, without being either printed or referred, be laid on the table, and that no further action whatever be had upon them. After an excited debate they were adopted, May 26; the first by a vote of 128 to 9; the second, 132 to 45; the third, 117 to 68. This action was signalized by the conduct of John Quincy Adams, who then began his remarkable course of opposition to slavery and defence of the right of petition. On the adoption of the last resolution he refused to vote. According to the sober journal of the House, "When the name of Mr. Adams was called, that gentleman arose and said: 'I hold the resolution to be a direct violation of the Constitution of the United States, the rules of this House, and the rights of my constituents.' Mr. A. resumed his seat amid loud cries of 'Order!' from all parts of the hall." His course was the more startling because he had previously presented abolition petitions and expressed his disapproval of their object.

It was at this time that his peculiarities of mind began entirely to dominate him. He was old, and without chance or desire for preferment. That he was willing, after having been President, to be a member of the House was deemed by many as evidence of eccentricity. Yet his age, experience, and unique power in debate rendered his position, despite the violent antipathy and ruthless treatment he encountered, formidable in that body and influential in the North. Probably nothing aided so much at that juncture in enlisting the attention of thoughtful men who had been hostile or indifferent to the antislavery agitation as Adams's persistent efforts in battling for the right of petition and against the slave interest. He possessed what the abolitionist agitators lacked — instinctive perception of every point that the fury of his adversaries made vulnerable. He wasted no energy on abstractions and met each concrete question with practical weapons. His strong mind, unwearied industry, and wide attainments formed a solid foundation for his courage and keenness in debate. He was far from being an orator in the usual sense. Before entering the House, although he had sat in the Senate, he had little experience in public speaking. But, with a motive, he was not long in that arena in becoming a dangerous antagonist.[1] In directness, sarcasm, ridicule, and retort he was nearly as withering as Randolph, though in a different style. Fear was unknown to him. He was often the centre of scenes of frenzied commotion that his bold sentiments and bitter words created. No denunciations, abuse,

---

[1] "Mr. Adams wrote with a rapidity and ease which would hardly be suspected from his somewhat measured style. Notwithstanding the finish of his sentences, they were, like Gibbon's, struck off at once and never had to be retouched."—*Everett's Works*, vol. ii. p. 590.

or threats could change his course. Nor did he lose his temper—men of such acrid intellect and caustic tongue seldom do. This made his opponents all the more exasperated and furious, and led them into conduct that steadily corroded friendly sentiment in the North.

Whatever the public interest in the action of the House, it was much greater in that of the Senate. The House was the theatre of so much incubating ambition and demagogic display that it did not impress the country like the Senate, which contained most of the political chieftains and public men of greatest ability and distinction. The proceedings of the House, therefore, on the subject of slavery, were largely dictated from the Senate, which thus became the focus of public attention. If anything had been lacking in Calhoun's recent course to show that he had become possessed by the one controlling purpose of guarding slavery, it was now disclosed. Thus far slavery had been the indirect object of his solicitude; to protect it directly was now sternly announced by him to be his paramount and unyielding aim. He was the acknowledged head and front of the slave interest and the dictator of its policy. His commanding position was yielded with full consent; his great prestige, powers, and intensity of purpose placed him beyond all envy and rivalry. He was the embodiment of his cause. Through the fiat of his example all apologetic defences of slavery were haughtily thrown aside. He and his followers defiantly proclaimed that it was not an evil, but a positive good, and that its security was the price of preserving the Union. His stand against abolition petitions and publications revealed the Southern determination to insist upon the most radical and extreme measures to further the dominant purpose.

In the preceding summer the excitement in Charleston was so intense that the post-office was, without much difficulty, rifled of a quantity of abolition publications, which were destroyed. The postmaster at New York was requested to prevent the further transmission of such matter. He applied for instructions to the Postmaster-General, Amos Kendall, who answered that there was no legal authority to exclude matter from the mails, and that such a power would be dangerous; yet he virtually advised that course. He assured the postmaster at Charleston that "we owe an obligation to the laws, but a higher one to the communities in which we live; and if the former be perverted to destroy the latter, it is patriotism to disregard them." The President, in his annual message, expressed himself pointedly in relation to "the painful excitement produced in the South by attempts to circulate through the mails inflammatory appeals addressed to the passions of the slaves, in prints and various sorts of publications calculated to stimulate them to insurrection and to produce all the horrors of a servile war"; and recommended the enactment of a law prohibiting under severe penalties the circulation of incendiary publications through the mails. Calhoun at once moved to refer this part of the message to a select committee. The motion met with some resistance. It was urged that the matter should be referred instead to the standing Committee on Post-offices; and that reference to a special committee would give the subject too much prominence and provoke unnecessary discussion and excitement. But Calhoun insisted, and the motion prevailed.

Pending the report, the other branch of the general question, already tormenting the House, was taken up. January 7, two petitions to abolish slavery in the District being presented, Calhoun moved that they be not received. He pronounced them "a gross, false, and malicious slander upon eleven States"; and argued that inasmuch as Congress had no jurisdiction over slavery either in the States or in the District, the petitions demanded a violation of the Constitution, and should therefore be peremptorily rejected. That the language of many of the petitions presented would have justified this rejection is undeniable; but this objection, had it been generally utilized, as it was occasionally, would have accomplished nothing except to render the wording of petitions less offensive; it did not go to the root of the matter. The assumption that Congress was without power to abolish slavery in the District was based on the theory that the States which ceded the District to the government being slave States, there was an implied condition or compact guaranteeing slavery in the District. But this proposition was indefensible and was entertained by few men. The procedure demanded by Calhoun would in effect have been the denial of the right of petition, and as such it was strongly opposed even by most of the Southern Senators. Some of them, indeed, severely criticised it as tending in itself to further the agitation. He frankly gave to the petitions a grave importance. "We must," said he, "meet the enemy on the frontier—on the question of receiving; we must secure that important pass—it is our Thermopylæ. The power of resistance, by a universal law of nature, is on the exterior. Break through the shell, penetrate the crust, and there is no resistance within. In the present contest the question on receiving constitutes our frontier. It is the first, the exterior question, that covers and protects all others. Let it be penetrated by receiving this petition, and not a point of resistance can be found within, as far as this government is concerned." January 11, Buchanan presented an abolition petition and moved that it be read and the prayer rejected. Calhoun at once demanded that the question whether the petition should be received be first taken. The debate continued intermittently until March 9, when the motion to receive was carried, 36 to 10.

Clay was emphatically in favor of receiving the petitions, and went as far as any Northern Senator in his desire to put them through the form of respectful consideration. In his opinion, the right of petition required of the servants of the people that they should examine, deliberate, and decide either to grant or refuse the prayer of a petition and to give the reason for the decision. This he thought would "carry conviction to every mind, satisfy the petitioners of the impropriety of granting their request, and thus have the best effects in putting an end to the agitation of the public mind on the subject." He further declared his belief that slavery was justified by its necessity; that were he a Southern man he would resist emancipation in every form, gradual or other, because the white race was superior, and because emancipation would necessarily give the blacks eventually a numerical preponderance. He proposed, as an amendment to Buchanan's motion to reject forthwith, a resolution asserting the practical reasons, without affirming or denying the Constitutional power, why Congress should not abolish slavery in the District. But as it did not meet with approval he withdrew it, and a few days afterward voted for the original motion, which was carried, 34 to 6. After some further discussion the subject was laid on the table for the session.

Meantime the select committee appointed on Calhoun's motion made its report. Much of it was not concurred in by a majority of the committee. It was written by Calhoun, and was substantially a treatise on his theory of the Constitution as well as of slavery, and the relations among the States in regard to it. The tendency of the views it expressed was regarded as inimical to the Union; even King, of Georgia, one of Calhoun's colleagues on the committee, so asserted. The report was accompanied by a bill which provided that it should be criminal for any postmaster knowingly to receive and put into mail any written, printed, or pictorial matter concerning slavery directed to any post-office or person in a State where the circulation of such matter was prohibited by law; and that if such matter should be deposited and not withdrawn within a month after notice to withdraw it, it should be destroyed. It was further made the duty of the entire department, from the Postmaster-General down, to co-operate in the enforcement of the law.

The bill was much debated. Clay opposed it. He argued that the harm of such matter did not come from sending it through the mails, but from the use of it afterward; hence that the States had exclusive jurisdiction to prevent its being taken from the post-offices to which it was sent. For this reason he denied the Constitutional power of Congress to enact such a law, which was really designed to aid the enforcement of State laws. He also challenged the right to designate persons or classes who should have the benefit of the mails and exclude all others. Moreover, he contended that the bill would be practically inoperative, as the postmasters were to be held accountable only when they *knowingly* delivered the prohibited matter—a condition difficult to prove. These views prevailed. After much political manœuvring, the bill was defeated, 25 to 19. The only Northern Senators to vote for it were Buchanan and the two from New York, Wright and Tallmadge, who were no doubt actuated by the political desire not to injure Van Buren. Indeed, it was so arranged that he gave the casting vote on a preliminary question, to show that he was not opposed to the bill.

These, however, were but the more conspicuous phases of the slavery question, that now began to assert itself through every avenue which the protection and advancement of the institution suggested. At this session Michigan and Arkansas applied for admission into the Union, the former as a free and the latter as a slave State. Both encountered varied opposition, but succeeded. Michigan had been an applicant for some three years and Arkansas for nearly as long; but Congress had not authorized either to form a constitution and provide for a State government. For this reason their action was deemed irregular by many. Clay so regarded it, and voted against the admission of both. The slavery question did not assume a formidable bearing, ostensibly because it was generally conceded, even by Adams, that the terms of the Louisiana purchase and the Missouri Compromise warranted slavery in Arkansas if the State chose to permit it. But the fact remains that neither State would have been admitted without the other. Their simultaneous admission preserved the sectional equilibrium for which the admission of Missouri and Maine had established the precedent.[1] The chief source of the opposition was the undoubted desire of the Whigs to postpone the admission of both States until after the Presidential election, which was soon to occur. It was quite certain that both would choose Democratic electors.

Notwithstanding the extreme sensitiveness on the subject

---

[1] The admission of Kentucky and Vermont, Mississippi and Indiana, undoubtedly prepared the way.

of slavery which the proceedings of the session had produced, Benton undertook the apparently impossible feat of enlarging Missouri. It was already one of the largest States in the Union, and the territory which it was proposed to annex, a fertile domain as large as Rhode Island, consisted of Indian lands under treaty. But the most serious obstacle was that the project involved a departure from the lines of the Compromise, thus converting free into slave soil. Yet there was manifest propriety in the plan, as it would symmetrize the proportions of the State by filling out the northwest corner. Perhaps it was this consideration mainly that allayed the danger of opposition; for Benton's efforts were entirely successful. The project was managed with so much tact that it received little public notice or discussion in Congress. The bill passed quietly through both houses and became a law. A new treaty with the Indians was made and ratified, and the State assumed its present outlines on the map.

Another phase of the slavery question that vexed the session in so many ways was the asserted independence of Texas. The first stage of Texan independence was the overthrow of Spanish dominion by Mexico, of which Texas formed a part. Early in 1824 Mexico established a republican constitution resembling that of the United States. It joined Texas and Coahuila as one State, and three years later a State constitution was formed. Both the national and State governments, however, were little more than nominal. The former was frequently shaken by changes of administration, usually accomplished by force; hence its authority sat lightly on the States more remote from the City of Mexico, the seat of the national government. In 1830 the vast area of Texas, nearly 270,000 square miles, contained a population of only 21,000, whites and negroes combined, of which the greater part had come from the United States. The joinder of Texas and Coahuila was ill-advised, the population of the latter being almost entirely Mexican. Coahuila dominated the legislature and caused the enactment of a law forbidding the further immigration of American settlers. But this law, like the provision in the constitution prohibiting slavery, had no practical effect except to embitter the Texans against everything Mexican. Although this law was afterward repealed, the dissensions among the irreconcilable elements of the State increased until at length the Texans demanded a separate State government. This being refused, they revolted, declared their independence, and began, under the leadership of Sam Houston, the war that eventually achieved it.[1]

The struggle for independence naturally aroused keen interest throughout the United States; and as the war at the outset was attended by barbarous atrocities on the part of the Mexicans, that interest was quickened into patriotic sympathy, which rapidly recruited the ranks of the revolutionists. Behind this was the ever-present desire for territorial expansion; for it was assumed that the establishment of independence by Texas would be followed by its admission into the Union. This outcome was the studied design of the South, as frankly declared by Calhoun, because it would bring an enormous accession to the slave interest; yet this consideration did not seriously influence popular

---

[1] It has been commonly asserted that Houston, with Jackson's tacit consent, went to Texas for the purpose of overthrowing the Mexican government there.—Parton's *Jackson*, vol. iii. p. 655; Von Holst's *Constitutional and Political History of the United States*, vol. ii. p. 562. This is denied, on apparently good grounds, by Houston's most recent biographer.—Williams's *Houston*, p. 74.

sentiment at the North, where that national pride which resisted secession in 1861 was more potent than the fear of sectional advantage to the South. As soon as information of the progress of the Texan cause spread through the country Congress was petitioned by individuals, public meetings, and legislatures, North and South, to recognize the independence of Texas. Precise information, however, upon which the government could act with propriety, came but slowly.

June 24, in response to a resolution of the Senate, the President reported that he was without such knowledge, but had taken measures to obtain it. Nevertheless, Congress was disposed to do something to gratify the popular demand. July 1, the Senate adopted resolutions declaring that "the independence of Texas should be acknowledged whenever satisfactory information has been received that it has in successful operation a civil government capable of performing the duties and fulfilling the obligations of an independent power," and expressing satisfaction with the effort of the President to gain that information. The first was introduced a month before by Clay, from the Committee on Foreign Relations, although he preferred not to have it acted upon at this session. With the development of the slavery question his attitude in regard to Texas had changed. He had severely criticised Monroe's administration for relinquishing to Spain, by the Florida treaty, our claim to Texas under the Louisiana purchase, and while Secretary of State he proposed the purchase of Texas from Mexico. He was now reluctant to promote in any way the growing discord over slavery. Pacification was his policy and his passion. The resolutions were empty and useless except to indicate what would be done if a suitable pretext offered.

Nine days later similar resolutions were adopted by the House. Thus closed the first scene of what was to prove a devious and bloody drama. Congress then adjourned.

A few days before the adjournment the venerable Madison died. He was the last of the eminent early statesmen, and was long regarded as the political mentor of the country. His writings shed invaluable light on some phases of our history, particularly Constitutional. The general scheme of the Constitution is more largely his conception than that of any other member of the convention. No American statesman except Hamilton so well deserves the title of publicist. The most serious disparagement of this title is his approval of the restrictive measures preceding the War of 1812. The purity of his character, the serenity of his mind, the poise of his judgment, the depth of his patriotism, and his watchful interest in public affairs naturally attracted throughout his long retirement the esteem and homage of public men without distinction of party. This is well illustrated by his relations with both Jackson and Clay. It is related that he was roused from his bed by Edward Livingston, the author of the nullification proclamation, to pass his opinion on the document before it was published; and that the suggestions and amendments he proposed, sitting in his night-dress between two spluttering candles, were eagerly adopted. Between him and Clay, despite their early disagreements, a strong friendship had developed. Their correspondence shows the cordial regard they had for each other. Shortly before Madison's death he expressed to a mutual friend his admiration of Clay's success in compromising differences that threatened the permanence of the Union, and the hope that he might be equally successful in pacifying the dread dissension over slavery.

"I wish," said Madison, "he could fall on some plan of compromising this, and then all parties, or enough of all parties, might unite and make him President."

For years Madison had been president of the American Colonization Society, which was formed in 1817, in accordance with a plan originally projected during the Revolution. The object of the society was the transportation of free negroes to Africa, primarily because of the fear that they would incite insurrections among the slaves. The society and its branches were long regarded with general favor, even by the abolitionists, and were aided by legislation, appropriations, and donations during the dubious vicissitudes attending the finally successful establishment of the colony of Liberia. From the first, Clay had been zealously interested in the society. He was chairman of the first meeting called at Washington preliminary to the formation of the society, and continued in active connection with it. Upon Madison's death he succeeded him as president. By this time, however, the society had lost favor with the abolitionists. With the progress of the antislavery agitation they had gradually come to the conclusion that the scheme of colonization, instead of being a valuable adjunct to their cause, was a disguised auxiliary to slavery, and as such they began to denounce it.[1] Garrison waxed violent against it, and therefore against Clay. Only a few years before, Clay had been his political idol. At the annual meeting of the society in 1827, Clay delivered an address extolling its

---

[1] In December, 1837, there were fifty-nine votes in the House against a motion to allow the society to hold its annual meeting in the hall, according to its custom. The reason for these adverse votes does not appear; but the number is about the same as supported Adams in his efforts to procure the reception of the abolition petitions.

operations and aspirations. He was so emphatic in declaring his antipathy to slavery as to gain the ecstatic admiration of its most radical opponents. "If I could be instrumental," he exclaimed, "in eradicating this deepest stain upon the character of our country and removing all cause of reproach on account of it by foreign nations; if I could only be instrumental in ridding of this foul blot that revered State that gave me birth, or that no less beloved State which kindly adopted me as her son, I would not exchange the proud satisfaction which I should enjoy for the honor of all the triumphs ever decreed to the most successful conqueror." And this is a fair specimen of the frankness with which he always expressed himself on slavery in the abstract. But there was a striking inconsistency in his characterization of the free negroes and his description of the results they would accomplish if transported. "There is," said he, "a moral fitness in the idea of returning to Africa her children, whose ancestors have been torn from her by the ruthless hand of fraud and violence. Transplanted in a foreign land, they will carry back to their soil the rich fruits of religion, law, and liberty. May it not be one of the great designs of the Ruler of the Universe, whose ways are often inscrutable by short-sighted mortals, thus to transform an original crime into a signal blessing to that most unfortunate portion of the globe? Of all classes of our population the most vicious is that of the free colored. It is the inevitable result of their moral, political, and civil degradation. Contaminated themselves, they extend their vices to all around them, to the slaves and to the whites. . . . Every emigrant to Africa is a missionary carrying with him credentials in the holy cause of civilization, religion, and free institutions." Yet this glaring inconsistency seems to have attracted no marked attention at the time; neither did the utter impracticability of the scheme to effect any diminution of the free negro population, although the results thus far totally refuted the arguments and promises of the society.[1] At all events, Garrison was satisfied. When Clay retired from the Department of State, in 1829, he made a speech at a dinner given in his honor which roused Garrison to the highest pitch of devoted enthusiasm. "Henry Clay," he wrote, "at this moment stands on a higher eminence than he ever before occupied. His attitude is sublime—his front undaunted—his spirit unsubdued. It is impossible to read his noble speech without mingled emotions of pride, indignation, reverence, and delight." And in the following year he described Clay as "the champion who is destined to save the country from anarchy, corruption, and ruin." Clay was then his candidate for President. But soon after this his ardor was quenched by his rapidly increasing frenzy against slavery; and he was finally to contribute in no small degree to defeat the Presidential aspirations of his former hero.

At the close of the first session of the Twenty-fourth Congress, Clay seriously contemplated retiring from the Senate. He decided, however, not to resign, but to complete his term, which expired March 3, 1837, intending to refuse a re-election. While the Senate was Whig there had been some satisfaction in leading the majority. But all branches of the government were now strongly Democratic. Even the political tendencies of the Supreme Court had changed.

---

[1] "The whole amount of the colonization of manumitted slaves in eighteen years ending in 1835 was eight hundred and nine, equal to the increase of the slave population for five days and a half! . . . Up to this time the funds raised by the society amounted to $220,449, and it had incurred a debt of $45,645."—Goodell's *Slavery and Antislavery*, p. 344.

Five of the seven justices were Jackson's appointees. The last two were Barbour and Taney. The confirmation of the latter was bitterly opposed by the Whigs and filled them with deep disgust. To Jackson it was a source of vindictive delight. The refusal of the Senate to confirm the nomination of Taney for Secretary of the Treasury infused Jackson with a fierce determination to place Taney on the Supreme Court bench, where his Constitutional views would work greater and more enduring havoc to the Whig party than any mere political influence could accomplish. Upon the resignation of Justice Duval, in January, 1833, Taney was nominated to fill the vacancy. But the Senate deferred action until the last day of the session, when the subject was indefinitely postponed on the pretext that a new arrangement of the circuits was proposed. This was equivalent to rejection. In the following summer Chief-Justice Marshall died; and, with the changes in the membership of the Senate, Jackson was able to compass his darling project more impressively than he had before conceived.[1]

Strongly intrenched in every avenue to power, the Democratic party was in a state of organization and discipline hitherto unknown in American politics. It appeared invincible for a long time to come. That Van Buren was to suc-

---

[1] "Mr. Clay had long ago, in the presence of Reverdy Johnson, made a personal apology for the style of his remarks upon his [Taney's] nomination to the Senate, and paid the highest possible tribute to his great judicial abilities. And ever after Mr. Clay, as his many letters to the Chief-Justice show, seemed to strive for the generous forgiveness of the Chief-Justice, and by his courteous and kind bearing. And the many instances in which Mr. Webster sought the counsel of the Chief-Justice on matters of state show his estimate of his great capacity and wisdom."—Tyler's *Taney*, p. 317. Because of Taney's opinion in the Dred Scott case, Sumner was very bitter toward him.—*Sumner's Works*, vol. ix. p. 274.

ceed Jackson was as well understood as any future political event can be. The design was undisguised, and all available means were employed to execute it. Had he been President the court and consideration he received could hardly have been more distinguished. His candidacy was generally acceptable to the party. The Jacksonian mandate was sufficient to remove all ordinary obstacles. But no adverse chance was to be taken by delay. In May, 1835, nearly eighteen months before the election, the Democratic National Convention was held at Baltimore. As this mode of nomination had been but recently instituted, it was not popular with the masses. Yet this mattered little. The convention was manned by office-holders and unflinching partisans of the administration. Van Buren was quickly and unanimously nominated. In the ensuing canvass there was no vital defection. Calhoun, of course, was still in lonesome hostility. Aside from this, the only open rebellion of any account centred in Tennessee; for, with all his influence, Jackson was unable to control his own State either as to the nomination or in the election. Hugh L. White, a former adherent of Jackson, and a Senator from Tennessee, was nominated in Tennessee, Alabama, and Illinois. Justice McLean, of Ohio, another of Jackson's former adherents, was also a candidate; but he received no electoral votes. Clay recognized the hopelessness of defeating Van Buren, and refused to be a candidate. The Whigs were therefore disintegrated and presented three candidates—Harrison, Webster, and Mangum. Harrison, however, was the most general representative of the party in the contest, and received 73 electoral votes. Webster was loyally supported by Massachusetts, and received her 14 votes. Mangum received South Carolina's 11 votes. White received

26 votes, those of Tennessee and Georgia. Van Buren received 170, a majority of 46 over the combined votes of his rivals. The Vice-Presidency had now relapsed into its former inconsequence. No candidate received a majority of the votes, hence the Senate dutifully elected Richard M. Johnson, who had been nominated with Van Buren. He was a worthy man, but without much political importance. He augured no hinderance to future designs.

Analysis of the Democratic victory over the dissociated elements of the opposition boded danger to the party. The popular vote of those elements was only about 25,000 less than Van Buren's, which was nearly 100,000 less than Jackson's in 1832. Van Buren's chief strength was in the North and East, then as now quickly responsive to the commercial and financial interests; and to thoughtful observers indications already portended the approach of disaster. That the West was so strong for Harrison vividly demonstrated that the tactics of the more active and practical managers of the Whig party, following the example that led to Jackson's elevation, were well grounded. They listened to the outcry of their Senatorial chieftains against military reputation as a means of Presidential preferment, but proceeded nevertheless with exclusive view to success and patronage. Van Buren's candidacy was an efficient illustration. It evoked no enthusiasm. His personality and career were the complete obverse of Jackson's. The popular taste, which had been cultivated by the bold and belligerent character and exploits of "Old Hickory," still plainly preferred military renown and martial vigor to merely civic qualifications. Clay was beginning painfully to perceive it; and he was soon to be the victim of it again.

He spent the recess at Ashland studying events, harvesting

his crops, and watching his fine herds of live-stock. The only incident to mar the quiet tenor of these occupations was to be attacked by one of his bulls, that gored and killed the horse Clay was riding. He was bruised by his fall, but not otherwise injured. Before the details of the election were fully known he was again at his post in the Senate. The session opened December 5, and proved a fitting climax to Jackson's public career.

Historical criticism that bestows upon opposing political elements about the same measure of praise and blame is not always difficult and has the aspect of fairness, but it is apt to be superficial. Yet a candid survey of our political history during the administrations of Jackson and Van Buren compels substantially this conclusion. For the heated and ofttimes frantic struggles during this period over questions that should have had no connection with politics, both parties were guilty in nearly the same degree. It is amazing that statesmen of experience, understanding, and ability should, through zeal for partisan advantage, have been so led to disregard the fundamental interests of the country. The first requisite of national prosperity is sound and undisturbed finance; yet for years this vital matter was the football of politics.

The remote origin of this protracted contest undoubtedly lay in Jackson's belligerent temperament and the swift and narrow working of his mind. Men do not become philosophers after sixty—much less do men of Jackson's type. He came into the Presidency with all his traits and defects not only incorrigible, but accentuated by his political success and the remarkable fealty of his party. The character and mental attributes of a human being were never more unmistakably revealed by physical appearance than by Jackson's. His figure was tall, spare, erect, and commanding. His features were worn and seamed, but fixed and strong. His steady, deep-set eyes, shadowed by shaggy brows, had a piercing gleam. His lips, when not suavely relaxed, had a rigidly firm and defiant expression. His hair was white, dense, and bristling, and an appropriate crown to a bearing and individuality that no stranger could meet without startling recognition. As with all such characters, he was somewhat superstitious: if he could avoid it he would not begin anything on Friday; and probably he was more or less a believer in his destiny. Any opposition to his plans and purposes he took as a personal affront; for he always ascribed the basest motives to his opponents. From this habit of mind, coupled with his tremendous resolution to accomplish whatever he desired to do, proceeded his implacable hatred of his political adversaries. He no doubt sincerely believed that Adams's election over him in 1824 was a dastardly political crime. Thenceforth he saw nothing good in anything proposed or done by any party to that transaction. He already hated Clay for his speeches on the Seminole war; and this feeling quickly embraced all who followed Clay's lead. Thus Jackson's temper and combativeness compressed the free elements that soon formed the Whig party, whose leaders fully reciprocated Jackson's hostility. The inevitable result was that partisanship too often excluded statesmanship. Had the bank kept scrupulously within its proper sphere, Jackson probably would not have seriously attempted its overthrow; certainly he could not have succeeded. In his annual messages a few abstract paragraphs against the institution would have satisfied his conscience and proved harmless. But when his enemies spurned all compromise and made the existing policy of the bank a political issue, and transformed the bank's enormous powers into political functions, war without quarter began, regardless of consequences. When Jackson conceived, on good grounds, that the public funds were loaned through political considerations in the interest of the Whig party, the most powerful instinct of his nature was aroused. He could not have been moved by a deep regard for the public interests or for the safety and proper use of the deposits, for in distributing the revenues among the "pet banks" he gave opportunity for the same charge against the administration that he had urged against the bank, although the danger of some improprieties in the deposit and use of the funds was removed by the bill passed soon afterward. Like all the other proceedings concerning the bank, his course was chiefly induced by political strategy. But the principal evil resulting from it was not favoritism to borrowers—though it was shown to the deposit banks—but the stimulus it gave to abnormal inflation of values, and hence to speculation. And this unhealthy condition was furthered and intensified by the vicious and demagogical scheme of depositing the surplus revenues with the States—a scheme upon which both parties had united a few months before the election. Jackson signed the bill for the same reason that most of the Senators and Representatives voted for it—the fear of popular disfavor. It is not probable that he would have sanctioned it without Van Buren's assent, as he was the one to be most directly affected politically. But so rapidly had the disastrous consequences of political finance begun to threaten that Van Buren, before the election, expressed emphatic disapproval of the scheme; and by the time Congress reconvened, Jackson had repented his approval of it. He now fully perceived its dangerous tendencies, and elaborately stated in his message the reasons against it.

Notwithstanding the manifest lessons and logic of the situation, distribution continued to be invincibly popular, and many prominent members of both houses of Congress were eager to press the policy beyond the scope of the deposit bill. Many other schemes were presented; the fungi of political and sectional rapacity multiplied and differentiated on this muck-heap of public plunder. Perhaps the worst feature of the whole matter was the lamentable condition into which the popular mind had fallen in the presence of this temptation. It was strikingly evinced by a wanton disregard of the express letter of the deposit bill, which explicitly provided that the funds were to be merely deposited with the States, *loaned*, and therefore subject to recall. This was bad enough, yet very few regarded the process as anything but an absolute distribution, *gift*. During the debates on the bill this purpose was openly proclaimed. The people generally so regarded it; and so it ultimately proved to be.[1] Aside from the popularity of the measure, the Whigs, to a large extent, favored it because it would materially reduce the federal funds in the deposit banks and thus deprive the administration of so much political leverage. From any point of view, it was a

---

[1] In a speech in January, 1841, Clay said: "The Senator from New York [Wright] has adverted to the twenty-eight millions of surplus divided a few years ago among the States. He has said, truly, that it arose from the public lands. Was not that, in effect, distribution? Was it not so understood at the time? Was it not voted for by Senators as practical distribution? The Senator from North Carolina [Mangum] has stated that he did. I did. Other Senators did; and no one, not the boldest, will have the temerity to rise here and propose to require or compel the States to refund that money. If, in form, it was a deposit with the States, in fact and in truth it was distribution. So it was regarded. So it will ever remain."

flagrant makeshift to remedy an unwholesome condition produced by equally pernicious causes.

Early in the session, Clay, undaunted by the previous failures of his land-money distribution bill, introduced it again; but it went no further, as the Committee on Public Lands, to which it was referred, reported a substitute providing that the lands should be only sold to actual settlers and in limited quantities. Two days after Clay had introduced his familiar bill, Calhoun presented one providing that the deposit law be extended to any surplus above $5,000,000 that might exist after January 1, 1838. In the South, distribution was considered rather as a partial recompense for the burden of an inequitable tariff than a matter of financial policy. Calhoun did not say this, but no doubt it was his opinion. He expressed the belief that inasmuch as the surplus was unavoidable it should not be left in the Treasury, and that it was more safe and equitable that the States should have the use of it in preference to the banks. "This, in fact," said he, "is the great and leading principle which lies at the foundation of the act of the last session — an act that will forever distinguish the Twenty-fourth Congress — an act which will go down with honor to posterity, as it has obtained the almost unanimous approbation of the present day. The passage has inspired the country with new hopes. It has been beheld abroad as a matter of wonder, a phenomenon in the fiscal world, such as could have sprung out of no institutions but ours, and which goes in a powerful and impressive manner to illustrate the genius of our government." It is hard to believe that this was Calhoun's candid judgment. It is more likely that he intended it for political effect. The bill was rejected. He then proposed the cession of all the public lands to the several States in which they were situate, to be sold by those States, one-third of the proceeds to be paid into the federal Treasury. This was vigorously opposed, and it failed. It was stigmatized, to Calhoun's irritation, as a direct bid for popular favor in the West.

Meanwhile the House was not barren of projects to dispose of the surplus. One member made bold to attempt the embodiment in law of the prevailing desire to declare the proposed deposits irreclaimable. He moved to instruct the Committee on Ways and Means to report a bill to that effect. The motion found strong support, but was defeated. Another member proposed the direct cession to the old States of lands equal in quantity to those which had been granted to the new States. This proposition was summarily laid on the table. Still another member moved Calhoun's first proposal, to extend the deposit bill. This was finally attached to the fortifications bill and passed. The Senate disagreed, but the House adhered; thus the bill failed, and its first object, appropriations for the defences of the country, was incontinently balked. Such were the efforts, not to mention the various amendments proposing minor and less inclusive schemes offered in both houses, by which unseemly greed and reckless political ambition sought to debauch the country. But here the problem remained until general bankruptcy solved it.

After the rally from the panic of 1833 the fairly sound condition of the currency was due to the force of circumstances rather than to the system. The status of the bank compelled it to extreme prudence, while the local banks, in order to satisfy the requirements of the Treasury Department before they could obtain deposits of the public money, had made themselves reasonably secure. The increase of population, the development of the country, the progress of invention, and the expansion of enterprise which the period exhibited, indicated phenomenal prosperity and promised still greater. Thousands of miles of new railroads and canals, hundreds of new steamboats, and the propulsive activities of commerce and business, inspired the people with industrial valor and energy seldom witnessed. Prices of all products rose steadily, and for a time healthily. Cotton and timber lands advanced in value wondrously and were briskly followed by agricultural and urban property.[1] The final extinguishment of the national debt, a marvel in European eyes, enormously enhanced American credit abroad, and a vast amount of foreign capital was immediately invested here. A large part of the bonded debts of the States was thus absorbed; and with such facility could money be borrowed in this way that many States were rashly precipitated into further debt for extravagant projects of public improvements. Private enterprise received similar impetus and aid, and with the same results.

To a certain degree much of this was sound; but it soon produced what extreme national prosperity always develops

---

[1] "Under this process prices rose like smoke. Lots in obscure villages were held at city prices; land bought at the minimum cost of government was sold at from thirty to forty dollars per acre, and considered dirt cheap at that. . . . Money, got without work, by those unaccustomed to it, turned the heads of its possessors and they spent it with a recklessness like that with which they gained it. The pursuits of industry were neglected, riot and coarse debauchery filled up the vacant hours. . . . The old rules of business and the calculations of prudence were alike disregarded, and profligacy, in all departments of the *crimen falsi*, held riotous carnival. Larceny grew not only respectable, but genteel, and ruffled it in all the pomp of purple and fine linen. Swindling was raised to the dignity of the fine arts. Felony came forth from its covert, put on more seemly habiliments, and took its seat with unabashed front in the upper places of the synagogue."—Baldwin's *Flush Times of Alabama and Mississippi*, p. 83.

—undue distension of values and the spirit of speculation. To accommodate the fictitious thrift that now set in, and without regard to real financial necessity or prosperity, new banks were organized on every side. Thus bank capital, circulation, and loans inordinately increased without a corresponding basis of specie. And for the lavish accommodation to borrowers the administration was partly responsible, for it expressly recommended to the deposit banks liberality in the use of the public money. The moneyed interest of the country seemed beset with financial dementia: banks were thought the magical means of creating wealth out of paper. It was this situation that rendered the scattering of the public funds among this rank growth of banks so harmful. Its encouragement to speculation, especially in the public lands, was prodigious. In the first instance, the lands were bought at the insignificant figure fixed by law. They were then sold and resold, and the multiplied proceeds invested in fresh purchases from the government. By these means the best and most attractive lands were being speedily disposed of. To dispassionate observers the results of this process had reached alarming proportions. Benton, with his usual acumen in such matters, perceived the situation and introduced a bill to prohibit the acceptance by the government of anything but specie in payment for the public lands; but the bill did not pass. Both parties were stubbornly against it. Many members of Congress were either deeply concerned in these speculations or had numerous constituents who were. Even the cabinet vigorously disapproved of any interference. But despite this untoward opposition, Benton convinced the President of the virtue of the measure, although he had recently declared in a message that the great increase in the revenue from the land sales was a gratifying mark of national prosperity and development of agriculture. And it should be remarked of Jackson that he was always ready to change his impulsive opinions—if his prejudices were not involved—when convinced that they were wrong. A conspicuous instance of this was his change of attitude toward distribution; for in two of his early messages he had announced his disapproval of that course. The incontestable fact was that the accumulating surplus came largely from the public lands, and it was apparent that unless Benton's plan was soon enforced the surplus would be in danger of being composed of irredeemable paper. Knowing that Congress would not interfere, the President accepted Benton's urgent advice and resolved to adopt an heroic measure. He waited until Congress adjourned; then, forthwith, over the remonstrance of a majority of the cabinet, carried out his purpose. At the President's request, Benton drafted an order requiring the Secretary of the Treasury to instruct the land officers to receive after August 15 only gold, silver, and land-scrip, for the public lands, except from actual settlers or *bona-fide* residents in the State where the sales were made. Until December 15 each of this latter class of purchasers was permitted to buy any quantity of land not exceeding three hundred and twenty acres, and pay in the usual way. These conditions were authorized by law. The order was at once obeyed by the issue of the "specie circular." It arrested many millions of dollars in process of transmutation into real estate.

The commotion this fiat produced was wide-spread and violent. Unlike the removal of the deposits, it had no partisan aspect and evoked no merely political demonstrations. Every individual, every interest, and every bank concerned directly or indirectly in land speculations felt the blow. Not only were the immediate operators checked and their hopes of affluence rudely blighted, but they suddenly found themselves in unexpected jeopardy of being land poor or paper poor; for the indirect consequences of the order were far-reaching and powerful. It was a vexatious inconvenience to transport specie from the East, whence it had to come; and its withdrawal made it scarce and costly. The money centres had begun to discern the phantasy of the paper system. Besides this, the time for making the order was most inopportune for speculation. The banks were providing for the first instalment of the distribution among the States. Foreign resources were also curtailed by fundamental causes similar to those existing here. Thus every financial influence was conspiring to embarrass the money-market; and the myriad of borrowers were driven to pay exorbitant rates to protect their inflated investments.

When the specie circular was issued, unforeseen and unimagined, the shock at first was paralyzing. There broke forth a wail of consternation, quickly followed by explosions of boisterous wrath. Many of Jackson's devoted followers turned upon him and reviled him. For those who had previously opposed him no epithets or denunciations were adequate in which to vent their feelings. All the time-worn terms that had been applied to Jackson's acts—absolutism, tyranny, usurpation, ignorance, perversity, and the like— were far too feeble. The terrible chorus of invective and reprobation that arose has never been equalled in our history. But the grim old man, hardened to clamor and obloquy, was unmoved. Though the appalling condition that menaced was in part his own creation, whether or not he recognized the fact, he did not falter in the course he had taken. He was ready to strike again if necessary. And it became necessary.

The meeting of Congress was anxiously awaited in the hope that the President's arbitrary edict, issued in recess, and in defiance of the well-known opinion of both the Senate and the House, would be abrogated. Shortly after Congress reconvened, the parliamentary process was started. Senator Ewing, of Ohio, a conspicuous figure in his day, impressively set it in motion by introducing joint resolutions, which afterward took the form of a bill, to rescind the specie circular and restore the former practice. A long and intermittent debate ensued. The Whigs led the onset with their accustomed vigor. They charged the President with every dishonorable motive, from a desire to aid the deposit banks to a wilful disregard of positive law, while Democrats mildly argued against the policy. Benton, almost single-handed, bore the brunt. His responsibility for the measure was understood, and the battle in the Senate became virtually his personal affair. At one time the discussion became so heated that he again nearly involved himself in a duel. But the most important result, as it proved, of his untiring labor, was to protract the debate until toward the close of the session. The main cause of this was that the debate was soon diversified by other related topics, particularly the currency, which for years had been Benton's almost incessant theme. It underlay all his various struggles against the bank. This primal thought in all his financial discussion is shown by a passage, which strikingly exhibits his characteristic combination of sense and pomposity, in one of his speeches on the bill to rescind the circular:

"The present bloat," said he, "in the paper system cannot continue; the present depreciation of money, exemplified in the high price of everything dependent upon the home market, cannot last. The revulsion will come, as surely as it did in 1819–20. But it will come with less force if the Treasury order is maintained and if paper money shall be excluded from the federal Treasury. But let these things go as they may, and let reckless or misguided banks do what they please, there is still a refuge for the wise and the good; there is still an ark of safety for every honest bank, and for every prudent man: it is the mass of gold and silver now in the country—the seventy-odd millions which the wisdom of President Jackson's administration has accumulated—and by getting their share of which all who are so disposed can take care of themselves. Sir, I have performed a duty to myself, not pleasant, but necessary. This bill is to be an era in our legislation and in our political history. It is to be a point upon which future ages will be thrown back and from which future consequences will be traced. I separate myself from it; I wash my hands of it; I oppose it. I am one of those who promised gold, not paper. I promised the currency of the Constitution, not the currency of corporations. I did not join in putting down the Bank of the United States to put up a wilderness of local banks. I did not join in putting down the paper currency of a national bank to put up a national paper currency of a thousand local banks. I did not strike Cæsar to make Antony master of Rome."

Calhoun's course was peculiar. He said that he put no faith in the measure to arrest the downward course of the country; that he believed the state of the currency was almost incurably bad, so that it was doubtful whether the highest skill and wisdom could restore it to soundness, and that it was destined at no distant time to undergo an entire revolution; that he considered an explosion inevitable, and so much the greater the longer it was delayed. Yet he declined to vote because he was not prepared to state his reasons at large for the vote that he might cast. Webster strove to give the bill the sanction of his ponderous legal authority; and Clay supported it in his usual style in a speech similar to one he had made to his constituents before the session opened. It was finally passed by the Senate, 41 to 5. The thoroughness of the debate there, however, deprived the House of an opportunity to invest the subject with any novelty; but there were sufficient discussion and delay to prevent the bill, which was passed by the House, 143 to 59, from reaching the President until the day before the dissolution of Congress and his own retirement. He neither signed nor vetoed it. In political parlance, he "pocketed it." He treated it as he had Clay's land bill. He announced his determination in a short message, but placed it on the ground that the provisions of the bill were too complex and of doubtful meaning. Perhaps he thought it unnecessary to state his paramount reasons— unalterable resolution to maintain the circular, and the assurance that Congress would override a veto. It was almost the last of his official acts and one of the most vividly characteristic of the man and his Presidential independence.

His subsequent critics, following the outcry raised at the time, have regarded his action in retaining the bill as a violation of the spirit of the Constitution. It is charged that he despotically thwarted the legislative power, preventing by his own individual caprice and obstinacy the enactment of any law whatever on the subject. That vague essence denominated the "spirit of the Constitution" has always

Ch. VII.] THE SPECIE CIRCULAR CONSTITUTIONAL 305

been the refuge of theorists as well as of those who have sought to distend the letter of that instrument for political purposes. It has thus been made to mean anything or nothing, according to the necessity of the occasion. The Constitution is the organic law; and, being such, the only safety in construing it lies in the logic of civilized jurisprudence. Where its terms are clear and express they are to be taken in their common and obvious meaning; and what they explicitly permit is Constitutional and valid whatever the consequences may be. The President is a factor in the legislative power. That he has the Constitutional right to retain a bill without approval or veto when it is not presented to him until within ten days of the adjournment of Congress is as certain as language can make it. Jackson's procedure, therefore, cannot be justly challenged on any Constitutional ground. That he had the legal right and power to make the specie order is likewise open to no rational doubt. Neither Webster nor Clay, nor any other competent lawyer in sympathy with their attitude toward the circular, could he have divested himself of his personal and political prejudices, would have argued before a judicial tribunal that it was not legally justified. That power was granted by a joint resolution adopted by Congress and approved by the President in 1816, which therefore had all the force of a formal statute. Simply stated, the question was, Does the word "or," as used in the resolution, mean "and"? The resolution directed the Secretary of the Treasury to adopt such means as he deemed necessary to cause "all duties, taxes, debts, or sums of money accruing or becoming payable to the United States to be collected and paid in the legal currency of the United States, *or* Treasury notes, *or* notes of the Bank of the United States as by law

20

provided and declared, *or* in notes of banks which are payable and paid on demand in said legal currency of the United States." It then needlessly added that "no such duties, taxes, debts, or sums of money . . . ought to be collected or received otherwise than in the legal currency of the United States, *or* notes of the Bank of the United States, *or* Treasury notes, *or* notes of banks which are payable and paid on demand in said legal currency of the United States." Beyond doubt the resolution granted the power of selection, and hence of exclusion. Nor was the practical construction of precedent wanting. The power of prohibiting the acceptance of specified classes of paper had been repeatedly exercised and without question. Crawford, while Secretary of the Treasury under Monroe, had exercised it several times; and Rush, under John Quincy Adams, had exercised it twice. Legally considered, therefore, the specie circular was valid. The question whether or not it was financially right is of course debatable; yet it scarcely admits of just criticism. It did not accomplish the good it might had it been issued sooner; but had it been, it would certainly have been overruled by Congress. As it was, it had comparatively slight effect, for the overshadowing crisis was close at hand. But it performed some service—to the prudent it was a warning, to the imprudent a restraint, and it stayed further waste of the public domain.

CHAPTER VIII

The Recognition of Texas — The Mexican Claims — International Copyright — Slavery — Benton's Resolution to Expunge the Senate's Censure of Jackson for the Removal of the Deposits — The Final Preparations — The Debate — Clay's Speech, Buchanan's Speech, and Webster's Protest — The Resolution Adopted and Executed — Jackson's Gratification — Analysis of his Presidency — Clay Decides to Remain in the Senate

BEYOND the usual routine laws, the session was not prolific of legislation. The three months of its duration were mostly consumed in debate. Like the distribution schemes and the bill to rescind the specie circular, an effort to reduce the tariff failed. Late in February, after stout opposition, the Senate passed a bill for that purpose; but it made little progress in the House, where a similar bill had already been under discussion without avail. Clay indignantly combated the plan, which he imputed to the administration, as an exhibition of bad faith toward the Compromise of 1833. He spoke with much feeling and narrated at some length his part in that measure, which for years was the source of explanation, accusation, and retort.

The disposition to recognize the independence of Texas was more successful. In a special message the President reported such information as he had acquired touching the status of Texas, but he was not satisfied that it yet warranted the government in recognizing it as an independent state. He advised delay, but expressed his willingness to co-operate with the judgment of Congress. By this time the popular desire was not to be overcome. March 1, the Senate adopted a resolution, 23 to 19, that Texas be recognized as an independent state. Clay was not present when the vote was taken, and probably he was not in favor of the resolution; but the next day he voted against a motion to reconsider, which was barely lost by an equal division. While the House was not disposed to adopt a formal resolution to recognize the independence of Texas, it inserted in the appropriation bill a provision for the expense of a diplomatic agent to the "republic of Texas" — whenever the President received satisfactory evidence that it was an independent power and he should deem it expedient to send a minister. As originally introduced, the provision was unequivocal and called for immediate action; the appropriation was for "the salary and outfit of a diplomatic agent to be sent to the independent government of Texas." But as modified it was regarded, as it was intended to be, as equivalent to an express declaration that independence be recognized. It answered the purpose.

Closely connected with this subject was a series of difficulties with Mexico, which had for some years been growing more aggravated, arising on one side from the claims of our citizens for injuries inflicted by the Mexicans, and on the other from the overbearing and hostile action of our government and of our troops along the frontier. The impulsive Mexican Minister at length involved himself in a violent quarrel with the administration, demanded his passports, and wrathfully left the country. Our claims were so strongly maintained by the government that they rapidly multiplied in number. Many of them were spurious or grossly exaggerated, and the friction between the two governments increased, Mexico being naturally angered at the feeling prevalent in this country in favor of Texas. And the conclusion is irresistible that the course of the administration was chiefly guided by the purpose of embroiling Mexico in the interest of the ultimate annexation of Texas. After unsuccessfully pressing the claims for a time with incontinent zeal, our *chargé d'affaires* left Mexico with a swaggering show of indignation. The administration was strongly inclined to forcible measures. In a special message, February 7, the President said: "The length of time since some of the injuries have been committed, the repeated and unavailing applications for redress, the wanton character of some of the outrages upon the property and persons of our citizens, upon the officers and flag of the United States, independent of recent insults to this government and people by the late extraordinary Mexican Minister, would justify in the eyes of all nations immediate war." But to evince "wisdom and moderation," he recommended the passage of an act authorizing reprisals if Mexico should not "come to an amicable adjustment of the matters in controversy between us upon another demand thereof from on board one of our vessels of war on the coast of Mexico." The Senate Committee on Foreign Relations, of which Buchanan was now chairman, made a report sustaining for the most part the views of the President, but presented a resolution that fell just short of approving the radical means he had proposed. It declared in careful and temperate phrase that the Senate concurred with the President that another demand for redress should be made, in the usual mode, and if the effort proved unsuccessful " a state of things will then have occurred which will make it the imperative duty of Congress promptly to consider what measures may be required by the honor of the nation and the rights of our injured fellow-citizens." It was unanimously adopted. In the House, resolutions of somewhat similar import, but more vigorous, were also adopted. In the face of this demonstration it was supposed that the weakness of Mexico would compel acquiescence. It should be observed that the Senate has, until of late years, usually shown more commendable caution in international complications than the Executive Department has been wont to practise. The House, on the contrary, has generally inclined, regardless of party, to countenance the President in such flourishes, because of its closer relations with the people. This has demonstrated the wisdom of excluding it from the treaty-making function.

Clay spoke in support of the Senate resolution, but took occasion nevertheless to criticise the report of the committee, and indirectly the administration. He said that the case against Mexico as stated by the committee was stronger than the evidence warranted; that the situation did not justify either war or reprisals; and that the Mexican Minister and our *chargé d'affaires* were both at fault, for their precipitate action. But he endeavored to soften the censure of the Minister's misconduct in publishing a pamphlet on the grievances of his country and himself by relating in his mellowest manner an anecdote of his experience while a peace commissioner at Ghent, and also recounting another circumstance that had recently occurred. To this talent for felicitous speech, so often employed by him, Clay owed much of his peculiar influence; and it is worth while, as an illustration, to quote this part of his impromptu remarks.

" While up," said he, " I will take the opportunity of saying that I do not concur in all the reasonings of the committee as to the publication of a pamphlet by Mr. Gorostiza, the Mexican envoy extraordinary. I will say, however, that it was a great diplomatic irregularity; but I do not think it makes out a case for war or for any serious disturbance. It is not an unusual case. I recollect an instance which occurred while the American commissioners were at Ghent, in 1814, at a most critical state of the negotiation—when it hung, as it were, on a balance, and when it was doubtful whether there would not be a rupture. While I was treating with Lord Gambier and the other British commissioners, a publication from the United States containing the correspondence between the governments of the United States and Great Britain found its way there. Lord Gambier, having seen it, expressed his surprise to me that my government should have given publicity to this correspondence, and said he could not see how they could justify the act. The other commissioners were equally displeased at the occurrence. I then explained to them that the course which had been adopted was one growing out of the peculiar structure of this government and which the people here demand of their servants. I mention this to show that what Mr. Gorostiza has done is not a thing unexampled. It will be remembered that the other day Mr. Pageot, the French Minister, just before embarking for France from New York, published a letter of the Duc de Broglie. Mr. Pageot has since returned to this country and has been received frankly and without any intimation of dissatisfaction on the part of our government. And I have no more doubt of the fact than of my standing on this floor at this moment that there had been information conveyed through some channel, official or unofficial, to France that Mr. Pageot's return to the United States would be welcomed without any displeasure being shown toward him in regard to his having published the letter of the Duc de Broglie; otherwise the French government would not have sent him to this country. Had Mr. Gorostiza not known the fact of this publication, he probably would not have pursued the example set him."

Clay's liberality of opinion in matters not political was shown by the interest he took in an effort by foreign authors to procure the benefit of copyright in this country. Their case was confided to his care. He presented their memorials and enforced them with brief observations favoring the request. Shortly afterward he also presented the petition of several American authors, doubtless prepared as a remonstrance, to amend the existing law in their interest. They complained that because American publishers could print British works without expense of copyright, they could not obtain a fair compensation for their works; and, carrying the theory of protection to its full limit, they besought Congress to prohibit entirely the publication of foreign works. This sordid suggestion, it is gratifying to know, met with no encouragement. In fact, it was soon repelled by a large number of other American authors, who, in enlightened contrast, urged that the benefit of our copyright laws be extended to foreigners. Clay took this just view. His remarks on presenting the first petition excellently stated the broad argument for international copyright. In the course of his remarks on presenting the petition of the hostile American authors, he gave this account of the piratical enterprise of American publishers in appropriating foreign works:

"I understand that the course of this business is that American booksellers have their agents in Great Britain, who as soon as a new work makes its appearance transmit it to them by the first packet. Sometimes it is received from the packet at The Narrows, and the vessel being detained there a short time, from some cause or other, by the time she arrives at the wharves the work is published and ready for distribution. This extraordinary despatch is effected by means of steam-presses and the hundreds of hands employed by some of the booksellers. The consequence is that the work is often slovenly published, on bad paper, with bad types, and omitting maps, diagrams, engravings, and other illustrations. This the first publishers feel themselves constrained to do, lest some rivals shall publish a cheaper edition than that which they have issued. Purchased in this defective form, no one can get the genuine production of the British author without sending abroad for it, as is sometimes done."

The petitions were referred to a select committee, of which Clay was made chairman. A report was soon presented and a bill introduced in accordance with his views; but it went no further.[1] Nor was the principle of this bill incorporated in the copyright laws until 1891, after several fruitless attempts.

At this session the slavery question would have engaged little attention but for an episode that occurred in the

---

[1] Buchanan said : "Cheap editions of foreign works are now published and sent all over the country so as to be within the reach of every individual ; and the effect of granting copyrights asked for by this memorial would be that the authors who were anxious to have their works appear in a more expensive form would prevent the issuing of these cheap editions ; so that the amount of republications of British works in this country, I think, would be at once reduced to one-half. But to live in fame is as great a stimulus to authors as pecuniary gain ; and the question ought to be considered whether they would not lose as much of fame by the measure asked for as they would gain in money. It is especially well worthy of the committee to go beyond publishers and ascertain what would be the effect on the acquisition of knowledge in this vast country."

House. Abolition petitions in the familiar forms were indeed plentiful, but in consequence of the prolonged excitement they had previously provoked they had lost much of their agitating effect and were taken largely as a matter of course. As soon as they were presented they were tabled under the "gag," which was now a fixture in the rules. Moreover, the other topics of the session had engrossed so much attention that the House had become quite indifferent to the tireless function of John Quincy Adams as the main channel of presenting the petitions. One morning, however, he aroused the slumbering fury of the Southern members in a most unexpected and exasperating way. After presenting some two hundred ordinary petitions he said that he had a paper on which, before it was presented, he desired the decision of the Speaker. It was a petition from twenty-two persons declaring themselves to be slaves. He wished to know whether such a paper came within the order of the House. The Speaker, James K. Polk, at once perceived, with evident embarrassment, what was imminent. He replied that he could not tell unless he was in possession of its contents. Mr. Adams also appreciated the consequences, and with that technical dexterity of which he was master, he took care not to render himself vulnerable. He said that if the paper were sent to the clerk's table it would be in possession of the House, and if sent to the chair the Speaker could see what were its contents. "Now I wish to do nothing," he continued, "except in submission to the rules of the House. This paper purports to come from slaves, and it is one of those petitions which have occurred to my mind as not being what they purport to be. It is signed partly by persons who could not write, by making their marks, and partly by persons whose handwriting would manifest that they had received the education of slaves. The petition declares itself to be from slaves, and I am requested to present it. I will send it to the chair." By this time the apathetic members of the House began to discover what was taking place. Objection was made to the paper going to the chair, and the Speaker anxiously expressed his desire to obtain the sense of the House.

The tumult and frenzy of the scenes and debate that followed were never exceeded in all the subsequent course of the antislavery agitation in Congress. The boundless rage of the Southern members at first blinded them to parliamentary law and usage as well as to the precise appreciation of what Adams had actually said and done. He was assailed with insult and vituperation. The first impulse of the enraged members vented itself in shouts to expel him. Then came resolutions that he be called to the bar and censured. For several days the storm of angry discussion continued, Adams maintaining his position with marvellous courage, coolness, and skill. Time after time resolutions were proposed and withdrawn, and amendments, modifications, and substitutes offered. But the turmoil gradually subsided, and when the House became sufficiently composed to appreciate the precise facts of the affair it reached a very temperate conclusion. It adopted two resolutions with a preamble. The latter did not even mention Adams's name, but merely stated the naked question first suggested by him, whether the petition came within the rule. The resolutions were, first, that the petition could not be received by the House without disregarding its own dignity, the rights of a large class of citizens in the South and West, and the Constitution of the United States; second, that slaves did not possess the right of petition secured to the people by the Constitution. Adams and seventeen others voted against both. Despite this fortunate outcome, candor must admit that admiration for the wonderful audacity and ability Adams displayed throughout the fearful ordeal should be tempered by the reflection that the affair was needlessly provoked and did more harm than good.[1]

In the Senate the slavery question remained quite inert. Aside from a pointed and threatening speech by Calhoun against abolition petitions, the only notable revival of it was over a petition of the colonization society, presented by Clay, for a corporate charter to enable it to hold and convey lands. Calhoun at once opposed it. He had become as strongly hostile to the society as the abolitionists had, but for entirely opposite reasons. His attitude was the result of that minute watchfulness and refined logic which led him to scrutinize every proposition suggested, to discern any lurking possibility of an adverse bearing on slavery.

"The Senator from Kentucky," said he, "must know that a great diversity of opinion exists among the wisest and best men of the country as to the ultimate good to be effected by this society; and that the prevailing opinion of the great body of the people of the South is against it. . . . A mysterious Providence has brought the white and black

---

[1] "I remember one day to have been on the floor of the House when he attacked Mr. Wise with great personality and bitterness. In allusion to the Cilley duel, with which he was connected, he spoke of him as coming into that assembly, 'his hands dripping with blood!' There was a terrible jarring tone in his voice, which gave added effect to the denunciation. Every person present seemed to be thrilled with a sort of horror, rather towards Mr. Adams than the object of his reproaches. In speaking of this scene to me afterward an eminent member of Congress said that 'Mr. Adams's greatest delight was to be the hero of a row.' There is no doubt that the rude personal passages which often occurred in the House of Representatives derived countenance from Adams's example."—Goodrich's *Recollections*, vol. ii. p. 404.

people together from different parts of the globe, and no human power can now separate them. The whites are a European race, being masters; and the Africans are the inferior race, and slaves. I believe they can exist among us peaceably enough, if undisturbed, for all time; and it is my opinion that the colonization society and all other schemes gotten up through mistaken motives of philanthropy, in order to bring about an alteration in the condition of the African, have a wrong foundation and are calculated to disturb the existing relations between the North and South. I believe the very existence of the South depends on the existing relations being kept up, and that every scheme which might be introduced, having for its object an alteration in the condition of the negro, is pregnant with danger and ruin. It is a benevolent object and highly desirable that the blessings of civilization and Christianity should be introduced into Africa; but this is a government of limited powers and has no more to do with free negroes than with slaves; and if Africa is to be civilized and Christianized, I hope it will not be done by this government acting beyond its Constitutional powers."

The petition was laid on the table by a vote of 24 to 12; and there it remained, notwithstanding Clay's exertions to procure further action upon it.

But whatever might have been the interest in these varied topics, the most conspicuous feature of the session was the expunging from the Senate journal of the resolution censuring Jackson for the removal of the deposits. Although the circumstance was merely a spectacular episode, it was nevertheless invested with an historical importance that makes it prominent in a period that was filled with striking events. It marked the zenith of Jackson's personal prestige and the nadir of the Whigs' humiliation. The occasion was surcharged with all the accumulated political passions that his Presidency had engendered, and it afforded the final and comprehensive opportunity to review from both sides his public career on the eve of his retirement. The result was the parting glorification of him by his zealous devotees over the prostrate hopes of his adversaries. With the strident note of triumph were mingled the execrations of conquered power and unconquered pride.

Immediately after the adoption of the censure, and again during the debate over the President's protest, Benton gave formal notice of his intention to move an expunging resolution, and pledged himself to prosecute this purpose until he succeeded or terminated his political life. During the next session he introduced such a resolution and made an elaborate speech in its behalf. As it could not then succeed, his efforts were designed for popular effect, and it was tabled without intention on his part to revive it during the session. But so obnoxious was the word "expunge" to the Whigs, and so fraught with danger in the opinion of many Democrats, that an attempt was made by mutual agreement to change the proposition to expunge to some other more consonant with Constitutional scruples. Accordingly the resolution was called up by one of its opponents with this object in view. At once Hugh L. White moved to strike out the words "ordered to be expunged from the journal" and insert "rescinded, reversed, repealed, and declared to be null and void." But as there was still some difference of opinion among Jackson's supporters as to what should be inserted, King moved to omit the proposed substitute from the motion. Such insistent pressure was brought to bear on Benton by several of his party colleagues that he was compelled to acquiesce. The motion was carried, 39 to 7. Most of the Senators now supposed that this display of conciliation would be followed by filling the blank with the formula White had proposed, or by some other substantially equivalent; and that if this were done expunging would be irretrievably relinquished. The astonishment was therefore extreme when Webster rose and theatrically proclaimed the triumph of the Constitution over the project to expunge, and moved to lay the maimed resolution on the table, asserting that he would not withdraw the motion for friend or foe. The motion precluded further amendment or debate, and prevailed by a party vote.

The Democrats were indignant, and most of them, abandoning their former scruples, determined to insist on expunging. Benton naturally was most deeply incensed. He at once resubmitted the original resolution, to stand over to the next session, and defiantly declared that he would not yield again for friend or foe. And he did not. With renewed and redoubtable energy he persisted in his purpose. Pursuant to the programme he had announced, he brought up the resolution at the next session and spoke with increased vigor. At the session following he presented it again and made another long harangue. Through his exertions expunging had become a test of Democratic loyalty. The party press, the local leaders, and the rank and file clamored for it, and a majority of the State legislatures elected and instructed Senators to execute it. One of the prevailing political theories of the period was that Senators and Representatives were bound by the instructions of their State legislatures. This absurdity, which substituted politics for the Constitutional tenure of office, and the opinions of State legislatures for the functions of Congress, long had the force of unwritten law. It was forcibly exemplified during the expunging agitation. When the legislature of Virginia adopted resolutions against the removal of the deposits, Rives, a supporter of the administration, felt obliged to resign, and Leigh took his place. But the legislature soon became Democratic, and instructed the Senators to vote for expunging. John Tyler refused to obey the mandate, and on his resignation Rives was returned. Leigh would not resign, and in consequence totally forfeited his political caste. Tyler received his reward later.

The number of Democratic Senators steadily increased until they formed a sufficient phalanx to render the final assault as imposing as it was irresistible. The time had come much sooner than Benton expected; and it came opportunely for the most dramatic effect—a consideration that he fully appreciated and adroitly utilized. Even if the resolution could have been adopted at the preceding session, he might well have been content to wait. The last session during Jackson's Presidency was the most fitting time to humble his opponents and exalt his hero. And it so chanced that the cruelty of this exultation was capable of refinement. December 7, two days after the session opened, he gave notice of his intention to present his resolution. But he waited until the 20th, the third anniversary of the day on which Clay moved the censure. The resolution, which was preceded by a long explanatory and declamatory preamble, was as follows:

"*Resolved*, That the said resolve be expunged from the journal; and, for that purpose, that the secretary of the Senate, at such time as the Senate may appoint, shall bring the manuscript journal of the session of 1833–34 into the Senate, and, in the presence of the Senate, draw black lines round said resolve, and write across the face thereof, in strong letters, the following words: 'Expunged by order of the Senate, this   day of   , in the year of our Lord, 1837.'"

January 12, he opened the debate by delivering a set speech on the resolution. This time the tone of his oration was changed from high-wrought argument and appeal to the dogmatic and gloating assurance he enjoyed in the prospect of the success he had so persistently toiled to achieve. He began by an elaborate display of personal and partisan egotism, which events, indeed, had to a large degree made pardonable. Complacently disdaining to renew the argument, which the popular voice had thus rendered superfluous, he proceeded in the full panoply of the Bentonesque style to pronounce a studied eulogy on Jackson and his administration. He was too practical to indulge in much vacuous rhapsody, although his ardor and impetuous feelings often impelled him to grotesque exaggeration; but combined with this were his practised mastery of facts and a brawny sarcasm that was exacerbating to the morbid resentment of his adversaries.

This speech was made on Monday, January 9. But four other speeches on the subject were delivered between that time and the following Monday, when the closing scenes were enacted. On Saturday a sort of Democratic caucus was held at Boulanger's, a noted restaurant, to canvass the situation fully. The task was not without difficulty. Benton and some others were for actual expurgation; but it was evident that some would not agree to this—the Constitutional objection still haunted them. Compromise and good cheer, however, at length surmounted the obstacles. The radical yielded, the reluctant were stimulated, the doubting were convinced; all harmonized on the hybrid plan as it stood. Benton confesses that "it required all the moderation, tact, and skill of the prime movers to induce and maintain the union upon details, on the success of which the fate of the measure depended." The conclave lasted until midnight; but when it broke up the final arrangements were perfected. Each Senator pledged himself to vote for the resolution and to sit up all night if needful to press it to a vote. Benton took care to provide for an ample supply of viands, wine, and coffee, to be served in an anteroom of the Senate chamber, where the wearied and hungered champions of expunging could snatch refreshment during the austerities and anxieties of a protracted session.

When the resolution was taken up at the appointed hour the debate proceeded. Evening set in. The chamber and its approaches were brilliantly lighted. Every available space not held by Senators in that historic room was occupied by members of the House and those who were favored with the envied privilege. The corridors and lobbies were eagerly thronged and the galleries were resplendent with the fashion and display that grace the boxes at grand opera on the opening night. The spectacle was all that the Senate in its greatest epoch could evoke. Such an occasion, awed and dignified by the presence of such a galaxy of justly distinguished public men, has not been possible in Washington since the memorable period that ended with their lives.

Chief among the various motives that brought this expectant assemblage together was the desire to hear the speech of Henry Clay. From the time that Benton first proclaimed the expunging design, Clay had maintained a contemptuous silence toward it. But that he would remain mute at the final hour was not to be supposed. More than any other man he was bound to remonstrate. No stronger provocation to antipathy and resentment could animate him than that which was boldly flaunted by Benton's resolution. And he of all men was best qualified to give expression to the sentiments and feelings of the Whigs toward Jackson and this unprecedented mode of hero-worship. Others could argue in justification of the censure and against its propriety and constitutionality as well as he could—possibly better; but no man possessed in so great a degree that subtle fusion of presence, manner, voice, speech, temperament, personality, and intellect which constitutes the highest type of the parliamentary orator. Thus it was rightly judged that the philippic he would pronounce on this aggravating occasion would remain to those who heard it one of the vivid memories of a lifetime. Apparently unconscious that he was the focus of attention and comment, he sat with grave countenance, yet with a gleam of suppressed rancor in the eye, until the appropriate moment came for him to speak. He then rose slowly, and, grimly surveying the hushed scene, proceeded in the modulated tones of his rich and wonderful voice with one of the most notable speeches of his long career.

His exordium was plain and serious and displayed that fluid ease of diction and indefinable quality of style so rare even among writers and extraordinary in public speech. He then entered upon a rapid and admirable *résumé* of the arguments originally advanced in support of the resolution of censure—Jackson's unwarranted assumption, as the Whigs maintained, of authority over the public money and of the power to dismiss Executive officials; justifying the resolution against the criticism that it was virtually an impeachment of the President without observing the Constitutional forms of procedure, and maintaining the right of the Senate to declare its opinion concerning any act of Executive usurpation. This was followed by an examination of the asserted right to expunge. After illustrating this argument, he turned to the prolix preamble to the resolution and commented with severity on the statement of facts it contained. Then came his peroration, in which his indignation and contempt reached the height of his oratorical expression. For many years it was printed in books on rhetoric with noted passages from the speeches of Otis, Henry, Wirt, and Webster, and declaimed by emulous school-boys.

Delivered as this peroration was, with all of his intensity of feeling and magnetic power, of which his language gives but slight token, the effect on his auditory was prodigious and thrilling.[1] Even Benton says: "He concentrated his wrath and grief in an apostrophizing peroration which lacked nothing but verisimilitude to have been grand and affecting." It certainly had as much verisimilitude as the profuse and fulsome panegyrics of Jackson displayed; and it would doubtless have defeated the resolution but for the extreme pressure of politics and the iron-clad pledge of the Democrats to force it through. The less determined among them writhed under his drastic scorn and sought the refreshment-room to revive their wincing courage.[2]

---

[1] Buchanan began his speech by saying: "Mr. President, after the able and eloquent display of the Senator from Kentucky, who has just resumed his seat, after having so long enchained the attention of his audience, it might be the dictate of prudence for me to remain silent."

[2] "I envy not," said Ewing, "the triumph of him who has pressed forward this resolution against the opinions and the feelings and the consciences of those whom he has found means to compel to its support—a resolution which he has urged on with passions fierce, vindictive, furious. Still less do I envy the condition of those who are compelled to go onward against all those feelings and motives which should direct the actions

Clay was followed by Buchanan in a very characteristic speech.[1] He was generally logical and candid, laborious and ineloquent. He plodded carefully over the entire original controversy, and then approached the difficulty which had taken him a long period of searching suspense to overcome. "I entered the Senate," said he, "in December, 1834, fresh from the ranks of the people, without the slightest feeling of hostility against any member on this floor. I then thought that the resolution of the Senator from Missouri was too severe in proposing to expunge." The manner in which he finally succeeded in satisfying his mind and overcoming his Constitutional doubt is a curious example of how able men can, under stress of politics, justify a palpably unwarranted thing by refined argument and casuistry. Without presenting the details of his reasoning, to quote a few sentences from his speech will suffice to explain his position, which was also that of a number of his associates.

"My own impression," said he, "is that, as the framers of the Constitution have directed us to keep a journal, a constructive duty may be implied from this command which would forbid us to obliterate or destroy. . . . Is any such proceeding as that of expunging the journal proposed by the resolution ? . . . Will this obliterate any part of the original resolution ? If it does, the duty of the secretary will be

---

of the legislator and the man. Why do I see so many pale features and downcast eyes unless it be that repentance and remorse go hand in hand with the perpetration of the deed?"

[1] Previous to 1824 Clay and Buchanan were close friends, so much so that Clay named one of his sons James Buchanan. But subsequently they became estranged in consequence of Buchanan's relations with Jackson. On several occasions, which Forney recounts, Clay treated him with indignity. "They frequently met in society in after years, especially at the dinner-table. If they did not become friends, they at least ceased to be enemies."—Forney's *Anecdotes of Public Men*, p. 182.

performed in a very bungling manner. No such thing is intended. It would be easy to remove every scruple from every mind upon this subject by amending the resolution so as to direct the secretary to perform his duty in such a manner as not to obliterate any part of the condemnatory resolution. Such a direction, however, appears to me to be wholly unnecessary. The nature of the whole proceeding is very plain. We now adopt a resolution expressing our strong reprobation of the original resolution; and for this purpose we use the word 'expunged' as the strongest term which we can employ."

In answer to the criticism that the word did not properly characterize the actual proceeding, he cited a number of authorities as sanctioning that use of it. But not one of them supported his assertion. Such circumstances are not suited to investigations in philology. Beyond question the resolution, in so far as the proposed writing across the face of the resolution of censure would cause defacement, was a violation of the Constitution, trivial indeed, but a violation.

Several other speeches were made before the debate closed, late at night. As the question was about to be put, Webster delivered an oral protest against the whole proceeding. He succinctly stated the argument against it, and the argument admitted of no answer. He justly summed up the matter thus: "We collect ourselves to look on in silence while a scene is exhibited which, if we did not regard it as a ruthless violation of a sacred instrument, would appear to us to be little elevated above the character of a contemptible farce." After Webster ceased, a short but impressive silence ensued. The struggle was over. On motion the blanks for the date were then filled and the resolution was adopted, 24 to 19. Clay did not wait to see it executed.

As soon as the vote was taken he stalked out of the chamber. As the secretary began to execute the mandate, such a volley of groans and hisses broke forth from one of the galleries that the presiding officer ordered it to be cleared. Benton was enraged at the disturbance, which, he shouted, was caused by "the bank ruffians." It marred the dignity with which he was anxious to have the scene invested. After venting his anger, he moved that the direction to clear the galleries be revoked, as it would cause the ejection of innocent spectators, and that the culprits be seized and brought to the bar. This was acceded to, but the raid of the sergeant-at-arms resulted in apprehending only one individual, who was brought before the Senate. This was deemed punishment enough for him, and he was discharged. The expunging was then consummated in peace.

The jubilation of Jackson's followers was unbounded. Benton's lasted for life. Long after the event, when he wrote his *Thirty Years' View*, that remarkable medley of the useless and the invaluable, his elation was unabated. "The gratification," he says, "of General Jackson was extreme. He gave a grand dinner to the expungers (as they were called) and their wives; and being too weak to sit at the table, he only met the company, placed the 'head expunger' in his chair, and withdrew to his sick-chamber. That expurgation! It was the 'crowning mercy' of his civil, as New Orleans had been of his military, life."

At this day, when the passions and strifes of that time are at most but the subjects of animated descriptions, we smile at what they provoked and marvel that the giants who then contended in the public arena should have devoted their powers to such barren displays. But such are the ways of politics. They change like the fashions; but at root political partisanship is ever the same, for it is grounded in human nature and fostered by its most potent characteristic —self-interest. Under its influence the strongest characters and the greatest minds are governed by the same impulses that drive savages to combat over a feather and children to tear one another's hair.

To Jackson, Van Buren's inauguration was, in his own phrase, "a glorious scene," not so much because of anything it represented for the public weal as because it signalized his own final and complete triumph. His paramount thought was that his successor was not only his personal choice, but he was the man whose nomination as Minister to England, to promote his succession, had been factiously rejected by a Whig Senate; and that by a singular coincidence he was sworn into office by Taney, whose nomination for the bench had once been likewise rejected because of the part he took in the removal of the deposits. To Jackson's mind it was a retribution, and aroused the keenest emotion he could feel—the thrill of victory over hated foes.

It had been the custom to treat his public career as the product of sheer will, and most of the prominent features of his Presidency as studied innovations in disregard of the Constitution, the laws, and the public welfare. The partisan views of his adversaries survived his time, and have generally been advocated by historical writers, who have to a large degree accepted them as just. This is not surprising. Most of the historical writing done since that time has been the work of those who were educated under the sway of the Whiggish culture of the country, and is thus imbued with Whiggish prepossessions. One source of this extraordinary influence will illustrate the assertion. No one occupies a higher place in American literature than Daniel Webster.

Regarded in their purely literary aspect, his works undoubtedly deserve their classic reputation. But this has insensibly carried with it the political bias that long dominated the educational centres, and is yet far from extinct.[1] After the Whig party, as such, became defunct, its intellectual, social, and political tendencies survived in the changed conditions, and impregnate most of the literature pertaining to the period of its existence.

The influence that Jackson exerted on the chief political events immediately preceding and during his Presidency, and for some time afterward, was indeed powerful. But this was mainly the natural consequence of his position. And many of his conspicuous acts were virtually forced upon him by the opposition. Some abiding effects followed the precedents and practices then established. Yet this is not peculiar to his Presidency. Moreover, he appeared at a juncture that made new departures inevitable. That he and his advisers were sometimes rash and precipitate, and unmindful of the indirect consequences beyond the immediate objects they had in view, is all too true; and it is the most serious criticism that can be justly preferred against them. This is a grave error in statesmanship, even when acts are right in themselves and founded on true principles. The interests of a people are multifarious and interwoven. When a condition is pervaded with mischievous elements produced by wrong policy, radical measures are perilous: it should be treated with caution and in progressive degrees. The proc-

---

[1] "At this moment the spirit that prevails in many institutions of learning in this country is at war, open and declared war, with the spirit of democracy. And if at the present time [1860] there is a class of intelligent and instructed men who feel with the people and are striving for popular objects, the fact is not due to the colleges."—Parton's *Jackson*, vol. iii. p. 700.

ess, however, is easier to prescribe in general than to apply in particular. This is eminently true of Jackson's predicament. The difficulty lay not so much in determining what ought to be done, abstractly viewed, as in what to do under all the circumstances, considering political exigencies, which could not be ignored, and absolute good, which politicians are always willing to compromise if necessary. Some palliation of Jackson's course is supplied by the novel state of affairs which confronted him, and of which all the consequences afford his critics an autopsical advantage. Had he avoided the conflicts that signalize his Presidency he would have been a marvel among statesmen or merely an official name. Such a result would have required him either to reconcile the Whigs to Democratic principles or submit to Whig dictation; for the attitude of his adversaries precluded any middle ground. If ever a Chief Magistrate can be pardoned for partisan excesses Jackson can. Parliamentary history contains no instance where the executive administration of a government was more sorely tried, baited, and assailed by a relentless opposition. The field of his operations was hedged about with enormous difficulties, for he was compassed by formidable foes intent upon present success, by whatever means and whatever the consequences.

Another stricture, not so merited, arises from the share Jackson had in the establishment of the spoils system. This criticism has grown, through the modern gospel of "civil service reform," from resentful accusation to absolute conviction, until Jackson is now generally regarded as personally responsible for the introduction of the proscriptive system into our national politics. While the fact cannot be gainsaid that it was under his administration that this policy was first avowedly practised, it is an imperfect and misleading idea that he is to be held accountable for it. The true considerations in regard to this subject have already been presented in the course of this narrative, but it is not superfluous to restate them briefly in this general review. Jackson's election was the overthrow of a long political régime and the beginning of a radically new one. There had been no pressing occasion for the application of the spoils doctrine on a national scale; yet it was not a novelty, as it had been operative for years in many of the States, and in some of them had attained consummate development. When, therefore, the opportunity and occasion came to apply it to federal offices the impulse was irresistible. There can be no reasonable doubt that under the conditions then existing Jackson did only what any President in his place would have been forced to do. As he did not originate or improve the system, but merely applied it under force of circumstances, he cannot be justly held responsible for it. And it is ascribing to him an unwarranted influence to say that the uniform practice of it by all parties ever since is due to his example.[1] The American people, whatever else may be their faults, should not be indicted for such a blind and unquestioning pursuit of the example or the precepts of any individual.

To attribute the leading characteristics of his Presidency to his initiative is the common and fundamental error that

---

[1] "Pernicious practices have been prevailing for the last fifteen years, which began with Jackson, which Van Buren had little need to exercise, but never repudiated, and which his party always pursued, which the Whigs of 1840 were afraid fully and heartily to disavow, and which when in power they carried out as far as any before them had done, and which now have become the standing rule of practice in this country."—*Life of R. H. Dana*, vol. i. p. 92.

has produced so many distorted notions concerning him. The premise is as false as it can be, if taken in connection with the fact that no man's conduct can be wholly separated from his personality. Had Jackson been born a few years earlier or later he would have died in obscurity. He did not possess, apart from adventitious circumstances, the intellect or the qualities to make an impression on any modern age, unless possibly in time of war. He was not and could not have become a statesman in the proper sense of the word. His type of mind is alien to statesmanship and is lacking in that patient, searching insight into widely diverse interests, public and private, present and future, and that comprehensive mastery and combination of these complex elements required in the genuine statesman.

He was not a thinker or a politician. He did not have the education and sustained habit of mind essential to the one, nor the ductility of disposition and conduct necessary to the other. His ideas were limited and fragmentary, but they were direct and concentrated, and came from his mind with a fascinating vigor and velocity. He could not express in speech or writing an orderly development of any subject with which he had to deal. Though he was not illiterate, it was only in his later years that he acquired the faculty of expressing himself fittingly in ordinary correspondence. Undoubtedly had he been educated and accustomed to the pen or public speech, and could he have maintained the patience, he would have learned to acquit himself respectably, perhaps powerfully; for his manner of stating facts and ideas partook of his virile temperament and often displayed the vivid force of Napoleon's bulletins. But he invariably depended on others for the composition of his official communications. As Parton shrewdly observes, he was always fortunate in his secretaries; and thus the state papers that bear his signature have seldom been surpassed in propriety and force of diction.¹

Some of the most striking acts of his Presidency would scarcely have been undertaken in his audacious and uncompromising way by any experienced public man, however he may have been advised and abetted by men of that description; for training in public affairs begets a politic circumspection that seeks the point of least resistance. These acts took a distinctive aspect from his personality and impetuous energy rather than from their character and effect. His guiding principle was, "Desperate courage makes one a majority." His intensity of purpose often impelled him to needless exertions. He would, so to speak, use a battery when a platoon of musketry was sufficient. This thorough-

---

¹ "Not one public paper of any description signed 'Andrew Jackson' ever reached the public eye exactly as Jackson wrote it. . . . Some of his most famous passages—those which are supposed to be peculiarly Jacksonian—he never so much as suggested a word of, nor saw till they were written, nor required the alteration of a single syllable before they were despatched." —Parton's *Jackson*, vol. i. p. 68. When Harvard University conferred on Jackson the degree of LL.D., Adams wrote: "Myself an affectionate child of our *alma mater*, I would not be present to witness her disgrace in conferring her highest literary honors upon a barbarian who could not write a sentence of grammar and hardly could spell his name."—Adams's *Diary*, vol. iv. p. 5. "I remember that in my youth, during his Presidency, it was generally believed in New England among his political opponents that he was an entirely illiterate man, who could not write an English sentence grammatically or spell correctly. This belief was too much encouraged by persons who knew better; and it was not until many years afterward that I learned how unfounded it was. There now lie before me autograph letters of General Jackson written wholly with his own hand, and written and punctuated with entire correctness, and with no small power of expression. The handwriting is sometimes rather better, for example, than Mr. Webster's. The spelling is perfectly correct throughout. General Jackson wrote better English than Washington; and as to King George III., the General was an Addison in comparison with his Majesty."—Curtis's *Buchanan*, vol. i. p. 129. See also *Memoirs of J. G. Bennett*, p. 90.

ness had the inevitable result of increasing the ardor and the assaults of the enemy, and enhanced the general effect in the popular mind. Such intense purpose and effort always have a prodigious influence over less determined minds. It explains the success of many men otherwise mediocre, and frequently produces reputation that the inherent quality of their achievements would not create. Great intellects are usually philosophical and not over-eager for material acquisitions or preferment. Narrow and combative minds are too often ambitious to attain objects unsuited to them. They confound transient position and power with genuine merit and enduring renown, which they never achieve, unless under exceptional circumstances, where celerity, resolution, and force are the prime requisites. But these conditions seldom occur, and hence the way-sides of history are strewn with bleaching bones—one of the saddest and most suggestive, yet one of the most natural spectacles wrought by human activity. Although Jackson was narrow-minded and fiercely energetic, he did not strive to force himself into a sphere to which he did not belong. In this respect he was a remarkable character, and he can only be understood by comparison with types of mind above and below him. He was not ambitious, nor was his nature alloyed by any selfish or ignoble element. His rise to the Presidency was not his design or achievement. His sole contribution to the result was that peculiarity of temperament which made him a hero in Indian warfare and in his solitary and fortunate battle of New Orleans. His exploits, thus performed, made him available by clever politicians as a Presidential candidate, and the temper of the times made him President. While President, as before, he was often absolute, it is true, in his ideas of what should be done, and utterly fearless in executing them. Yet seldom did the initiative proceed from his own reflections. No President ever listened more intently to his advisers; and he usually followed the counsels of those in whom he had most confidence, albeit the manner of accomplishing the objects determined upon were generally and distinctively Jacksonian. This is true of his struggles over financial questions. His combative instinct quickly penetrated the heart of the bank controversy; but for the scheme of the contest Benton is mainly responsible. And so he was in a large degree for most of the more noted acts of Jackson's Presidency. From this it is not to be inferred that Jackson was a passive instrument in the hands of others. Far from it. None were more ready to acknowledge his masterful individuality than those who stood closest to him. But the fact tends to qualify the common opinion that it was his domineering will that shaped his entire policy and controlled others to execute it according to his behests.

Von Holst formally characterizes Jackson's Presidency as a "reign";[1] and the appellation has clung with the tenacity usually incidental to tersely put error. The ill-balanced judgment of this distinguished writer is shown by his coupling this theory of Jackson's Presidency with the unphilosophical and pessimistic criticism that it "systematically undermined the public conscience and diminished the respect of the people for the government."[2] The two characterizations are manifestly inconsistent, and were it not

---

[1] This is not original with Von Holst. It is to be found incessantly in the Whig utterances of Jackson's time.—See Sargent's *Clay*, p. 186.

[2] No student of our political history can fail to appreciate the industry of Dr. Von Holst; but it must be recognized that his work is a polemical treatise, not a philosophical history. The stress he lays upon many facts and events is entirely out of proportion to their real importance and significance, a result due to his alien training and congested theories.

that the ideas they represent are so prevalent they might be dismissed without further comment. To form a correct estimate of a public man and his career, the actual conditions in which he was placed must be ascertained and considered —not only the political features, but the quality of the times and the temper and tendency of popular thought and feeling. The material facts are easily determined, and when sedulously followed they lead to sound conclusions. Mere sentiments and abstractions are dangerous and deceptive and tend to substitute imagination and prejudice for investigation and truth. Jackson has long been the victim of the latter process.

The management of our foreign affairs has never been conducted with more signal effect than under Jackson. No President has ever done more to compel respect for our national rights and American citizenship. A similar spirit was displayed in his prompt and forceful resistance to disunion. No President has demonstrated greater practical loyalty to the larger aims of the Constitution and more devotion to the Union and the democratic theory on which the Constitution and the Union rest. The charge, incessantly repeated, that he autocratically exercised powers in disregard of the Constitution, cannot be sustained. For everything he did in which his Constitutional warrant has been questioned, and where he did not act under express powers, the argument in his support is stronger than that against him. And no important instance where his action was professedly under statutory authority can be adduced that was not sanctioned by a fair and reasonable interpretation of the law. It does not answer to inveigh against infractions of the "spirit" of the Constitution and the laws when the letter or necessary implication furnished ample authority for the acts assailed. In a constitutional government there can be no more vicious tendency than to ignore, even in the name of patriotism and natural justice, the plain injunctions either of the organic law or of statutes validly enacted. Far greater harm has always, under the plea of propriety, followed lax construction than has ever been inflicted by the strict enforcement of improper or unjust provisions. Bad laws that are executed will soon be repealed or modified at the demand of public sentiment; but if through mere opinion they lose their stringency or effect they inevitably become the pretext under which incalculable evil is perpetrated. Underneath almost every position taken by the Whigs was the presumptuous but imposing fallacy that whatever they advocated was right, and therefore that their opponents were public enemies. This kind of assumption has sanctified error since the pretensions of creeds and dogmas first began to impress and mould the credulity of man. It is fortunate that occasionally a man appears who is strong and willing enough to recur to first principles and quell the sophistries that steal into the thought and destroy the robust instincts of the people. Jackson did not "reign." He administered the government under the guidance of democratic principles and according to the plain purport and purpose of the Constitution, and against the strained constructions and strenuous efforts of a party undemocratic in its tenets and its tendencies. When he retired, every feature of our governmental institutions was unimpaired and unaffected. He never manifested or entertained the slightest design or inclination wilfully to transcend his lawful province. Under the stress of extreme provocation and excitement, he sometimes carried the war into the enemy's country; but his patriotism was unchallenged. Had he at any time evinced the faintest sinister design he would have been repudiated and disgraced instantly and by his own party.

It is absurd to say that he "undermined the public conscience" or bred among the people a spirit of lawlessness that asserted itself in riot, tumult, and disrespect for social and governmental institutions. No one man or set of men could have done or can do that in this country. It was not respect for the government that was affected, but acquiescence in the dictation of a small number of distinguished Senators, who were more zealous to promote the interests of their party than the well-being of the country. By this it is not meant that those Senators were at any time actuated by unpatriotic motives, but that their erroneous principles, under the crucial test of partisan strife, forced them to acts that were indefensible and injurious. During this period there were many unfortunate exhibitions of disorder in all parts of the country. In Washington several members of Congress were assaulted for what they had said in debate. But these outbreaks were not peculiar to Jackson's Presidency nor legitimately traceable to him or his policy. Similar acts were common before and after his Presidency. Many of them grew out of the antislavery developments and were committed by men who were least affected by Jackson's principles. Even classic Boston presented unseemly spectacles of this kind, perpetrated by its most exclusive, if not aristocratic, elements. Jackson himself narrowly escaped assassination by a lunatic whose pistols miraculously failed to discharge. The motive for the act was engendered in a disordered mind by hearing Whig Senators denounce Jackson as an enemy to the country. But no reasonable mind would attribute such a baleful incident to the principles and precepts of the Whigs, no more than that Conkling would be held guilty of the frightful but crazy crime of Guiteau. The application of unbiased common-sense is alone needed to dispel such notions. Jackson was not an anarchist and inculcated no anarchical principles. Nor was he a demagogue. Democracy is not license, even though its manifestations sometimes shock the bigotry and complacency of that class which would be more at home under a monarchy.[1] The restlessness of the people that is incidental to some periods, accompanied with the violence of men who always chafe under the restraint of the criminal law, bespeaks more for our institutions than is shown by passive and comfortable indifference to the stealthy encroachments of favoritism and class advantage. But apart from this it is a fallacious view of social phenomena that does not penetrate beyond mere external symptoms into the remote and complex causes that produce them.

The characteristics of Jackson's period were not due to his influence, but to the direction of the popular mind, which made his elevation and doings possible. It was a time of remarkable development, expansion, and activity. When he appeared before the public eye a new stream of thought and action had started. It swept about him and carried him with its torrent. The economic and political cleavage of the North and South was becoming more and more apparent. The attention and interest of the people were directed toward politics as they had never been before. The democratic impulse, through natural and necessary

---

[1] In 1840 the "aristocratic elements" of Boston were tired of our political tendencies. Otis predicted that in thirty years our republican system would end. Allston said that in "eighty years there would not be a gentleman left in the country."—Pierce's *Sumner*, vol. iii. p. 8.

causes too large and various to possess a single, much less a personal, source, was revived and increased. That Jackson chanced to be the personage to whom it was attracted, and that his personality contributed to intensify it, are not to be regretted. With all his defects and administrative errors the sum of his influence was beneficial. The sentiment of patriotism which he inculcated far outweighs the transient evils he may have caused or furthered; and the day may come when the example of his Presidency will prove a bulwark in the hour of the nation's need.

It is noticeable that Clay now took less interest than had been his wont in minor matters that came before the Senate. Formerly there were few subjects of any moment that did not enlist his attention and comment. His suggestions upon matters not involved in politics were accorded great respect, and betoken a largeness of view and an understanding of national and international bearings only possible to a mind long accustomed to public affairs. There were that increased weight and reposeful power in his utterances which always develop in the speech of public men of protracted experience and prestige. He was nearly sixty years of age, and almost half his life had been conspicuously passed in the public councils. He no doubt felt, and rightfully, that he had performed his due share of routine legislative labors. The Senate no longer had any strong attraction for him; yet when he was confronted, as he was during the session, with the necessity of retiring or remaining, he reversed his determination to withdraw and accepted a re-election. His friends and partisans throughout the country, who admired and supported him with an enduring fervor and enthusiasm never surpassed in the career of a statesman so long in public life, insisted that he continue in the body of which they and his political adversaries alike regarded him almost as an essential figure. But he had not conquered his repugnance. All the efforts of the Whigs, under his leadership, had been unavailing to resist the triumphant course of Jackson and the Democrats, and another Democratic administration was to follow. He was almost in a state of political despair and felt little hope of Whig supremacy in his time. A year before, when he had determined to leave the Senate at the end of his term, he wrote: "If I were persuaded that by remaining longer in the public service I could materially aid in arresting our downward progress, I should feel it my duty not to quit it. But I am not sure that my warning voice has not too often been heard. Perhaps that of my successor may be listened to with more effect." And after the adoption of the expunging resolution, when he had been re-elected, he still continued to express his earnest desire for retirement, not, however, in a strain of lamentation, but of acute disgust. "I shall hail," he wrote, "with greatest pleasure the occurrence of circumstances which will admit of my resignation without dishonor to myself. The Senate is no longer a place for a decent man." And again: "I shall escape from it with the same pleasure that one would fly from a charnel-house."

This resolution he eventually carried out, but not until five years later, after a period hardly less exciting and laborious than during Jackson's Presidency, and when at last the goal of his great ambition seemed within his grasp.

CHAPTER IX

Van Buren's Intellectual and Political Characteristics — His Policy as Jackson's Successor—The Crisis of 1837—The Tactics of the Whigs—Webster's Speech at Niblo's—The Appeal of the New York Merchants to the President—The Extra Session of Congress, the President's Message, and the Democratic Programme—Clay Organizes the Opposition, and Calhoun Supports the Administration—The Opening Debate on the Independent Treasury—The Banks and Resumption—The Regular Session—Renewal of the Excitement Over the Slavery Question—Calhoun's Attitude

THE Presidency is a precarious honor. With its possessor chance plays curious tricks. Jackson and Van Buren illustrate both extremes of this peculiar fortune. Notwithstanding his extraordinary political success thus far, Van Buren came to the Presidency under conditions that were extremely unpropitious and trying. When he attained the coveted distinction his good fortune forsook him, and the very causes of his elevation operated against him. The opposite of Jackson in everything but his political principles, he was entirely without Jackson's popular resources. It did not avail that he had been Jackson's close adviser and in full accord with his policy, if not partly responsible for it. He was devoid of every attribute to continue effectively Jackson's executive methods. He had no personal prestige among the masses, even of his own party. Without the popular influence that invested Jackson with his peculiar power, he was regarded merely as an official President rather than an important political force. To the Whigs he was the creature of Jackson's favor, thrust into power by his desire and dictation. From the hour his Presidential prospects opened he was not only assailed and denounced, but sneered at and lampooned as a mere politician and deft manipulator. "The Little Magician" was the sobriquet most commonly applied to him. And, in truth, had his rise from the Senate to the Presidency been due to craft alone, it would have presented much the same appearance. His service in the Senate was too short to assure his position as a statesman and reveal his truly great talent and ability for public life. Every move after that was a step for and toward the Presidency, and as such instigated the attacks of the Whigs, and the jealousy of his Democratic rivals.[1]

Without opportunity to justify his pretensions or meet his adversaries with their own weapons, he acted on the only plan open to him: he took advantage of the conditions in which he was placed, and with the utmost adroitness and skill. It is unfortunate for his fame that the combination of circumstances that fixed his destiny precluded him from participating directly in the events to which he owed his advancement, and thus from forcibly carving his own career in the great forum of the Senate.

---

[1] Such opinions, though in some degree justified by his tactical skill, have been immensely magnified by the asperity of political warfare prior to and during his term, and were subsequently still further aided by the spleen of his former friends because of his candidacy on the Free-soil ticket in 1848.—See *Democratic Review*, vol. iii. p. 121. "Mr. Van Buren had won the favor of the hero just as the jackal wins the good-will of the lion. He was called the 'mistletoe politician,' nourished by the sap of the hickory-tree."—Wise's *Seven Decades of the Union*, p. 121. It is significant that Von Holst's disparaging opinions of him are largely drawn from Mackenzie's virulent and abominable compilations. The corrective of the common and erroneous views concerning Van Buren is in an unbiased study of the leading facts and events in his career. See Shepard's *Van Buren*, p. 387.

His entire mental and physical composition was not such as to create any striking impression on the popular mind. His most inherent intellectual qualities made him deliberate, circumspect, and politic.[1] The success of his early public life in the narrow theatre of State politics was largely the result of the methods these qualities had induced; and subsequent circumstances so encompassed him that his sterling powers of mind and capacity for public affairs were scantily called into play. No doubt Jackson was drawn to him by the very fact that they were so completely unlike, for this is one of the most common sources of friendship and confidence between men. Van Buren was unassertive, insinuating, and amiable.[2] He seldom gave cause for personal dislike. He was too conservative and complaisant for his own advantage. His disinclination to assert his opinions naturally led to the common notion that he had no convictions contrary to his political interests. His mode of thought and calmness of temper made him slow to take offence or

---

[1] Martineau's *Retrospect of Western Travel*, vol. i. pp. 74, 77; Quincy's *Figures of the Past*, p. 355.

[2] "There are many features in the character of Mr. Van Buren strongly resembling that of Mr. Madison—his calmness, his gentleness of manner, his discretion, his easy and conciliatory temper. But Madison had none of his obsequiousness, his sycophancy, his profound dissimulation and duplicity. In the last of these he much more resembles Jefferson, though with very little of his genius."—Adams's *Diary*, vol. ix. p. 369. "He will be a party President, but he is too much of a gentleman to be governed by the rabble who surrounded his predecessor and administered to his bad passions. As a man, a gentleman, and a friend, I have great respect for Mr. Van Buren; I hate the cause, but esteem the man."—Hone's *Diary*, vol. i. p. 246. In a speech, Clay said: "I have always found him, in his manners and deportment, civil, courteous, and gentlemanly; and he dispenses in the noble mansion which he now occupies, one worthy of a great people, a generous and liberal hospitality. An acquaintance with him of more than twenty years' duration has inspired me with respect for the man, although I regret to be compelled to say I detest the magistrate."

harbor resentment. Had he been more positive and combative he would have received more respect and deference; he certainly could not have been more bitterly opposed. His qualities of mind and character were thus to a large extent obscured, and it was not until extortionate events compelled it that his firmness and strength of intellect were revealed. He was generally regarded as the most non-committal of politicians, and, despite his acts while President and afterward, the idea still persistently attaches to his reputation. His face gave no especial indication of his intellectual powers. It displayed sanity and practicality, without any admixture of the eccentric or the ideal. The keenness of his glance qualified the appearance of benignity and philosophic breadth his features otherwise possessed. Apart from the healthy good-nature that beamed from it, his countenance was imperturbable.[1] It was never the index of his thoughts; and as for emotions, he had none that were acute or violent. With him self-control was not an

---

[1] "He looks very well, and from his ease of manner and imperturbable good temper it might be supposed that he had less to occupy his mind than any man in New York. His outward appearance is like the unruffled surface of the majestic river which covers rocks and whirlpools, but shows no marks of agitation beneath."—Hone's *Diary*, October 26, 1835; vol. i. p. 168. These lines went the rounds of the newspapers:

"Good Lord! what is Van! for though simple he looks,
'Tis a task to unravel his looks and his crooks;
With his depths and his shallows, his good and his evil,
All in all he's a riddle must puzzle the devil."

"Mr. Van Buren was rather an exquisite in appearance. His complexion was a bright blond, and he dressed accordingly. On this occasion [at church in Rochester in 1828] he wore an elegant snuff-colored broadcloth coat with a velvet collar; his cravat was orange with modest lace tips; his vest was of a pearl hue; his trousers were white duck; his shoes were morocco; his neatly fitting gloves were yellow-kid; his long-furred beaver hat with broad brim was of a Quaker color."—Stanton's *Random Recollections*, p. 32.

effort, but an involuntary instinct. It was altogether natural, therefore, that he should without unnecessary effort utilize the opportunities that arose, and sail with the current so long as it moved toward the haven he sought.

The difficulties he was to encounter had long been generating and they were close at hand; yet his inaugural address displayed no apprehension, if indeed he felt any. It was thoroughly Democratic and optimistic, but gave little indication of concrete purposes, save in regard to slavery. On this subject he declared himself explicitly, as he had done before election, firmly opposed to any interference, either in the States or in the District of Columbia. This declaration, however, had no novel political significance, for it coincided with the opinion of the great majority of the people of all parties except the abolitionists, who were not yet regarded as a political factor. But touching the extension of slavery he was silent. This topic had not yet attained the character of an actual problem. Like most inaugurals of new Presidents, his was essentially a salutatory, inspired by the satisfaction of his newly acquired honor and hopeful expectations not yet disturbed by opposition and adversity. His main design was sufficiently understood without his dwelling upon it —he proposed to sustain so far as he could the measures of his predecessor. His respect for Jackson verged to extreme humility, and was doubtless deemed by him politically advantageous as well. In his letter accepting the nomination he said: " I consider myself the honored instrument, selected by the friends of the present administration, to carry out its principles and policy; and that as well from inclination as from duty I shall, if honored with the choice of the American people, endeavor to follow generally in the footsteps of President Jackson; happy if I shall be able to perfect the work which he has so gloriously begun." And he closed his inaugural address with a venerating tribute to Jackson that evinced no change of sentiment or purpose.

This general plan was at once evidenced by the retention of Jackson's cabinet. One place, however, was vacant —that of Secretary of War, through the appointment of Cass as Minister to France in 1836. Butler, the Attorney-General, performed the functions of the position until Van Buren came into office. Poinsett, one of the few prominent men of South Carolina who had opposed nullification, was then appointed. The old cabinet had been largely of Van Buren's choice, hence no change was expected. Nevertheless, it is not unlikely that at first he contemplated several changes. Benton's leadership of the administration forces in Congress had been so conspicuous and masterly that he was urged to accept a portfolio; but he wisely declined. The cabinet as then constituted was still personally acceptable to Van Buren, and as it could not be materially strengthened from those who were available after Benton refused to enter it, he concluded to retain it as it was.[1] But there was urgent need that it be as strong as he could make it; for the new administration had hardly been installed when the storm which had been so long gathering broke with appalling fury. The crisis of 1837, here and elsewhere, was without parallel, and none more severe has occurred since; and no financial and commercial disturbance has been more fraught with economic instruction. It seldom happens that so many of the causes that produce monetary and business crises are operative in combination. So suddenly did it come and so rapidly and widely devastat-

---

[1] For Van Buren's frank statement of the difficulties in forming a good cabinet, see his *Political Parties in the United States*, p. 68.

ing were its consequences that on May 15, but a few days over two months after Van Buren's inauguration, he was constrained to convoke an extra session of Congress to meet the emergency. It was called for September 4. Meantime the ravages were complete, and a terrible and exacting situation confronted the public councils.

If the relative importance of different periods of national history were to be judged by statistics alone, the period under review would not deserve the attention it demands. In 1837 the population was about 15,000,000. In his last annual message to Congress, in December, 1836, Jackson estimated that the total public expenditure for the ensuing year would not exceed $32,000,000. These two facts furnish a fair idea of the physical proportions of our national life and government at that time. But principles are not dependent on mere numbers or the size or extent of the objects on which they operate. Thus it is that a thorough and correct understanding of the history of this country is a liberal education in political philosophy and economy. It is unfortunate that this is not more generally recognized and applied in the higher education of American youth. And it is still more unfortunate that Senators and Representatives in Congress, not to speak of other public men, should exhibit, as they commonly do at the present day, ignorance of the history of their country. Such incapacity in the practice of any profession would be akin to criminal; but in public life, where the consequences involve the interests of every citizen, it excites little surprise or condemnation. Comprehensive knowledge of the country's history among our public servants would prevent the periodical recurrence of time-worn fallacies and mistakes and lead to a general and abiding acquiescence in many principles that should be elementary in the political creed of every public man.

The premonitory signs of the impending crisis were proximately caused by the specie circular. The blow it inflicted made the vast hollow of the financial system loudly resound. Those who were not involved in paper transactions made haste to guard their interests as best they could—many by hoarding gold or withdrawing as far as possible from danger. The alarm quickly spread, and the reckless confidence upon which the monetary system of the country rested crumbled and fell. The most serious effects of the distribution policy followed close upon those of the specie circular. It commonly happens that the consequences of error come at the most inopportune times. It was so with these. As we have seen, the deposit banks, to provide for the instalments to the States, were forced to contract their loans. In ordinary times this would have strongly affected the money market, but now under the circumstances the pressure was prodigiously increased. Of necessity it bore hardest upon those who were most instrumental in creating the plethoric condition that existed. Gold rose with fatal rapidity. The situation of the speculators grew from bad to worse. Those who were not engaged in speculation, but whose fortunes were inseparably linked with legitimate business interests, were soon affected also, and finally were likewise drawn into the widening vortex of failure.[1] Many

---

[1] "There are certainly wild speculators, blind and desperate gamblers here also; but the objects of their schemes are almost always enterprises of public utility. The spirit of speculation in the United States has strown this vast country with useful works—canals, railroads, turnpikes, with manufactories, farms, villages, and towns; amongst us it has been more rash, wild, and foolish, and much less productive in useful results. It is with us mere stock-jobbing."—Chevalier's *Society in the United States*, p. 166.

of the strongest business houses, unable longer to withstand the fearful strain, collapsed like the weakest.¹ The puny paper-made banks succumbed to the first gust of the tempest; and when the oldest and stanchest suspended specie payment, as nearly all had by the middle of May, the prostration and consternation were complete and universal. Some idea of the extent of these calamities may be formed from the estimate that nearly half a million persons became bankrupt; and this, of course, makes no account of the hardships of the vastly greater number dependent on wages and salaries. There is little wonder, therefore, that in some cases stores and warehouses were despoiled by mobs.

One of the most forbidding features of politics is that no national catastrophe is so dire and universal that politicians will not utilize it for partisan advantage. Despite the dismal havoc of the crisis, the Whig leaders seemed to hail it with malign delight. With vociferous acclaim they paraded their past prophecies and pointed to the wreck and ruin on every side as proof of their realization. Again all the familiar accusations and denunciations of Jackson were revived and volleyed forth with inflamed zeal. That most of them had done service through two Presidential campaigns and had been signally voted down only swelled the energy with which they were now renewed. What could be more convincing! Every phase of the grievous situation had been foretold; for years it had been the constant text of Whig

---

[1] "For the last two weeks there has been a succession of enormous failures in New Orleans and New York, extending to Philadelphia, Boston, and partially to other cities."—Adams's *Diary*, May 4, 1837, vol. ix. p. 355. "The number of failures is so great daily that I do not keep a record of them, even in my mind." — Hone's *Diary*, May 2, 1837, vol. i. p. 253. Nevertheless, there were some light tints in the general scene of distress. Hone records that in September nine theatres were running in New York city.—Ibid., p. 266.

orators and writers. Jackson had been honored and trusted by the people, but he had betrayed them. The proof was only too manifest. His ignorance, perversity, and despotic will had stopped the sources of public blessings and blasted national prosperity. Argument was no longer needful. The broadcast ruin was demonstration. The masses, inclined, as they always are, to trace their misfortunes to something immediate and tangible, instead of remote and complex causes, absorbed the quackery thus dinned into their eager and willing ears.

After the charter of the bank expired, the institution, with amazing effrontery and corruption, transmigrated into a State corporation under the hybrid name of "Pennsylvania Bank of the United States." It did not follow the usual and legal course of liquidation and winding-up, but merely transferred its assets and obligations to the new corporation and proceeded without material interruption, even reissuing the old notes. Moreover, as it afterward transpired, the business methods and operations now prosecuted were shockingly irregular and dishonest; yet Biddle and his allies,[1] with practised skill, at once assumed the initiative in a new agitation against the policy it was believed the new administration would pursue. In short, before Van Buren was inaugurated, the campaign to elect a Whig suc-

---

[1] Notwithstanding the action of the bank, Biddle had lost nothing of his influence among the Whigs. March 28, a meeting of merchants was held in New York for the purpose of inducing the bank to do something to mitigate the distress. Hone wrote: "I was invited to attend this meeting; never was such an assemblage of woe-begone countenances. Despondency had taken the place of that indomitable spirit which usually characterizes the merchants of New York, and Nicholas Biddle, the insulted and proscribed of Andrew Jackson and his myrmidons, is the sun to which they alone can look to illumine the darkness."—*Diary*, vol. i. p. 249.

cessor was begun. And such was the greedy zeal to take advantage of the coming events whose lurid shadows already lay athwart the activities of the land, that the formal and spectacular opening of the campaign was arranged for March 15, but eleven days after the inauguration. It took place, according to the programme, at the city of New York, with all the accompaniments of such occasions. Daniel Webster was the medium. Elaborate preparations were made to greet him on his return after the close of the session. He came by steamboat from Amboy and was escorted to the American Hotel by a great procession. In the evening he spoke at Niblo's for two hours and a half to a rapt audience of thousands. His speech was a powerful and animated résumé of the financial controversies which had vexed the country during Jackson's Presidency, and was laden with dismal forebodings of calamities to come unless the measures of the Whig party were adopted. It was not only a political harangue, but it was calculated to intensify the distress that was daily becoming more manifest and terrifying. No man ever lived more capable of mastering the problems of national finance than Webster. During his early career he evinced consummate understanding and grasp of the fundamental principles of the whole subject, and the genius to state them with comprehensiveness, lucidity, and power. But he soon receded from his original principles—principles that cannot die or change. He lacked mental integrity. He was faithless to his own intellect. In his eager efforts to gain the Presidency he sacrificed great opportunities for the public good and for his own lofty reputation, and sank in the mire of partisan advocacy. Had his force of character and will been equal to his mind he would not have become merely a serviceable auxiliary to lesser men who dominated him and then rewarded his servility with cold indifference to his ambition.

His reception and speech were but the first phase of the prearranged plan to make political capital of the distress of the country. April 25, it was followed by another imposing demonstration in the same city. It was styled a meeting of merchants, and resulted in the adoption of a set of resolutions ascribing the crisis to governmental interference with business and commerce, intermeddling with the currency, the destruction of the bank, the attempt to substitute metallic for credit currency, and the issuing of the specie circular; admonishing the administration against maintaining the policy of its predecessor; and directing the appointment of a committee of fifty to urge the President to withdraw the circular, forbear the enforcement of importers' bonds, and call an extra session of Congress. And, to enhance the popular effect, other cities were invited to co-operate in this crusade. It was also provided that another meeting be called to receive the report of the committee.

May 3, the committee waited on the President with formality and display, and presented a long and harrowing statement of the existing situation and the alleged causes that produced it. The relief proposed was the adoption of the entire Whig programme contained in the resolutions of the merchants' meeting, with the addition of Clay's land-money plan. The arraignment of Jackson was harsh and unstinted and in the usual style of the Whig diatribes. It was rashly imprudent, if not insolent, unless the committee acted under the delusion that Van Buren was so terrorized and susceptible that he could be forced into compliance. If so, the character and temper of the man were radically misunderstood. He received the committee with his accustomed urbanity, and calmly listened to the address. Had he been like Jackson he would have treated it as an insult and shown the committee the door. But this was not his method. When the presentation was concluded he suavely bowed the gentlemen out, promising a written reply the next day. It was accordingly delivered. Although couched in temperate phrase, it was a firm refusal to accede to any of the demands, except that he promised reasonable indulgence to the importers. He assured the committee that before his election he had declared his approval of the measures of his predecessor; that knowing this, the people had elected him; and that he proposed to adhere to them. The committee returned to New York professedly indignant, but probably without poignant disappointment; for the outcome was doubtless supposed to be politically efficacious. Biddle, also, had not neglected the opportunity. He had followed at the heels of the committee, and took occasion to pay his respects to the President. He was likewise treated with all the gracious civility that any distinguished caller would have received. But as his counsel was not solicited—as he expected it would be—he, too, felt slighted and aggrieved.

May 8, another public meeting was held, at which the committee made its barren but rhetorical report, and revealed the animus of the whole performance by declaring that the only hope left for the sorely afflicted country was the arbitrament of the ballot-box. New resolutions reasserting the declaratory substance of the previous ones were adopted. They virtually constituted the platform that was again to serve the Whig party.[1] On the 10th, the banks of New

---

[1] "It is a very common fact that for thirty-four years (since 1828) very few merchants of the first class have been Democrats. The mass of large

York suspended specie payment, and most of the banks of other cities immediately followed their example. Their action, however, was at once legalized by the State legislatures. The suspension of all but six of the deposit banks compelled the Treasury Department to retain most of the incoming revenues in the hands of the collectors or on special deposit. This situation rendered an extra session of Congress indispensable. There was no other recourse, and the President yielded to the necessity.

The climax of the crisis had now been passed. The whirlwind of ruin had spent itself, and the strain and excitement were followed by a period of commercial stagnation. The suspension of the banks required them to accept each other's paper, and in consequence gold and silver coin vanished.[1] Even the government was forced to receive and disburse depreciated notes. Inasmuch as no paramount authority was exerted over paper currency, it was issued in every form and by any individual, firm, and corporation that chose to do so. It was often a medium of coarse and insulting caricature to influence the masses against the administration, for they were instructed by all available means to regard Jackson as the cause of the distress and Van Buren as the obstacle to its alleviation. Nor did the Whig leaders relax their efforts to solidify their political advantage. Not long after Webster delivered his

---

and little merchants have, like a flock of sheep, gathered either in the Federal, Whig, Clay, or Republican folds. The Democratic merchants could easily have been stowed in a large Eighth Avenue railroad-car."—Barrett's *Old Merchants of New York* (first series), p. 81.

[1] Gold, "Jackson money," had come into common circulation and was ostentatiously carried by the Democrats. The gold eagle had not been previously coined for thirty-five years.—Chevalier's *Society in the United States*, p. 147; *Niles's Register*, vol. lv. p. 321.

speech in New York he made a long Western tour and spoke in several places in much the same vein, endeavoring to the utmost to decry and cripple the administration. He was already working for the nomination in 1840. His utterances furnished the stock ideas that were elaborated and diffused by the press and the orators of the Whig party. The Treasury was soon in critical straits. Aside from difficulties that were arduous and perplexing without forced aggravation, it was in the serious dilemma of having to pay to the States, under the deposit law, what it urgently needed for current expenses. But in this situation, however pressing the necessities, the interim between the calling of the special session and its convening was none too long to allow the excitement to abate and for the formulation of plans to meet the emergency.

The personnel of the Twenty-fifth Congress was remarkably strong and brilliant. The prolonged political contests had directed the ambition of many able men toward public life; and neither the Senate nor the House has ever contained a greater number of men already distinguished and to attain distinction than met on the first Monday of September, 1837, to deal with the unprecedented condition of the country and the national finances.[1] Yet it would doubtless have been better had there been less political animosity, ambition, and insistence; for such conditions are extremely ad-

---

[1] Adams's opinion, however, of the personnel of Congress was unfavorable; but his estimates of men were seldom complimentary. December 27, 1838, he wrote: "When I look upon the composition of these two bodies, the Senate and the House of Representatives of the United States—the cream of the land, the curled darlings of fifteen millions, scattered over a surface of two millions of square miles—the remarkable phenomenon that they present is the level of intellect and of morals upon which they stand, and this universal mediocrity is the basis upon which the liberties of the nation repose."—*Diary*, vol. x. p. 78.

verse to the rational solution of financial problems. The chief benefit of the political struggles about to be renewed in Congress were the lessons that they were to teach in the future. The strenuous character of the impending contest and the extremity of political danger in which the administration stood were plainly indicated by the slender majority by which Polk, the administration candidate, was elected Speaker of the House. The vote was 116 to 103. But if any doubt existed as to Van Buren's firmness it was dissipated by his message, which had been anxiously awaited.[1] It is one of the ablest messages ever presented to Congress, evincing profound insight into the situation that existed, the causes that produced it, and the right policy to pursue. In later times it has received the general and decisive sanction of economists and financiers, and the constrained approval of writers, like Von Holst, adversely disposed toward Van Buren and his administration.

He first adverted to the immediate reasons for convoking Congress—the suspension of the deposit banks, which rendered nugatory the provisions of law in regard to the "deposit and safe-keeping" of the public moneys; the want of means to defray the expenses of the government; the inability of the importers to meet their bonds for duties; and the difficulty of the Treasury in maintaining specie payments. He then entered upon a clear and forcible exposition of the causes of the crisis. He ascribed them to "over-action in all departments of business—an over-action deriving, perhaps, its first impulses from antecedent causes, but stimulated

---

[1] "The President's message was brought on to this city by railroad, steamboats, and horsemen, and carried from hence to Boston, which place it reached in the incredibly short space of twenty-four hours from Washington, a distance of five hundred miles."—Hone's *Diary*, vol. i. p. 268.

to its destructive consequences by excessive issues of bank paper and by other facilities for the acquisition and enlargement of credit." "The consequences of this redundancy of credit, and of the spirit of reckless speculation engendered by it," were the vast foreign debt contracted here; the investment of many millions in unproductive Western lands, and the creation of a prodigious amount of debt for other real estate equally unproductive and at prices disproportionate to its actual value; the improvident expenditures for public improvements; the diversion of labor that should have been applied to agriculture, resulting in the necessity for large importations of grain; and the growth of luxury founded on fancied rather than real wealth. To these he added, as aggravating influences, the loss of capital by the great conflagration in New York city in 1836; the disturbing effects of transferring the public funds under the deposit law; the measures of foreign creditors to reduce their loans, and the consequent withdrawal from the United States of a large portion of our specie. He then adverted to the situation abroad, always an element necessarily to be considered in properly investigating the financial and commercial condition of this country. "It has since appeared," said he, "that evils similar to those suffered by ourselves have been experienced in Great Britain, on the Continent, and indeed throughout the commercial world; and that in other countries as well as our own they have been uniformly preceded, as with us, by unprecedented expansions of the systems of credit."[1]

---

[1] "Great gloom then gathered over our commerce, a panic set in in earnest, and bankruptcies, cessation of business, depreciation of goods and securities, prostration of trade, followed each other with wonderful rapidity. . . . At Manchester there were 50,000 hands out of employment, and most of those employed were working only on half-time. In Scotland

Such was the introduction to the leading measure to which Van Buren committed his party—the establishment of an independent Treasury, "to separate the fiscal operations of the government from those of individuals or corporations." It was necessarily followed by an elaborate declaration against the re-establishment of a national bank in any form. He emphatically denounced this plan, which was the chief feature of the Whig policy, maintaining that it would be incompetent to effect any beneficial purpose and would "impair the rightful supremacy of the popular will, injure the character and diminish the influence of our political system, and bring once more into existence a concentrated money power hostile to the spirit and threatening the permanency of our republican institutions." He cogently demonstrated that a national bank was not needed to facilitate domestic or foreign exchange, and asserted that it is not the proper and Constitutional province of the government to aid individuals in the transfer of their funds except through the post-office.

He was equally averse to the use of State or local banks as depositories for the public moneys. They had been thus employed during three periods—anterior to the first national bank, during the interval between the first and the second, and since 1833—and had proved unsuccessful notwithstanding the precautions and safeguards provided by

---

there were many failures, and in Ireland the state of trade was still worse."—Levi's *History of British Commerce*, p. 233. "The accounts from England are very alarming; the panic prevails there as bad as here. Cotton has fallen; the loss on shipments will be very heavy, and American credits will be withdrawn. The paper of Southern and Western merchants is coming back protested." "Everything in England is tending to a commercial crisis like that in which we are placed."—Hone's *Diary*, March 20, May 12, 1837, vol. i. pp. 248, 259.

law. This forced the inquiry whether the government could not and should not be entirely severed from all connection with banks, however convenient such agencies might be in ordinary times. He reached the conclusion that "the collection, safe-keeping, transfer, and disbursement of the public money can be well managed by the officers of the government." This, in brief, was the general scheme of the proposed independent Treasury, the details and difficulties of which he carefully considered. He incidentally discussed the character of the funds that should be received and disbursed by the government, and urged, as a salutary check upon issues of paper currency, the continuance of the policy instituted by the specie circular, and the propriety of a general bankruptcy law that would include corporations and banks as well as individuals. He also desired that the remainder of the undistributed surplus, nearly $9,400,000, should be retained to meet government necessities instead of being turned over to the States. The sentiment pervading the message was, as expressed at its close, that the real duty of the government "is to enact and enforce a system of general laws commensurate with, but not exceeding, the objects of its establishment, and to leave every citizen and every interest to reap, under its benign protection, the rewards of virtue, industry, and prudence."

As soon as the reading of the message was concluded in the Senate, Silas Wright, who was to be chairman of the Committee on Finance, and who sustained much the same relation to Van Buren that Benton had to Jackson, made the usual motion to print. Clay immediately seconded the motion, but took occasion to assail the President's policy. "While I am up," said he, "I cannot forbear saying that after attentively listening to the reading of this message I feel the deepest regret that the President, entertaining such views and proposing such a plan for the relief of the country as he had presented, has deemed it his duty to call an extra session of Congress at this inconvenient period of the year." This was only a slight, yet sufficient indication of the gantlet through which the project of the independent Treasury was to run. Nor was it the first intimation that Clay had given of his intention to wage systematic warfare on whatever policy the administration might announce. Immediately after the election he proposed to his followers an organized opposition, grounded on the theory that Van Buren had been designated by Jackson as his successor and triumphed through the machinery and patronage of the government. "Now I think," he wrote to a correspondent, "that no wisdom or benefit in the measures of the new administration can compensate or atone for this vice in its origin."

Clay was apparently too anxious for the Presidential nomination in 1840 to be honest with himself or regardful of the true interests of the country. Prompted by similar motives, he had denounced the opposition to the administration of John Quincy Adams as factious and culpable.[1] Although this plan of campaign was meditated before the beginning of the crisis, it was not changed afterward. The calamitous situation of the country only encouraged the efforts to break down the administration and to frustrate every measure it proposed. And within this general movement, in which all the Whig leaders were feverishly active and united, were the operations of the friends of the several candidates, who sought to avail themselves of the final re-

---

[1] *Clay's Correspondence*, p. 116.

sults. Clay's adherents were early in the field. Soon after Van Buren's inauguration a meeting was held in New York to promote Clay's interests. He was formally notified of the proceedings, and in August replied in an artfully composed letter, which was widely published. He stated that the agitation of the subject was premature, especially in view of the distracted condition of the country. Yet he was careful not to rebuke his partisans for their zeal or to advise a long postponement. He agreed that in regard to a candidate for the Presidency " some mode should be adopted of collecting the general sense of those who believe it important to the preservation of our liberties involved, the correction of abuses, and a thorough reform in the Executive administration, that there should be a change in the Chief Magistracy." He then revealed his ardent desire for the nomination, but in the temperate and diplomatic language peculiar to candidates in his situation.[1]

Therefore, Clay's immediate announcement of disapproval of the policy outlined by the message was not surprising. However his candidacy for the Presidential nomination was regarded by his rivals, he was the chief spirit of the opposition; his leadership was still paramount. In their hostility to the administration there was little discord among the Whigs. That any measure emanated from the administration was sufficient reason for them to oppose it if it had a political bearing. Measures were soon proposed. They were in the form of seven bills, reported by Wright from

---

[1] November 22, 1837, the Whigs of New York city held a celebration of their local victory. "The indications of public feeling during the day, which I have watched carefully, have been in my opinion decidedly in favor of Mr. Clay as the Whig candidate for President."—Hone's *Diary*, vol. i. p. 280.

the Committee on Finance, and incorporated substantially the recommendations of the President and the Secretary of the Treasury: to postpone indefinitely the fourth instalment of deposit with the States; to authorize the issue of Treasury notes to relieve the necessities of the government; to extend the time of payment of importers' bonds; to adjust the remaining claims upon the deposit banks; to provide for the placing of imports in the public stores and the payment of duties when the goods were withdrawn; to impose additional functions upon certain public officers—the independent Treasury system; to revoke the charters of such banks in the District of Columbia as should not within a fixed time resume specie payments, and to suppress the issue of small notes in the District. They were also introduced in the House to expedite debate. With the exception of the bills in regard to the revenue bonds and to adjust the claims on the deposit banks, they were at once attacked with all the vigor and ingenuity the opposition commanded.

The bill to postpone the fourth instalment of deposit was rancorously assailed as a breach of faith, on the theory that the States had already incurred obligations on the prospect of receiving it. The condition of the Treasury and the source of the fund did not influence the absurd and demagogical efforts to defeat it. It passed both houses, however, and was the first of the proposed measures to become a law. But so many Democrats in the House were reluctant to yield the scheme of distribution that it was there insisted that the postponement be made definite—January 1, 1839— and the Senate concurred. The bill also took from the Secretary of the Treasury the power of recalling the past instalments, and left it with Congress—a sufficient guarantee that it would not be exercised. Despite the intention to carry out the original plan, the fourth instalment was not delivered. January 1, 1839, the condition of the Treasury still forbade it, and the instalment was at length relinquished. But the funds that had been "deposited" with the States have never been recalled. It is not probable that another distribution will ever be attempted. The profligacy of Congress is likely to prove an adequate solvent of any surplus that may threaten, even should there be a disposition to ignore the lesson of the surplus of 1837.

The bill to authorize the issue of Treasury notes (to the amount of $10,000,000) was denounced as a proposed emission of paper currency, and ridiculed as an ignominious retreat from the much-vaunted purpose to establish an entirely metallic monetary system. In truth, the proposition was distasteful to many friends of the administration, notably Benton. Their support was gained only by the urgency of the situation and by removing the notes as far as practicable from the function of currency. They were to be issued in denominations of not less than $50, interest bearing, payable one year from their date, and transferable only by endorsement. Though receivable for public dues, they were not legal tender and not reissuable. With every precaution thus taken to prevent the issue from assuming the character of currency, it did not merit the animadversion it received. Under the circumstances, it was probably the best method of providing the means indispensable to the Treasury, as it was more expeditious and advantageous than a direct loan would have been. It encountered more opposition in the House than in the Senate, where Clay grotesquely assailed it as attempting to create a government bank of issue in disguise. It was the second bill of the session to become a law. Within the next five years this mode of procuring means was several times resorted to without much question.

The main struggle of the session was, of course, waged over the proposed independent Treasury — the "divorce bill," as it was styled. It involved all the principal elements of the great controversy between the two parties. As originally proposed, it provided that the revenues should be disbursed by the proper government officials at the Treasury and the Sub-Treasuries to be established at the chief commercial centres. In this form the measure was radical and far-reaching, as it would entirely terminate the use of banks for any purpose by the government; but the possibilities of the system were not fully disclosed until Calhoun offered an amendment providing that by gradual degrees, until January 1, 1841, the revenues of the government from all sources should be paid only in gold and silver or paper issued under the authority of the United States and expressly permitted by law to be received.

Calhoun had severed his late alliance with the Whigs and engaged with his usual vigor in support of the financial measures of the administration. And his support was so able and important that he perforce shared the Democratic leadership with Wright and Benton. His speech on the specie amendment covered with clearness and power the whole subject of the proposed financial policy and the causes and conditions that prompted it. He necessarily found it awkward to reconcile the views he expressed with some phases of his opposition to Jackson's measures; yet he was hampered by no radical inconsistency so far as his purely financial opinions were concerned. His new alliance was not unexpected. For some time, in fact, Clay and other prominent Whigs had chafed under the necessity and circumstances that induced co-operation with the nullifiers,[1] and they were not much averse to the change of situation that dissolved it. They expected soon to need no aid from without the party to execute their designs. Calhoun's explanation of his attitude—for his peculiar political position did not require him to furnish party justification—was that a new political and financial era had arrived and that he was free to act *de novo*. "I move off," said he, "under the States-rights banner, and go in the direction in which I have been so long moving."

The debate was long and earnest, most of the Whig Senators participating and vying with one another in ingenuity to adduce arguments against the Democratic policy. Most of the arguments, however, are so blended with political and partisan considerations as to render them of little service to the science of finance. The principal reasons urged against an independent Treasury were that it would place too much power in the hands of the Executive, by increasing the patronage and by affording opportunity for favoritism in one way and another to political friends; that it was calculated to impair the entire banking system of the country and abnormally contract the currency; that it would necessitate the exclusive use of coin by the government and paper by the people; that the public funds would be insecure; and that the scheme was opposed to the principles of our government and would be a return to antiquated methods.

Webster was looked to as the chief exponent of the strictly financial views of his party; but while his utterances contain much that is true and valuable, he was too

---

[1] Clay wrote in April, 1834: "The nullifiers are doing us no good here."
—*Clay's Correspondence*, p. 382.

much imbued with partisanship to render his speeches invulnerable. Like all his Whig colleagues, he suggested no remedy in place of the one he decried, except the institution of another national bank.

Clay spoke toward the close of the debate. As might be expected, his speech was mainly political. A large part of it was but a repetition in new form of his previous speeches attributing the financial condition of the country entirely to Jackson's measures. He, therefore, took issue with the President's statement with regard to the causes of the crisis as set forth in his message. He imputed to the administration the design to subvert the State banks and place them at the mercy of the federal government, and argued strenuously in favor of a convertible paper system through the medium of the banks. He then repeated the current objections to the measure: insecurity of the public funds through danger of peculation, "the liability to favoritism," "the fearful increase of Executive patronage," "the perilous union of the purse and the sword"; and that the system was "destined to become, if it was not designed to be, a vast and ramified connection of government banks, of which the principal will be at Washington and every Sub-Treasury will be a branch," on the theory that the drafts of the Secretary on the Sub-Treasuries would operate as a general currency in the place of bank-notes. After alleging inconsistency between the views of the late and the existing administrations on the subject of regulating the exchanges, he passed to a discussion of the Whig panacea for the ills of the country — a national bank. "I declare," said he, "that, after the most deliberate and anxious consideration of which I am capable, I can conceive of no adequate remedy which does not comprehend a national bank as an essential part." He challenged the statement in the message that the popular will had twice been "solemnly and unequivocally expressed" against it, and argued that Jackson's re-election after his veto of the bill to recharter the bank did not signify that the people were adverse to any bank, but to the one proposed, because Jackson himself had declared in his veto message that if he had been consulted he could have furnished a model free from objection. "I am perfectly persuaded," said Clay, "that thousands and tens of thousands sustained his re-election under the full expectation that a national bank would be established during his second term." If he really believed this he deceived himself. Political issues have seldom been more clearly defined than that in the campaign of 1832 over rechartering the bank. And Van Buren's election after the struggles in relation to the bank during Jackson's last term made the result absolutely unequivocal. His argument in favor of a bank presented nothing new. "We are all," said he "— people, States, Union, banks—bound up and interwoven together, united in fortune and destiny, and all, all entitled to the protecting care of a parental government. . . . A government, an official corps — the servants of the people — glittering in gold, and the people themselves — their masters — buried in ruin and surrounded by rags!" The principal idea of the speech was that little public good was to be expected until there were a Whig administration and a Whig Congress.

October 3, Calhoun's amendment was adopted by a majority of one, and on the next day the bill as amended was passed by the Senate, 26 to 20. But in the House the administration was not strong enough to carry it. On the

14th, two days before the adjournment, it was laid on the table by a vote of 119 to 107. Nevertheless, the delay of the measure was of little practical consequence, as the system it proposed was already by force of circumstances in practical operation. Moreover, the momentum was started that was finally to carry the measure through.

Notwithstanding the opposition to the independent Treasury system, both houses were strongly adverse to a national bank. Many petitions were of course presented in favor of a bank. In the Senate they were referred to the Finance Committee, which reported a resolution stating "that the prayer of the petitioners ought not to be granted." When it was called up, Clay said that he could see no utility in a negative resolution; that he could recollect but one example— Randolph's resolution that it was inexpedient to declare war against Great Britain. He preferred that the resolution be laid on the table, but if that course was not taken he moved as a substitute "that it will be expedient to establish a United States bank whenever it shall be manifest that a clear majority of the people of the United States are in favor of such an institution." This was rejected and the original resolution adopted, 31 to 14. A few days later a resolution declaring "that it is inexpedient to charter a national bank" was adopted by the House, 123 to 91.

The proposition to enact a bankruptcy law for banks met with scant encouragement. Benton was almost alone in his advocacy of it. Despite his indefatigable support of the administration, his personal relations with Van Buren were not cordial. Shortly after the inauguration he warned the President of the impending crisis, and strongly urged precautions concerning the government funds; and his pride met a rude rebuff, which he never fully pardoned, when Van

Buren blandly told him, "Your friends think you a little exalted in the head on that subject."

Several bills of minor importance became laws; but the only ones to succeed connected with the leading policy of the administration were those postponing the fourth instalment of deposit with the States, authorizing the issue of Treasury notes, and to adjust the claims against the deposit banks. But they relieved the most urgent necessities of the government and left the administration in a position to continue the struggle for the regular establishment of the independent Treasury.

The brief interval between the adjournment of the special and the beginning of the regular session, December 4, developed no marked change in the general condition of the country. The excitement and acute symptoms of the crisis had subsided, but the ravages were too serious to be repaired save by the gradual return of confidence and the slow process of normal recuperation. Yet some improvement was visible. The business houses that had escaped the common devastation were the nucleus of that potential energy which always revives and supports the activities of the people, however severe the revulsion that overwhelms them. This never-failing phenomenon is the most convincing demonstration that the natural laws of trade and finance, when unimpeded, work more sound and enduring good than legislative stimulants can produce. One evidence of improvement was the decrease in the premium on gold, which had fallen from eight and seven-eighths to five per cent. Besides this was the movement on the part of the sound banks to resume specie payments. The chief obstacle was the Pennsylvania Bank of the United States, which still wielded great influence. Its precarious condition was known only to its officers, who took all available means to delay the final catastrophe. As resumption would be the beginning of the end, it was industriously but diplomatically opposed. The bank pleaded its own cause in disguise through the specious pretext of a paternal desire to aid the weaker banks, to which further time was an absolute necessity. The situation of the New York banks was wholly the reverse. The State law legalizing their suspension required them to resume within a year, which would expire May 15, 1838. To them, therefore, resumption was vital. Moreover, their condition as well as their relations to the commerce and finance of the country were such as to impel them to pursue a sound banking policy. Accordingly, before the extra session of Congress, they proposed a convention of representatives of all the banks of the country, to agree upon a time for general resumption. But at the instance of the Pennsylvania Bank it was delayed until Congress rose, to await legislative action.

Shortly after the adjournment the New York banks again took the initiative and issued invitations for a convention to be held in New York city, November 27. It met on that day, but the object was again frustrated. Resolutions to resume specie payment on March 1 and July 1, 1838, were defeated. The convention then adjourned to April 15. At that time there was still a strong opposition to immediate resumption, and the result was to fix January 1, 1839, as the date for resumption, although it was agreed that banks so desiring could resume sooner. When the convention ended, the premium on gold in New York, which had been steadily declining, was less than one per cent. This was due to the position of the New York banks, which were now compelled to act alone to save their charters. They all resumed specie payment on May 10, and their example was speedily followed by many banks in other States.

The results of the elections in the fall of 1837 caused the Whigs much rejoicing. The popular tide had set strongly in their favor—even in New York, notwithstanding the reconciliation of the "Locofoco"[1] faction with the main body of the Democratic party. This faction had for some time been in revolt, but it was now in accord with the policy of the administration. While Van Buren was sensitive to these manifestations of popular sentiment, he was not influenced by them. He expressly recognized them in his annual message, but professed that the decisive factors in the various elections were local rather than national,[2] and strongly renewed his recommendation of the independent Treasury plan. In this connection he called attention, in severe terms and very justly, to the fact that over $27,000,000 of the notes of the former Bank of the United States were still uncancelled and over $10,500,000 still in circulation, through the illegal and adventurous operations of its

---

[1] This name was applied in the fall of 1835. In a contest between the two factions of Tammany Hall, the regulars were unexpectedly outnumbered and turned off the gas. Apprehending this, the other faction had brought candles and locofoco matches and at once relighted the hall. "The latter, in 1836, organized the Equal Rights party, and declared it an imperative duty to the people to 'recur to first principles.' Their 'declaration of rights' might well a few years later have been drawn by a student of Spencer's *Social Statics*."—Shepard's *Van Buren*, p. 293.

[2] This reference to the elections provoked Clay's criticism. "I am shocked," said he, "at the President having undertaken in his message to comment on the result of local elections. It is unprecedented, and, I must be allowed to say, undignified. It is the first example in which the President spoke of elections, not of the general government, but of State governments. . . . A State Chief Magistrate may in his message refer to the result of the elections in his own State; but what decent pretext has a President of the United States to take notice of the result of State elections and assign causes, dishonorable causes, for them?"

successor. He also pronounced in favor of the policy of disposing of the public lands so long advocated by Benton—low prices, graduated according to their relative value, and liberal pre-emption privileges, with the leading object of inducing settlement and cultivation. The only other topics of particular interest in the message were that referring to the controversy of long standing with Great Britain over the northeastern boundary, and that with Mexico over the claims which had during the preceding administration been pushed so vigorously. Neither had been much advanced, and both afforded opportunity for patriotic display.

The proceedings of the session, which lasted until July 7, were unusually varied and of lively public interest, although comparatively little important legislation reached the statute-books. The first topic to engross attention was slavery. Notwithstanding the financial and political questions apparently uppermost, the antislavery agitation was again obtruded with enhanced energy. From the startling increase in the number of abolition petitions and their signers it was evident that the cause was progressing and augmenting its forces. Most of the petitions were, as formerly, for the abolition of slavery in the District of Columbia, and frequently described slavery in terms so severe and ill-restrained that the Southern Senators and Representatives, as well as the Southern people and press, regarded them more acutely than ever before as flagrant insults, and were thus in their dread and rage driven to a more uncompromising and vindictive stand than they had previously assumed. The most portentous aspect of the agitation, and that which most influenced the South, was the fact that the abolitionists were becoming a political force. The legislature of Connecticut had repealed the "black law," under which Prudence Crandall's school had been suppressed. The legislature of Massachusetts had, by a large majority, adopted resolutions censuring Congress for its treatment of abolition petitions, and asserting the Constitutional power of Congress to abolish slavery in the District. The legislature of Vermont had not only adopted similar resolutions, but went so far as to protest against the annexation of Texas because it would be a slave State. And this was the theme of many petitions.

The feelings of the Southern members now passed the bounds of mere excitement, and the most ominous scenes which had thus far been enacted took place in the House. The swelling multitude of petitions and petitioners was alone sufficient to create profound alarm, and but slight provocation was needed to disclose the determination of the Southern members to take radical action. December 20, Slade, of Vermont, who had previously presented some petitions praying for the abolition of slavery in the District, and moved to refer them to a select committee with instructions to report a bill for that purpose, began a speech in support of his motion. The speech, so far as he proceeded, was an attack on slavery in general, after the type common to abolitionist agitators. As soon as its purport was manifest it met with obstreperous objections; and after much wrangling and confusion the House adjourned. During the tumult the members from several of the Southern States had been requested to withdraw; and when the result of the motion to adjourn was announced, Campbell, of South Carolina, mounted a chair and with stentorian voice gave notice that the gentlemen who represented the slave-holding States were invited to meet in the District committee-room. The conclave was quickly organized. Many of those present were ready for extreme measures. Rhett, of South Carolina, proposed resolutions declaring that the "Constitution having failed to protect the South in the peaceable possession of their rights and peculiar institutions, it is expedient that the Union be dissolved," and to provide for the appointment of a committee of two members from each State to report upon the best means of peaceably dissolving it.

Though the proposition met with some favor, the majority of those who attended the conference were convinced that it was unnecessary to press it at that juncture, and decided instead to again employ the "gag." As this was generally acceptable to the Northern politicians, there was no serious difficulty the next day in procuring its adoption in the most stringent form, despite vigorous opposition under the lead of Adams. To do it required the suspension of the rules by a two-thirds vote, which was easily obtained. Debate was quickly silenced by carrying the previous question, and the "gag" resolution was adopted. Some of the Northern members, however, who voted to suspend the rules voted against the resolution in order to satisfy their constituents; but in voting to suspend the rules they did what was most needful to aid the Southern policy. Thus, in the House, further discussion of slavery was prevented for the session. Rhett's proposition attracted wide attention. While the plan it contained was by no means novel, it was the first time it had been formally presented, and the "memorable secession" from the House became a stock phrase, and secession of the South a standing threat. It had the effect which its author subsequently explained was his purpose to produce—to give formal notice of the attitude of the South in the event of any interference with slavery.

That scenes similar to those in the House, in consequence

of the abolition petitions, did not take place in the Senate was mainly due to the character of this body, for the same provocation existed, and the disposition of the Southern Senators was alike to that of the Southern Representatives. A few days before the adoption of the " gag " by the House, Clay, perceiving the increase in the number of petitions, remarked: " It is manifest that the subject of slavery in the District of Columbia is extending itself in the public mind, and daily engaging more and more of the public attention. I have no hesitation in saying the Congress ought not to do what is asked by the petitioners without the consent of the people of the District of Columbia. I am desirous of inquiring whether the feeling of abolition in the abstract is not extending itself, or whether it is not becoming mixed up with other matters—such, for instance, as the belief that the sacred right of petition has been assailed. It becomes the duty of the Senate to inquire into this business and understand the subject well."

Discussion at once ensued, the Southern Senators taking ground against receiving the petitions. Calhoun was especially pronounced. He was "for no conciliatory course, no temporizing," and appealed to the Southern members to stand by him. "There is but one question," said he, "that will ever destroy this Union, and that is involved in this principle. Yes, this is potent enough for it, and must be early arrested if the Union is to be preserved." Uninfluenced by the outcry of Calhoun, Clay plainly expressed his opinion as to what should be done—that the petitions should be received, referred, acted upon, and argued down.

The motion to receive the petitions was laid on the table. But the subject did not remain there. The next day Swift, of Vermont, presented the memorial and resolutions of the legislature of that State in relation to slavery in the District and the annexation of Texas. King hotly pronounced them "an infamous libel and insult on the South." Calhoun was nearly benumbed with astonishment, as this was the first he had heard of them. He admitted that he was not prepared to discuss them, and desired that they be received and laid on the table, that he might " prepare his mind for action on the subject, determined that it should not rest until it had received the final action of the Senate." At Clay's request the documents were withdrawn with notice that they would be presented later. On the two following days occurred the proceedings in the House over Slade's motion and the adoption of the "gag." Thus Calhoun had ample incentive to exert himself to the utmost in defence of his political doctrines. And he did so. On the 27th he presented a series of six resolutions asserting his principles.

Of all men of that day whose utterances survive, none understood so clearly the real character and import of the issue over slavery. He was doubtless sincere in the belief he steadfastly expressed that slavery was right and should be preserved for the interest of both the master and the slave. This, we may assume, was the fundamental premise upon which the entire superstructure of his defence was reared. Yet underlying this was the imperious fact that slavery had become a controlling element in the social fabric of the South, the chief basis of its activity and wealth, and hence the dictator of its public and political sentiment. Even the ministers of the gospel were hardly less zealous than the politicians in upholding the institution, for which they found abundant sanction in Holy Writ. Under such circumstances the moral aspect of slavery, as viewed where slavery did not exist, could not appeal to the Southern people; and the fierce criticism and agitation in the North only rendered the South more obdurate to reason and more energetic to fortify and extend the institution.

Perhaps the most singular phase of the whole matter is that the South was so blind to its true material interests. In this same year, in a commercial convention of the Southern States, the relative conditions of the North and South were vividly contrasted. The steadily increasing superiority of the North over the South in population and wealth, and industrial and commercial interests, was complainingly recognized and admitted. The cause was largely ascribed to the tariff, internal improvements, the two national banks, the paper system, pensions, and governmental extravagance and abuses, which gave the North such an advantage as to make the South its tributary; and, as a partial remedy, direct trade between Southern and foreign ports was proposed. This explanation contained some truth, but it was not sufficient to account for the disparity in the conditions of the two sections. The main cause was in the fatal disadvantage of the system of slave labor and its attendant evils as compared with that of free labor. As the subject is studied at this distance of time, when every motive for ignoring or obscuring the truth is removed, it seems surprising that the economic superiority of free labor was not perceived and utilized. Had this phase of the question been properly and dispassionately considered, the course of events would doubtless have been changed. But the obstacles were twofold—the slaves were negroes, whom the most enlightened people of the South were in any case afraid to liberate; and the associations and habits of life were such as to exclude the contemplation of such an alternative. The philosopher may calmly reason now on the subject of slavery extinct; but then the planter had to deal with property that constituted a large part of his possessions and with conditions created generations before him.

That Calhoun was inconsistent with his former views whenever they conflicted with the development of his new theories in defence of slavery did not deter him. Any opinions he had ever expressed were resolutely abandoned if contrary to the logical exigencies of his position. A striking instance of his change of mind was in relation to the Missouri Compromise. While in Monroe's cabinet, when the bill was passed and signed, he favored it; but he now emphatically disapproved it as being a "dangerous measure," which had "done much to rouse into action the present spirit." He asserted that "had it been met with uncompromising opposition, such as a then distinguished and sagacious member from Virginia (Mr. Randolph), now no more, opposed to it, abolition might have been crushed forever in its birth." He had no faith in palliatives to allay the agitation. He saw that there could be no pacification of the agitators, and that the only mode of meeting their efforts was in the rigid denial of the right to assail slavery in Congress or by political action. He sought to interpose legal propositions as a barrier against the rising tide of moral sentiment against slavery. He admitted his doubts as to the efficiency of his plan, but presented it as the most promising one. He desired that the Union be preserved, but not unless slavery could be secure within it; yet he foresaw with prophetic certainty the inevitable danger with which the slavery question was fraught. Most of the Senators, whatever their opinions upon the question, deprecated his aggressive policy. They preferred to avoid discussion by merely receiving the petitions and memorials and laying them on the table without debate. Northern Senators, anxious to give the South all reasonable support, felt, out of regard for their own political safety at home, that Calhoun's extreme demands were more onerous than he ought to impose. But he would not swerve from his purpose. The stifling of discussion was not what his haughty spirit desired. He invoked the Constitution as the sufficient guarantee of security to slavery, and insisted that the time had come to make a test of the Senate's disposition toward the South. His resolutions were the means.

CHAPTER X

The Debate on Calhoun's Slavery Resolutions and Clay's Substitutes—The Independent Treasury again Defeated—Minor Financial Legislation—The Doctrine of Instructions—The Subsidiary Coin—Clay's Set Speech on the Slavery Question and Calhoun's Comments—Clay's Northern Tour—The Obstacles to His Nomination—The Whig National Convention—Harrison and Tyler Nominated—Clay's Disgust and Acquiescence

CALHOUN's resolutions were designed to embrace the entire legal status of slavery and to furnish a complete "platform" of its Constitutional rights. The essential propositions of the first three were that in the adoption of the Constitution the States acted as free, independent, and sovereign, and "entered the Union with the view to its increased security and against all dangers, domestic as well as foreign, and the more perfect enjoyment of its advantages, natural, political, and social"; that they "retained, severally, the exclusive and sole right over their own domestic institutions and police, and are alone responsible for them, and that any intermeddling of any one or more States, or a combination of their citizens, with the domestic institutions and police of the others, on any ground or under any pretext whatever, political, moral, or religious, with the view to their alteration or subversion, is an assumption of superiority not warranted by the Constitution, insulting to the States interfered with, tending to endanger their domestic peace and tranquillity, subversive of the objects for which the Constitution was formed, and by necessary consequence tending to weaken and destroy the Union itself"; that the government was instituted by "the several States" as a common agent to carry into effect the powers they had delegated by the Constitution; "and that in fulfilment of this high and sacred trust this government is bound so to exercise its powers as to give, as far as may be practicable, increased stability and security to the domestic institutions of the States that compose the Union; and that it is the solemn duty of the government to resist all attempts by one portion of the Union to use it as an instrument to attack the domestic institutions of another, or to weaken or destroy such institutions instead of strengthening and upholding them, as it is in duty bound to do."

These three resolutions formed the groundwork of general principles applied in the remaining resolutions. They contained the ultra doctrine of States-rights, and Calhoun's familiar theory of the formation and character of the Union. Yet they encountered little opposition for that reason. The first was adopted, 31 to 13. The second received some slight verbal amendment, and the words "insulting to the States interfered with" were stricken out. An effort was also made to strike out the words "moral and religious," but it was unsuccessful, for Calhoun earnestly maintained that they were vital. Webster criticised the resolution as being too broad and too vague and "at variance with the correct interpretation of the Constitution," although he admitted the necessity of some definite action on the subject by Congress. "If the resolutions," said he, "can be modified to meet the Constitutional requisitions, asserting that the Constitution *permits* slavery and protects the institution, I will then vote for them. An assertion here that the Constitution cannot meddle with domestic institutions, if supported, utterly deprives it of power or effect." The second resolution was adopted, 31 to 9.

The third evoked more discussion. The objection was urged that it was not the duty of the government to increase the stability and security of the domestic institutions of the States or to strengthen and uphold them. The argument in behalf of this objection was so cogent and so generally entertained that Calhoun acquiesced, and the clauses were eliminated. A proviso was then proposed asserting that the resolutions should not be construed as adverse to "these fundamental principles of this government: That all men are created equal; that they are endowed by their Creator with certain inalienable rights; that among these are life, liberty, and the pursuit of happiness. That the freedom of speech and of the press and the right of the people peacefully to assemble and petition the government for redress of grievances shall never be abridged. That error of human opinion may be tolerated while reason is left free to combat it. That the Union must be preserved." Calhoun vigorously protested, and at length a substitute was adopted declaring that "nothing in the foregoing resolutions is intended to recognize the right of Congress to impair in any manner the freedom of speech or of the press or the right of petition as secured by the Constitution to the citizens of the several States, within their States respectively." Presumably Calhoun regarded it as harmless because of the last phrase, which fell short of the express provision of the Constitution. An addition was then moved that "the right of the people to speak, write, print, and publish anything whatever is indisputable; and that they are amenable only to the State in which they may be at the time."

By this time the spirit of opposition began to manifest

itself more strongly; and many of the Senators who were willing to vote for the resolutions expressed their disapproval of the whole proceeding, as likely to produce more harm than good. To these criticisms Calhoun replied with intense earnestness, asserting that the Senate did "not sufficiently comprehend the extent and magnitude of the existing dangers." He pointed them out with truth that grated on the political sensibilities of the Senators. Disunion was the spectre that he kept constantly before their eyes. His independent position left him free to bend his energies to the defence of Southern interests, without regard to ulterior political considerations. Clay wrote that Calhoun's aim was "to advance the political interest of the mover and to affect mine";[1] but there is no good ground to suppose that in this course Calhoun had any political purpose apart from the cause he represented. His entire conduct was the reverse of politic, and it may be safely assumed that he was governed by the belief that it was necessary to take positive action in support of slavery as the only method of protection. The motion was defeated. It was followed by another to strike out the words "the several States" and insert "the people of the United States." This was intended to counteract Calhoun's basic theory. In regard to it Clay remarked: "If the Senator will frame his amendment according to the historical fact in the adoption of the Constitution I will vote for it. The historical fact is that the Constitution was adopted by the people of the several States, acting within their respective limits."[2] This motion

---

[1] "I am greatly deceived," he continued, "if in both respects he has not signally failed. He was caught in his own trap."—*Clay to Brooke, January* 13, 1838.

[2] In a subsequent speech on this subject he said : "With regard to the point so much insisted upon in this debate, and which has produced great

also failed, and the resolution as it then stood was adopted, 31 to 11.

The fourth specifically applied the general doctrines of the three first to the institution of slavery, and declared that all attacks upon it " are in manifest violation of the mutual and solemn pledge to protect and defend each other given by the States respectively on entering into the Constitutional compact which formed the Union, and as such are a manifest breach of faith and a violation of the most solemn obligations, moral and religious." The preceding resolutions precluded debate on this one, and it was adopted, 34 to 5, after the words " moral and religious " were stricken out.

Thus far the resolutions had met with no effective opposition; but it was apparent after the fourth was disposed of that the two last could not be adopted. Calhoun had carried his doctrines too far. The fifth resolution was: "That the intermeddling of any State or States, or their citizens, to abolish slavery in this District or any of the Territories, on the ground or under the pretext that it is immoral or sinful, or the passage of any act or measure of Congress with that view, would be a direct and dangerous attack on the institutions of all the slave-holding States." It was plainly not acceptable to the majority. One Senator contended that the resolution was not declaratory of Constitutional rights, but of expediency — a legitimate field for difference of opinion and discussion. Others disapproved of the phraseology while agreeing with the general purport. The suggestion

---

controversy in former times, whether the Constitution is to be regarded as the work of the people of the United States collectively or of the separate States composing the confederacy, I have always thought that more importance is attached to it than it deserves. The real question in considering the instrument is not how the Constitution was made, but what is it as it is?"

was made that Calhoun should consent to insert "on any pretext whatever" instead of "on the ground or under the pretext that it is immoral or sinful"; but he refused. A motion was then made to insert "also a violation of the public faith implied in the cession of this District by the States of Virginia and Maryland." Calhoun said that he had always been of the opinion that any interference with slavery in the District would not only be a violation of the public faith, but also unconstitutional; and that he had not thought proper to assert it, as he knew that a majority of the Senate was of a different opinion, and therefore his "object was to place the question on no particular portion of the Constitution, but on its general character and structure, which was much stronger and much less liable to be disputed." He neither objected nor consented to the proposed amendment, which was then carried. These details are essential to a full understanding of the origin of the causes that led to the repeal of the Missouri Compromise and the final defence of slavery that resulted in the Rebellion.

At this juncture Clay, who had taken but small part in the previous discussions, spoke at some length, and in the course of his speech presented a series of resolutions to conform to his own conception of what should be declared. He declined to vote for either the fifth or sixth of Calhoun's resolutions, and asserted that he had voted for the others "not from any confidence in their healing virtues." Considering all the circumstances, especially the manner in which Calhoun had "pressed them on the Senate," he was of the opinion that at the North they might "increase and exasperate instead of diminishing and assuaging the existing irritation."

The sixth resolution was designed, in inferential terms, to protect slavery in Texas, should that country be annexed to the United States. To this Clay objected as blending "the two unhappy causes of agitation together." He also condemned Calhoun's plan to create what was afterward called the "solid South," on the States-rights platform, and to place in the keeping of one party, instead of all, the peculiar interests of the slave-holding States. He then discussed the right of petition, declaring himself in favor of rejecting petitions that prayed for relief which Congress clearly did not possess the Constitutional power to grant, but in other cases to receive them and dispose of them respectfully. His policy was to keep the abolitionists "separate and distinct from all other classes," and "the subject of abolition separate and distinct from all other subjects." He believed in argument to quiet the agitation. To preserve our institutions and the Union, he "would argue with any one, with lunatics themselves in their lucid intervals, and argue again and again." He had no apprehension for the safety of the Union. "We allow ourselves," said he, "to speak too frequently and with too much levity of a separation of the Union. It is a terrible word, to which our ears should not be familiarized. I desire to see in continued safety and prosperity *this* Union and no other Union. I go for this Union as it is, one and indivisible, without diminution. I will neither voluntarily leave it nor be driven out of it by force. Here in my place I shall contend for all of the rights of the State which has sent me here. I shall contend for them with undoubting confidence and in all the security which the Union confers, under all the high sanctions which the guarantees of the Constitution affords, and with perfect conviction that they are safer in the Union than they would be out of the Union. I am opposed to all separate confederacies and to all sectional conventions. No state of actual danger exists to render them expedient or to justify deliberation about them. This Union, this government, has done nothing, nothing whatever, to excite the smallest alarm. It will do nothing; but if it should, if contrary to all human probability the rights of the slave-holding States shall be assailed by any authoritative act emanating from this capital, a state of things for resistance, forcible resistance, will then occur. It will be time enough then to act."

His resolutions were eight in number. The two first declared that slavery in the States was exclusively subject to the power and control of those States respectively; that no other State nor the people of any other State had any Constitutional authority to interfere with it; and that all petitions touching slavery in the States be therefore instantly rejected; the fourth and fifth, that slavery ought not to be abolished in the District, but that in deference to the right of petition Congress was bound to and would receive, respectfully treat, and refer to the appropriate committee, petitions on that subject if couched in decorous language; the seventh and eighth, that Congress was without power to prohibit the slave-trade between the States; and that while the Senate had seen with painful regret the antislavery agitation, it beheld "with the deepest satisfaction, everywhere prevailing an unconquerable attachment to the Union, as the sure bulwark of the safety, liberty, and happiness of the people of the United States." As no action was taken on these six resolutions, their only interest lies in their statement of Clay's opinions, on the points upon which they touched; but as the other two became the basis of substitutes for Calhoun's fifth and sixth resolutions, they possess historical importance.

The third recited that when the District was ceded by Virginia and Maryland slavery existed in both States, including the ceded territory, and that as it still continued in both States "it could not be abolished within the District without a violation of that good faith which was implied in the cession and in the acceptance of the territory, nor unless compensation were made to the proprietors of slaves, without a manifest violation of an amendment to the Constitution of the United States, nor without exciting a degree of just alarm and apprehension in the States recognizing slavery, far transcending in mischievous tendency any possible benefit which could be accomplished by the abolition." The sixth of the series declared that "it would be highly inexpedient to abolish slavery in Florida, the only Territory of the United States in which it now exists, because of the serious alarm and apprehensions which would be thereby excited in the States sustaining that domestic institution; because the people of that Territory have not asked it to be done, and when admitted as a State into the Union, they will be exclusively entitled to decide that question for themselves"; also because it would be in violation of the Compromise of 1820. The latter reason, however, was omitted when the resolution was considered. After some further observations, in which he said that there was nothing abstract or metaphysical in his resolutions, and that he did not concur in declaring that the abolition of slavery in the District would be a *direct* attack upon the institution of slavery in the States, Clay proposed to offer the third and sixth as amendments to Calhoun's fifth. He concluded by formally moving the third for that purpose.

A vigorous discussion followed, principally between Calhoun and Clay; for Calhoun was extremely averse to yielding on any part of his programme. He thoroughly disapproved of Clay's conciliatory method, and declared that the difference between them was "as wide as the poles." But in the main Clay's propositions received decided approbation. The proposed amendment went through the usual process of verbal change, and was finally adopted, 36 to 9, in this form: "That the interference by the citizens of any of the States with the view to the abolition of slavery in this District is endangering the rights and security of the people of the District, and that any act or measure of Congress designed to abolish slavery in this District would be a violation of faith implied in the cessions by the States of Virginia and Maryland, a just cause of alarm to the people of the slave-holding States, and have a direct and inevitable tendency to disturb and endanger the Union."

The resolution in the form originally submitted by Clay was much the better, as it stated the concrete reasons for the sentiment it expressed. But Clay never stood out for any particular formula of words when the substance he sought was stated; results were always his object, though they could only be attained by sacrifice. In 1836 he admitted the Constitutional power of Congress to abolish slavery in the District, and that there was no condition in the cession to prevent its exercise. The "violation of faith" asserted in the resolution was not placed on either ground, but on the inexpediency of abolition in the District under all the circumstances; and this position was unquestionably sound. Webster showed conclusively that there would be no violation of anything contained in the statutes and instruments which effected the cession if slavery were abolished in the District, and he objected to the terms of the resolution, though he was opposed to any interference with slavery there. He voted against all the resolutions because he could not approve the terms in which they were expressed.

Clay's sixth resolution was then taken up. Reference to the Compromise was omitted, and the resolution was made to apply to "any Territory of the United States" instead of to Florida. The additional reason was inserted that any attempt to abolish slavery in such Territory "would be a violation of good faith towards the inhabitants who have been permitted to settle with and hold slaves therein." Thus changed, the resolution was adopted, 35 to 9. Calhoun's last resolution was laid on the table, and the debate, which had extended over two weeks, was terminated.[1] The Senate turned with relief to other things; for not only was discussion of the slavery question distasteful to nearly all the members, and in their judgment unwise and impolitic, but they did not regard the subject as of sufficient importance to receive the attention that Calhoun compelled.[2] And in the public mind it was of minor conse-

---

[1] Webster spoke on March 12 and 13. "The House was deserted again this day. Webster finished his speech in the Senate, universally thought the most splendid and powerful of his efforts. There was no possibility of keeping a quorum in the House."—Adams's *Diary*, vol. ix. p. 509.

[2] The action of the Senate on these resolutions is styled by Von Holst "cheap and cowardly cunning," and Clay's compromises, "opiates to stupefy the thought and especially the moral feeling of the people." This author, here as elsewhere, is unmindful of the true and practical considerations : that constitutionally and legally the resolutions, as adopted, were for the most part sound ; that Congress was, as it always will be, influenced by practical considerations ; and that under all the circumstances the temporizing policy was the only practical and efficacious one to pursue. The only logical alternative is to say that all the Constitutional guarantees of slavery should have been overthrown, and slavery forcibly abolished. Such criticism hardly deserves refutation.

quence as compared with the state of the country and the political and financial questions of the hour.

The leading topic before Congress was again the independent Treasury. A bill similar to the one that failed at the special session was soon introduced. The debate upon it was even more extended and elaborate than before, although substantially the same arguments were employed. It was passed by the Senate by a majority of two votes, but not until the provisions requiring specie payments to the government were stricken out, which caused Calhoun and his followers to vote against it. In the House the bill was defeated by a majority of 14, the defection from the administration being still the obstacle. But the system continued as before, *de facto*.

The chief interest aroused by the debate centred in an encounter between Clay and Calhoun, which is notable in our parliamentary annals. February 15, Calhoun delivered a set speech on the measure. It was a plain argument, stating with more care and deliberation the views he had previously expressed, and containing no personalities. Clay spoke on the 19th. It was manifest that his speech had been thoroughly considered and that it was designed for political effect, and incidentally the castigation of Calhoun, to which the latter part of it was devoted. For seven years Clay, Webster, and Calhoun had co-operated in the leadership of the opposition to the Jackson party; and when Calhoun forsook them to join in the support of Van Buren it naturally aroused in his former allies a feeling of resentment bound to be revealed, notwithstanding their growing aversion to an alliance with the nullifiers. Indications of it were shown during the special session; but that his attack might have all the force possible, Clay patiently bided his time.

The plan was devised with great skill and executed with his wonted oratorical power.

He began by an impressive statement of his sense of responsibility, and continued: "Never before have I risen to express my opinions upon any public measure fraught with such tremendous consequences to the welfare and prosperity of the country, and so perilous to the liberties of the people, as I solemnly believe this bill to be.... And I have thanked my God that he has prolonged my life until the present time to enable me to exert myself in the service of my country against a project far transcending in pernicious tendency any that I have ever had occasion to consider." After briefly describing the "eminently prosperous" condition of the country before "Andrew Jackson, not by the blessing of God, was made President of the United States," he compared the country in its existing condition to a ship "helpless and immovable upon breakers, the surge beating over her venerable sides, and the crew threatened with instantaneous destruction," brought there "by his bungling navigation or by his want of skill and judgment."

He then set out to prove five propositions: that it was the deliberate purpose of the late administration to establish a Treasury bank to be administered and controlled by the Executive Department; that with this end in view the intention was to overthrow the entire banking system of the country; that the attack was first confined to the Bank of the United States, and after its overthrow the attack was directed against the State banks; that Van Buren's administration was pledged to complete and perfect the principles, plans, and policy of Jackson's administration; and that the independent Treasury bill was intended to execute that pledge "by establishing upon the ruins of the late Bank of the United States and the State banks a government bank, to be managed and controlled by the Treasury Department acting under the commands of the President of the United States." The argument in support of these propositions presented nothing that was novel except a new arrangement of materials which, for the most part, Clay had employed many times before. The first three propositions were based on Jackson's messages and farewell address, and the argument was interspersed with specimens of Clay's long-practised art of denouncing Jackson, which these passages amply illustrate:

"War and strife, endless war and strife, personal or national, foreign or domestic, were the aliment of the President's existence. War against the bank, war against France, and strife and contention with a countless number of individuals. The wars with Black Hawk and the Seminoles were scarcely a luncheon for his voracious appetite. And he made his exit from public life denouncing war and vengeance against Mexico and the State banks. . . . His administration consisted of a succession of astounding measures which fell on the public ear like repeated bursts of loud and appalling thunder. Before the reverberations of one peal had ceased another and another came, louder and louder and more terrifying. Or rather, it was like a volcanic mountain emitting frightful eruptions of burning lava. Before one was cold and crusted, before the voices of the buried villages and cities were hushed in eternal silence, another more desolating was vomited forth, extending wider and wider the circle of death and destruction."

In connection with the fourth proposition—that the administration was pledged to carry out the policy of its predecessor—Van Buren became the object of Clay's invective.

He exultingly cited the passage in Van Buren's letter of acceptance saying that he was "the honored instrument selected by the friends of the present administration to carry out its principles and policy," and that if elected he should "endeavor generally to follow in the footsteps of President Jackson." "The honored instrument!" Clay exclaimed. "That word, according to the most approved definition, means tool. He was, then, the honored tool—to do what? To promote the honor and advance the welfare of the people of the United States and to add to the glory of the country? No, no; his country was not in his thoughts. Party, party filled the place in his bosom which country should have occupied. He was the honored tool to carry out the principles and policy of General Jackson's administration."

That Van Buren was striving to execute Jackson's financial policy was undisputed, hence there was no difficulty in demonstrating the fact; but that there was an ulterior design to create a government bank in hostility to the State banks, as Clay contended, was not true, and his argument was far-fetched. His reasoning was practically the same as that of his speech at the special session, and failed to justify the awful apprehensions he had expressed with such dramatic solemnity in his exordium.[1]

After concluding this part of the speech, in which all that Calhoun had opposed was vividly arrayed, he characterized him as the one, next to Van Buren, "most conspicuous of those who pressed this bill upon Congress and the

---

[1] "And what was the question at issue? It was whether Nicholas Biddle should have the custody of the public money and use the average balance in discounting notes, or whether Mr. Cisco should keep it at New York in an exceedingly strong vault and not use any of it in discounting notes."—Parton's *Famous Americans*, p. 46.

American people," and referred to the disparaging estimates of Van Buren that Calhoun had often expressed. "On one occasion, not very distant, denying to him any of the nobler qualities of the royal beast of the forest, he attributed to him those which belong to the most crafty, most skulking, and one of the meanest of the quadruped tribe." Calhoun had intimated that the course of Clay and his friends was unpatriotic. Clay denied the justice of the reproach.

"We united," said he, "if indeed there were any alliance in the case, to restrain the enormous expansion of Executive power, to arrest the progress of corruption, to rebuke usurpation, and to drive the Goths and Vandals from the capital, to expel Brennus and his horde from Rome. . . . And how often have we witnessed the Senator from South Carolina, with woful countenance and in doleful strains, pouring forth mournful and touching eloquence on the degeneracy of the times and the downward tendency of the republic. Day after day in the Senate have we seen the displays of his lofty and impassioned eloquence. . . . At the critical moment the Senator left us; he left us for the very purpose of preventing the success of the common cause. He took up his musket, knapsack, and shot-pouch, and joined the other party. He went, horse, foot, and dragoon, and he himself composed the whole corps. . . . We did no wrong to the distinguished Senator from South Carolina. On the contrary, we respected him, confided in his great and acknowledged ability, his uncommon genius, his extensive experience, his supposed patriotism; above all, we confided in his stern and inflexible fidelity. Nevertheless, he left us and joined our common opponents, distrusting and distrusted. He left us, as he tells us in his Edgefield letter, because the victory which our common arms were about to achieve was not to inure to him and his party, but exclusively to the benefit of his allies and their cause. I thought, actuated by patriotism, that noblest of human virtues, we had been contending together for our common country, for her violated rights, her threatened liberties, her prostrate Constitution. Never did I suppose that personal or party considerations entered into our views."

He then passed to Calhoun's speech, which he slightingly characterized as "plausible, ingenious, abstract, metaphysical, and generalizing," not "adapted to the bosoms and business of human life"; and replied to it without further personalities except to say that Calhoun's opinions as to the constitutionality of a national bank had entirely changed. And there was no need of any—his blow had struck home.

As soon as he had concluded, Calhoun arose and said that Clay had misstated and perverted every argument he had advanced; that he intended to pay his respects to the Senator at the first opportunity; and that when he did so the debt between them would be fully discharged. Clay rejoined that whether or not he had misstated or perverted Calhoun's arguments was not for that Senator to say—he would appeal to a less partial judge, the Senate; that as to any intention of paying on the Senator's part, he was as ready to receive as the Senator was to pay; that he sought a contest with no man and should not avoid one with the Senator.[1] The significance of the affair was well understood.

---

[1] "The galleries were all filled two hours before the time of the Senate's meeting. . . . Mr. Clay rose to the order of the day at one o'clock and spoke until half-past five. In the course of the speech, Mr. Clay bore somewhat hard upon Mr. Calhoun for his recent apostasy and replied to his arguments in favor of the bill, to which the latter replied in a few exceedingly harsh and ill-natured remarks. . . . I thought there was a degree

Clay had put Calhoun on trial for inconsistency; and the charges were so grave that he was obliged to meet them with all the ingenuity, eloquence, and power that he possessed. Clay's indictment was so well matured and effectively preferred that Calhoun fully appreciated the necessity of a defence prepared with equal deliberation and the utmost thoroughness. It was to be, as he declared, the vindication of his public life and character. He was in no haste. Not until March 20 did he deliver his reply.[1]

The first part of his speech related to his former arguments, which he alleged Clay had perverted. He then proceeded with his personal defence. So far as concerned his position on financial questions while acting with the Whigs, he was successful in showing that his present attitude was not inconsistent. Had he been able to rest his case there it would have been quite secure. He was not a Whig, and he was under no obligation to co-operate with the Whig party. His support of Van Buren's administration, therefore, involved in itself no treachery and no breach of political propriety toward his late allies. But while he stoutly contended for this he had admitted in his Edgefield letter—a communication to friends in South Carolina in which he declined a public dinner—that in supporting Van Buren he was influenced by another motive than to abide by his convictions as to the right financial policy for the government to pursue: that by continuing his alliance with the Whigs

of acrimony and ill-nature in his reply much greater than the occasion justified."—Hone's *Diary*, vol. i. p. 290.

[1] "I happened to know that in this time he refreshed his reading of the Oration on the Crown; and, as the delivery of the speech showed, not without profit. Besides its general cast, which was a good imitation, there were passages of a vigor and terseness — of a power and simplicity — which would recall the recollection of that masterpiece of the world."— Benton's *Thirty Years' View*, vol. ii. p. 98.

at the new juncture of events it was "clear that the victory would inure not to us, but exclusively to the benefit of our allies and their cause." Nor did he in his speech disavow or qualify the truth of that statement: he strove to justify his course in that respect as being legitimate political tactics to preserve the States-rights party and its principles. It was at best but slippery ground upon which to stand; and although his justification was presented with his usual subtleness and ability, it manifestly lacked that quality of sterling political rectitude which he would have sustained in the early part of his career.

To Clay's characterization of his speech as metaphysical, he made a keen reply. "I cannot retort," said he, "on the Senator's charge of being metaphysical. I cannot accuse him of possessing the powers of analysis and generalization, those higher faculties of the mind (called metaphysical by those who do not possess them) which decompose and resolve into their elements the complex masses of ideas that exist in the world of mind—as chemistry does the bodies that surround us in the material world; and without which those deep and hidden causes which are in constant action and producing such mighty changes in the condition of society would operate unseen and undetected. The absence of these higher qualities of mind is conspicuous throughout the whole course of the Senator's public life. To this may be traced that he prefers the specious to the solid and the plausible to the true. To the same cause, combined with an ardent temperament, it is owing that we ever find him mounted upon some popular and favorite measure, which he whips along, cheered by the shouts of the multitude, and never dismounts till he has ridden it down. . . . It is the fault of his mind to seize on a few prominent and striking advantages, and to pursue them eagerly without looking to consequences."

He then reviewed his own public life, in the effort to show that he had uniformly acted according to his convictions, regardless of party trammels; and cited his opposition to the restrictive system, his support of the navy, and his attitude toward "Mr. Dallas's bank of 1814-15" to justify his contention. Then "passing the intervening instances," he extolled his administration of the War Department. The Vice-Presidency, he said, afforded him the leisure and opportunity "to study the genius of the prominent measure of the day, then called the American System; of which I profited. I soon perceived where its errors lay and how it would operate. I clearly saw its desolating effects in one section and corrupting influence in the other; and when I saw it could not be arrested here I fell back on my own State, and a blow was given to a system destined to destroy our institutions, if not overthrown, which brought it to the ground."

Such was the tenor of his defence. He had studiously avoided the most vulnerable features of his career, which were caused by his radical change of views and his conduct in relation to the tariff, internal improvements, and a national bank; and by asserting that the nullification proceedings had crippled protection, he gave Clay precisely the advantage best suited to his method and style of attack. Clay was now relieved of the necessity of making veiled allusions and general statements. Calhoun had opened the way for particular denunciation, and Clay promptly and with impassioned zeal seized the opportunity.[1]

---

[1] Salmon P. Chase wrote in his diary, April 10, 1880: "It is said that he [Calhoun] was desirous of supporting the administration of Mr. Adams,

He began by expressing his regret at precipitating a personal controversy, and by asserting that what he had said was in the performance of a public duty. He had long served with the Senator, admired his genius, and struggled to think well of him; but the Edgefield letter had changed his opinions. He indignantly repelled the assertion that nullification overthrew the protective system. "At the commencement of the session of 1832," he said, "the Senator was in any other condition than that of dictating terms. Those of us who were then here must recollect well his haggard looks and his anxious and depressed countenance. A highly estimable friend of mine, Mr. J. M. Clayton, of Delaware, alluding to the possibility of a rupture with South Carolina, and declarations of President Jackson with respect to certain distinguished individuals he had denounced and proscribed, said to me on more than one occasion, referring to the Senator from South Carolina and some of his colleagues, 'They are clever fellows, and it will never do to let old Jackson hang them.'" Clay maintained that nullification, instead of overthrowing protection, had, by aiding the Compromise, expressly sanctioned the Constitutional

---

but was overruled by his native State. 'He proposed,' a gentleman who had ample means of knowing the truth, recently remarked to me, 'to support the administration, in a caucus of South Carolinians.' The proposition was received with disgust, and Governor Taylor rose and exclaimed: '*Crucify him!*' So decided disapprobation alarmed and discouraged him. He fell in with the prevailing sentiment and went for Jackson."—Warden's *Chase*, p. 214. Certainly he at once entered actively into the opposition, and as Vice-President appointed the Senate committees adversely to the administration.—Sumner's *Jackson*, p. 111. He declared that "Such was the manner in which it came into power that it must be defeated at all hazards, regardless of its measures."—Von Holst's *Calhoun*, p. 65. This was the leading sentiment of the opposition. "In the words of one of the most distinguished of General Jackson's supporters, the administration must be put down, 'though as pure as the angels at the right hand of God.'"—Sargent's *Clay*, p. 123.

power and perpetuated the system; and that in every instance where he and Calhoun had disagreed concerning the terms of the Compromise Calhoun had yielded. "Nullification!" he exclaimed; "a strange, impracticable, incomprehensible doctrine, that partakes of the character of the metaphysical school of German philosophy, or would be worthy of the puzzling theological controversies of the Middle Ages!"

He admitted that "no one, in the commencement of the protective policy, ever supposed that it was to be perpetual. We hoped and believed that temporary protection extended to our infant manufactures would bring them up and enable them to withstand competition with those of Europe." He commented caustically on Calhoun's acknowledged political motive in dissolving the alliance, and explained his own action in voting for Adams in 1824, to which Calhoun had alluded, and his change of opinion in 1816 in regard to a national bank, the only time he had ever changed his "deliberate opinion upon any great question of national policy." "The distinguished Senator," said he, "sticks long to no hobby. He was once gayly mounted on that of internal improvements. We rode that double, the Senator before and I behind him. He quickly slipped off, leaving me to hold the bridle." This he showed by stating what Calhoun proposed in his advocacy of that policy. In the same manner he illustrated Calhoun's early favor of a national bank. He closed in a strain of mingled sarcasm and contempt.

"How profound he may suppose his power of analysis to be, and whatever opinion he may entertain of his own metaphysical faculty, can he imagine that any plain, common-sense man can ever comprehend how it is Constitutional to prolong an unconstitutional bank for twelve years? ... I do not speak of this in any unkind spirit, but I will tell the Senator when he will be consistent. He will be so when he resolves henceforward never to pronounce that word again. We began our public career nearly together; we remained together throughout the war and down to the peace. We agreed as to a Bank of the United States—as to a protective tariff—as to internal improvements—and lastly, as to those arbitrary and violent measures which characterized the administration of General Jackson. No two prominent public men ever agreed better together in respect to important measures of national policy. We concur now in nothing. We separate forever."

The speeches then subsided into a colloquy, in which Calhoun endeavored to explain away Clay's assertions as to his early career and Constitutional views; but he was not and could not be successful. He had radically changed his opinions, and there was no escape from the fact.[1] The liberal statesman had become the chief defender of the slavery interest, and by necessary consequence had revised and metamorphosed his former tenets to conform to his new creed. On

---

[1] "It will excite some surprise at the present day," says Edward Everett, in his *Memoir of Webster*, "in the consideration of the political history of the last thirty years, to find how little difference as to the leading measures existed in 1816 between these distinguished statesmen [Clay, Calhoun, Webster, Lowndes, and Cheves]. No line of general party difference separated the members of the first Congress after the peace." And this similarity of opinion continued until 1824. In the Presidential campaign of that year, before the election by the House, Benton, Buchanan, Tyler, Blair, and others who afterward stood high in the Democratic party, were warm supporters of Clay. At that period Van Buren also shared the prevailing opinions in favor of internal improvements and protection. In the Senate he supported the tariff of 1828. He was among the first, however, to change his ground, and he led the way to the reconstruction of the Democratic creed. See Shepard's *Van Buren*, pp. 83, 85.

the whole, therefore, Clay had the advantage both on the merits of the subject and in the superiority of his talent for that kind of controversy;[1] and the result of the encounter afforded the Whigs keen delight, for the debate was printed and read throughout the country.

Several financial measures of less importance than the proposed independent Treasury were enacted. In accordance with the recommendation of the President, the issue and circulation of all bills, notes, and other securities of corporations whose charters had expired were prohibited and made penal, the law being particularly aimed at the notes of the former Bank of the United States. The banks in the District were compelled to adopt the financial policy of the administration. They—and by another act, all corporations, firms, and individuals also—were required to cease the issue and circulation of all paper currency of a lower denomination than five dollars; and those that had issued such paper were required to redeem it. The District banks

---

[1] "The truth and the victory were with Clay, who closed with the taunting hope that the settlement of accounts was as satisfactory to the Senator from South Carolina as it was to him. Clay spoke of the South Carolina nullification with such insulting contempt that it brought out Preston, who complained of it bitterly. Preston's countenance was a portraiture of agonizing anguish. The personal oratorical encounters between Clay and Calhoun are Liliputian mimicry of the orations against Ctesiphon and for the Crown or the debate of the second Philippic."—Adams's *Diary*, vol. ix. p. 505. In Calhoun's speech in 1817 on the bill to set aside the dividends and the bonus of the bank as a permanent fund for internal improvements, he expressed these sentiments: "I am no advocate for refined arguments on the Constitution. The instrument was not intended as a thesis for the logician to exercise his ingenuity on. It ought to be construed with plain good sense." "If we are restricted in the use of our money to the enumerated powers, on what principle can the purchase of Louisiana be justified?" "The uniform sense of Congress and the country furnishes better evidence of the true interpretation of the Constitution than the most refined and subtle arguments."

were also required to resume specie payments on or before January 1, 1839, or sooner if the banks of Baltimore and Richmond should do so. Clay opposed the measures. He vigorously condemned the suppression of small notes in the District. Among other things he said: "The committee have wholly reversed the natural order of things; they have begun at the wrong end. They were looked to for some remedy to the disordered state of the currency; we had hoped for some cure to the general disorder; but instead of that they begin with this little District. . . . This bill is aimed at the poor, the miserable, the wretched portion of the community; against slaves, negroes, and beggars; against women and children! Here are fines to punish boys and girls if they go to market or offer to buy anything with the only money you have enabled them to have in their possession." And again: "The committee have since the commencement of the session strained every nerve, and have produced this sixpenny bill to put down shin-plasters." He was persistent in his advocacy of paper currency. Before the time arrived for the New York banks to resume specie payments he introduced a joint resolution to permit the demand notes of sound banks to be paid for all public dues and to be disbursed to public creditors willing to receive them. His professed purpose was to aid resumption; his real object was to aid the delinquent banks and indirectly restore the paper system by rescinding the specie circular. The resolution was vigorously opposed by the leading supporters of the administration; but its tactical efficiency carried it through after an entire change of phraseology. Late in the session it was adopted in this form: "That it shall not be lawful for the Secretary of the Treasury to make or continue in force any general order which shall create any difference between the different branches of revenue, as to the money or medium of payment in which debts or dues accruing to the United States may be paid." The Secretary of the Treasury, however, was enabled to preserve the policy of the specie circular under provisions of law which Congress had apparently overlooked.

Some other topics were discussed. Notwithstanding his position as the expectant Whig nominee for the Presidency, he spoke on them with his usual freedom. On presenting one of the many petitions for the establishment of a national bank, he took occasion to detail his plan for such an institution. He opposed the public-lands policy of the administration; and supported a bill to prohibit duelling, which became a law at the next session.[1]

He also expressed his views on three international questions. In regard to the proposal to erect a Territorial government for Oregon, he urged such a course as would obviate difficulty with Great Britain over the mooted northwestern boundary. But concerning the affair of the *Caroline*, which had recently occurred, his attitude was bolder. The *Caroline* was a steamboat owned by American citizens, and was seized and destroyed in our waters by Canadian militia,

---

[1] "It is well known," said he, in the course of his remarks, "that in certain quarters of the country public opinion is averse to duelling, and no public man can fly in the face of that public opinion without having his reputation sacrificed; while there are other portions again which exact obedience to that fatal custom. The man with a high sense of honor and nice sensibility, when the question is whether he shall fight or have the finger of scorn pointed at him, is unable to resist, and few, very few, are found willing to adopt such an alternative. When public opinion is renovated and chastened by reason, religion, and humanity, the practice of duelling will at once be discontinued. It is the office of legislation to do all it can to bring about this healthful state of the public mind."

who killed several men in the affray. The act was instigated by the fact that the vessel was employed in aid of the insurgents. It was one of the numerous disturbances along the border which arose from the Canadian rebellion. Clay denounced the affair as an "unparalleled outrage," and vigorously maintained that redress should be demanded. On the subject of the Mexican claims he expressed himself in much the same manner as he had when it was previously before Congress. "The want of dignity," said he, "and the want of temper that have been manifested by persons connected with the government in relation to this whole matter are greatly to be deplored." The session ended July 9.

The last session of the Twenty-fifth Congress — from December 3 to March 3, 1839 — developed little of historic interest. The Sub-Treasury question was allowed to rest until the next session, as the political conditions were still unfavorable to the passage of the bill. Much useful and necessary legislation was enacted; but having no relation to politics, it did not cause prolonged debates. Besides the law against duelling, the most conspicuous acts of general interest were those abolishing imprisonment for debt, on process issued out of the Federal courts in States where that policy was adopted; and to authorize the President to maintain, by force if necessary, our claim to the territory in the extreme northeast, to which the British government had thus far refused to accede. On this subject there was considerable public excitement.

The administration bill to reduce and graduate the prices of the public lands was finally passed by the Senate. Clay earnestly opposed it, but Webster supported it. It failed, however, in the House. In connection with some resolutions adopted by the legislature of North Carolina declaring the expunging resolution unconstitutional, the question incidentally arose as to what extent Representatives were bound by such instructions. Clay thus expressed the theory then commonly entertained:

"What is the basis and what the principle of the doctrine of instruction? To a certain extent I have always believed in this doctrine and have been ever ready to conform to it. But I hold to the doctrine as it stood in 1798, that in general, on questions of expediency, the Representative should conform to his instructions, and so gratify the wishes and obey the will of his constituents, though on questions of constitutionality his course might be different. . . . Is it not that we are to conform to the wishes of our constituents? Is it not that we are here to act, not in our own, but in a delegated character? And will any who stand here pretend that whenever they know the wishes or will of those who sent them here they are not bound to conform to that will entirely? Is it not the doctrine that we are nothing more than a mirror to reflect the will of those who called us to our distinguished office? That is the view I take of the doctrine of instruction."

It originated in the early distrust of centralized government. It prevailed very generally prior to the Civil War, and was often applied. The constitutions of several States expressly authorized it, although no method was provided for enforcing it in case the Representatives declined to follow the instructions they received; public sentiment, however, was commonly efficacious. But the doctrine gradually fell into disuse, and has been superseded by the English theory, as enunciated by Blackstone and Burke, that representatives do not serve their local constituencies alone, but the whole nation, and therefore they are not subject to instructions, and that their tenure is fixed by their election. This has proved to be the wiser and more orderly practice as applied to members of legislative bodies.

Another topic of interesting, though brief, discussion was the subsidiary silver coin. In some localities there was a dearth of it. "I happened," said Clay, "to receive, but a few days ago, a communication from an intelligent gentleman in one of our principal seaports, affirming that the scarcity of silver change was one of the effects of the passage of the gold bill; because by reducing the standard of gold coin it became less valuable as an article of exportation than silver, and therefore the latter was always exported. Now this is exactly what was predicted by myself and others at the time of the passage of the law for the adjustment of the value of the two coins; and the result has proved the correctness of the prediction. Gold cannot be exported under that law without disadvantage unless exchange is greatly against us; but silver can profitably be exported, and when exportation becomes necessary it is of course made in that species of coin in which it can be sent abroad without loss."

His statements were at once challenged. "I think," said Niles, " there is no such scarcity; I know that in many places it is abundant. Within my own experience banks have refused to receive it. This is convincing proof that there is an abundance of it. It is known to every one who has inquired into the subject that silver change is never exported, because its nominal value would be lost and it could only be disposed of as bullion to be recoined, occasioning much loss by the process. There may be a scarcity of change in some States, but that is the result of their paper systems. The hostility of paper to silver is well known; indeed, so hostile is it that where it has the power even silver fippenny bits are driven out of circulation. What was the result in Philadelphia, where the mint was located, during the late suspension? In that city, which previous to the suspension was thoroughly saturated with silver change, after the barrier was broken down and the emission of shin-plasters authorized, no change whatever could be procured. In a single night the state of things was completely changed. Instead of an abundance of silver change there was an entire absence of it. And a similar result will always follow a similar cause; and to the extension of our paper system, the circulation of one-dollar notes, and notes for a fractional part of a dollar, may we much more appropriately look for the scarcity of silver change than the operation of the gold bill of 1834."

Niles was corroborated by others, particularly Benton. The truth is that silver had been undervalued by the act of 1834, which had to some extent caused its exportation and conversion into bullion; and paper had forced it out of circulation in some parts of the country. The lessons are obvious.

At this session Clay made another of his calamitous mistakes. But for his blunder he would probably have been nominated and elected President in 1840. It was occasioned by a set speech on the subject of slavery. Aside from it and Calhoun's comments on it, there was no other discussion of the question in the Senate. In the House the usual "gag" was at once adopted; but this time it was prefaced by several resolutions introduced by Atherton, of New Hampshire, which echoed the Senate resolutions adopted at the preceding session. Clay was the leading Whig candidate for President, and the prospect of his nomination seemed certain. But he was not satisfied to rest upon his record in regard to slavery; he determined to speak again on abolition, and this time more fully and deliberately than he had ever spoken before, in the effort to placate, so far as possible, hostility to him on the part of the people of the South, and those of the North who were not radical in their antislavery opinions. He was manifestly becoming alarmed at the spread of the agitation and the feeling toward it in the South. It is not unlikely that the speech, which was delivered February 7, was prepared at Ashland during the recess. That he was anxiously revolving the question in his mind appears from his correspondence.¹

It was unusual for him to revise a speech after he had made it, much less to write it out before; but in this case he not only wrote it, but he read it to a number of his close political friends for their opinion as to its expediency. It may be inferred from what little is known of this consultation that he was advised against delivering the speech. He nevertheless pursued his common course, of listening to counsel, but following his own judgment. It was on this occasion that he made his famous remark: "I had rather be right than be President."² The Presidency, however,

---

¹ In a letter to his friend Brooke he expressed solicitude on account of the introduction of the abolition element into the elections, the first time it had been known, and the fear that the contagion would spread through all the free States, which might ultimately result in the abolitionists gaining control of the government, proscribing slave-holders, abolishing slavery in the District and the slave-trade between the States. "And," he continued, "the end will be—— My own position touching slavery at the present time is singular enough. The abolitionists are denouncing me as a slave-holder and the slave-holders as an abolitionist, while the both unite on Mr. Van Buren."—*Clay's Correspondence*, p. 430.

² Colonel Thomas "says that Mr. Clay himself got up, and, he believes wrote, the anti-abolition petition from the District upon which he made his

was his object, and the speech limped sorely behind this ideal pretension. For so important a speech it was delivered on an unusual pretext—the presentation of a petition signed by numerous residents of the District praying against the abolition of slavery there.

He recurred to the opinion he had repeatedly expressed, that the wisest way to treat abolition petitions was "to receive and refer them without opposition and report against them in a calm and dispassionate and argumentative appeal to the good sense of the whole community." As this had not been done, he proposed "to advert to some of those topics which might have been usefully embodied in a report by a committee of the Senate, and which, he was persuaded, would have checked the progress, if it had not altogether arrested the efforts, of abolition." He divided those who were opposed to slavery into three classes: "those who from sentiments of philanthropy are conscientiously opposed to the existence of slavery, but who are no less opposed at the same time to any disturbance of the peace and tranquillity of the Union or the infringement of the powers of the States composing the confederacy," notably the Society of Friends; "apparent abolitionists—that is,

---

anti-abolition speech at the last session of Congress, and that its effect has been to demolish his last possible chance for the Presidency. . . . Preston has avowed in a speech at a Whig meeting and in a public letter that he was one of a small party of friends to whom Clay read his speech before he delivered it in the Senate."—Adams's *Diary*, vol. x. p. 116. Preston, who was Clay's chief supporter in the South,'said in the speech to which Adams refers: "On one occasion Mr. Clay did me the honor to consult me in reference to a step which he was about to take, and which will perhaps occur to your minds without more direct allusion. After stating what was proposed, it was remarked that such a step might be offensive to the ultras of both parties, in the excitement which then existed. To this Mr. Clay replied: 'I trust the sentiments and principles are correct; I had rather be right than be President.'"

those who, having been persuaded that the right of petition has been violated by Congress, co-operate with the abolitionists for the sole purpose of asserting and vindicating that right"; and "the real ultra-abolitionists, who are resolved to persevere in the pursuit of their object at all hazards and without regard to any consequences, however calamitous they may be." The latter class he denounced in terms so passionately severe as absolutely and permanently to complete their alienation from his support, and he thus defeated, as events demonstrated, the possibility of his election to the Presidency.[1] "It is," said he, after his terrible arraignment, "because these ultra-abolitionists have ceased to employ the instruments of reason and persuasion, have made their cause political, and have appealed to the ballot-box, that I am induced upon this occasion to address you."

He reviewed the different periods during which the spirit of abolition had displayed itself, and ascribed the agitation then existing principally to "the example of British emancipation of the slaves in the islands adjacent to our country," and to "persons in both parts of the Union who sought to mingle abolition with politics and to array one portion of the Union against the other," but denied that either of the two great political parties had "designs or aim at abolition." He discussed the power and expediency of abolishing slavery in the District and the Territory of Florida, and of prohibiting the slave-trade between the States, repeating and

---

[1] Clay's "speech in the United States Senate, on February 7, 1839, apropos of the petitions for abolition in the District, was his bid for the Presidency, and as such was the most notable event of the year. It destroyed the last shred of his antislavery reputation at the North, except among the Friends, whom he was cunning enough to flatter."—*Life of Garrison*, vol. ii. p. 282.

amplifying the arguments he had advanced in connection with the resolutions on those subjects. But these subjects, he asserted, "are but so many masked batteries concealing the real and ultimate point of attack. That point of attack is the institution of domestic slavery as it exists in these States. It is to liberate three millions of slaves held in bondage within them."

To the abolition of slavery he urged three obstacles. The first was the want of Constitutional power, which he showed and which was incontestable. The second was the presence of three millions of slaves. "In the slave States," said he, in maintaining this proposition, "the alternative is that the white man must govern the black or the black govern the white. In several of those States the number of the slaves is greater than that of the white population. An immediate abolition of slavery in them, as these ultra-abolitionists propose, would be followed by a desperate struggle for immediate ascendency of the black race over the white race, or rather it would be followed by the instantaneous collision between the two races, which would break out in civil war that would end in the extermination or subjugation of one race by the other. In such an alternative who can hesitate? Is it not better that the existing state of things should be preserved instead of exposing them to the horrible strifes and contests which would inevitably attend an immediate abolition? This is our true ground of defence for the continued existence of slavery in our country. It is that which our Revolutionary ancestors assumed. It is that which, in my opinion, forms our justification in the eyes of all Christendom." The third obstacle was the vast amount of capital invested in slave property, which he estimated at twelve hundred millions of dollars. He asserted the legality and rightfulness of property in slaves,[1] and that if the scheme of abolition were to be executed the slave property should be paid for, and its value assessed entirely upon the free States.

He contended that the agitation had retarded the prospect of any kind of emancipation, gradual or immediate, in any of the States, and "increased the rigors of legislation against slaves in most if not all of the slave States." Though he had favored gradual abolition, he now declared that he would "oppose any scheme whatever of emancipation because of the danger of an ultimate ascendency of the black race or of a civil contest which might terminate in the extinction of one race or the other." In his opinion, emancipation would also result in the emigration of hordes of negroes to the North, which would increase the hardships of free labor there. He condemned the opposition of the abolitionists to colonization and to a separation of the two races, "which by their physical structure and color ought to be kept asunder, should not be brought together by any process whatever of unnatural amalgamation." The question whether or not the negroes were to remain forever in bondage he hopefully left to the future, but predicted that "in the progress of time, some one hundred and fifty or two hundred years hence, but few vestiges of the black man will remain among our posterity." Notwithstanding his sanguine opinions at the preceding session, he now said that "abolition should no longer be regarded as an imaginary danger." Union on one side would beget union on the other. "And this process of reciprocal consolidation will

---

[1] Webster said, in 1848: "I am not at the present moment aware of any place on the globe in which this property of man in a human being as a slave, transferable as a chattel, exists, except in America."

be attended with all the violent prejudices, embittered passions, and implacable animosities which ever degraded or deformed human nature, a virtual dissolution of the Union will have taken place, while the forms of its existence remain. The most valuable element of union—mutual kindness, the feelings of sympathy, the fraternal bonds—which now happily unite us will have been extinguished forever. One section will stand in menacing and hostile array against the other. The collision of opinion will quickly be followed by the clash of arms."

"I am," he continued, "no friend of slavery. The Searcher of all human hearts knows that every pulsation of mine beats high and strong in the cause of civil liberty. Wherever it is safe and practicable, I desire to see every portion of the human family in the enjoyment of it. But I prefer the liberty of my own country to that of any other people, and the liberty of my own race to that of any other race." He palliated slavery as "a stern and inexorable necessity," for which his generation was not responsible, and closed with an eloquent appeal to desist from further agitation for abolition.

The speech was received in the Senate and through the country with profound surprise. By it Clay practically abjured the peculiar antislavery character he had hitherto maintained. Not only had he been in the Senate the leading defender of the right of petition, but he had uniformly uttered the loftiest sentiments of freedom. Although he was a slave-holder and had strongly deprecated the antislavery movement, his personal situation was assigned to his unavoidable surroundings, and provoked no serious disfavor except among the most radical abolitionists, and with these chiefly because of his efforts in behalf of colonization.

The arguments presented by his speech were by no means novel, and, in the main, were generally entertained by the conservative elements in the North; yet the speech was inspired by a sentiment totally different from that which had distinguished his former utterances on slavery. It varied little, except as to the right of petition, from the anti-abolition speeches of the champions of slavery. Despite his proud vaunting of consistency and his criticism of Calhoun's oscillations, he now subjected his own conduct to the same rebuke. His protestations that there was nothing thus far in the extent and effect of the agitation that boded danger to the Union were still fresh in the public mind. Certainly there were no new developments within the last few months to render the situation more critical. Besides all this, his course was so unexpected and gratuitous that his motive was imputed—as it deserved to be—to the hope of political advantage.[1] The speech, therefore, gave the prevailing opinion of him a rude shock. And evidence of the effect of his performance was soon forthcoming. Calhoun at once commended him in terms that contained a sardonic tone of triumph. He began by alluding to the change in Clay's sentiments, which he warmly commended, and then spoke of the Senate resolutions of the preceding session, the Atherton resolutions in the House, and an address to the people signed by a number of public men, as breaking the force of the abolition movement. "The work is done," said he. "The spirit of abolition is overthrown, of which

---

[1] "The Governor of Kentucky and the members of the delegation from that State in the House are now so deeply committed upon all slavery questions that it is impossible to get the vote of Massachusetts for Mr. Clay; and his only chance of election is by the Southern and slave-holding interest. . . . There is no good-will lost between Mr. Clay and Mr. Webster."—Adams's *Diary*, vol. x. p. 77.

we have a strong confirmation in what we have this day heard. . . . Of all the dangers to which we have ever been exposed this has been the greatest. We may now consider it as passed. The resolutions to which I have referred, with the following movements, gave the fatal blow, to which the Senator from Kentucky has given the finishing stroke."

Calhoun was soon to see how utterly mistaken he was in supposing that any progress had been made in allaying the agitation; but neither he nor Clay was to see how greatly they erred in thinking that emancipation would be followed by a violent struggle for race supremacy. What Clay's feelings were while Calhoun was complacently discoursing on his conversion and his own fallacies cannot be known, but they may be imagined. The candidate had renounced the sentiments of the man, and he bore his self-sought humiliation mutely. He looked for compensation in the success of his ambition. But he had vaulted too far.

He returned to Ashland confident that he would be nominated for President at the Whig national convention to be held at Harrisburg, Pennsylvania, December 4. The prospect, indeed, seemed flattering. He was the acknowledged chief of the party, the foremost champion of its principles, and the most popular among its masses. He had sustained its organization and morale through adversity and defeat. If ever any great political party owed its existence and endurance mainly to one man the Whig party is an example. He had able and dexterous coadjutors, yet no Whig could be compared with him in leadership and influence. In point of prominence and public service no one in the party could be named with him except Webster; but Webster was markedly deficient in the attributes of leadership. There was never a day when he had the remotest possibility of becoming President, for at no time did he have any considerable support in his continuous candidacy for the nomination. Perhaps no statesman of genius and intellectual power was ever so barren of political influence. His supporters for the Presidency were always mostly confined to a small coterie of his New England admirers. Though mighty in serious debate, he lacked those indefinable qualities that inspire popularity among the masses and political deference among leaders. Nevertheless, his ambition to attain the Presidency was morbidly intense, and he cherished a degree of envy toward Clay that led him to interpose, so far as he could, to thwart Clay's preferment.[1] This want of magnanimity toward Clay, under all the circumstances, was not creditable to him. Had not Clay pre-eminently deserved from his party the distinction he sought, it is not probable that he would have allowed his rivalry to impede Webster's elevation if he saw no reasonable prospect of his own. Perhaps this quality partly explains his great popularity and his capacity for leadership. Selfishness was not among his faults. It was soon apparent that he would be stoutly opposed. Webster was in the field, if not to obtain the nomination, at least to aid covertly in defeating him. He was forced to decide upon the latter course. He withdrew, advised his friends that Clay was not the most available candidate, and spent the summer in Europe. But the danger from Webster's attitude was the least that con-

---

[1] "Some years after Mr. Webster's death John J. Crittenden said: 'We all desired to see Clay and Webster elected to the Presidency, and we felt that to accomplish this object it was necessary that Clay should come first ; but we were never able to make Webster and his friends see this, and therefore neither of them won the prize.'"—Stanton's *Random Recollections*, p. 151.

fronted Clay; it was but a small factor in the combined forces that were to accomplish his defeat.

John Randolph once remarked that the principles of the Whig party were seven—five loaves and two fishes. This sarcasm contained much truth. The party was a heterogeneous composition. It had its origin in Clay's factious opposition to Monroe's administration and matured in opposition to Jackson's. It of course assumed certain distinctive Constitutional principles, the outgrowth of which were protection, internal improvements, and a national bank. But to these policies were added one by one through the exigencies of political opposition other features, such as the distribution of the surplus, the disposition of the public lands, and the various assaults on Jackson's financial policy. The disaffected and recalcitrant elements of the Democratic party were made welcome in the Whig fold; and to accommodate them, concessions were made. Moreover, a large part of the Northern wing of the party, though not abolitionist, was averse to slavery, and to mollify and restrain it had been a studied feature of the party policy. In short, efforts had been directed to combine with the Whigs, so far as practicable, all who were not Democrats, but who could be reconciled to the wide and variegated mosaic of the Whig platform. And now to all these elements of this complex array was added the host of victims of the late crisis, whose main political desire was a change of administration. The feelings of this class had no relation to persons. Any suitable candidate would answer, and all the better if he were not prominently identified with the theories and measures over which the past struggles had been so fiercely waged.

The practical effect of these conditions upon the party was to beget a type of managers similar to those who had brought the Democratic party into power. They were professional politicians.¹ They may be likened to horse-hairs in a pool, moved by animalculæ. They were not hero-worshippers. Party principles were only among their weapons. Their object was victory. Prestige, worth, past service, alone weighed little with them. The base of their operations was the choice of candidates who could poll the most votes. This decided, their processes and manipulations were directed to that result with a skill and an adroitness which politicians of the present day have not surpassed. These methods, as we have seen, were not new in the Democratic party. They began to be applied in Burr's time and were brought to perfection by Van Buren and the Albany Regency. They started Jackson on his career as candidate and President. They had now been adopted by the Whigs, particularly in the State where they originated, and their chief practitioners were William H. Seward and Thurlow Weed. Such was the new danger to which Clay but slowly and partially awoke.

It was more difficult to contend with this obstacle than with those which resulted from his former positions on various public questions. The latter he had for some time labored to counteract by letters and speeches designed to mitigate the impression that his opinions were extreme and inflexible. He had been assured by friends in the State of New York that he was decidedly the favorite of the Whigs there; and that Seward, then Governor, and Weed,² and the

---

¹ "When, as in the United States, republican institutions, instead of being slowly evolved, are all at once created, there grows up within them an agency of wire-pulling politicians, exercising a real rule of the people at large. . . . So that in the absence of a duly adapted character, liberty given in one direction is lost in another."—Spencer's *Sociology*, vol. ii. p. 662.

² "On one important question Mr. Weed and I were antipodes. Be-

machine of which they were the head, were "warmly and zealously" for him, notwithstanding that they deemed it at the time "inexpedient to make public declaration of their preference." But as his information grew more reliable he became suspicious of duplicity and determined to visit the State to do something for himself. Accordingly, in July and August he made a tour through some parts of Canada, ostensibly for health and pleasure. He stopped, however, at Buffalo, where he was accorded an enthusiastic reception and made a brief speech. In the course of his remarks he touched cautiously on politics, and then referred to his candidacy. On the latter subject he advanced the argument that was to accomplish his defeat. "If my name," said he, "creates any obstacle to cordial union and harmony, away with it, and concentrate upon some individual more acceptable to all branches of the opposition. What is a public man worth who is not ever ready to sacrifice himself for the good of his country? I have unaffectedly desired retirement; I yet desire it, when, consistently with the duties and obligations which I owe, I can honorably retire. No veteran soldier, covered with scars and wounds inflicted in many hard campaigns, ever received his discharge with more pleasure than I should mine. But I think that, like him, without presumption, I am entitled to an honorable discharge."

He proceeded from Montreal by way of Lake Champlain to Saratoga, where he arrived August 9, and remained several days. There, as at all places he visited, he was re-

---

lieving that a currency in part of paper kept at par with specie and current in every part of our country was indispensable, I was a zealous advocate of a national bank; which he as heartily detested, believing that its supporters would always be identified in the popular mind with aristocracy, monopoly, exclusive privilege, etc." — Greeley's *Recollections of a Busy Life*, p. 314.

ceived with enthusiasm and display.¹ While there he had interviews with Weed, who was now ready to disclose the disposition of the Whig managers toward his candidacy. He was informed that in their judgment he could not succeed in the election, notwithstanding the preference for him in the party. But he was too familiar with unfavorable counsel and adverse circumstances, as well as too much impressed with his apparent popularity, to be persuaded that he would not be as strong as any other candidate. He did not intimate that he understood the true significance of Weed's deliverance—that the delegation from the State would be against him in the convention.² Presumably he relied on the majority of the party, which was undoubtedly in his favor, to override the plans of the leaders. If so, he totally misjudged their power.

He reached the city of New York, his principal destination, on the 21st, and was greeted by a demonstration of exceptional magnitude and fervor.³ All that he saw and heard touching himself and his candidacy confirmed his confidence. To all appearances the tour had produced the effect he sought. His return to Ashland was followed by the usual occupation of a leading candidate for Presidential nomination—conducting a profuse correspondence and receiving zealous friends and advisers.

---

[1] Hone's *Diary*, vol. i. p. 374.
[2] Thurlow Weed's *Autobiography*, vol. i. p. 480.
[3] Hone's *Diary*, vol. i. pp. 376-7. "In the summer of 1839 I heard Mr. Clay deliver an elaborate speech on the bank and Sub-Treasury question from an open barouche at the steps of the New York City Hall. He had been conducted by a long cavalcade of horsemen from the bank of the Hudson, and he was surrounded by an immense concourse. I stood at the junction of Broadway and Park Row. His voice rang so loud and clear that his words were distinctly reverberated from the wall of the Astor House."—Stanton's *Random Recollections*, p. 153.

The operations of his opponents were already well under way. In New York the Whig leaders were undoubtedly opposed to his nomination for the reasons they professed. The State was the centre of the Anti-masonic element, which was against Clay; and the abolitionists, continually increasing in number, were irrevocably hostile. Besides, the State was nominally Democratic. Thus, while Clay was preferred by the Whig leaders, as well as by most of the regular rank and file of the party, they were sincere in their assertions that he could not be elected, and determined that the advantages and spoils of victory should not be imperiled by sentiment if they could prevent it. Yet it was impolitic to affront Clay and his steadfast friends by openly advocating the nomination of Harrison, his chief rival, who possessed the requisite qualifications of an "available" candidate. General Scott, therefore, was made the foil of their real design and the medium of their operations. Clay was fervently eulogized; his ability, services, and desert were eloquently recognized; his unfortunate position and political weakness pathetically mourned. Every contrivance of political ingenuity was utilized to circumvent the choice of delegates pledged to his support. Perhaps the most successful was what became known as the "triangular correspondence." The leader in one locality would regretfully write to the leaders in others that Clay's prospects were hopeless in his district, and therefore advise extra efforts elsewhere; the others would reply in the same strain, and the replies would be industriously circulated. In many cases this device worked so well as to prevent the selection of delegates for Clay, contrary to the decided preponderance of sentiment for him. The outcome of these dexterous manipulations was that Clay had but ten votes from the State of New York, while Harrison had two avowedly, Scott twenty nominally, but subject to orders.

The convention [1] was held in a Lutheran church; and the incongruity of the place with the occasion was made still more anomalous by the most extraordinary machinations that ever shaped the results of a national political convention. The most decisive part of the proceedings began at the Astor House [2] in New York city, where Weed stopped on his way to Harrisburg to confer with other leading pilgrims on their mission to save the country. Among them were Ashmun and Jones, two of Webster's lieutenants, who were authorized by him "to support the candidate," as Weed mellowly states, "most likely to strengthen the ticket." Harrison was of course agreed upon as that candidate. But it was found, before the convention opened, that a large plurality of the delegates favored Clay, and that he was apt to carry the convention. Then ensued more conferences and cogitations, by which more schemes were evolved. No serious difficulty was experienced in uniting all the adverse interests upon Harrison.

---

[1] It should be remarked that as there had previously been no Whig national convention there was no regular organization formally to call one, and the movement for this one was instituted by the "opposition members of Congress without distinction of party."—*Niles's Register*, vol. lvii. p. 47.

[2] "There was reserved for Mr. Weed's exclusive use during these years of active political leadership a room in the Astor House, which he always occupied when called to the city. 'He retained room 11,' writes one who knew him well. 'Could that room but speak, what a story it might tell! It was an audience chamber and council closet, where all sorts of persons went month after month, year after year. In it caucuses were held, campaigns arranged, Senators, members of the cabinet, Governors, Ministers, and even Presidents were made and unmade. For nearly a quarter of a century more political power and influence probably emanated from that little apartment than from any other source in the entire republic.'"—Barnes's *Life of Weed*, p. 237.

This done, it was resolved to adopt the "unit rule," then originated—that the majority of each delegation should decide the full vote of its State. In conjunction with this, to prevent any contagious eloquence in Clay's behalf, it was determined that a committee of not more than three should be appointed from each delegation "to receive the views and opinions of such delegation and communicate the same to the assembled committee of all the delegations, to be by them respectively reported to their principals." Thereupon each delegation was to meet separately and ballot for candidates, after which the committees were to assemble and compare results. This process was to be repeated until a majority vote was reached. In consequence, the real deliberations of the convention were to be held by detachments outside of it. This crafty scheme assured success.[1] The method was opposed in the convention, but Clay's partisans lacked his energy and persistence, and the resolution was adopted. The result of the first ballot was 103 for Clay, 94 for Harrison, and 57 for Scott. The influences to disintegrate Clay's strength were then brought to bear. Seven ballots were taken, Harrison gaining mainly by the transfer to him of Scott's previous votes. His nomination was certain, but, in the eager and imploring efforts to reconcile Clay's angered and rebellious supporters, the last ballot was delayed twenty-four hours. The final ballot stood 148 for Harrison, 90 for Clay, and 16 for Scott. Thus the result of twelve years of Whig uproar and exertions to preserve our imperiled institutions was to nominate the *tertium quid*, as Wise sarcastically called Harrison, and by methods more intriguing, unfair, and tyrannical than

---

[1] Benton's *Thirty Years' View*, vol. ii. p. 204.

Jackson or the Albany Regency, so long and so vehemently denounced by the Whigs, had ever conceived. Even Greeley in after years piously apologized for the transaction as being the only means to nominate a candidate who could be elected and thus carry out the patriotic purpose of the party.[1]

In Harrison's nomination, however achieved, Clay's adherents were compelled to acquiesce. Treason to the party, under the conditions that existed, could not be contemplated. But the dread of it and the provocation for it caused the victorious managers deep anxiety. As soon as the result of the last ballot was announced to the convention one of the Kentucky delegation declared its concurrence in Harrison's nomination. He was followed by another member, who spoke to the same effect, and asked that a letter from Clay, which had been for some days in the possession of a delegate, but which, to avoid the appearance of intent to excite sentiment for Clay, had not been shown, be read to the convention. Permission was given, and the letter was produced and read. In it Clay stated that should any other candidate be chosen he would cordially support him, and adjured his friends to be guided solely by the motive of uniting the party, that its success in the election might be attained. When he sent this letter he could not foresee the unprecedented means that were used against him; hence it was feared by some that he would not consider himself bound by the pledge to support the ticket, and would remain fatally inactive throughout the canvass. But the letter was none the less hailed with exuberant approval. Speeches in the most laudatory style were made

---

[1] Greeley's *Recollections of a Busy Life*, p. 131.

upon his character and devotion. "I envy Kentucky," exclaimed one of the speakers, "for when he dies she will have his ashes!" Yet the sombre countenances of his discomfited friends seemed to bode ill, and the gloom was deepened by the difficulty in finding a suitable man willing to accept the nomination for Vice-President.

Long before the convention, Weed had offered to Webster the support of the New York delegation for the place, if Harrison were nominated for President; but Webster haughtily declined the proposition. Clay's friends were eagerly besought to make the selection, and four of them —Leigh, Clayton, Tallmadge, and Southard—successively refused to stand. At length, as the last resource, John Tyler was proposed. His political career and principles had been hybrid—partly Democratic and partly Whig. While Senator he had disapproved the removal of the deposits; and, refusing to vote for the expunging resolution in compliance with the instructions of the Virginia legislature, he had resigned his seat. By the aid of the Whigs, under Clay's advice, he was defeated in his attempt to be re-elected; but he was promised, as the reward for his martyrdom, the nomination for Vice-President. At all events, he was one of Clay's most ardent supporters in the convention, and confessed, it was said, that he had wept at Clay's defeat.[1] He was nominated. The convention neither formulated a platform nor adopted resolutions defining the programme of the party. This was left to the conjectures that each element of voters should deem most consistent with its

---

[1] "Mrs. Tyler says that she once remarked on this tale to her husband, and that he laughed heartily, and said that he wished that was the greatest of the falsehoods propagated concerning him."—*Letters and Times of the Tylers*, vol. i. p. 595.

principles and desires. "Efforts were made," says Weed, "during the last hours of the convention to awaken some enthusiasm for the ticket. But the deep mortification of the friends of Mr. Clay rendered those efforts but partially successful. The delegates separated less sanguine than usual of a united and zealous effort to elect the ticket." So terminated this remarkable convention, the consequences of which are without parallel in our history.[1]

Clay was at Washington attending the first session of the Twenty-sixth Congress, which began December 2, when the result of the convention was made known to him. His feelings overcame all dignity and restraint. He strode back and forth in violent excitement and wrath, bitterly and profanely accusing his ill-fortune and the impotence of his friends.[2] But he was

> . . . . "the engineer
> Hoist with his own petar."

---

[1] The Democratic press was as outspoken as Clay's friends in regard to his defeat. Among other things the *Democratic Review*, of February, 1840, said : "We cannot dissemble an indignant contempt—not less sincere that we have but few political sympathies in common—for the mean ingratitude which has thus so basely betrayed him in the last hours of his public life, to sacrifice him, his rights, and his fame to a cunning intrigue and to a cold calculation of party expediency, which we verily believe to have been as shallow and impolitic as it was heartless and false. In the words of Fouché, it was worse than a crime—it was a blunder."

[2] "Such an exhibition we never witnessed before, and we pray never again to witness such an ebullition of passion, such a storm of deprecations and curses. He rose from his chair, and, walking backwards and forwards rapidly, lifting his feet like a horse string-halted in both legs, stamped his steps upon the floor, exclaiming : 'My friends are not worth the powder and shot it would take to kill them.' He mentioned the names of several, invoking upon them the most horrid imprecations, and then turning to us approached rapidly with a violent gesture and in a loud voice said : 'If there were two Henry Clays one of them would make the other President of the United States.' Trying to bring him to his senses, we replied : 'If there were *two* Henry Clays the continent would not be large enough to hold them, and

Availability had carried the day. Clay had laboriously built up a conglomerate party, of many elements and interests, and a various combination of policies, with but one purpose in common—the overthrow of the Democratic régime. The test of the candidates of such a coalition is always availability. He had recognized it by his own recent course as a trimmer; and doubtless the poignant appreciation of his corresponding sacrifice of political character intensified his disgust. But his acute disappointment quickly subsided. He was soon absorbed in his customary functions in the Senate. He was still chief of the Whigs, and he maintained all his zeal for the success of the party.¹

---

they would not leave a morsel of each other; they would mutually destroy themselves. You were warned by Judge White of this result when it might have been prevented, but you would not take heed.' 'Ah! yes,' said he; 'you and Judge White are like the old lady who knew the cow would eat up the grindstone. It is a diabolical intrigue. I now know which has betrayed me. I am the most unfortunate man in the history of parties; always run by my friends when sure to be defeated, and now betrayed for a nomination when I or any one else would be sure of an election.'"—Wise's *Seven Decades of the Union*, p. 172.

¹ "After the adjournment of the Harrisburg convention many of the members went to Washington, where it was found that of these were one or more delegates from eighteen out of the twenty-two States, which had been represented in that patriotic and enlightened body. They called in a body upon Mr. Clay to do homage to the high moral principle which had influenced his conduct. The friends of Harrison and Scott, with those originally enlisted for Webster, were as ready to acknowledge the high claims of Clay to the proud distinction of their nomination as he and his friends had been to surrender those claims in favor of a candidate who was thought to be more available. The particulars of this touching ceremony, together with those of the great Whig dinner given on the same day, are detailed admirably in the *National Intelligencer*."—Hone's *Diary*, vol. i. p. 399.

CHAPTER XI

The Financial and Political Situation—Organization of the House—The Independent Treasury Established—Other Proceedings of Congress—Slavery and International Law — The Democratic Convention — The Campaign of 1840—Clay's Platform for the Whig Party—William H. Harrison and his Opinions—The Election—Harrison and Clay and the Construction of the Cabinet—The Inaugural Address—The Clamor for the Spoils—Strained Relations Between Clay and Harrison—The Death of the President—John Tyler—The Close of the Jacksonian Epoch

WITH the partial recovery of the country from the effects of the crisis, the prospect of a Whig victory diminished. About the time when Clay started on his tour, Van Buren did likewise, visiting several places in Pennsylvania, New Jersey, and New York. His reception, especially in the city of New York, was most gratifying to him and encouraged his belief that, by the time of the election in 1840, the factitious promise of a Whig triumph would disappear. Popular demonstrations of regard for public men, however, are rarely significant of political strength: there is commonly in most places a sufficient number of the admiring and the curious to form an imposing crowd. But aside from the greeting Van Buren received on his tour, there were other causes to make him sanguine. Business was reviving, and foreign commerce was rapidly regaining its normal volume. The revenues, from customs duties and the public lands, were steadily approaching their former level. All signs of returning prosperity seemed propitious. In the fall of 1838 the results of the elections indicated a renewal of confidence in the administration. But in October of the following year the promising aspect of the situation began to fade. England had experienced a relapse of the crisis, and the effects were quickly communicated to this country. The banks in Philadelphia, including the Philadelphia Bank of the United States, suspended, and their example was generally followed, save in New York and in New England, with some few exceptions.[1] The manifestations of distress were not so acute as before, but the general situation was much the same. A paralyzing stupor fell upon trade and business, from which they were slow to recover. Nevertheless, Van Buren, with laudable firmness, met Congress with his usual recommendations of sound finance, retracting nothing of his former policy. He was now strong enough in both houses of Congress to carry the great measure of his administration.

The legislative proceedings of the session were delayed two weeks by an acrimonious struggle over the organization of the House. There was a contest for the five New Jersey seats, the possession of which would be vital to either party, as they would determine the political control of the House. The formal credentials were held by the Whigs. The Congressmen from that State were voted for on a general ticket. The returns from two election districts were thrown out for alleged irregularities, although the Democrats insisted, justly in all probability, that this action was wrongful; at all

---

[1] September 17, 1839, Senator Linn wrote from London: "Since my arrival, money affairs here have been in the worst possible condition—men looked into each other's faces with suspicion and turned with disgust from every proposition relating to American property and security, and the recent protest in Paris of a million and a half of drafts drawn by the Bank of the United States I fear will give the finishing blow to everything American."—*Life of Linn*, p. 110

events, it decided the result of the election and engendered much excitement and asperity. On calling the roll the clerk declined to include either delegation or to put any motion whatever, even to adjourn. After four days of confusion and tumult John Quincy Adams was asked to suggest some mode of solving the difficulty. He did so in a very characteristic way. Briefly addressing the members, he proposed that the House proceed to organize itself; and when several members asked who would put the question he made the historic reply, " I will put the question myself." He was made chairman, and presided until the 16th, when R. M. T. Hunter, of Virginia, was elected Speaker by a union of the Whig members with Calhoun's friends, who were incensed at the refusal of some of the administration Democrats to vote for one of their number. Hunter was an Independent, but a States-rights man and supporter of the Sub-Treasury plan. Neither of the New Jersey delegations was allowed to vote. The contestants were finally seated.

The proceedings of the session were heavily charged with politics. Party feeling was intense. Both sides labored to the utmost to gain every possible advantage for effect in the pending Presidential campaign. The chief struggle, which occurred over the independent Treasury bill, was waged with extreme energy and bitterness. The administration was determined to force the measure through, and the confidence of the Whigs in their success at the ensuing election gave them additional ground for denouncing the programme. The bill was early introduced in the Senate, and its progress hastened by every available means. Clay delivered the most conspicuous speech against it. None of his speeches so well exhibit his versatility as the series on this much-debated subject; but unfortunately they are better evidence of his skill as a debater, with a view to influencing public opinion, than they are of his wisdom and judgment on questions of national finance. While this speech contained no new arguments, those which he had urged before were stated in a form well adapted to the uses of campaign literature. Moreover, the degree of his zeal in support of Harrison was a matter of deep and general interest, which his speech amply satisfied. His description of the financial condition of the country is so faithful and complete that it should be quoted.

"The general government," said he, "is in debt, and its existing revenue is inadequate to meet its ordinary expenditure. The States are in debt, some of them largely in debt, insomuch that they have been compelled to resort to the ruinous expedient of contracting new loans to meet the interest on prior loans; and the people are surrounded by difficulties, greatly embarrassed, and involved in debt. While this is, unfortunately, the general state of the country, the means of extinguishing this vast mass of debt are in constant diminution. Property is falling in value; and all the great staples of the country are declining in price, and destined, I fear, to further decline. The banks are rapidly decreasing the amount of their circulation. About one-half of them, extending from New Jersey to the extreme Southwest, have suspended specie payments, presenting an image of a paralytic, one moiety of whose body is stricken with palsy. The banks are without a head; and instead of union, concert, and co-operation between them, we behold jealousy, distrust, and enmity. We have no currency whatever possessing uniform value throughout the whole country. That which we have, consisting almost entirely of the issue of banks, is in a state of the utmost disorder, insomuch that it varies, in comparison with the specie standard, from par to fifty per centum discount. Exchanges, too, are in the greatest possible confusion; not merely between distant parts of the Union, but between cities and places in the same neighborhood; that between our great commercial marts of New York and Philadelphia, within five or six hours of each other, vacillating between seven and ten per centum. The products of our agricultural industry are unable to find their way to market from the want of means in the hands of traders to purchase them, or for want of confidence in the stability of things; many of our manufactories are stopped or stopping, especially in the important branch of woollens; and a vast accumulation of their fabrics on hand, owing to the destruction of confidence and the wretched state of exchange between different sections of the Union."

January 23 the bill was passed by the Senate, 24 to 18. In the House it encountered still more strenuous opposition; but, as there was now a majority for it, it was pushed with vigor. As Benton says: "The shortest road was taken to its passage; and that was under the debate-killing pressure of the previous question. That question was freely used, and amendment after amendment cut off, motion after motion stifled, speech after speech suppressed; the bill carried from stage to stage by a sort of silent struggle chiefly interrupted by the repeated process of calling yeas and nays, until at last it reached the final vote—and was passed—by a majority not large, but clear—124 to 107. This was the 30th of June, that is to say, within twenty days of the end of a session of near eight months." The spirit of the opposition is shown by the ridiculous motion to amend the title of the bill so as to read, "An act to reduce the value of property, the products of the farmer, and the wages of labor, to destroy the indebted portions of the community, to place the Treasury of the nation in the hands of the President, and to enable the public money to be drawn from the public Treasury without appropriation made by law." This motion received eighty-seven votes.

This was the only measure of general importance, other than the ordinary legislation, to become a law. A bankruptcy bill was passed by the Senate, but in the House it was laid on the table. The principal objections to it were those urged by Clay — to compulsory proceedings against individuals and to making the bill applicable to banks and other corporations. But the bankruptcy throughout the country was not confined to corporations or persons. The most striking examples of it were furnished by many of the States, which had incurred vast debts, largely abroad, for the prosecution of unremunerative public works. At least thirteen States were thus virtually bankrupt. Some of them even repudiated their obligations, to the serious injury of American credit and the American character.[1] An effort was made, originating in London, to induce the government to assume the State debts. Benton offered a series of resolutions denouncing the scheme as unconstitutional and unwise. Crittenden proposed an amendment, asserting that it would be just and proper to distribute among the States

---

[1] "It is impossible to conceive anything more painful and mortifying to one, either by birth or adoption an American, than the contemptuous and reproachful comments which any mention of the United States is sure to elicit. The commercial and financial delinquencies of some of the States, but principally of Pennsylvania, have created a universal impression throughout Europe of utter want of faith, honor, and integrity on the part of the whole nation."—Mrs. Butler's (Fanny Kemble) *Year of Consolation*, vol. i. p. 37. See, also, *Democratic Review*, vol. xi. p. 212; ibid. vol. xiv. p. 1; *Life of Clay* (anonymous), vol. i. p. 182; *De Tocqueville*, vol. i. p. 165.

the proceeds of the sales of the public lands to aid them in paying their debts. As this was the favorite feature of Clay's programme he supported it; but it was defeated, and Benton's resolutions were adopted.

The Committee on Foreign Relations made a temperate and pacific report in regard to the difficulty with England over the northeastern boundary. Clay concurred in the report, but contended that if the two governments should, through the ordinary course of diplomacy, be unable to agree, the question could be submitted to arbitration under a provision in the treaty of Ghent. Should these means fail to settle the dispute, he scouted any dread of the result of war. Van Buren favored any expedient rather than force. This attitude made him unpopular in Maine in the same manner as his firm stand for neutrality during the Canadian rebellion injured him in the northwestern counties of New York. This was doubtless the motive for Clay's bellicose encomium on our power and our prowess.

On presenting an abolition petition Clay reasserted the right of petition, but took occasion to remark that he thought the crisis of the agitation was passed, and also to express the gratification he had derived from the perusal of some valuable works from Northern pens on the subject of abolition. He mentioned several such works, and approved the argument presented by one of them, that "two communities of distinct races cannot live together without the one becoming more or less in subjection to the other." The tenor of his remarks shows that his real opinions on the slavery question had undergone no change, and that his respect for the right of petition had not abated. And his instinctive sentiment against slavery was manifested not long afterward in connection with some resolutions that Calhoun had introduced.

In 1830 the American coasting schooner *Comet* was wrecked on one of the Bahamas. A number of slaves on board who were being transported from the District of Columbia to New Orleans, were freed by the local authorities. Four years later the *Encomium* was wrecked near the same place, and the slaves she carried were treated in a similar manner. In 1835 the brig *Enterprise* was driven by storm into Port Hamilton, Bermuda, and the slaves on board of her were likewise liberated.[1] In all these cases the owners of the slaves besought our government to procure redress. After protracted negotiations the British government paid the value of the slaves taken in the two first cases, but absolutely refused to make compensation in the last—for the reason that it had taken place, unlike the previous ones, after the abolition of slavery in the British West Indies. Calhoun made the matter the subject of resolutions applying to slave property the ordinary law of nations protecting vessels with persons and property on board, when lawfully engaged, but forced by stress of weather into ports of friendly powers; and therefore declaring that the act of the local authorities of Port Hamilton in freeing the negroes on the *Enterprise* was in violation of international law. He argued at length in support of his proposition, which was denied by nations that did not recognize slavery. No Senator voted against the resolutions, although but thirty-three of the fifty-two Senators voted. Clay voted for them, but emphatically disapproved the introduction of them on the ground that negotiations concern-

---

[1] *Niles's Register*, vol. xlviii. p. 44.

ing the subject were closed by language so decisive as to preclude expectation that they would be resumed, and that the resolutions were without practical utility. "I think," he added, "a too frequent use of the expression of opinions on subjects merely abstract by a body of such high and grave authority as the Senate will have a tendency to bring our opinions into disrepute." Calhoun replied, and Clay, in rejoining, made the grounds of his objection more explicit and more significant of his dislike to the assertions of international law in behalf of slavery.

The standing feud between Calhoun and Clay was vigorously displayed again in course of the discussion of a land bill which Calhoun had introduced, similar to the one he had urged two years before. What led to the renewal of the personal debate was Clay's inquiry whether the administration favored the bill. "The inquiry," said he, "I should not make if the recent relations between the Senator who introduced the bill and the head of that administration continued to exist; but rumors, of which the city, the *cercles*, and the press are full, assert that those relations are entirely changed and have within a few days been substituted by others of an intimate, friendly, and confidential nature." Calhoun pronounced the inquiry indecorous and his personal relations with the President none of Clay's concern. "But," said he, "the Senator assumes that a change in my personal relations involves a change of political position; and it is on that he founds his right to make the inquiry. He judges, doubtless, by his own experience; but I would have him to understand that what may be true in his case on a memorable occasion is not true in mine. His political course may be governed by personal considerations; but mine, I trust, is governed strictly by my principles, and is not at all under the control of my attachments or enmities." Clay insisted that the public was entitled to know whether the bill was an administration measure. "Is it," he asked, "of no importance to the public to learn that these pledges and compromises have been entered into? — that the distinguished Senator has made his bow in court, kissed the hand of the monarch, was taken into favor, and agreed henceforth to support his edicts?" Calhoun then recurred to the coalition scandal of 1824, and reasserted his own independence and consistency. Clay repeated the details of his justification for supporting Adams, and referred to Calhoun's compliant part in the Compromise of 1833. "But for that Compromise," he added, "I am not at all confident that I would now have the honor to meet that Senator face to face in this national capital." This allusion to Jackson's threat to prosecute Calhoun for treason brought him to his feet again.

"As the Senator," said he, "has thought proper to refer to it [the Compromise] and claim my gratitude, I in turn now tell him that I feel not the least gratitude towards him for it. The measure was necessary to save the Senator politically; and as he has alluded to the subject, both on this and on a former occasion, I feel bound to explain what might otherwise have been left in oblivion. The Senator was then compelled to compromise to save himself. Events had placed him flat on his back, and he had no way to recover himself but by the Compromise. This is no after-thought. I wrote more than half a dozen letters home at the time to that effect." He then went on to explain that Jackson's course had rallied around him the friends of protection; that Clay was thus left in a hopeless condition, and that Webster "would have reaped all the political honors and advantages of the system had the contest come to blows." For these reasons, he asserted, Clay was obliged to compromise as his "only means of extrication." "I had the mastery over him on that occasion. I have never taken any credit for my agency in the Compromise act. I claim a higher—that of compelling the Compromise; and I would have dictated my terms . . . had not circumstances not proper to explain here prevented it. . . . I never contemplated a sudden reduction of duties. I never desired to destroy the manufactures, and at no time contemplated a full reduction under six or seven years."

"The Senator from South Carolina," replied Clay, with indignant emphasis, "said that I was flat on my back and that he was my master. Sir, I would not own him as my slave. He my master! and I compelled by him! And as if it were impossible to go far enough in one paragraph, he refers to certain letters of his own to prove that I was flat on my back! and that I was not only on my back, but another Senator and the President had robbed me! I was flat on my back and unable to do anything but what the Senator from South Carolina permitted me to do! Why, sir, I gloried in my strength, and was compelled to introduce the Compromise bill, and was compelled, too, by the Senator, not in consequence of the weakness, but of the strength of my position. If it were possible for the Senator from South Carolina to introduce one paragraph without showing the egotism of his character, he would not now acknowledge that he wrote letters home to show that I was flat on my back, while he was indebted to me for the measure which relieved him from the difficulties in which he was involved."

He then gave his version of the case, asserting that he produced and carried through the Compromise notwithstanding Webster's unceasing opposition; that he was influenced by no personal considerations, but was actuated by the motive of pacifying the country and preventing the effusion of blood. "There was," he continued, "another reason that powerfully operated on me. . . . I saw that the protective system was in danger of being swept away entirely, and probably at the next session of Congress, by the tremendous power of the individual who then filled the Executive chair; and I felt that the greatest service that I could render it would be to obtain for it 'a lease for a term of years,' to use an expression that has heretofore been applied to the Compromise bill."[1]

However interesting these explanations of the Compromise may be, they were but a brief interlude to the ardent attention devoted to the existing political situation. The Presidential campaign began as soon as the Whig convention adjourned, and was carried on with increasing energy until the day of election. Exciting as some of the previous campaigns had been, there has never been one that could compare with this. In the methods employed it was a new departure. The dexterity of the Whig managers in procuring Harrison's nomination was fully equalled by the novel skill employed in arousing popular sentiment in his support. There was no necessity to await the formal action of the Democratic party, for it was well understood that Van Buren would be renominated, as he was in several States and by the Democratic national convention at Baltimore May 5. The nomination for Vice-President was left to the party organizations in the States, most of which renominated Johnson. The convention did not imitate the

---

[1] Even John Tyler, in an address delivered in March, 1855, gave Clay the credit of the Compromise.—*Letters and Times of the Tylers*, vol. i. pp. 601-2.

non-committal policy of the Whig convention, but adopted a clearly worded and explicit platform, asserting the cardinal tenets of the party. It declared for strict construction of the Constitution, and therefore against the power to carry on a general system of internal improvements, fostering one branch of industry to the detriment of another, chartering a national bank, interfering with slavery and the abolition movement in all its objects; for economy in every department of the government, and the raising of only sufficient revenue for administrative purposes, and the granting of liberal privileges to foreigners becoming citizens and acquiring lands. This was supplemented by an address repeating more fully these principles, denouncing the abolitionists, whose fanatical zeal was imputed to the instigation of the Whigs, defending Van Buren's administration, asserting that Harrison was a Federalist and that his military glory was doubtful, and criticising the pageantry of the Whig campaign as addressed merely to the senses. The convention, however, was gloomy, for the prospect of success was dubious. Already the country was stirred with the commotion created by the exertions and enthusiasm of the Whigs.

Public meetings and political harangues were by no means a novelty in Presidential canvasses, but the extent to which they were now employed far surpassed that of all previous campaigns. The speeches were generally made in the open air before vast concourses of people.[1] In some cases these

---

[1] "The people rose almost *en masse*. The whole country was divided, as if in civil war, in hostile factions. Banners flouted the sky; the people met in armies; the pursuits of business were neglected for the strife and strivings of political canvassing; and an excitement careered over the land, which in any other country would have drenched it in blood and upheaved the government from its foundation stones. At Nashville a multitude

gatherings were so large that the places they occupied were surveyed and measured to determine the number of acres of people that attended. Clay and Webster, as well as the less conspicuous Whig leaders, joined with unprecedented fervor in this party service. Nor did they wait until Congress adjourned, but began their operations early in the session. Clay spoke in Baltimore, May 4, before an immense crowd—twenty thousand, he estimated—drawn together by a national convention of young men. He declared himself unreservedly for Harrison and buoyantly predicted an overwhelming victory. "This," he exclaimed, "is no time to argue; the time for argument has passed; the nation has already pronounced its sentence."[1] Yet he did argue on many occasions and in several States. His principal speech was delivered in his native county in Virginia, June 27, and became one of the text-books of the campaign.

He began by asserting his earnest support of Harrison and gracefully referring to his visit to the county of his nativity. "Why," he then asked, "is the plough deserted, the

---

which no man might number, composed of the old enemies of Clay, hung upon his accents, and as he denounced the principles and measures of Jacksonism, rent the air with thunder-shouts of applause which invaded even the peace of the Hermitage."—Baldwin's *Party Leaders*, p. 344.

[1] "The convention itself consisted of thousands; an immense, unwieldy mass of political machinery to accomplish nothing—to form a procession polluted by a foul and unpunished murder of one of their own marshals, and by the loss of several other lives. I am assured that the number of delegates in attendance from the single State of Massachusetts was not less than twelve hundred. And in the midst of this throng Henry Clay, Daniel Webster, William C. Preston, Senators of the United States, and four times the number of members of the House of Representatives have been two days straining their lungs and cracking their voices to fill this multitude with windy sound for the glorification of William Henry Harrison and the vituperation of Martin Van Buren."—Adams's *Diary*, vol. x. p. 282.

tools of the mechanic laid aside, and all are seen rushing to gatherings of the people? What occasions those vast and universal assemblages which we behold in every State and in almost every neighborhood? Why those conventions of the people at a common centre, from all extremities of this vast Union, to consult together upon the sufferings of the community and to deliberate upon the means of deliverance? Why this rabid appetite for public discussion? What is the solution of the phenomenon which we observe of a great nation agitated upon its whole surface and to its lowest depths, like the ocean when convulsed by some terrible storm? There must be a cause, and no ordinary cause." This led him to his accustomed theme of "the encroachments and usurpations of the Executive branch of the government — subordination of the entire official corps, from the highest to the lowest, to the will of the President; political proscription and abuse of the power of dismissal; seizure of the Treasury; all tending, if not designed, to concentrate the powers of the government in the hands of the Executive. He excepted the army and navy from this influence, but asserted, as evidence of design to bring the military into partisan subjection, that two officers of the army had been court-martialed for purchasing supplies from Whigs instead of Democrats; and he assailed, as further proof of a sinister purpose, a recent recommendation of the Secretary of War to increase the militia to two hundred thousand. He ridiculed and combated the charge that the Whigs were really Federalists.[1]

---

[1] That the Whig principles were substantially those of the former Federal party was early and candidly admitted by John Quincy Adams in a letter to Clay, April 21, 1829. "The objection," he wrote, "there appears to me to be against applying the denomination of Federalists to

The necessity he proclaimed for a change of administration implied the adoption of positive and corrective measures; and he did not hesitate, unlike the Whig convention, to assert his own programme, though he was careful to speak only for himself. Under the circumstances he could not do otherwise; but he doubtless spoke with much assurance that his views would be decisive. He proposed that no person should be eligible to the Presidency after serving one term; that "the veto power should be more precisely defined and be subjected to further limitations and qualifications"—particularly, that provision should be made for bills passed within ten days of the close of a session of Congress, to prevent "pocket vetoes," and that a majority of all the members of each house should override a positive veto; that "the power of dismission from office should be restricted and the exercise of it rendered responsible"—particularly in cases of the removal of officials appointed with the concurrence of the Senate, and that in such cases where removals should be necessary the reasons should be fully communicated; that "the control over the Treasury should be confided and confined exclusively to Congress, and all authority of the President over it, by means of dismissing the Secretary of the Treasury or other persons having the immediate charge of it, be vigorously precluded"; and that "the appointment of members of Congress to any office, or any but a few specific offices, during their continuance in office and for one year thereafter, should be prohibited." These propositions, it will be observed, were suggested by his contests with Jackson and Van

---

the opposers of protection to manufactures and internal improvements is that I believe the fact to be otherwise. The old Federalists were generally friendly to those interests. Washington was pre-eminently so."

Buren. None of them have ever been adopted. He intimated the opinion that the establishment of a national bank was necessary to the creation of a sound currency; but he was careful not to pledge himself to that policy. The public lands he would treat as provided for in the bill that Jackson rejected. The protective system should "be adhered to and maintained on the basis of the principles and in the spirit of the Compromise." "A pruning-knife, long, broad, and sharp, should be applied to every department of the government." The States having made so much progress in their systems of internal improvement, and having been so much aided by the distribution under the deposit act, they should receive no further assistance from the government, except the payment of the last instalment under that act, the absolute relinquishment to them of the previous instalments, and the proceeds of the sales of the public lands, as prescribed in his bill. "The right to slave property, being guaranteed by the Constitution and recognized as one of the compromises incorporated into that instrument by our ancestors, should be left where the Constitution had placed it, undisturbed and unagitated." This speech was the most authoritative exposition of the Whig creed, and may be taken as the type of the innumerable Whig speeches of the campaign.

The most powerful aid to the Whig ticket was the condition of the country resulting from the financial crisis. No argument was necessary to make that plain, and that, in itself, was enough to convince a large portion of the people that the government was at fault.¹ Want and logic seldom

---

[1] "Hundreds and thousands of persons, destitute of employment and almost destitute of bread, found relief in swelling the Harrison processions and gatherings, in singing patriotic songs, and shouting for reform."—Goodrich's *Recollections*, vol. ii. p. 350.

consort. It is not supposable that at such a time the mass of the people reasoned much whether there should be a national bank or an independent Treasury, or what was the best system upon which to deal with the public lands. Multitudes, moved by destitution and encouraged by clamor, naturally believed that a change of administration would be beneficial. "They feel," said Clay, "the absolute necessity for a change, that no change can render their condition worse, and that any change must better it. This is the judgment to which they have come; this is the brief and compendious logic which we daily hear." And this impulse was urged on by all the arts of stump declamation. The argument of most weight in the popular mind was that the administrations of Jackson and Van Buren were characterized by prodigal and profligate extravagance and waste of the public funds. It was in this that the highly spectacular feature of the campaign had its impetus.

The charge was more than specious. The new political temper displayed after Jackson's election, begetting an inordinate desire for office, which was furthered by the spoils system, led insidiously to the creation of new places to be filled, new expenditures to be made, and the concoction of innumerable schemes to plunder the government by indirection. In times of great political activity and excitement the public eye is too little directed to the minor means that ingenious and unscrupulous men employ to filch the public funds. During the Revolution these plunderers enriched themselves through the woes of the country. Similar operations prevailed during the War of 1812 and the Rebellion. During the Jacksonian period, after the national debt was paid, there set in a spirit of laxity that increased and spread until the results became scandalous. Wherever the public moneys presented temptation they were in danger. After the method was instituted of keeping and disbursing the revenues through the medium of the officials instead of the banks, defalcations and peculations became so common that only the more flagrant cases attracted attention.[1] Swartwout, collector of customs at the port of New York, was a defaulter to the extent of nearly $1,250,000,[2] and the United States district-attorney at the same place, $72,000. Many of the land officers were guilty in lesser degrees.[3] The

---

[1] "Defalcations are no crime. Mr. Van Buren in his message proposes to make defalcations of public money felony and punishable in the state-prison. Nonsense! Neither party will agree to such an absurdity! Never!"—*New York Herald*, December 10, 1838.

[2] "Swartwout's appointment was opposed by the leading friends of General Jackson and Mr. Van Buren in New York. Mr. Van Buren opposed it most earnestly." "This man [Hoyt] was a pet of Van Buren's. I have understood he was a grocer, and became bankrupt. He was afterward appointed by Van Buren collector of the port of New York. He certainly then purloined a large amount of the public money."—*Reminiscences of J. A. Hamilton*, pp. 125, 126. Swartwout wrote to Hoyt, March 14, 1829: "Your very beautiful and entirely interesting letter of the 8th was received in due course. I hold to your doctrine fully, that no d——d rascal who made use of his office for the purpose of keeping Mr. Adams in and General Jackson out of power is entitled to the least lenity or mercy, save that of hanging. So we think both alike on that head. Whether or not I shall get anything in the general scramble for plunder remains to be proven; but I rather guess I shall."

[3] "Out of sixty-six receivers of public money in the new States, sixty-two were discovered to be defaulters; and the agent sent to look into the affairs of the peccant office-holder in the Southwest reported him *minus* some tens of thousands, but advised the government to retain him for a reason one of Æsop's fables illustrates—the agent ingeniously surmising that the appointee succeeding would do his stealing without any regard to the proficiency already made by his predecessor; while the present incumbent would probably consider, in mercy to the Treasury, that he had done something of the pious duty of providing for his household."—Baldwin's *Flush Times of Alabama and Mississippi*, p. 85. "A list of some of the most prominent of the defalcations exhibits that this sad condition of things was not sectional or local, and had increased lamentably within a brief period. The public Treasury had been plundered of about twenty millions of dollars within a few years."—*Memoirs of J. G. Bennett*, p. 257.

government was more or less blamable for inattention; yet something should be allowed for inexperience with the system which had so recently come into existence.

A still greater loss to the Treasury came through extravagant appropriations, fraudulent contracts, and the like, for which Congress, without regard to party, was more responsible than the administration. The details of this source of waste were not known during the campaign; it was only after subsequent investigation that they were ascertained. Still, the idea was abroad. The total expenses of the government had rapidly increased, and this furnished abundant ground for denunciation. During the last session some inquiries were started in Congress which resulted in showing that Van Buren's life in the White House was conducted in an elegant style. Speeches were made in the House, in which his mode of living was graphically contrasted with the simpler manner of his predecessors; and these speeches were profusely circulated as campaign documents, with telling effect. It was said that golden goblets and spoons, gilt candelabra, silver plate, knives and forks, costly china and fine linen, satin chairs and damask sofas, carriages and servants were his portion, while the masses toiled and suffered to pay for them. He was charged with being an aristocrat and a monarchist, and thus unworthy of support by true Americans.

Early in the campaign a Richmond newspaper observed derisively of Harrison: "Give him a barrel of hard cider and a pension of two thousand dollars, and our word for it he will sit the remainder of his days contented in a log-cabin." It was an unfortunate remark; for it was at once taken up by the Whig journals and speakers, and prompted the spectacular features of the extraordinary canvass that followed.[1] Log-cabins and hard cider became the symbols of a popular crusade and an irresistible argument against the extravagance of the government and the alleged contempt of the administration for the people. And there was enough truth in the idea of Harrison they represented to give them more than merely picturesque effect.

Harrison was nearly sixty-eight, poor, plain, and unassuming.[2] But his descent and career were highly honorable. He was the son of a distinguished citizen of Virginia, who was repeatedly Speaker of the colonial Congress, and a signer of the Declaration of Independence. At the age of nineteen, while a medical student, he left his studies, and was commissioned as an ensign in the arduous Indian war during Washington's administration. He served with gallantry, and retired in 1797, with the rank of captain, to take the appointment of secretary of the Northwest Territory. A year later he became a delegate in Congress. Soon after-

---

[1] "In an evil hour the Locofocos taunted the Harrison men with having selected a candidate who lived in a log-cabin and drank hard cider, which the Whigs, with more adroitness than they usually display, appropriated to their own use, and now on all their banners and transparencies the Temple of Liberty is transformed into a hovel of unhewn logs; the military garb of the general, into the frock and shirt-sleeves of a laboring farmer. The American eagle has taken his flight, which is supplied by a cider barrel, and the long-established emblem of the ship has given place to the plough."—Hone's *Diary*, vol. ii. p. 22.

[2] In April, 1840, Horace Mann visited Harrison, and in a letter gave a minute description of his rustic abode and simple habits of life. "The house was a building with two wings. Part of the central building was veritable logs, though now covered externally by clapboards and within by wainscoting. This covering and these wings have been added since the log nucleus was rolled together. The furniture of the parlor could not have drawn very largely upon any one's resources. The walls were ornamented with a few portraits, some in frames, some disembodied from a frame. The drawing-room was fitted up more in modern style; but the whole furniture and ornaments in these rooms might have cost two hundred or two hundred and fifty dollars."—*Life of Horace Mann*, p. 127.

ward the Territory was divided, and of that part of it made to constitute the Territory of Indiana he was appointed Governor, serving thirteen years with honesty and ability. In the Indian war with Tecumseh he commanded at the successful battle of Tippecanoe. In 1812, at the desire of the soldiers, he was made major-general of the Kentucky militia, and had performed some service when he was appointed commander of the Northwestern army. He conducted the operations that resulted in the victory of the Thames. While none of his military achievements were of much magnitude, they were all successful and brought peace throughout a wide region. From 1816 to 1819 he served in the House of Representatives, and from 1825 to 1828 in the Senate, from Ohio. In 1828 he was appointed Minister to Colombia, but in the following year he was removed by President Jackson, because he defended Clay against the charge of bargain and corruption. Returning to Ohio, he had recourse to farming for a livelihood, which was aided by his acting as the clerk of a court.[1]

Like all other men who have served the public for any considerable length of time, he had not escaped censure

---

[1] "I met with one incident in Cincinnati which I shall long remember. I had observed at the hotel table a man of about medium height, stout and muscular, and of about the age of sixty years, yet with the active step and lively air of youth. I had been struck with his open and cheerful expression, the amenity of his manners, and a certain air of command which appeared through his plain dress. 'That is,' said my friend, 'General Harrison, clerk of the Cincinnati court of common pleas. . . . He is now poor, with a numerous family, neglected by the federal government, although yet vigorous, because he has the independence to think for himself. As the opposition is in the majority here, his friends have bethought themselves to come to his relief by removing the clerk of the court of common pleas, who was a Jackson man, and giving him the place, which is a lucrative one, as a sort of retiring pension.'"—Chevalier's *Society in the United States*, p. 196.

and abuse; but there was nothing in his career to justify severe criticism. His humble circumstances were good evidence of his honesty; and his inferior position was equally good evidence that, with the opportunities he had had, he possessed little talent for political advancement and influence. He understood perfectly that his nomination was made solely because of his availability; but naturally he was not unwilling to profit by it. He acknowledged his situation very frankly to Clay, to whom he wrote several months before the convention. "I can only say that my position in relation to yourself is to me very distressing and embarrassing. How little can we be judge of our future destinies! A few years ago I would not have believed in the possibility of my being placed in a position of apparent rivalry to you, particularly in relation to the Presidency, an office which I have never dreamed of attaining, and which I ardently desired to see you occupy. I confess that I did covet the second, but never the first office in the gift of my fellow-citizens. Fate, as Bonaparte would say, has placed me where I am, and I await the result which time will determine." Certainly he had no political record to warrant his elevation. His opinions on the questions which had agitated Congress during the last twelve years were quite unknown to the people. His candidacy in 1836 had, under the circumstances, attracted no especial attention to his political convictions, though the fact that he ran in that year as a Whig candidate no doubt created a presumption as to his position. After his nomination the subject necessarily arose; not only was he personally belittled and lampooned, but he was accused of being a Federalist and an abolitionist. The truth was that his official career had small political significance and no material bearing on his present situation. That he had been removed from office by Jackson for favoring Clay was the most prominent political fact that appeared.

But he was not slow to express himself. He began by letters, which for the most part were high-sounding generalities, avoiding so far as practicable the expression of his views on particular questions. It was well enough for him to say that the President should not be devoted to his party rather than to the whole country, that he should commit no usurpations or abuse of power, that he should not resort freely to the veto, and that proscription on account of party should not prevail; the real difficulty is in the application of these excellent principles. A President is easily convinced that his party is the true exponent of what is best for the country and that only its members should be intrusted with the execution of its policy. In his speeches, for he made several, Harrison became somewhat more explicit as the pressure increased. He admitted in complimentary terms the superior attainments and claims to preferment of Clay and Webster, and thus indirectly sanctioned their views of public policy and courted their co-operation. He declared himself distinctly in favor of only a single term for the President, and pledged himself not to stand for another if elected. In 1822 he maintained that a national bank was absolutely unconstitutional; in 1836 he had overcome his scruples sufficiently to say that he would consent to approve a bill to charter a bank if the collection and disbursement of the revenue would suffer without one; but he now intimated, although he professed that his Constitutional views were unchanged, that such a result would follow without a bank, and that the popular will, if clearly expressed, in favor of a bank should not be resisted. "Methinks," said he, on one occasion, "I hear a soft voice asking, 'Are you in favor of paper money?' I am." He favored protection, but accepted the Compromise as inviolate. He denied the charge that he was an abolitionist, declared that slavery should not be abolished in the District without the consent of Virginia and Maryland, and that while the right of petition should be observed, the antislavery agitation was not sanctioned by the Constitution. He did not dwell on the subject, but it cannot justly be said that he veiled his opinions concerning it. In the latter part of his Governorship of the Indiana Territory he incurred unpopularity for a time by opposing the abolition of slavery there; and his votes in the House on the Missouri bill were against the restriction of slavery. But notwithstanding this record and his avowed sentiments, he did not repel the Whigs who favored the abolition movement; for the character of the campaign made the slavery question a minor consideration.[1] Though little was said as to Anti-masonry, Harrison was acceptable to its adherents, and this was a secret but powerful element in his support in several States.

It was soon evident that Van Buren would be defeated. However motley the array that effected Harrison's nomination, the supporters of his election were still more varied, as they included large numbers who had never before acted with the Whig party. Whatever their political principles, and however they may have differed from those which Clay had so long advocated, hostility to the administration was the sufficient motive for supporting Harrison.

---

[1] "In spite of General Harrison's trimming on the subject of slavery, and the evidence of his consistent hostility to the abolition movement, his candidacy carried off their feet an alarming number of Whig abolitionists, while the Third Party had captured another class."—*Life of Garrison*, vol. ii. p. 414.

Log-cabins, decked in frontier style with coon-skins, bunches of corn, strings of peppers and dried apples, and the like,[1] were built in the cities and villages. Inside these cabins copious supplies of cider were on tap to be drunk from gourds; on the outside crowds assembled to absorb still more copious and inflaming harangues.[2] Huge processions, music, campaign songs, cartoons, banners with such legends as "Matty's policy, fifty cents a day and French soup; our policy, two dollars a day and roast beef," were now first introduced as a prominent feature of Presidential campaigns. Besides this, all the devices that could be resorted to were used to swell the Harrison enthusiasm and recruit the ranks of his followers.[3] Benton, indulging in his usual frenzy against the influence of banks, asserts that they

---

[1] A broom at the door represented the "clean sweep" that Harrison was to make. And it was not forgotten that he had told his old soldiers that they would never find his latch-string pulled in.—*Life of Seward*, vol. i. p. 490.

[2] Julian's *Political Recollections*, pp. 10, 16.

[3] "Tippecanoe song-books were sold by the hundred thousand. There were Tippecanoe medals, Tippecanoe badges, Tippecanoe flags, Tippecanoe handkerchiefs, Tippecanoe almanacs, and Tippecanoe shaving-soap. All other interests were swallowed up in the one interest of the election. All noises were drowned in the cry of 'Tippecanoe and Tyler too.' The man who contributed most to keep alive and increase the popular enthusiasm, the man who did most to feed that enthusiasm with the substantial fuel of fact and argument was, beyond all question, Horace Greeley. On the 2d of May the first number of *The Log-Cabin* appeared, by 'H. Greeley & Co.,' a weekly paper to be published simultaneously at New York and Albany, at fifty cents for the campaign of six months. It was a small paper; but it was conducted with wonderful spirit, and made an unprecedented hit."—Parton's *Greeley*, p. 181. "The *Herald* had much to do with the election, and kept pace with the enthusiasm of the times. It astonished newspaperdom. Its reports of speeches at Patchogue, in Wall Street, and other localities were given to the public with a fulness and with a speed never known before to the press."—*Memoirs of J. G. Bennett*, p. 263. See, also, Benton's *Thirty Years' View*, vol. ii. p. 205; Adams's *Diary*, vol. x. pp. 352, 355; Weed's *Autobiography*, vol. i. p. 467; Sherman's *Recollections of Forty Years*, vol. i. p. 48.

contributed largely to defray the expenses of this political pandemonium and to provide an abundant corruption fund; but with how much truth it is impossible to know. Regarded from any point, the campaign was no credit to our institutions, although not an unnatural consequence of the conditions that existed. The total vote, including 7059 for the Liberty ticket, was 2,410,778—912,573 more than in 1836. The Whig majority was 139,256; yet the Democratic vote was 367,153 more than in 1836. But seven States—only one Northern state, Illinois—went Democratic. Harrison and Tyler received 234 electoral votes; Van Buren, 60. The Democratic votes for Vice-President were divided, Johnson receiving 48.

Van Buren accepted the result with his usual composure. He was at once proclaimed as the choice of the party for its candidate in 1844, and he was confident of his eventual success. He met Congress, which convened December 7, as firm as ever in the maintenance of his policy. He reported a satisfactory condition of the finances and the successful operation of the independent Treasury system under the recently enacted law, and opposed with renewed vigor the establishment of a national bank. This part of the message was manifestly intended by him as a defence of the principles of his administration. It was composed with great ability and in an elevated style. It is perhaps the best of his state papers.

As this Congress still contained a Democratic majority in both houses, but expired at the same time as the administration, little was accomplished beyond passing the necessary appropriation bills. The principal debate in the Senate related to the public lands. It was occasioned by a preemption bill, which was finally passed by the Senate, but not by the House. On January 28 and 29 Clay spoke on the general subject of distributing the proceeds of the public lands. His speech had no particular reference to the bill, but was entirely devoted to a justification of the distribution plan he had so long advocated. It was of course designed to prepare the way for the adoption of that plan under the incoming administration. How imperfectly he divined the future progress of the nation may be judged from some of his closing remarks.

"If to the other ties," said he, "that bind us together as one people, be superadded the powerful interest springing out of a just administration of our exhaustless public domain, by which for a long succession of ages, in seasons of peace, the States will enjoy the benefit of the great and growing revenue which it produces, and in periods of war, we shall be forever linked together with the strength of adamantine chains. No section, no State, would ever be mad enough to break off from the Union and deprive itself of the inestimable advantages which it secures. . . . Age after age may roll away, State after State arise, generation succeed generation, and still the fund will remain not only unexhausted, but improved and increasing, for the benefit of our children's children to the remotest posterity."

Clay did not repress his exultation over the Whig victory. Nor did he wait until the Whigs were in power, and Harrison could formally define the policy of his administration, to assail the Sub-Treasury system. Early in the session he introduced a resolution declaring that the "act ought to be forthwith repealed." He spoke with extreme elation. "It has never," said he, "been my purpose in offering this resolution to invite or partake in an argument on the great measure to which the resolution relates, nor is it my purpose now. I would as lief argue to the convicted criminal, when the rope is around his neck and the cart is about to remove from under his body, to persuade him to escape from the gallows, as to argue now to prove that this measure of the Sub-Treasury ought to be abandoned."[1] The ordinary forms should be dispensed with. The measure had been under discussion for three years and a half, hence further argument would be unnecessary and misapplied. "This nation, by a tremendous majority, has decided against the Sub-Treasury measure. And when the nation speaks and wills and commands, what is to be done? There is no necessity of the forms of sending to a committee for a slow process of inquiry; but there is a necessity for doing what the country requires, and to reform what Senators have been instructed to reform."

Wright, in reply, denied that the result of the election implied the popular disapproval of the Sub-Treasury. "How is it ascertained? By what declaration of policy or principle on the part of that party which has become predominant? Why, I should suppose, if the result of the late election can be claimed as proving anything, it is to prove that we are to take down the splendid edifice in which I now stand and erect a log-cabin in its place; that instead of the rich draperies and valuable pictures before us we are to hang around our chamber coon-skins, cat-skins, and other trophies of the chase." Clay winced under this sarcasm and retorted with much earnestness; but as usual he

---

[1] He afterward complained that this "casual expression" had been "terribly perverted by the public prints. The papers have represented me as having compared the gentlemen of the Senate who differ from me in opinion with regard to that measure as a company of convicts with halters around their necks."

relied mainly on the well-known character of his own principles as the guarantee of what those of the new administration would be. Calhoun maintained that "the election decided nothing but that General Harrison should be elected President for the next term," and protested "against the attempt to make any other inference the basis of official action," and in doing so he "but took the ground taken by the Senator and those with whom he acted when it was attempted to construe in a similar manner a former election to have decided against the renewal of the charter of the bank and in favor of certain measures to which he was opposed." In response to the question as to what was to be done after the Sub-Treasury was removed, Clay said, haughtily: "'Sufficient unto the day is the evil thereof.' We have nothing now but the Sub-Treasury to handle. That is an obstacle in the way of any measure. Let us first remove that, and it will then be time for the Senator from New York to hand in his inquiries." The resolution served its purpose, and toward the close of the session it was laid on the table.

If Clay seemed officious he no doubt felt that there was abundant reason for it. There was no Whig platform apart from the policy with which he was inseparably identified and for which he was largely responsible. The real Whig party was the Clay party; and it is this unquestionable fact that renders his career so important historically. It is not surprising, therefore, that Harrison at the outset should have recognized Clay's support as indispensable, and willingly conceded his leadership. Harrison's letter to him before the nomination was followed by another soon after that event, in which he expressed his gratitude to him. "I must," he continued, "beg you also to believe that if the claims derived from your superior talents and experience (so universally acknowledged by my supporters) had prevailed over those which accidental circumstances had conferred upon me, and enabled the convention to name you as the candidate, you would have had no more zealous supporter in the Union than I should have been."

After the election they first met at the home of Governor Letcher, at Frankfort; and soon afterward Clay entertained Harrison at Ashland. There can be no doubt that during this time Clay's counsel was paramount in all important matters of party policy. In these interviews the composition of the cabinet was discussed. Clay was offered the choice of any appointment he desired in the administration; but he at once declined any official position, preferring to remain in the Senate until the principal measures decided upon were enacted, and then retire, in view of his prospective candidacy in 1844. This was distinctly understood; and both concurred in the expediency of an extra session of Congress to enact these measures. Harrison's inaugural address was subsequently submitted to Clay, and all his suggestions but one were adopted.[1] Clay advised the elimination of the allusions to the Greeks and Romans, which Harrison had inserted from an habitual fondness for that kind of historical illustration, but he insisted on retaining them.[2] It is related, however, that Clay was so peremptory

---

[1] "The first draft of his inaugural was so wantonly offensive to the antislavery Whigs who had aided in his election that even Mr. Clay condensed it and prevailed on the General to modify it. He had declared that 'the schemes of the abolitionists were fraught with horrors upon which an incarnate devil only could look with approbation.'"—Julian's *Political Recollections*, p. 25.

[2] It appears that the address was also submitted to Webster, who wrote a substantially new one for Harrison to recite. "Twelve Roman procon-

in some things that he drew from Harrison the remark: "Mr. Clay, you forget that I am the President."[1]

Clay was willing that Webster should enter the cabinet, although he told Harrison that his "confidence in Webster had been somewhat shaken during the last eight years; he did not see how any Whig President could overlook him."[2] The cabinet as then and afterward constructed was exceptionally strong and made up chiefly from Clay's stanchest friends—Crittenden, his colleague in the Senate, for Attorney-General; Ewing, of Ohio, for Secretary of the Treasury; Bell, of Tennessee, for Secretary of War; Badger, of North Carolina, for Secretary of the Navy. Webster was selected for Secretary of State, and his friend Granger for Postmaster-General.

In his inaugural address Harrison deplored the tendency of the Executive to absorb powers vested by the Constitution in the other departments of the government. He declared himself explicitly in favor of limiting the eligibility of

---

suls and several citizens" have I slain, "and yet they are not all dead." Harrison, however, declined to use Webster's production.—Schouler's *History of the United States*, vol. iv. pp. 360, 362.

[1] The authority for this assertion is a letter in the New York *World* of August 31, 1880, written by James Lyons, who entertained Harrison in Richmond in February, 1841.

[2] *Clay's Correspondence*, p. 447; Hone's *Diary*, vol. ii. p. 54. "On the morning of the day when President Harrison was expected to send to the Senate the names of the members of his cabinet some one remarked, in the presence of Mr. Clay, Mr. Crittenden, and several other members of Congress, that Mr. Webster was to be Secretary of the Treasury. 'Oh no,' said Mr. Clay, 'Mr. Webster is to take the Department of State.' 'That,' said the first speaker, 'was the original programme, but as Mr. Webster prefers the Treasury Department, the President has consented to appoint him to the Treasury.' Instantly, and in his most impassioned manner, Mr. Clay replied: 'I will oppose it; I will denounce it in open Senate. The State Department is the proper place for Mr. Webster.'"—*Century Magazine*, vol. xxiii. p. 182.

the President to one term, and renewed his pledge that he would not consent to serve a second term. He maintained that the President is not a part of the legislative branch; that the veto power should be exercised only to preserve the Constitution from violation and the people from the consequences of hasty legislation, and "to prevent the effects of combinations violative of the rights of minorities." He asserted the "right and privilege of the people to decide disputed points of the Constitution arising from the general grant of power to Congress to carry into effect the powers expressly given." He declared against the union of the sword and the purse. "It was certainly a great error," said he, "in the framers of the Constitution not to have made the officer at the head of the Treasury Department entirely independent of the Executive. He should at least have been removable only upon the demand of the popular branch of the legislature." The Executive should exert no influence over the elective franchise, and he should not interfere with the absolute freedom of the press nor with legislation, particularly with the ways and means of raising revenue. As to a bank, he was silent, and touched the subject of the currency only to declaim against metallic money "as fraught with more fatal consequences than any other scheme having no relation to the personal rights of the citizen." He was against any interference with slavery either in the States or in the District. Concerning the financial embarrassment of some of the States, he vaguely suggested that it was "our duty to encourage them to the extent of our Constitutional authority to apply their best means and cheerfully make all necessary sacrifices and submit to all necessary burdens to fulfil their engagements and maintain their credit." He announced his desire to maintain peaceful and honorable relations with foreign powers and to treat the Indians with justice and liberality; and closed with a rather sophomoric appeal to the people to refrain from the violence of party spirit. On the whole, the address was satisfactory to the leading Whigs, and betokened Harrison's readiness to co-operate in the execution of the party policy.¹

Weeks before the new administration was installed it was evident that the pressure for office would be tremendous. The desire of the Whigs for the spoils of their victory proved even more general and urgent than that of the Democrats after Jackson's first election. Washington was overrun with office-seekers, and every one supposed to have influence in the quest for place was overwhelmed with applications, while those who dispensed the patronage were soon dismayed.²

---

[1] "It was not creditable to the manliness of Mr. Adams and his cabinet that none of them remained at their posts to receive their successors. They all fled as if an enemy was in hot pursuit. A beautiful contrast was exhibited by Mr. Van Buren and his friends twelve years afterwards. Mr. Van Buren, on General Harrison's arrival in the city, invited him to the White House, made him acquainted with its inmates, and entertained him as his guest until the inauguration. The members of his cabinet remained in their several offices until their successors made their appearance, received them courteously, and introduced them to their subordinates"—Kendall's *Autobiography*, p. 308. Van Buren's "tact is admirable, and whatever may be his feelings in regard to the success of his distinguished rival, he will never afford his political opponents the triumph of letting them be known."—Hone's *Diary*, vol. ii. p. 59.

[2] The scene was long fresh in Greeley's memory. In 1854 he wrote to Seward: "Now came the great scramble of the swell-mob of coon minstrels and cider-suckers at Washington. . . . Several regiments went on from this city." At the time, he wrote of the "large and numerous swarms of office-hunting locusts sweeping on to Washington daily. All the rotten land speculators, broken bank directors, swindling cashiers, etc., are in full cry for office, office." "Mr. Fry made a speech one evening at a political meeting in Philadelphia. The next morning a committee waited upon him to know for what office he intended to become an applicant. 'Office?' said the astonished composer. 'No office.' 'Why, then,' said the

Webster, representing the President, issued a circular to the heads of departments declaring that assessments and partisan interference with popular elections on the part of government officials and employés would be cause for removal; but the work went on none the less. Clay prudently decided to have nothing to do with appointments. "Without the principle of non-interference," he wrote, "if the day had a duration of forty-eight hours instead of twenty-four, I should be unable to attend to the applications I receive."

Before Harrison went to Kentucky he wrote to Clay suggesting that it would be better for them to communicate with each other by means of a third person, from the fear that their "personal meeting might give rise to speculations, and even jealousies, which it might be well to avoid." Although this notion, which could occur only to a mediocre man, was waived for the time, the dread of danger to his dignity seems to have grown upon him after he reached Washington, and was doubtless increased by those who sought to lessen Clay's influence with him. At all events, but a few days after the inauguration Harrison intimated to Clay that he preferred to have him communicate in writing the suggestions he desired to offer, instead of calling personally.[1] The incident was caused by the efforts to procure the appointment of one Edward Curtis as collector of customs at New York. Curtis was an adroit political schemer and strategist, and was supported by Seward and Weed, but was distasteful to Clay because of his activity in opposing him at Harrisburg. He was appointed.[2] Harrison's rebuff vexed

---

committee, 'what the h—— did you speak last night for?'"—Parton's *Greeley*, p. 190. See also Coleman's *Crittenden*, vol. i. pp. 136, 149; *Woodbury's Writings*, vol. i. p. 128.

[1] Sargent's *Public Men and Events*, vol. ii. p. 116.

[2] "There is a pretty good hit in one of the Southern papers upon the

30

Clay sorely, and it might have led to estrangement had the President lived. After a few days, Clay's vexation somewhat cooled, and he wrote to Harrison a mildly reproachful letter resenting the imputation that he had sought to dictate to him in any manner.¹ He then left for Ashland, and the two men met no more. On April 4, after a brief illness, Harrison died.² As events proved, his nomination, election, and inauguration were but a mere episode. The important result was incidental—it made John Tyler Vice-President.

Tyler at once took the oath of office as President, and assumed the title as well as the functions. This being the first instance where the President had died during his term, there were no precedents to guide the formalities of the succession. There was some transient criticism of Tyler's styling himself President instead of Acting President; but it was more finical than substantial, and his course has since

---

rather redundant introduction of classical illustrations in the President's inaugural address. . . . The writer says that General Harrison was prevailed upon to consent to the appointment of Edward Curtis as collector at New York by being told that he was a lineal descendant of the Curtius of Rome."—Hone's *Diary*, vol. ii. p. 70.

¹ *Clay's Correspondence*, p. 452.

² The following, from Hone's *Diary*, sufficiently illustrates the sentiments that prevailed throughout the country as soon as Harrison's death became known: "On receipt of the news here yesterday morning a spontaneous exhibition of the badges of woe was seen throughout the city; the flags on all public places, as well as on all the shipping in the harbor (not excepting Tammany Hall), were exhibited half-mast, and some of them shrouded in black. The courts in session immediately adjourned. The newspapers were clothed in mourning, all but the *Evening Post*, whose . . . editor, Bryant, says he regrets the death of General Harrison only because he did not live long enough to prove his incapacity for the office of President. Most of the places of amusement were closed in the evening. The last words uttered by the President, as heard by Dr. Worthington, were these: 'Sir, I wish you to understand the true principles of the government; I wish them carried out, nothing more.'"—vol. ii. p. 72.

been followed in similar cases. It was of vastly greater moment to the Whigs that he should succeed to Harrison's policy as well as to his title. Whether he would was at least a doubtful question. Danger was apprehended that he would prove refractory. There was abundant reason for the fear. He had been long in public life, his course had not been uncertain, and it was well known.[1]

He was of an old and distinguished Virginian family, and had strengthened his already high social position by an advantageous marriage. He was well educated, and possessed a fine presence, engaging manners, and very respectable powers of public speech.[2] He was admitted to the bar at the age of nineteen and soon acquired practice and popularity. In 1811 he was elected to the State legislature, and began his political career as an unbending strict-constructionist. He was opposed to the recharter of the Bank of the United States, and signalized his views by proposing resolutions censuring the Senators from Virginia for voting for the recharter contrary to their instructions. He served five years in the legislature, and was then elected to Congress, where he served five years. While in the House he

---

[1] Adams wrote on the day of Harrison's death: "Tyler is a political sectarian, of the slave-driving, Virginian, Jeffersonian school, principled against all improvement, with all the interests and passions and vices of slavery rooted in his moral and political constitution—with talents not above mediocrity, and a spirit incapable of expansion to the dimensions of the station upon which he has been cast by the hand of Providence, unseen, through the apparent agency of chance."—*Diary*, vol. x. p. 457.

"[2] A man of striking, manly beauty, with hair of silky, soft chestnut brown, flowing in curls imperial as those of Jove when Olympus shook with his nod; a strong gray eye, which glowed as he breathed forth his inspirations of intellect and heart; a finely chiselled mouth, expressing the most delicate taste and sweet benevolence; and a nose and chin of manly fortitude;—one could but inwardly exclaim when looking at him and listening to him, '*Os nomine sublime dedit.*'"—Wise's *Seven Decades of the Union*, p. 139.

was conspicuously rigid in his advocacy of States-rights and strict-construction. He was opposed to the policy of internal improvements and protective tariffs, and declared his opinions in numerous speeches. In 1818 he joined in an elaborate report against the bank. He opposed Clay's resolutions looking to the recognition of the South American states, but supported those in censure of Jackson's proceedings in the Florida war. He followed Randolph in opposing the Missouri Compromise, maintaining that Congress had no power to impose restrictions upon a Territory in the formation of a State constitution, or to control slavery in any way in the territorial domain.

In 1821 he retired from Congress on account of ill-health; but two years later he was returned to the State legislature, mainly to promote his election to the Senate. He was defeated, however; but in 1825 he was elected by the legislature Governor of the State. In 1824 he favored Crawford for the Presidency; but after the coalition outcry against Adams and Clay he wrote a letter to Clay extolling his action in supporting Adams and entering the cabinet. This letter afterward became known and gave him some trouble.[1] He did not retract the sentiments he expressed, although he was an opponent of Adams's administration. His ambition while Governor was still to enter the Senate, and he was finally elected over Randolph, taking his seat in December, 1827.

During Jackson's first term Tyler acted chiefly with the administration party, and he supported Jackson's re-election in 1832. He evinced no change in the principles he had followed in the House. He was still opposed to internal

---

[1] Schurz's *Clay*, vol. i. p. 279; *Clay's Correspondence*, p. 119; *Letters and Times of the Tylers*, vol. i. p. 41.

improvements, particularly to further aid in the construction of the Cumberland road. He opposed Clay's bill to distribute the proceeds of the public lands. He was also strongly against the tariffs of 1828 and 1832. While he did not approve nullification, his language against the injustice of the tariff system that prompted it was not less vigorous than Calhoun's. He zealously supported the Compromise, but voted against the force bill. He had ranked as an administration man with independent leanings. He was held in high estimation, and his conduct was ascribed to worthy motives and his Constitutional principles. But what he deemed strict adherence to those principles gradually led him into the opposition. The first indication of this course was to oppose the action of the President in employing diplomatic agents without the consent of the Senate. His hostility to the principles of Jackson's nullification proclamation and the force bill marked an increasing alienation that soon became complete. Though still maintaining the opinion that the bank was unconstitutional, he disapproved the removal of the deposits, voted for Clay's resolution of censure, and drew the report of the Senate committee asserting the solvency of the bank. In 1833 he was re-elected to the Senate; but in 1836 he resigned because of his refusal to obey the instructions of the Virginia legislature to vote for Benton's expunging resolution. Then occurred his effort for re-election, from which he was induced to withdraw by the prospect of the Vice-Presidency.[1] This office must have held strong attraction for him, for he was anxious to run with Harrison in 1836; but through Clay's influence Granger was nominated instead.

---

[1] Wise's *Seven Decades of the Union*, pp. 157, 161.

From these leading facts of Tyler's previous political career, it is obvious that his only pretension to be a Whig was through his having acted with the Whigs in the Senate, not on any positive Whig measure of policy, but solely in opposition to Jackson. His acceptance of the nomination for Vice-President can only be explained by an intense desire for the honor of the office; and the action of the convention in nominating him, by the lack of a willing and orthodox candidate, a sentimental impulse, and an indifference to the contingency that came to pass on Harrison's death.

Before the convention, when Clay's nomination seemed probable, Tyler wrote to him for a statement of his views on several political subjects, saying that he was regarded "as a Republican of the old school, who had indulged, when the public good seemed to require it, somewhat too much in a broad interpretation to suit our Southern notions." Clay said in his reply: "We disagree about absolute questions of policy, and make that disagreement available to prevent our uniting in wresting the Constitution from the hands of men who have put them into its living vitals." Repeatedly during the campaign, in answer to inquiries, Tyler declared his adherence to the opinion that a national bank was unconstitutional. One reason why Clay had so much interested himself in Virginia politics was that in the expectation of being nominated he was anxious that his native State should be for him in the election. The prevailing opinion of its public men had long been against the constitutionality of a national bank. Hence when he failed to receive the nomination, and the Whig ticket was successful without the aid of Virginia, he was outspoken in his disregard for the opinions of the Virginia school. In a letter to his constituents in September, 1842, Wise wrote: "The first salutation I met from Mr. Clay, after the election of 1840, and when we met in Congress in December of that year, flushed with victory and all rejoicing, was, 'Well, sir, it is not to be lamented that old Virginia has gone for Mr. Van Buren, for we will not now be embarrassed by her peculiar opinions.'"

Notwithstanding the apprehensions of the Whigs that Tyler would not stand firmly by their programme, they were given ground for confidence by his cordial retention of Harrison's entire cabinet, and by an address to the people promulgated a few days after he took the oath of office. From the general tone and sentiments of this address, it might well have been written by a stalwart Whig. Its references to the late administrations were severe enough to warrant the belief that Tyler was ready to go as far as any one in reversing the Democratic policy. He did not declare himself in favor of a national bank, but his remarks on the subject of currency and finance created the impression generally that he would approve the establishment of one. "In deciding," said he, "upon the adaptation of any such measure to the end proposed, I shall resort to the fathers of the great Republican school for advice and instruction, to be drawn from their sage views of our system of government and the light of their ever-glorious example."

Clay was not wholly reassured by the promising sound of this address: he was too familiar with the wide orbit of action that plausible generalities permit. He at once wrote to Tyler to ascertain his views more definitely; but he gained little satisfaction. The only topics upon which he was explicit were the Sub-Treasury, the repeal of which he regarded as inevitable, and the distribution of the proceeds of the public lands, which he favored, if the annual appropriations for rivers and harbors were excluded. He said that he had formed no plans; but that some additional burdens might be necessary for the relief of the Treasury, and that the condition of the military defences required immediate attention. As to a bank, his remarks were portentous. He said that, if the other subjects he had mentioned were attended to, Congress would accomplish much good; and he suggested several reasons why a bank should not be insisted on. He added, however, that he should leave the matter wholly to the discretion of Congress, and be governed, so far as his action was concerned, by the character of the measure proposed; but he significantly requested Clay to consider whether he could not "so frame a bank as to obviate all Constitutional objections." A few days after receiving this letter Clay wrote to Brooke: "I repair to my post in the Senate with strong hopes, not, however, unmixed with fears. If the Executive will cordially co-operate in carrying out the Whig measures all will be well. Otherwise everything is at hazard."

It was to be otherwise. The Whig triumph was to prove barren—blasted by Tyler's fortuitous accession. The national bank question, which had so long been the chief source of political turmoil, was now to receive its quietus from Tyler, and to lie entombed under Webster's epitaph— "an obsolete idea." Again political conditions had developed a new stage. Tyler's pro-slavery principles had made him available to strengthen the Whig ticket. In his hands, sustained by Calhoun's determined efforts, the pro-slavery policy was to be advanced until it dominated all others. The Jacksonian epoch had come to a close.

www.ingramcontent.com/pod-product-compliance
Lightning Source LLC
Chambersburg PA
CBHW051847300426
44117CB00006B/300